America Now

Short Readings from Recent Periodicals

America Now

Short Readings from Recent Periodicals
Fourth Edition

Edited by

ROBERT ATWAN

Exercises prepared with the assistance of

Mark Bellomo
State University of New York, New Paltz

Jennifer Ivers
Boston University

Bedford/St. Martin's   Boston ◆ New York

For Bedford/St. Martin's
Developmental Editor: Aron Keesbury
Production Editor: Deborah Baker
Production Supervisor: Catherine Hetmansky
Marketing Manager: Brian Wheel
Editorial Assistant: Joshua Levy
Copyeditor: Tara Masih
Text Design: Jean Hammond
Cover Design: Hannus Design Associates
Cover Art Direction: Donna Lee Dennison and Zenobia Rivetna
Cover Digital Photography: Lightstream
Composition: Pine Tree Composition, Inc.
Printing and Binding: Haddon Craftsmen, Inc.

President: Charles H. Christensen
Editorial Director: Joan E. Feinberg
Editor in Chief: Karen S. Henry
Director of Marketing: Karen Melton
Director of Editing, Design, and Production: Marcia Cohen
Managing Editor: Elizabeth M. Schaaf

Library of Congress Control Number: 00–106436

Acknowledgments

Ad Council National Campaign Against Youth Violence (advertisement). "Children Aren't Born Violent." Reprinted by permission of the Ad Council.

Acknowledgments and copyrights are continued at the back of the book on pages 371–74, which constitute an extension of the copyright page. It is a violation of the law to reproduce these selections by any means whatsoever without the written permission of the copyright holder.

Preface for Instructors

About the Book

People write for many reasons, but one of the most compelling is to express their views on matters of current public interest. Browse any newsstand, library magazine rack, or Web portal home page and you'll find an abundance of articles and opinion pieces responding to current issues and events. The fourth edition of *America Now* retains its generous sampling of this timely and provocative material.

The collection is designed to immerse introductory writing students in the give-and-take of public dialogue and to stimulate thinking, discussion, and composition. Its overriding instructional principle—which informs everything from the choice of readings and topics to the design of questions—is that participation in informed discussion will help generate student writing. The book systematically encourages its users to view reading, thinking, discussion, and writing as closely interrelated activities. It assumes that (1) attentive reading and reflection will lead to informed discussion; (2) participation in open and informed discussion will result in a broadening of viewpoints; (3) an awareness of different viewpoints will stimulate further reflection and renewed discussion; and (4) this process in turn will lead to thoughtful papers. The book's general introduction, "The Empowered Writer," briefly takes the student through the process and offers some useful guidelines for engaging in productive discussion.

Exciting Professional Selections

The book's thirty selections from professional writers are drawn from twenty-seven recent periodicals, ranging from such literary and news-oriented magazines as *Fourth Genre, Time, Newsweek,* and the *New York Times Magazine* to such general interest periodicals as *Civilization* and *Life.* With its emphasis on public discourse, this collection draws a generous sampling of material from America's leading political magazines: *The Nation, The Progressive, Mother Jones, American Prospect,* and *The New Republic.* Magazines appealing primarily to men (*Esquire*) and to women (*Ms.* and *Essence*) are also represented. In general, the selections illustrate the variety of personal, informative, and persuasive writing read daily by millions of Americans. In addition to their range and interest, the selections are short —many under three pages, and some no longer than a page—to keep student interest and to serve as models for students' own writing, generally assigned to be about the same length.

NEW TO THIS EDITION: Because issue-oriented anthologies tend to become stale and dated so quickly, I have continued to keep the selections fresh and topical. Every selection by a professional writer is new to this edition and—perhaps more important—has appeared within a year or two of the book's publication. Each is therefore truly contemporary.

Relevant Student Selections

America Now retains the strong presence of student writing that marked previous editions of the book. The collection features twenty published student essays, almost all of which appeared in college newspapers across the country that are available on the Internet. These recent essays reveal student writers confronting, in a public forum, the same topics and issues that challenge some of our leading social critics and commentators and show how student writers can enter into and influence public discussion. In this way, *America Now* encourages students to view the act of writing as a form of personal and public empowerment. Too frequently, students see the writing they do in a composition class as having little connection with real-world problems and issues.

The student selections in the book prove that writing can make a difference, and since they clearly display what students write about on their own outside of class, the student selections are sure to spark lively and interesting discussion inside the classroom.

NEW TO THIS EDITION: As with the professional selections, every selection by a student writer is new to this edition.

The Role of the Internet

As in the third edition, nearly all of the student pieces were located on the Internet. *America Now* was the first composition reader to draw heavily on this rapidly expanding resource for readers, writers, and anyone interested in discussion of current political and cultural affairs. As Web pages, chat rooms, online forums, and other discussion sites proliferate, students will find a wide-open environment for sharing information, opinions, and concerns. All kinds of public forums are quickly growing more convenient and accessible;

most periodicals, for example, now welcome e-mail responses, and today student writers can enter the public sphere as never before. More than simply a source of student essays, the immediacy and urgency of online student discussion ensures that the essays gathered there represent the subjects that motivate students. In addition to student essays from Internet sources, we have also included in this edition selections from several online magazines.

NEW TO THIS EDITION: Since keeping abreast of today's America means keeping abreast of the Internet as well as what is published there, *America Now*, Fourth Edition, now features a larger number of Internet sources.

Opposing Viewpoints

For instructors who want to concentrate on developing argumentation skills, I have expanded the number of "Opposing Views." These sets now include student debates on gender differences, affirmative action, religion and the First Amendment, hate crime legislation, and capital punishment. The collection also features a debate between two prominent experts on whether the Scholastic Achievement Test (SAT) should account for race and class differences.

NEW TO THIS EDITION: Responding to the comments of instructors who found these sets of essays most effective in beginning student discussions, I have tripled the number of them in this edition, and the book now features six sets of opposing views on controversial topics.

Timely Themes

Student essays not only make up a large percentage of this edition, they also shape the volume's contents. As we monitored at Bedford/St. Martin's the broad spectrum of college newspapers available on the Internet—and reviewed several hundred student essays—we gradually found the most commonly discussed campus issues and topics. Nearly 50 percent of the issues have been changed in this edition to reflect the changing interests of students over the past few years. Certain issues, such as religion and the Constitution, capital punishment, affirmative action, and hate crime legislation, have provoked so much recent student response that they could have resulted in several single-topic collections. Many college papers do not restrict themselves to news items and editorial opinion but make room for personal essays as well. Some popular student topics were gender, group identity, role models, relationships, and negative stereotyping, all of which are reflected in the book's table of contents.

To facilitate group discussion and in-class work, *America Now* features fifteen bite-sized units. These tightly focused chapters permit instructors to cover a broad range of themes and issues in a single semester. Each unit can be conveniently handled in one or two class periods. With the exception of the first unit, the chapters move from accessible, personal topics (for example, body image, identity, and moral decisions) to more complex public issues, thus accommodating teachers who prefer to start with personal writing and gradually progress to exposition, analysis, and argument.

Since composition courses naturally emphasize issues revolving around language and the construction of meaning, this edition also includes several chapters designed to encourage students to consider the powerful influence of words and symbols. Language issues surface in the chapters on the media and public opinion, body image, words, religion and the Constitution, and hate crimes.

NEW TO THIS EDITION: This edition includes seven controversial topics designed to stimulate discussion and writing. These new topics are media and public opinion, today's moral decisions, the future, religion and the Constitution, the legalization of drugs, hate crime laws, and the culture of violence.

The New Visual Focus of Public Discussion

Throughout this fourth edition more attention is paid to the persuasive power of language and image. Reflecting the growing presence of advertising in public discussion, the book now features ten carefully selected advertisements designed by various groups and organizations to initiate public change. The ads—all new to this edition—are distributed throughout the book; students are encouraged to uncover the visual and verbal strategies of recent "opinion advertising" employed by various advocacy groups and intended to influence the consciousness and ideology of large audiences.

Aside from the advertisements, the book features several other visual texts aimed at demonstrating the persuasive combination of word and image. The all-new first unit is intended to show students the ways that controversial news events can be shaped and interpreted by the media's selectivity of text and photography. The unit focuses on one of the unforgettable news stories of 2000—the seizure of a Cuban child, Elián González, by armed government agents in a successful attempt to return him to his father and eventually back to Cuba. A "front page portfolio" displays news coverage from the *Los Angeles Times*, the *Miami Herald*, and the *New York Times* and is followed by three essays offering a diversity of opinion on the different ways the media portrayed the story. The unit offers instructors the opportunity to discuss with students some of the ways the media can manipulate public opinion through photography.

Photography is also introduced in a more personal fashion with a photo essay that explores the childhood significance of body image and which originated as a Literacy through Photography project in the Durham, North Carolina, public schools. In "The Best Part of Me" (see p. 28), photographer Wendy Ewald offers a sample of how elementary school children responded when asked to "choose the part of their body they liked best or that explained the most about them."

NEW TO THIS EDITION: This edition contains a greater number and variety of visual elements, including ten striking and controversial "opinion advertisements," a photo essay on body image, and a portfolio of newspaper front pages illustrating the way the media can use photography to shape public opinion.

The Editorial Apparatus:
Before, During, and After Reading

The apparatus of *America Now* supports both discussion-based instruction as well as more individualized approaches to reading and writing. Taking into account the increasing diversity of students (especially the growing number of non-native speakers) in today's writing programs, the apparatus offers extensive help with college-level vocabulary and features a "Words to Learn" list preceding each selection. This vocabulary list with brief definitions will allow students to spot ahead of time some of the words they may find difficult; encountering the word later in context will help lock it in memory. It's unrealistic, however, to think students will acquire a fluent knowledge of new words by memorizing a list. Therefore, the apparatus following each selection includes additional exercises under the headings "Vocabulary/Using a Dictionary" and "Responding to Words in Context." These sets of questions introduce students to prefixes, suffixes, connotations, denotations, tone, and etymology.

To help promote reflection and discussion, the book includes a prereading assignment for each main selection. The questions in "Before You Read" provide students with the opportunity to explore a few of the avenues that lead to fruitful discussion and interesting papers. A full description of the advantages gained by linking reading, writing, and classroom discussion can be found in my introduction to the instructor's manual.

Along with the discussion of vocabulary, incrementally structured questions follow individual selections. Picking up on the vocabulary lists preceding each selection, another question set, "Responding to Words in Context," supplements the existing "Vocabulary/ Using a Dictionary" questions and asks students to use what they have learned from the dictionary exercises and vocabulary lists. Following the vocabulary questions, the "Discussing Main Point and Meaning" and "Examining Sentences, Paragraphs, and Organization" questions help to guide students step by step through the reading process, culminating in the set of "Thinking Critically" questions. As instructors well know, beginning students can sometimes be too trusting of what they see in print, especially in textbooks. Therefore, the "Thinking Critically" questions invite students to take a more skeptical attitude toward their reading and to form the habit of challenging a selection from both analytical and experiential points of view. The selection apparatus concludes with "In-Class Writing Activities," which emphasize freewriting exercises and collaborative projects.

In addition to the selection apparatus, *America Now* also contains end-of-chapter questions designed to stimulate further discussion and writing. The chapter apparatus approaches the reading material from topical and thematic angles with an emphasis on group discussion. The introductory comments to each chapter highlight the main discussion points and the way selections are linked together. These points and linkages are then reintroduced at the end of the chapter through three sets of interlocking study questions and tasks: (1) A suggested topic for discussion, (2) questions and ideas to help students prepare for class discussion, and (3) several writing assignments that ask students to move from discussion to composition — that is, to develop papers out of the ideas and opinions expressed in class discussion and debate. Finally, instructors with highly diverse writing classes may find "Topics for Cross-Cultural Discussion" a convenient way to encourage an exchange of perspectives and experiences that could also generate ideas for writing.

The Instructor's Edition

Jennifer Ivers of Boston University and Mark Bellomo of the State University of New York, New Paltz, prepared the instructor's manual (which is found in the instructor's edition of this book), bringing to the task not only a familiarity with the text but years of classroom experience at all levels of composition instruction. The manual contains an essay for each unit, offering suggestions for teaching the selections in the unit together and separately; and suggested answers and possible discussion topics based on every question posed in the text. Anyone using *America Now* should be sure to consult the manual before designing a syllabus, framing a discussion topic, or even assigning individual selections. Liz deBeer of Rutgers University also contributed a helpful essay on designing student panels ("Forming Forums") and advice on using the book's apparatus in both developmental and mainstream composition classes.

Acknowledgments

While putting together the fourth edition of *America Now* I was fortunate to receive the assistance of many talented individuals. In addition to their work on the instructor's manual, Mark Bellomo, Jennifer Ivers, and Liz deBeer offered many useful suggestions for the book's instructional apparatus.

To revise a text is to entertain numerous questions: What kind of selections work best in class? What types of questions are most helpful? How can reading, writing, and discussion be most effectively intertwined? This edition profited immensely from the following instructors who generously took the time to respond to the last edition: Kim M. Baker, Roger Williams University; Diane Bosco, Suffolk County Community College; Steven Florzcyk, the State University of New York, New Paltz; Patricia W. Julius, Michigan State University; Jessica Heather Lourey, Alexandria Technical College; Michael Orlando, Bergen Community College; Hubert C. Pulley, Georgia Southern University; Andrea D. Shanklin, Howard Community College; Linda Weiner, the University of Akron; and Martha Anne Yeager-Tobar, Cerritos College.

Other people helped in various ways. I'm indebted to Barbara Gross of Rutgers University, Newark, for her excellent work in preparing the instructor's manual for the first edition. Two good friends, Charles O'Neill and Jack Roberts, both of St. Thomas Aquinas College, went over my early plans for the book and offered many useful suggestions.

As always, it was a pleasure to work with the superb staff at Bedford/St. Martin's. *America Now* began with Bedford's editorial director, Joan E. Feinberg, who conceived the idea—and I thank her for it. Jane Betz, my editor on the first edition, shaped the book in lasting ways and helped with the planning of the revision. Of all the people acknowledged, I owe the most gratitude to this edition's developmental editor, Aron Keesbury. His insightful suggestions, remarkable good sense, and uncanny ability to keep track of so many minute details made this collection a pleasure to work on from start to finish. I appreciate, too, the efforts of Josh Levy, who tackled a variety of editorial tasks. Donna Ashley cleared permissions under a tight deadline. Deborah Baker guided the book through production with patience and care, staying on top of many details, and Elizabeth Schaaf managed the production process with her usual attentiveness. I was fortunate to receive the careful copyediting of Tara Masih. In the advertising and promotion department, manager Hope Tompkins as well as Pelle Cass and Jill Chmelko deserve warm thanks for their work.

Finally, I would like to thank Bedford's president, Charles H. Christensen, for his deep and abiding interest in college composition. It is a great pleasure and privilege to work with him.

R. A.

Contents

1 Do the Media Manipulate Opinion?   1

Can you trust the images you see in the news? Do photographs and videotapes always provide objective pictures of an event? In April 2000 Americans found themselves uncomfortably confronted by these key questions as the media launched a barrage of conflicting images occasioned by the U.S. government's seizure of a six-year-old Cuban boy from the home of his Miami relatives. Front page stories from three of the nation's leading newspapers graphically reveal the various ways a single event can be interpreted by the press.... An online magazine reminds us that pictures, "like words, can project illusions and take events out of context." ... "Which photo do you believe?" asks a noted political commentator.... If all stories have two sides, claims a Northwestern junior, then the Elián González episode is truly "a tale of two images." ... A cartoon from the *Iowa State Daily* makes a satirical point about the power of photojournalism.

2   Our Body Image—
   How Early Does It Begin?   27

Opinion polls show that most Americans are discontented with their appearance. Usually, women want to lose pounds and men want to gain muscle in the hopes of achieving their "ideal" body images. Does this obsession with the way we look begin in adulthood, adolescence, or much earlier? As part of a Literacy through Photography project in a North Carolina school system, an art teacher discovers what elementary school children think of their bodies. . . . A *New York Times* reporter wonders why people are more inclined to lie about their height than their weight or age. . . . A University of Nebraska broadcasting major worries that too many young people are killing themselves because of a "cultural expectation to be thin."

3   Are Gender Differences Real?   49

Do males and females truly behave as though they come from different planets? Can gender differences be bridged by mutual understanding, or are they so innate that a communication gap between men and women will always remain? Are girls given fewer opportunities in our society than boys? A reporter reviews the current scientific evidence for gender differences, examining the roles of both culture and body chemistry in the formation of male and female personalities. . . . Popular television quiz shows, such as *Who Wants to Be a Millionaire*, may be biased toward men, reports a leading liberal journal. . . . In an elegantly concise anecdote, an essayist reveals a fundamental difference between men and women. . . . Two Kansas City Metropolitan Community College students heatedly debate a favorite American topic: Do men or women make better drivers?

4   How Important Is Ethnic Identity?   76

Do you ever see yourself as a representative of an ethnic or racial group? How important is it to your sense of identity to belong to this particular group? How do you identify yourself if, like many Americans, you belong to more than one ethnic group? A young traveler revisits his native Vietnam and unexpectedly discovers who he really is. . . . A Kansas State political science major believes that "politically correct" multiculturalism is destroying American unity. . . . "What are you?" is not a simple question, explains a writer whose ethnic and cultural backgrounds are not easily classified. . . . An ad questions the government's charges against a Chinese American scientist.

5 Do Words Matter?   96

Do the ordinary words we use in our daily lives make any difference? Can they create hostile environments or facilitate relationships? Do we always know what they mean, even when we use such common words as *love* and *hate*? How can mere words persuade us to make extravagant purchases? A New York University student would like to restore the awesome power of a four-letter word—*love*. ... The simple word *sorry* can be one of the most powerful terms we can use in private or in public, argues one of the nation's leading linguists. ... Why are SUVs so popular? asks a noted cultural critic who believes the key to their success is neither their size nor their expense but their phony "Western names."

6 Who Should Our Heroes Be?   120

Does everyone grow up with heroes and role models? Can we judge a society by the kinds of individuals its young people decide to imitate? If so, what does America's obsession with media celebrities and professional athletes say about us? Is it possible to find our heroes closer to home? A contributor to *Newsweek*'s online weekly explains why his mother has become a greater hero to him than all the comic-book superheroes of his childhood. . . . We would all be better off if we resisted our fascination with media personalities and discovered our heroes among community activists, says a University of Kansas economics major. . . . One of America's most popular historians disputes our traditional list of heroes and proposes a new pantheon of extraordinary though lesser-known individuals.

7   Today's Choices — How Do We Decide What to Do?   138

At a time when nearly all traditional moral values are being challenged, how do we make serious personal decisions? On what grounds do we base our conduct: communal, religious, individualistic? Should we follow conventional moral guidelines? Be politically correct? Do what our conscience dictates? A medical student ponders a personal dilemma: Should she learn how to perform abortions and risk her career and possibly her life?. . . An advertisement for the National Abortion Federation regrets that doctors increasingly need to wear bulletproof vests to work. . . . In a controversial *New York Times* essay, a famous philosopher raises moral responsibility to unprecedented levels. . . . If a successful marriage means being able to live together harmoniously, then isn't it a good idea, argues a Central Missouri State columnist, to try living together before getting married?

8 The Future — What Can We Expect?   163

The recent millennium celebrations inspired a great deal of retrospection, as writers looked back and evaluated the past. But not everyone felt nostalgic. Many used the occasion to wonder what the future held in store. What will life be like in the twenty-first century? Will there be more incredible technological change? Will society be radically transformed? A leading commentator for *Time* magazine wonders how biogenetic breakthroughs will fundamentally alter traditional male-female relationships. . . . Noting increases in intermarriage and the erosion of racial barriers, an African American essayist cautiously considers the disappearance of race. . . . The next frontier of scientific exploration should be the mysterious human brain, argues a Western Illinois University student. . . . An advertisement worries about overcrowding.

9 Can We Resist Stereotypes?   189

Why are we so quick to label people? Where do stereotypes come from? What harm can they do? Are some group stereotypes accurate? Are stereotypes an inevitable part of everyone's life in all societies? On a trip to Africa, the assistant director of the New York Civil Liberties Union observed male behavior that would have provoked slurs or stares back in the United States. . . . A magazine editor who wanders into the wrong part of town confronts the "poisonous thought" of racial stereotyping. . . . A Filipino student can understand why she is stereotyped because she herself has done the same to others: "Stereotypes exist for a reason, and prejudices die hard," she argues. . . . By asking a disturbing question, a stark advertisement drives home the effects of stereotyping.

10   Affirmative Action Programs— Are They Still Needed?

Have recent state policies ended affirmative action programs in the United States, or will these programs continue in one form or another? Can admissions officers find ways to circumvent state legislators and ensure greater diversity and better minority representation in the classroom? Two authorities on affirmative action policies debate whether the SATs should take race and ethnicity into account when calculating scores. . . . A University of Rochester senior takes issue with a campus newspaper column condemning affirmative action programs, while another student argues for retaining them.

11   God and the Constitution — Must They Be Separate?   232

When the nation's founders agreed on a First Amendment that prohibited Congress from establishing a religion or from denying anyone religious freedom, how far did they intend their restrictions to go? Did they want to prohibit all forms of religious language and displays in public? A noted Boston columnist wonders why the Ohio State motto "With God All Things Are Possible" is unconstitutional while all U.S. currency proclaims "In God We Trust." ... The Anti-Defamation League urges Americans to maintain a strong "wall separating church and state." ... With the recent epidemic of school violence, a number of community leaders have advocated posting the Ten Commandments in public schools: The editorial board of a Virginia Tech online paper sees this suggestion as clearly unconstitutional, whereas a columnist at Truman State University in Missouri finds nothing wrong with the idea.

12   Is the War on Drugs Worth Waging?   251

Are U.S. drug laws obsolete? Do they do more harm than good? And if marijuana, heroin, and other substances are illegal, why isn't alcohol prohibited? Isn't alcohol similarly dangerous? Doesn't it cause irreparable social harm? The publisher of a Latino political journal explains why the "government's escalating battle to keep people from consuming illegal drugs has been a miserable failure." . . . If legalizing alcohol doesn't work, why should we think legalizing drugs will help solve social problems? asks a UCLA columnist. . . . A prominent *Newsweek* essayist argues that "beer and booze are not the same as illegal drugs. They're worse.". . . Mothers Against Drunk Driving (MADD) issues a warning for parents. . . . Concerned about unjust sentencing for drug offenders, an advocacy group offers some practical advice based on historical precedent.

13   How Do We Define "Hate Crime"?   277

Should certain crimes—violent or otherwise—targeted at members of a different race, or at gays, or at people with disabilities be specially designated as "hate crimes"? Are such crimes worse than other crimes? Do they deserve greater penalties? A world-renowned feminist explains why hate crimes are so often committed by heterosexual white males. . . . When poverty and social class enter the picture, hate crime can become especially violent, as it did, a *Nation* essayist recounts, in the ritual murder of a young gay man in Laramie, Wyoming. . . . A Brigham Young University newspaper editorial thinks that a hate crime designation will only result in greater conflict. That opinion is challenged in a response that argues for the necessity of such legislation. . . . An advertisement for an online magazine isn't afraid to offer a politically incorrect opinion.

Few people would dispute the fact that violence is a main feature of American films, video games, and television. But to what extent can violent behavior, especially among the young, be attributed to violence in the media? What other cultural and social factors are involved? A communications professor believes our investigations into the "culture of violence" should be more "holistic" and include an examination of our socially stratified consumer culture. . . . In a monthly column, the chair of US Airways believes that we can successfully respond to the alarming violence in our schools only if we make a concerted effort on many levels. . . . A Tulane student attempts to explain a curious fact: Why is it that as the overall crime rate has fallen, the number of mass murders has skyrocketed?.... Children aren't born violent, the Ad Council assures us, but they can learn to be.

15 Is the Death Penalty Necessary?   327

Is capital punishment the most effective way to deal with convicted murderers? Is it fair to those who died to let their murderers go on living? Can we always be certain we are not executing an innocent person? These questions invariably arise in discussions of one of America's most divisive issues: the death penalty. Writing for a controversial photography project sponsored by the United Colors of Benetton, a journalist evaluates his experiences with death row inmates. . . . A professor and author seriously wounded by the Unabomber believes that revenge has its virtues in a morally responsible society. . . . A Bismarck State College student systematically rejects anti–death penalty arguments such as those voiced by a University of Texas sociology major. . . . The latest arguments against capital punishment are concisely advanced in a recent advertisement from the American Civil Liberties Union. . . . In a brief excerpt from the best-seller *Dead Man Walking*, Sister Helen Prejean considers the morality of execution as retribution.

Introduction: The Empowered Writer

What Is America Now?

America Now collects very recent essays and articles that have been carefully selected to stimulate reading, discussion, and writing. The philosophy behind the book is that interesting, effective writing originates in public dialogue. The book's primary purpose is to help students proceed from class discussions of reading assignments to the production of complete essays that reflect an engaged participation in those discussions.

The selections in *America Now* come from two main sources— from popular, mainstream periodicals and from college newspapers available on the Internet. Written by journalists and columnists, public figures and activists as well as by professors and students from all over the country, the selections illustrate the types of material read by millions of Americans every day. In addition to magazine and newspaper writing, the book also features a number of recent opinion advertisements (what I call "Op-Ads" for short). These familiar forms of "social marketing" are often sponsored by corporations or nonprofit organizations and advocacy groups to promote policies, programs, and ideas such as gun control, automotive safety, family planning, literacy, civil rights, or conservation. Such advertising texts allow one to pinpoint and discuss specific techniques of verbal and visual persuasion that are critical in the formation of public opinion.

The selections of *America Now* are gathered into fifteen units that cover today's most widely discussed issues and topics: violence, capital punishment, hate crimes, body image, affirmative action initiatives, racial and ethnic stereotypes, and so on. As you respond to the readings in discussion, debate, and writing, you will be actively taking part in the major controversies of our time.

Participation is the key to this collection. I encourage you to view reading and writing as a form of participation. I hope you will read the selections attentively, think about them, be willing to discuss them in class, and use what you've learned from your reading and discussion as the basis for your papers. If you do these things, you will develop three skills necessary for successful college work and beyond: the ability to read critically, to discuss topics intelligently, and to write persuasively.

America Now invites you to see reading, discussion, and writing as closely related activities. As you read a selection, imagine that you have entered into a discussion with the author. Take notes as you read. Question the selection. Challenge its point of view or its evidence. Compare your experience with the author's. Consider how different economic classes or other groups are likely to respond.

Remember, just because something appears in a newspaper or book doesn't make it true or accurate. Form the habit of challenging what you read. Don't be persuaded by an opinion simply because it appears in print or because you believe you should accept it. Trust your own observations and experiences. Though logicians never say so, personal experiences and keen observations often provide the basis of our most convincing arguments.

When your class discusses a selection, be especially attentive to what others think of it. It's always surprising how two people can read the same article and reach two entirely different interpretations. Observe the range of opinion. Try to understand why and how people arrive at different conclusions. Do some seem to be missing the point? Do some distort the author's ideas? Have someone's comments forced you to rethink the selection? Keep a record of the discussion in your notebook. Then, when you begin to draft your paper, consider your essay as an extension of both your imaginary conversation with the author and the actual class discussion. If you've taken detailed notes of your own and the class's responses to the selection, you should have more than enough information to get started.

Participating in Class Discussion: Six Basic Rules

Discussion is a learned activity. It requires a variety of essential academic skills: speaking, listening, thinking, and preparing. The following six basic rules are vital to healthy and productive discussion.

1. *Take an active speaking role.*   Good discussion demands that everyone participates, not (as so often happens) just a vocal few. Many students remain detached from discussion because they are afraid to speak in a group. This fear is quite common—so common that psychological surveys show that speaking in front of a group is generally one of our worst fears. A leading communication consultant suggests that people choke up because they are more worried about how others will respond than about what they themselves have to say. It helps to remember that most people will be more in-

terested in *what* you say than in how you say it. Once you get over the initial fear of speaking in public, your speech skills will improve with practice.

2. *Listen attentively.*   No one can participate in group discussion who doesn't listen attentively. This may sound obvious, but just think of how many senseless arguments you've had because either you or the person with whom you were talking completely misunderstood what was said. A good listener not only hears what someone is saying but understands *why* he or she is saying it. One of the most important things about listening is that it leads to one element that lively discussion depends on: good questions. When the interesting questions begin to emerge, you know good discussion has truly begun.

3. *Examine all sides of an issue.*   Good discussion requires that we be patient with complexity. Difficult problems rarely have obvious and simple solutions, nor can they be easily summarized in popular slogans. Complex issues demand to be turned over in our minds so that we can see them from a variety of angles. Group discussion will broaden our perspective and deepen our insight into difficult issues and ideas.

4. *Suspend judgment.*   Class discussion is best conducted in an open-minded and tolerant spirit. To fully explore ideas and issues, you will need to be receptive to the opinions of others even when they contradict your own. Remember, discussion is not the same as debate. Its primary purpose is communication, not competition. In discussion you are not necessarily trying to win everyone over to your point of view. The goal of group discussion should be to open up a topic so that everyone in the group will be exposed to a spectrum of attitudes. Suspending judgment does not mean you shouldn't hold a strong belief or opinion about an issue; it means that you should be willing to take into account rival beliefs or opinions. An opinion formed without an awareness of other points of view—one that has not been tested against contrary ideas—is not a *strong* opinion but merely a stubborn one.

5. *Avoid abusive or insulting language.*   Free and open discussion can only occur if we respect the beliefs and opinions of others. If we speak in ways that fail to show respect for differing viewpoints— if we resort to name-calling or use demeaning and malicious expressions, for example—we not only embarrass ourselves but we close off the possibility for an intelligent and productive exchange of ideas. Contrary to what you might gather from some popular radio and

television talk shows, shouting insults and engaging in hate-speech are signs of verbal and intellectual bankruptcy. They are usually the last resort of someone who has nothing to say.

6. *Come prepared.* Discussion is not merely random conversation. It demands a certain degree of preparation and focus. To participate in class discussion, you must consider assigned topics beforehand and read whatever is required. You should develop the habit of reading with pen in hand, underlining key points and jotting down questions, impressions, and ideas in your notebook. The notes you bring to class will be an invaluable aid in group discussion.

Group Discussion as a Source of Ideas

Group discussion can stimulate and enhance your writing in several important ways. First, it supplies you with ideas. Let's say that you are participating in a discussion about how we express group identities (see Unit 4). One of your classmates mentions some of the problems a mixed ethnic background can cause. But suppose you also come from a mixed background, and, when you think about it, you believe that your mixed heritage has given you more advantages than disadvantages. Hearing her viewpoint may inspire you to express your differing perspective on the issue. Your perspective could lead to an interesting personal essay.

Suppose you now start writing that essay. You don't need to start from scratch and stare at a blank piece of paper or computer screen for hours. Discussion has already given you a few good leads. First, you have your classmate's opinions and attitudes to quote or summarize. You can begin your paper by explaining that some people view a divided ethnic identity as a psychological burden. You might expand on your classmate's opinion by bringing in additional information from other student comments or from your reading to show how people often focus on only the negative side of mixed identities. You can then explain your own perspective on this topic. Of course, you will need to give several examples showing *why* a mixed background has been an advantage for you. The end result can be a first-rate essay, one that takes other opinions into account and demonstrates a clearly established point of view. It is personal, and yet it takes a position that goes beyond one individual's experiences.

Whatever the topic, your writing will benefit from reading and discussion, which will give your essays a clear purpose or goal. In that way, your papers will resemble the selections found in this book: They will be a *response* to the opinions, attitudes, experiences, issues, ideas, and proposals that inform current public discourse. This is why most writers write; this is what most newspapers and magazines publish; this is what most people read. *America Now* consists entirely of such writing. I hope you will read the selections with enjoyment, discuss the issues with an open mind, and write about the topics with purpose and enthusiasm.

The Practice of Writing

Suppose you wanted to learn to play the guitar. What would you do first? Would you run to the library and read a lot of books on music? Would you then read some instructional books on guitar playing? Might you try to memorize all the chord positions? Then would you get sheet music for songs you liked and memorize them? After all that, if someone handed you an electric guitar, would you immediately be able to play like Jimi Hendrix or Eric Clapton?

I don't think you would begin that way. You would probably start out by strumming the guitar, getting the feel of it, trying to pick out something familiar. You would probably want to take lessons from someone who knows how to play. And you would practice, practice, practice. Every now and then your instruction book would come in handy. It would give you basic information on frets, notes, and chord positions, for example. You might need to refer to that information constantly in the beginning. But knowing the chords is not the same as knowing how to manipulate your fingers correctly to produce the right sounds. You need to be able to *play* the chords, not just know them.

Learning to read and write well is not that much different. Though instructional books can give you a great deal of advice and information, the only way anyone really learns to read and write is through constant practice. The only problem, of course, is that nobody likes practice. If we did, we would all be good at just about everything. Most of us, however, want to acquire a skill quickly and easily. We don't want to take lesson after lesson. We want to pick up the instrument and sound like a professional in ten minutes.

Wouldn't it be a wonderful world if that could happen? Wouldn't it be great to be born with a gigantic vocabulary so we instantly knew the meaning of every word we saw or heard? We would never have to go through the slow process of consulting a dictionary whenever we stumbled across an unfamiliar word. But, unfortunately, life is not so easy. To succeed at anything worthwhile requires patience and dedication. Watch a young figure skater trying to perfect her skills and you will see patience and dedication at work; or watch an accident victim learning how to maneuver a wheelchair so he can begin again an independent existence; or observe a new American struggling to learn English. None of these skills is quickly and easily acquired. Like building a vocabulary, they all take time and effort. They all require practice. And they require something even more important: the willingness to make mistakes. Can someone learn to skate without taking a spill? Or learn a new language without mispronouncing a word?

Writing as a Public Activity

Many people have the wrong idea about writing. They view writing as a very private act. They picture the writer sitting all alone and staring into space waiting for ideas to come. They think that ideas come from "deep" within and only reach expression after they have been fully articulated inside the writer's head.

These images are part of a myth about creative writing and, like most myths, are sometimes true. A few poets, novelists, and essayists do write in total isolation and search deep inside themselves for thoughts and stories. But most writers have far more contact with public life. This is especially true of people who write regularly for magazines, newspapers, and professional journals. These writers work within a lively social atmosphere in which issues and ideas are often intensely discussed and debated. Nearly all the selections in this book illustrate this type of writing.

As you work on your own papers, remember that writing is very much a public activity. It is rarely performed alone in an "ivory tower." Writers don't always have the time, the desire, the opportunity, or the luxury to be all alone. They may be writing in a newsroom with clacking keyboards and noise all around them; they may be writing at a kitchen table, trying to feed several children at the same time; they may be writing on subways or buses. The great English novelist D. H. Lawrence grew up in a small coal miner's cottage with no place for privacy. It turned out to be an enabling experience. Throughout his life he could write wherever he happened to be; it didn't matter how many people or how much commotion surrounded him.

There are more important ways in which writing is a public activity. Much writing is often a response to public events. Most of the articles you encounter every day in newspapers and magazines respond directly to timely or important issues and ideas, topics that people are currently talking about. Writers report on these topics, supply information about them, discuss and debate the differing viewpoints. The units in this book all represent topics now regularly discussed on college campuses and in the national media. In fact, all of the topics were chosen because they emerged so frequently in college newspapers.

When a columnist decides to write on a topic like affirmative action, she willingly enters an ongoing public discussion about the issue. She didn't just make up the topic. She knows that it *is* a serious issue, and she is aware that a wide variety of opinions have been expressed about it. She has not read everything on the subject but usually knows enough about the different arguments to state her own position or attitude persuasively. In fact, what helps make her writing persuasive is that she takes into account the opinions of others. Her own essay, then, becomes a part of the continuing debate and discussion, one that you in turn may want to join.

Such issues are not only matters for formal and impersonal debate. They also invite us to share our *personal* experiences. Many of the selections in this book show how writers participate in the discussion of issues by drawing on their experiences. For example, Deborah Blum's "What's the Difference between Boys and Girls?" is based largely on Blum's observations and personal experience, though the topic — gender differences — is one widely discussed and debated by educators, psychologists, and biologists. Nearly every unit of *America Now* contains a selection that illustrates how you can use your personal experiences to discuss and debate a public issue.

Writing is public in yet another way. Practically all published writing is reviewed, edited, and re-edited by different people before it goes to press. The author of a magazine article has most likely discussed the topic at length with colleagues and publishing professionals and may have asked friends or experts in the field to look it over. By the time you see the article in a magazine, it has gone through numerous readings and probably quite a few revisions. Though the article is credited to a particular author, it was no doubt read and worked on by others who helped with suggestions and improvements. As a beginning writer, it's important to remember that most of what you read in newspapers, magazines, and books has gone through a writing process that involves the collective efforts of several people besides the author. Students usually don't have that advantage and should not feel discouraged when their own writing doesn't measure up to the professionally edited materials they are reading for a course.

What Is "Correct English"?

One part of the writing process may seem more difficult than others—correct English. Yes, nearly all of what you read will be written in relatively correct English. Or it's probably more accurate to say "corrected" English, since most published writing is revised or "corrected" several times before it appears in print. Even skilled professional writers make mistakes that require correction.

Most native speakers don't actually *talk* in "correct" English. There are numerous regional patterns and dialects. As the Chinese American novelist Amy Tan says, there are "many Englishes." What we usually consider correct English is a set of guidelines developed over time to help standardize written expression. This standardization—like any agreed-upon standards such as weights and measures—is a matter of use and convenience. Suppose you went to a vegetable stand and asked for a pound of peppers and the storekeeper gave you a half pound but charged you for a full one. When you complained, he said, "But that's what *I* call a pound." What if you next bought a new compact disc you've been waiting for, and when you tried to play it you discovered it wouldn't fit your CD player. Life would be very frustrating if everyone had a different set of standards: Imagine what would happen if some places used a red light to signal "go" and a green one for "stop." Languages are not that different. In all cultures, languages—especially written languages—have gradually developed certain general rules and principles to make communication as clear and efficient as possible.

You probably already have a guidebook or handbook that systematically sets out certain rules of English grammar, punctuation, and spelling. Like our guitar instruction book, these handbooks serve a very practical purpose. Most writers—even experienced authors—need to consult them periodically. Beginning writers may need to rely on them far more regularly. But just as we don't learn how to play chords by merely memorizing finger positions, we don't learn how to write by memorizing the rules of grammar or punctuation.

Writing is an activity, a process. Learning how to do it—like learning to ride a bike or prepare a tasty stew—requires *doing* it. Correct English is not something that comes first. We don't need to know the rules perfectly before we can begin to write. As in any activity, corrections are part of the learning process. You fall off the bike and get on again, trying to "correct" your balance this time. You sample the stew and "correct" the seasoning. You draft a paper about the neighborhood you live in and as you (or a classmate or teacher) read it over, you notice that certain words and expressions could stand some improvement. And step by step, sentence by sentence, you begin to write better.

Writing as Empowerment

Writing is one of the most powerful means of producing social and political change. Through their four widely disseminated gospels, the first-century evangelists helped propagate Christianity throughout the world; the writings of Adam Smith and Karl Marx determined the economic systems of many nations for well over a century; Thomas Jefferson's Declaration of Independence became a model for countless colonial liberationists; the books and essays of numerous feminists have altered twentieth-century consciousness. In the long run, many believe, "the pen is mightier than the sword."

Empowerment does not mean instant success. It does not mean that your opinion or point of view will suddenly prevail. It does mean, however, that you have made your voice heard, that you have given your opinions wider circulation, that you have made yourself and your position a little more visible. And sometimes you get results: a newspaper prints your letter; a university committee adopts your suggestion; people visit your Web site. Throughout this collection you will encounter writing specifically intended to inform and influence a wide community.

Such influence is not restricted to professional authors and political experts. This collection features a large number of student writers who are actively involved with the same current topics and issues that engage the attention of professionals—affirmative action, group identity, capital punishment, gender differences, labeling and stereotyping, and so on. The student selections, all of them previously published and written for a variety of reasons, are meant to be an integral part of each unit, to be read in conjunction with the professional essays, and to be criticized and analyzed on an equal footing. The student writing holds up.

America Now urges you to voice your ideas and opinions—in your notebooks, in your papers, in your classrooms, and, most important, on your campus and in your communities. Reading, discussing, and writing will force you to clarify your observations, attitudes, and values, and as you do you will discover more about yourself and the world. These are exciting times. Don't sit on the sidelines of controversy. Don't retreat into invisibility and silence. Jump in and confront the ideas and issues currently shaping America.

Do the Media Manipulate Opinion?

It is often said that "one picture is worth a thousand words," meaning that a picture can convey a message more effectively and more economically than words could ever do. The expression is now so much a driving principle of journalism that no news story can be considered complete without its photographs or videos. Such images, it is argued, can show us at a glance something that might take a writer several pages to describe. And such images, the argument continues, offer us reliable, eyewitness testimony to what has occurred, for unlike a writer's words, as we are often told, the photographer's camera doesn't lie.

On Saturday, April 22, 2000, Americans were confronted by two sets of photographs that depicted two opposing sides of a dramatic news story the national media had been covering for months: the fate of a six-year-old Cuban boy who had been rescued off the coast of Florida. When the small craft being used by his mother and others to flee Fidel Castro's Cuba capsized, the boy's mother drowned and the rescued Elián González was allowed to stay with relatives in Miami for several months until the decision was reached that he should be reunited with his father. The incident touched off powerful emotions in Miami, where the predominantly anti-Castro Cuban community felt that it was in the boy's best interest to remain in the United States. The U.S. government, however, believed it was obliged to return Elián to his native land and into the custody of his father.

The deadlock came to a dramatic conclusion in the early-morning hours of April 22, when—under orders from the attorney general—Immigration and Naturalization Service agents broke into the Miami relatives' house, seized the six-year-old, and whisked him off to Washington. As the media turned its full attention to the raid and the subsequent reunion, two photographs quickly captured the public's attention: One depicted an armed and helmeted agent seizing the boy at gunpoint, while the other showed a smiling boy in his father's arms. For the news media, the two pictures—the raid and the reunion—perfectly represented the opposing sides. Those who supported the anti-Castro cause of the Cuban Americans focused on the shot of Elián being forcibly removed by armed agents, while those who supported the government's position pointed to the shot that showed a happy boy where they believed he should be—in his father's care.

The purpose of this unit is to examine those controversial photographs and to discuss how they were employed by the news media to shape public opinion. To begin with, a portfolio of front pages from a few leading newspapers—the *Miami Herald,* the *Los Angeles Times,* and the *New York Times*—will display how different papers covered the issue by making different editorial decisions about which pictures to use, how to lay them out, and what headlines would best accompany them. These verbal/visual texts are followed by several essays that place the photographs in the context of public opinion.

Writing for the online magazine *Slate,* William Saletan carefully analyzes each photograph and reminds us that "pictures, like words, can project illusions and take events out of context." The noted political columnist William Safire, on the other hand, does not see two attempts at propaganda, but asks us which picture we trust more—one taken by a professional photojournalist at the scene or a snapshot taken by someone closely involved with Elián's seizure. Although she doesn't distrust either photograph, student columnist Lindsay Cohen "reads" the gunpoint image in an unexpected fashion, seeing it as one that reinforces the power of the U.S. Constitution. Finally, Iowa State cartoonist Carmen Cerra makes a subtle and compelling visual point about the power of photography itself.

Front Page Portfolio

[THE MIAMI HERALD, THE LOS ANGELES TIMES, THE NEW YORK TIMES/
April 23, 2000]

TAKEN BACK: Armed federal agents are ready to seize Elian Gonzalez from Donato Dalrymple's arms, above, to return him to his father, Juan Miguel Gonzalez, with whom he was reunited hours later, top.

▶ **HOW IT HAPPENED**

Lightning move took agents just 154 seconds

Herald Staff Report
The lightning raid that plucked Elian Gonzalez from his great-uncle's Little Havana house capped 44 hours of near round-the-clock negotiations, filled with near-agreements, stubbornness and subterfuge, with some of Miami's most prominent citizens trying to mediate a peaceful resolution to the five-month saga of the child rather.
Attorney General Janet Reno and the Gonzalez family attorneys were in fact still on the phone with the

▶ **THE REACTION**

Tense scenes played out on Miami streets

BY SANDRA MARQUEZ GARCIA,
TYLER BRIDGES AND CURTIS MORGAN
Five months of pent-up passion spilled over Saturday into a bitter daylong series of seesaw clashes in the streets of Little Havana between hundreds of protesters and nearly as many police in full riot gear.
Demonstrators, outraged at the seizure of Elian Gonzalez by a gun-toting federal SWAT team, shouted, wept, waved flags and signs and — in isolated angrier outbreaks —

GRIEF: Elian's cousin Marisleysis Gonzalez cries after boy was taken.

▶ Attorney General Janet Reno polled advisors and got unanimous support to go ahead with "Opera-

As angry protests dwindle, strike called for Tuesday

BY MANNY GARCIA, CAROLYN SALAZAR
AND ANDRES VIGLUCCI
sviglucci@herald.com
It took five months for the custody battle over Elian Gonzalez to build to a tense standoff. It took federal agents less than three minutes to end it.
In a cleanly executed predawn raid that caught Elian's Miami relatives off guard, armed and helmeted U.S. Border Patrol officers pushed aside a handful of demonstrators to batter in the door of their Little Havana home. At gunpoint, they took the boy from the grip of his Thanksgiving Day rescuer, fisherman Donato Dalrymple.
"We're taking you to see your pa-

pa," a Spanish-speaking female agent, Betty Mills, told the terrified boy as she carried him out of the house to a government van.
Before most of Miami awoke Saturday to what had occurred, Elian had been reunited with his father, Juan Miguel Gonzalez, at Andrews Air Force Base outside Washington, D.C.
Gonzalez, who asked U.S. officials for five minutes alone with his son, boarded the airplane that brought Elian from Homestead Air Reserve Base. He emerged carrying the boy, who held his father in a bear hug.

▶ PLEASE SEE ELIAN, 2A

Los Angeles Times

Sunday Final

ON THE INTERNET: WWW.LATIMES.COM
CIRCULATION: 1,108,347 DAILY / 1,381,387 SUNDAY

SUNDAY, APRIL 23, 2000
COPYRIGHT 2000 / THE TIMES MIRROR COMPANY / CC/ 402 PAGES

$1.50 SUNDAY
DESIGNATED AREAS HIGHER

SUNDAY REPORT

Life Grim for State's Racetrack Workers

■ Decrepit housing and lack of overtime pay are common for grooms and other 'backstretch' employees. Industry long ago won exemptions from some labor standards.

By JOE MOZINGO
TIMES STAFF WRITER

Behind the grandstands and opulent turf clubs, workers who take care of horses at California's racetracks inhabit a dusty, isolated world where normal labor and living standards don't apply.

They often work every day of the week without overtime. Most live in small equipment rooms in the stables, with plywood walls, bare concrete floors and no running water.

In Pomona, they sleep and cook on county property under Fire Department signs warning: "Use as Living Quarters and Cooking Prohibited." At Santa Anita Park in Arcadia, they use filthy communal restrooms infested with flies and deemed unsanitary by the health department.

The stable areas at California's six racetracks and nine fairgrounds lack some of the most basic employee protections for approximately 4,000 workers, records and interviews show.

This situation is no accident. The horse-racing industry has long enjoyed exemptions from labor and living regulations that apply to other California workers, including

Please see TRACKS, A31

ALAN DIAZ / Associated Press
A federal agent confronts Donato Dalrymple, holding Elian Gonzalez in closet of Miami home.

Associated Press
Juan Miguel Gonzalez holds son Elian after they were reunited in Maryland.

Elian, Dad Reunited After Raid

■ **Reconstruction:** Atty. Gen. Reno decides to act after forming unusual alliance with Juan Miguel Gonzalez. Their bond reverses predictability of post-Cold War politics.

More Inside

■ **MAD IN MIAMI**—The anger of Miami's Cuban Americans exile community spills onto the streets. Hundreds are arrested. **A17**

■ **WHAT'S NEXT**—Immigration experts predict case could be resolved soon now that Elian is in the custody of his father. **A20**

■ **HEALTH CONCERNS**—Psychology experts are divided over the emotional health of boy who has lived in the media's glare. **A20**

■ **FACE OFF**—Elian has been transformed into a living visual aid, Howard Rosenberg writes. **A20**

■ **QUIET IN CUBA**—In Havana, the atmosphere was almost as if nothing had happened. **A24**

■ **Immigration:** U.S. agents swarm home of Cuban boy's Florida relatives, ending five-month impasse. He joins father at Maryland military base. Protesters roam Miami streets.

By RICHARD A. SERRANO
TIMES STAFF WRITER

WASHINGTON—For Janet Reno, the eleventh hour came at 4 in the morning.

Tired, exasperated, unable after hours of negotiations to reach a peaceful solution to the impasse over Elian Gonzalez, she sat at her desk in the Justice Department early Saturday and asked half a dozen top advisers whether the time had come to use force. Each of them said yes.

It was an excruciating moment for the attorney general, who has always maintained that the care of children is her priority but whose tenure began tragically with the bungled raid of the Branch Davidian compound near Waco, Texas, in which 19 children died.

It was time to act, Reno decided, not only for the sake of 6-year-old Elian but also for Juan Miguel Gonzalez, the 31-year-old father who had made an indelible impression on Reno when they met only two weeks earlier.

Reno spoke into her telephone headset.

"Go," she said.

A few minutes later, the phone rang. Intermediaries working with Elian's relatives in Miami were on the line. They wanted more time to negotiate.

But it was too late. White vans carrying a score of helmeted and heavily armed agents already were caravaning toward the relatives' tiny white stucco house. Using a battering ram to break through the door, they retrieved Elian at gunpoint from the family members who wanted to keep him in America forever.

Within a few hours, father and son were reunited.

For Reno, the bond forged with Juan Miguel Gonzalez was complete.

It was an odd combination from the start: a hotel doorman and self-avowed communist in common cause with the highest law enforcement official in the world's biggest democracy.

For a while, their unusual alliance reversed the polarity of post-Cold War politics and brought about a rare alignment of two traditionally hostile governments.

For more than 40 years, since Fidel Castro seized control of the Caribbean island south of Florida, the two nations have rarely seen eye to eye. Yet on the question of Elian Gonzalez, both governments found themselves in fundamental agreement: Juan Miguel Gonzalez is Elian's rightful legal guardian, and father and son should be reunited as soon as possible.

It was a relationship patched together by each nation's anguish over the fate of the young shipwreck survivor whose mother perished in her attempt to reach America and freedom last November.

It was a relationship that deepened along with Reno's growing conviction that Juan Miguel Gonzalez truly loved his son and that he had come to America in good faith as the boy's only surviving parent.

What follows is a reconstruction of key moments in that relationship, based on U.S. government documents and interviews with the

Please see REVIEW, A18

By RICHARD A. SERRANO
and MIKE CLARY
TIMES STAFF WRITERS

MIAMI—Elian Gonzalez was reunited with his father Saturday after a SWAT team of federal agents, armed with semiautomatic weapons and firing pepper spray, rushed the home of the Cuban boy's Miami relatives and seized the child near a back bedroom closet.

Crying "Help me! Help me!" in both English and Spanish, the frightened 6-year-old was hurried from Miami's Little Havana neighborhood in a predawn raid, taken by helicopter to a waiting government jet and flown to Andrews Air Force Base in suburban Washington, where he was turned over to the long-waiting arms of his father, Juan Miguel Gonzalez.

The reunion was warm and emotional, said the father's attorney, Gregory B. Craig. It followed five months of anxiety and extremely harsh feelings that have consumed the case of the little refugee, whose mother drowned as he was set adrift on an inner tube in the Florida Straits.

"There was a huge relief on Juan Miguel's face and a huge smile," Craig said after watching the initial embrace of father and son. "I saw

absolutely no evidence of any kind of trauma or any kind of fear or any kind of uncertainty" on Elian's part.

Indeed, even as Elian's Miami relatives flew to Washington to try to see the boy Saturday, photos showed a smiling Elian with his father, stepmother and little half-brother, Hianny. In one shot, Elian, dressed in a blue Batman shirt, beamed as his father held him in front of the camera.

Those images were starkly different from the pictures and TV footage from Miami. In one Associated Press photograph, a federal agent in full attack gear, a large firearm in the general direction of the terrified child, the agent's finger is poised near the trigger.

Or, television, a crying Elian was seen being whisked by an Immigration and Naturalization Service agent out of the house and into a police van. Outside, agents fired pepper spray to control a small crowd of Cuban Americans, some of them hurling rocks and other debris in anger.

As the sun came up on a startled Miami, protesters roamed through the streets. Sometimes the crowds were more than 1,000 strong. More rocks and debris were thrown at

Please see REUNION, A18

After Such Strife, Vietnam Fades From Campuses

By KENNETH R. WEISS
TIMES EDUCATION WRITER

The Vietnam War, which tore the fabric of American society for a decade, has dwindled on college campuses to just another case study of foreign policy during the Cold War.

It's not for lack of scholarly interest. Since 1990, academics have been churning out more books on Vietnam than on World War II. The trend has continued through the decade, with a regular crop of

LESSONS AND LEGACIES

25 Years After Vietnam

■ One in a series

finger-pointing exposes, revisionist theories, revisions of the revisionists and incessant searches for lessons amid the rubble of defeat.

Nor is it a lack of student interest. At many campuses, students mob the few available classes. They hunger for insight into the war, hoping to learn more about events that reverberate through

Please see CAMPUSES, A30

Janitors Reach Tentative Accord

The union representing striking janitors reached a tentative agreement with cleaning contractors Saturday night. The janitors strike will continue, however, pending a union vote Monday on the proposed pact. **B1**

CAROLYN COLE / Los Angeles Times
Elian Gonzalez is carried by an Immigration and Naturalization Service agent from the home of his Miami relatives to an awaiting police van.

'Operation Reunion' Seen as Harsh but Necessary

■ **Tactics:** Family, others say predawn raid on home amounted to overkill. But some experts disagree.

By LISA GETTER
and ROBERT J. JACKSON
TIMES STAFF WRITERS

WASHINGTON—In the end, it took just three minutes. But it was three minutes of raw intimidation.

Family lawyer Kendall Coffey, on the phone with a mediator, heard the front door being smashed off its hinges. Federal agents stormed into the little white house. One agent, in green riot gear, armed with an automatic rifle, burst into a bedroom where Elian Gonzalez was being hidden. A Spanish-speaking female agent grabbed the scared 6-year-old and ran to an unmarked white van.

Elsewhere in the house, agents pushed through doors, menaced occupants and shouted at cousin Marisleysis Gonzalez, "Give me the boy! Give me the . . . boy!" she

said later. Outside, federal agents dressed in riot gear sprayed the anti-Castro crowd with pepper spray.

Then, as suddenly as it had begun, Operation Reunion was over.

The raid was part of a plan that had been in the works for weeks. There were opportunities to grab the child before Saturday—at the Miami hospital where Elian's cousin was admitted, at a park in Miami Beach where the family met with Atty. Gen. Janet Reno 10 days ago.

But when the mission was finally launched, the images of gun-toting officers shocked more than just those in the house in Little Havana, as camera crews quickly beamed the scene to television audiences around the world.

Reno and Immigration and Naturalization Service Commissioner

Please see TACTICS, A22

New England Final
Boston: Periods of light rain and fog continue, high 50. Tonight, still cloudy, low 45. Tomorrow, clouds slowly crumble, brighter late, high 58. Weather map and details are on Page 25.

The New York Times

VOL. CXLIX .... No. 51,367   Copyright © 2000 The New York Times   SUNDAY, APRIL 23, 2000   THREE DOLLARS

Drug Makers Reap Profits On Tax-Backed Research

By JEFF GERTH and SHERYL GAY STOLBERG

MEDICINE MERCHANTS

Birth of a Blockbuster

On Jan. 7, 1982, in a laboratory at Columbia University, a little-known science professor, Laszlo Z. Bito, finished a nine-month experiment on the eyes of cats. In his handwritten data, carefully charted in gray hardcover notebooks, lay the origins of what every pharmaceutical company longs for: a blockbuster drug.

The drug is Xalatan, a best-selling eyedrop for glaucoma. With $507 million in sales last year — and the potential for billions more, most of it pure profit — the four-year-old medicine is the equivalent of liquid gold for its manufacturer, The Pharmacia Corporation. The eyedrop earned Columbia University about $20 million in royalties last year, and it has made a millionaire of Dr. Bito as well.

Yet there are other, unseen, partners in the creation of Xalatan: the American taxpayers, who backed Dr. Bito's work with $4 million from the National Institutes of Health. The taxpayers have reaped no financial return on their investment; their reward, government officials say, is the eyedrop itself.

Xalatan costs patients $45 to $50 for a tiny bottle that lasts six weeks. That price — about $1 a day for a drug that staves off

This drug to fight glaucoma, developed with government help, is not cheaper because of it.

blindness — may not seem excessive. But the key ingredient in that daily dose costs Pharmacia only pennies to make, and Americans, who live in the only industrialized nation that lacks government restraints on drug prices, pay more than twice what Europeans patients pay for the drug.

That puts Xalatan out of reach for patients like Albert Russell, a retired optician and part-time blues singer from Prince George's County, Md. Mr. Russell, whose glaucoma has left him nearly blind, lives on an $832-a-month Social Security check. He is among the one-third of elderly Americans who lack prescription drug coverage, and when he talks about Xalatan, he uses the word "outrageous" to describe its price.

To officials at Pharmacia, the price is fair. "We are bringing forth innovation," said Dr. Anders Harfstrand, the company's vice president for ophthalmology, "and innovation always brings a premium."

In this election year, the cost of prescription medicines is at the center of the political debate. With the biomedical revolution yielding a flood of new medicines, drugs are now the fastest-growing component of the nation's trillion-dollar-a-year medical bill. As Congress contemplates expanding Medicare to include prescription drug coverage, and some states move to bring drug prices more in line with those in foreign countries, the industry is struggling to fend off federal regulation that might limit its ability to set prices.

At the heart of the fight is Dr.

Continued on Page 20

Federal Welfare Overhaul Allows Albany to Shift Money Elsewhere

By RAYMOND HERNANDEZ

ALBANY, April 22 — In the four years since the overhaul of the nation's welfare laws, New York has taken at least $1 billion given to it by the federal government for new antipoverty programs and used it instead to indirectly finance huge tax cuts and other programs that appeal to middle-class voters, according to government and private estimates.

The budgetary switch has also been employed by other states, prompting Congress to open an investigation to determine the scope of the practice nationwide. But New York, with the nation's second-largest welfare population, appears to be among the most aggressive states in using its federal welfare dollars to help pay for other programs it would otherwise find difficult to afford.

To date, New York has taken in roughly $6.1 billion in federal welfare funds and earmarked about $5 billion of it — that's in state disagreement as to the exact figure — to finance traditional programs for the poor,

like public-assistance grants. But it has spent very little of the remaining money to create programs intended to help welfare recipients make the transition to permanent employment, as proponents of the new federal welfare law intended.

Instead, the state used that money, as much as $1.3 billion by some estimates, for welfare programs the state and local governments once financed themselves. That has freed an unprecedented amount of state money, which has been used to help pay for politically popular programs, like a host of new tax cuts and more state aid for local governments.

The situation represents a missed opportunity, say advocates for the poor, who have been urging the state to invest its welfare money in the kinds of innovative anti-poverty programs envisioned by proponents of the welfare overhaul, including its emphasis on job placement

Continued on Page 26

INSIDE

An Internet Shakeout
Internet executives say the market will soon shake loose some industry losers. Most think that means the other guy, not them.   PAGE 11

Wide Debate on Abortion
The Supreme Court will soon review

Alexander H. Cohen Dies
The producer of 101 shows on Broadway and in London's West End and the originator of the annual Tony Awards television was 78.   PAGE 36

Desert Grandeur in Arizona
Hopi artisans turn clay into ancient

CUBAN BOY SEIZED BY U.S. AGENTS AND REUNITED WITH HIS FATHER

OUTRAGE IN MIAMI

Child Is Reported Calm After Tense Moments in Little Havana

By RICK BRAGG

MIAMI, April 22 — Armed United States immigration agents smashed their way into the Little Havana home of Elián González's Miami relatives before dawn today, took the sobbing 6-year-old boy from a bedroom closet and flew him to a reunion with his father outside Washington.

As demonstrators wept in rage and coughed from pepper spray and tear gas, the agents wrapped the child in a blanket and carried him to an airport to fly him to Washington. The action touched off a fury in the streets outside the home where Cuban exiles have kept a vigil since November.

"What's happening? What's happening?" Elián said in Spanish as he was taken away. "Help me. Help me."

The raid ended a bitter standoff between the federal government and the boy's defiant great-uncle, after federal officials finally gave up fruitless negotiations with an exile community that saw Elián as a symbol of freedom and a precious victory, now perhaps lost, over President Fidel Castro of Cuba.

"God, how could you have performed only half a miracle?" asked a frantic, weeping Marisleysis González, a 21-year-old cousin who had been the boy's closest companion since he was rescued at sea on Nov. 25 in a failed crossing from Cuba that drowned his mother.

The United States Justice Department said this morning that Elián was taken safely from the home at about 5:15 a.m. and was flown to Andrews Air Force Base near Washington, where his father, Juan Miguel González, waited.

Later in the morning, Mr. González was seen carrying Elián from a car at the base. They are together, said Myron Marlin, a Justice Department spokesman.

Within minutes of being reunited with his father, stepmother and 6-month-old half-brother, Elián was "totally at ease" and laughing, said Gregory B. Craig, Juan Miguel González's lawyer.

Photographs released by the lawyer showed a beaming Elián. The family will be taken to an undisclosed location in the Washington area, where it can be assured of privacy, officials said.

Elián, one Justice Department spokesman said, was satisfied and calm on the flight from Miami, a federal agents gently explained what was happening.

An hundred of unhappy Cuban-American demonstrators clashed with the police keen this afternoon, the distraught Miami relatives, say they wanted to assure themselves that the boy was happy and safe, boarded a plane to Washington, seeking a meeting with Mr. González, who had not yet decided whether to grant one.

The relatives — Lázaro, Delfin and Marisleysis González — were met at Reagan National Airport by a police escort. They had hoped to go directly to Andrews to see Elián, but were

Continued on Page 14

90 Miles Away

Castro's revolution has divided many Cuban families, but none as publicly as Elián González's feuding clan.   MAGAZINE

Juan Miguel González with his son Elián yesterday after Elián's 9:42 a.m. arrival at Andrews Air Force Base, in a photo released by the family's lawyer. Mr. González's wife, Nersy, held their 6-month-old son, Hianny.

For Reno, a Difficult Call in the Last Minutes

By DAVID JOHNSTON

WASHINGTON, April 22 — Their agonizing deadline was 3 a.m., and as the minutes ticked away before federal law-enforcement officials had to decide whether to seize Elián González at gunpoint, Attorney General Janet Reno was on the phone to lawyers for the boy's Miami relatives, appealing to them one last time to end the impasse.

"You are running out of time," an aide to the attorney general recalled Ms. Reno as having said, describing her tone in explicit but tense emotional and fatigue after allnight negotiations. "You've got to decide now." Ms. Reno said, "That's all the time you have."

With that, as Ms. Reno held the phone in her office at the Justice Department, a team of eight agents, some of them armed and wearing body armor and jumpsuits, swarmed into the house of Elián's great-uncle, Lázaro González. It was just the kind of raid, armed and confrontational and carried out under darkness, that the officials had said for weeks was the situation they wanted to avoid. In fact the specter of an armed federal agent grabbing the boy from a closet was displayed in television all day.

Within three minutes the agents were gone, taking the child in a waiting minivan, ending a five-month-long custody battle that had haunted Ms. Reno, who had tried, and repeatedly failed, to coax him the case without the use of force.

This morning after the raid, President Clinton said that Ms. Reno had made the right decision and that he supported her. "The law has been upheld," he said, "and that was the right thing to do."

"She made the decision," Mr. Clinton said. "She managed this. But I fully support what she did. And it was clear to me from our long conversations that we was in agreement that they were on the phone with Ms. Reno asking for more time and with Ms. Reno asking for more time as the agents stormed the house. Ms. Reno made confirmed the account, but said that she had warned them for hours that time for negotiations was rapidly coming to an end.

About 4 a.m., Ms. Reno learned representatives of the relatives that

Continued on Page 17

Lawyers for the relatives complained that they were on the phone with Ms. Reno asking for more time as the agents stormed the house. Ms. Reno made confirmed the account, but said that she had warned them for hours that time for negotiations was rapidly coming to an end.

Doris Meissner, the immigration service commissioner who was by Ms. Reno's side throughout the night, said the agents' commanders had asked to be told no later than 3 a.m. whether to begin the raid, a deadline that stretched another hour as the talks dragged on.

Elián González was carried out of the home of his Miami relatives before dawn by agents of the Immigration and Naturalization Service.

WILLIAM SALETAN

The Elián Pictures

[SLATE/April 24, 2000]

Before You Read

What is the purpose of photographs? Are they pictures of a frozen moment, or do they tell a whole story? When you look at your photographs, do you stop and consider what was happening immediately before or immediately after you took the picture? Have you ever critiqued a photograph?

Words to Learn

foment (para. 1): to stir up (trouble); instigate (v.)

demonstrably (para. 5): in a manner that can be demonstrated or proved (adv.)

relinquish (para. 6): to give up; abandon (v.)

noncompliance (para. 6): failure to comply; refusal to yield (n.)

iconographic (para. 11): representative, illustrative; often symbolic (adj.)

credence (para. 12): belief, credentials (n.)

cropped (para. 13): cut off the tops or ends of (v.)

glosses (para. 18): makes appear right by showy argument or by minimizing (v.)

attributes (para. 19): designates as a cause (v.)

WILLIAM SALETAN _(b. 1964) is a frequent contributor to_ Slate, The New Republic, Mother Jones, The National Review, _and_ George, _among other publications. He is the recipient of a Washington Monthly Journalism Award, and he has a book forthcoming on politics (2001). Saletan lives in the Washington, D.C. area._

We saw the pictures on television and in the papers all weekend. The first shows a federal agent, machine gun at the ready, seizing Elián González from the home of his Miami relatives before dawn Saturday. The second shows Elián smiling with an arm around his father, Juan Miguel, hours later in Maryland. The Miami family and its supporters have used the first picture to foment outrage against the government's raid. Juan Miguel and his supporters have used the second picture to reassure the public that Elián is safe and happy. Don't believe it. Pictures, like words, can project illusions and take events out of context. Look again at each picture. Notice what it disguises and what it omits.

Start with the image that dominated the weekend, the picture of the Miami raid.

1. Whose house is it?   "The chilling picture of a little boy being removed from his home at gunpoint defies the values of America," says George W. Bush. But that's not what the picture shows. Elián isn't being removed from his home. He's being removed from the house in which his great-uncle and cousins, against his father's wishes and without legal custody, have kept him. The picture doesn't convey whose house it is. Instead, by capturing Elián's moment of terror, it suggests to the eye that the house is Elián's.

2. Who's holding Elián?   The man holding Elián isn't his father, his cousin, or even a longtime family friend. He's Donato Dalrymple, one of the fishermen who plucked Elián out of the ocean last November. "They took this kid like a hostage in the nighttime," Dalrymple protested to reporters after the raid. But if Elián is the hostage in this scene, who's the kidnapper?

3. What is Elián doing?   Sunday's *New York Times* said the picture showed Elián "hiding in a closet in the arms of" Dalrymple. But the only person who's demonstrably hiding is Dalrymple. Since Elián is in Dalrymple's arms, he has to go wherever Dalrymple takes him. If Dalrymple had carried Elián to the front door and presented him to the agents, Elián would have gone along. But that wouldn't have proved that Elián wanted to leave the house, any more than this picture proves Elián wanted to stay. It turns out, according to Monday's *Times,* that Dalrymple "grabbed [Elián] and hid in a closet, trying to protect the boy."

4. How did we get here?   A picture captures a moment, omitting the events that led to it. In this case, the missing context includes months of effort by the U.S. Justice Department to get the Miami relatives to relinquish Elián to his father, a government order stripping the relatives of custody, the relatives' failure to turn over the boy, and a final, all-night negotiating session in which the relatives again dragged their feet and tried to set conditions for a father-son visit.

According to the *Times*, Attorney General Janet Reno warned the relatives during the night that the time for noncompliance had run out and that if they didn't agree right away to hand over Elián, "We're going to take a law-enforcement action." The raid was the last act of the play. But it's the only act shown in the picture.

Even that act has been reduced to its final scene. The agents had 7 arrived with a warrant to search the house for Elián and retrieve him. They had knocked on the door, announcing who they were and why they were there. Only after the relatives failed to respond had the agents broken into the house and entered the room where Dalrymple held Elián. None of these precautions shows up in the picture.

5. *What does the agent see?* It seems clear from the picture that 8 Dalrymple is unarmed. But this seems clear only because the raid is now over and no weapons were found in the house. The agent in the picture doesn't know that. He's sizing up the situation in real time. He and his colleagues are heavily armed because Justice Department officials had heard there might be weapons in the house. They were wrong. But they weren't reckless.

6. *What's going on outside?* The picture shows only what is 9 going on inside the house. Outside, a crowd of anti-Castro demonstrators that has dwindled from hundreds earlier in the evening is erupting in outrage. Federal officials say they wanted the agents well-armed in case extremists in the crowd made good on threats of lethal violence. That didn't happen, though some of the demonstrators scuffled with the agents and tried to block the door.

7. *At whom is the gun aimed?* Sen. Connie Mack, R-Fla., says 10 the agent in the picture is "pointing a gun at the head of a 6-year-old boy." House Majority Whip[1] Tom DeLay says the agent is "waving a machine gun at" Elián. But the reason you can see the agent's trigger finger clearly is that it's extended *alongside* the gun, *not* curled around the trigger. And the impression that the gun is pointed at Elián is an optical illusion caused by compressing a three-dimensional scene into a two-dimensional photograph. In the vertical dimension, Reno says the gun is pointed down, which agents call the "search po-

[1] *Whip:* An officer of a political party in Congress, Parliament, and so on, whose duties include maintaining discipline and enforcing attendance.

sition." That's not clear, but the more salient point is that in the horizontal dimension, the gun is pointed in the direction of Dalrymple rather than Elián—which is logical, because Dalrymple is holding Elián, and the agents had been warned of violence at the house and were under orders to protect Elián. If you saw the picture on CNN Saturday morning, you had no idea the gun was pointed at anyone other than Elián, because Dalrymple had been squeezed out of the picture.

8. Why does the agent look scary? Many critics have cited the agent's combat gear, helmet, goggles, and heavy weapon as evidence that the government used overkill. The agent's outfit and weapon certainly are intimidating—and that's the point. "A great show of force can often avoid violence," explained former Solicitor General Walter Dellinger on ABC's *This Week*. "It allowed [the agents] to get in and out in three minutes before a crowd could build up through which they might have had to fight their way out. Look again at that iconographic picture and you will see that Mr. Dalrymple . . . is stunned by the officer in his display of a weapon. . . . His jaw goes slack, his arm loses its grip, and that avoided a physical tug-of-war which could have severely injured" Elián. The momentary image is designed to look bad so that the real outcome will be good. But the picture doesn't capture the real outcome. It only captures the momentary image. 11

9. Has the gun been fired? At a press conference Sunday, an attorney for the Miami relatives accused the agents of "going in with guns blazing." The picture lends credence to that charge. In fact, however, no shots were fired. The picture leaves out the key piece of information that would have dispelled this illusion: a soundtrack. 12

10. Who took the picture? Every photograph taken during a complex sequence of events entails two interwoven biases. First, it conveys only the moment and image that the photographer chooses to convey. You're looking at this particular scene from this particular perspective because this is the moment at which the photographer chose to snap a picture, and this is the perspective from which he chose to snap it. Second, having immortalized these two choices, the camera, by its nature, conceals the person who made them. In this case, that person is Alan Diaz, a freelance photographer. The *Washington Post* says Diaz "had developed a relationship with the González family and was standing nearby when the boy was discovered in the closet." The *Times* says Diaz "was guided into the bedroom where the boy was being held" before the agent got there. The caption on the photograph, however, tells you none of this. All it says 13 is "Associated Press." (Joshua King of SpeakOut.com has written a brilliant, thorough analysis of how Diaz got the picture and how it was composed and cropped. To read his report, go to http://www .speakout.com/activism/opinion/king0424.asp).

11. What happened afterward?   According to news accounts,   14 once the agents got Elián out of Dalrymple's arms, they wrapped the boy in a blanket, whisked him outside to a van, assured him that everything would be all right, fed him, gave him toys, and took him by helicopter and plane to his father in Maryland. None of this shows up in the picture. Instead, the still photograph, carried by protesters in the streets of Miami and replayed endlessly on television, immortalizes the episode's worst moment and obscures its actual conclusion.

Recognizing the political damage done by this picture of the raid,   15 Juan Miguel's attorney, Greg Craig, released a different picture of Elián, showing the boy smiling after being reunited with his father. But this picture, too, should be scrutinized.

1. What does Elián know?   Craig and his congressional allies   16 say Elián's smile proves that the boy is in good hands. But a smile doesn't prove that the person who's smiling is in good hands. It only proves that he *thinks* he's in good hands. Does Elián understand his situation? The agents who took him from Miami say that he told them he didn't want to go back to Cuba. They assured him he was only going to see his father. Does Elián understand that the U.S. government expects the courts to reject the Miami relatives' appeals to keep Elián in the United States—and that once this happens, Juan Miguel intends to take Elián back to Cuba?

2. Where is Elián's mother?   The impression created by the pic-   17 ture is that this is Elián's nuclear family, and the woman on the left is his mother. On *Meet the Press,* Craig reinforced this impression by discussing decisions about Elián which "Juan Miguel, in consultation with his wife and family, will make." But Juan Miguel's wife, the woman in the picture, is *not* Elián's mother. Elián's mother, who was divorced from Juan Miguel, is missing from the picture because she drowned while bringing Elián to the United States. Had she been alive, she would hardly have cooperated with Craig's reassuring message. Dead men tell no tales, and dead women appear in no pictures.

3. Whose house is it?   The family picture, like the raid picture,   18 generates the impression that Elián is at home. He isn't. In this picture, he's at a house at Andrews Air Force Base in Maryland. According to the *Post,* "A crib and children's bed had been set up in the living room, with a double bed in the bedroom. U.S. marshals had moved in next door. Several Cuban officials were present, along with a few beefy INS officers." The *Post* says, "Cuban government officials are believed to have access to" the family. The AP says Elián has been "holed up" with the family. The *Orlando Sentinel* reports that Saturday, "Only Craig, [the Reverend Joan Brown] Campbell and a small group of confidants and government officials had access to Elián and his family"; and Sunday, Juan Miguel "refused through a base spokesman to meet with" the Miami relatives. Who controls the premises? Who has access to Elián and Juan Miguel? Who has influence over them? Who gets to interpret their words and deeds? The picture glosses over these questions.

4. *Who took the picture?* In a caption, the *Post* attributes the picture to "González family via AP." But the AP neither took the picture nor received it directly from Juan Miguel—much less from the "González family," a title of authenticity to which Elián's Miami relatives arguably have a better claim than Elián's stepmother does. The picture was provided to the AP by Craig. There's no evidence that Craig is allied with Fidel Castro, as some critics charge. But Craig's role is certainly open to question, since Juan Miguel obviously can't afford to pay Craig's bills. The danger is not, as the Miami relatives foolishly suggest, that the picture has been "doctored." The danger is that just as the photographer in Miami chose to capture Elián at his most terrified, the photographer in Maryland chose to capture Elián at his most relaxed.

> *Reality is one thing.*
> *Pictures are another.*
> *To confuse the two,*
> *you'd have to be blind.*

The media and the players in the Elián saga are busy congratulating themselves on their use of the pictures to convey what happened this weekend. "One of the beauties of television is that it shows exactly what the facts are," says Reno. "The two pictures . . . captured the story from start to finish," agrees a *New York Times* editor. Nonsense. Reality is one thing. Pictures are another. To confuse the two, you'd have to be blind.

Vocabulary/Using a Dictionary

1. In paragraph 1, what does *foment* mean ("The Miami family and its supporters have used the first picture to *foment* outrage against the government's raid")? What is the origin of the word?

2. What does the word *iconographic* mean (para. 11)? What words do you recognize within it?

3. "Joshua King of SpeakOut.com has written a brilliant, thorough analysis of how Diaz got the picture and how it was composed and *cropped*," comments Saletan in paragraph 13. What does the author suggest by his use of the word *cropped*?

Responding to Words in Context

1. In paragraph 9, Saletan states: "Federal officials say they wanted the agents well armed in case *extremists* in the crowd made good on threats of lethal violence." What do you think the word *extremist* means? What word do you think *extremist* derives from? What is the definition of this word?

2. "The agents had arrived with a *warrant* to search the house for Elián and retrieve him," states Saletan in paragraph 7. In this context, what does the word *warrant* mean? In what other ways can you use the word?

3. In step three ("Whose house is it?") of analyzing the second picture, Saletan fires some questions at the reader: "Who controls the premises? Who has access to Elián and Juan Miguel? Who has influence over them? Who gets to interpret their words and deeds? The picture *glosses* over these questions" (para. 18). What does the word *glosses* mean? From where do you think the word took its meaning?

Discussing Main Point and Meaning

1. Explain, according to the author, who supports each picture, and why the photograph has been supported by the group. Further, describe Saletan's opinion of media photography.

2. While analyzing the photograph of the Miami raid in paragraph 4 ("Who's holding Elián?"), why does the author inquire of the reader "if Elián is the hostage in this scene, who's the kidnapper?"

3. What do we learn about the background of Alan Diaz, the man who took the picture of the Miami raid (para. 13)? Why does Saletan think this information is important?

4. If, as the author claims in paragraph 19, "the danger is not, as the Miami relatives foolishly suggest, that the [Elián smiling] pic-

ture has been 'doctored,'" then, according to the author, what is the danger of the picture?

Examining Sentences, Paragraphs, and Organization

1. What is the purpose of the first sentences of paragraphs 3–6, 8–14, and 16–19? Why is the author posing these sentences as questions?

2. A transition, by definition, is "a passing from one condition, form, state, activity, place, etc., to another." Transitional paragraphs smoothly relate the preceding topic to the next one. Locate the transitional paragraph or paragraphs in Saletan's essay and describe how this paragraph effects a transition.

3. An essay is *unified* when all its paragraphs clarify or help support the main idea (thesis). Unity is lost if an essay strays from the topic by including sentences and paragraphs unrelated to the main idea. Keeping this definition of *unity* in mind, does Saletan's essay have unity? Explain how you know.

Thinking Critically

1. Throughout Saletan's essay, he arrives at many different conclusions based on interpreting and observing the two different media photos. Are his conclusions sound? Do you agree with all of them?

2. After reading Saletan's essay, do you feel more or less informed about the Elián situation? More or less confused about the outcome? Do you consider Saletan to be an authority on the Elián seizure? Why or why not?

In-Class Writing Activities

1. Have you ever had a serious discussion about the Elián situation outside of the classroom? In a short essay, describe the dialogue (exchange of ideas and opinions) that took place.

2. Pretend that you are engaging in a correspondence with young Elián González. Write him a letter giving him any warnings, guidance, or advice that you would like to share.

WILLIAM SAFIRE

In the Dead of Night

[THE NEW YORK TIMES/April 24, 2000]

Before You Read

When you watch the news or read a newspaper, do you scrutinize the information you receive? If you see two different views on a topic, how do you decide which opinion is right? Do you trust the media? To what extent?

Words to Learn

dismaying (para. 3): afraid at the prospect of danger; daunting (adj.)

cajoling (para. 4): coaxing with flattery and insincere talk (v.)

admonished (para. 5): cautioned against specific faults; warned (v.)

fiats (para. 8): orders issued by legal authority (n.)

arrogate (para. 10): to seize without right; appropriate (v.)

impunity (para. 10): exemption from punishment, penalty, or harm (n.)

circumvented (para. 10): circled around; got the better of by craft or ingenuity (v.)

defiance (para. 12): bold resistance to authority or opposition (n.)

preemptive (para. 12): having to do with an action taken to check another action beforehand (adj.)

ludicrous (para. 12): laughably absurd (adj.)

Photograph #1 shows a helmeted, goggled, grimacing man   1
pointing a fearsome automatic weapon toward a terrified child being protected by the man who rescued him from the ocean five months ago.

WILLIAM SAFIRE *(b. 1929) is a longtime journalist and speechwriter. He consistently provides a conservative voice for the* New York Times *through his editorial columns and, from 1969 to 1973, was a speechwriter for President Nixon.*

Photograph #2 shows the same child hours later, posing smiling   2
and relaxed in the arms of his father.

The first photo was shot by Alan Diaz of the Associated Press,   3
who will presumably provide its reporters with full details surrounding the politically dismaying spot-news photo. Diaz, who was waved into the house by its residents' shocked attorney, could respond credibly to such questions as: Were other shots taken in the instants before and after? Was anything posed? Who was first to grab the child? What were the subjects saying? The news organization is objective; we'll believe its report.

The second photo was credited "courtesy of Juan Miguel   4
González," carefully posed for propaganda purposes. It was taken—after nobody knows how much cajoling—by Gregory Craig, President Clinton's personal lawyer, who was hired by the left-wing church group serving Fidel Castro's interests.

> *Which photo do you believe illuminates the truth of this drama—the spot-news shot or the propaganda pose?*

Attorney General Janet Reno's spokes-   5
man, Eric Holder, admonished us yesterday "not to focus on" the photo taken by the free press. "The picture that Americans should focus on," he says, is #2, of the happy family taken and distributed by the Clinton-Craig-Cuban connection.

Which photo do you believe illumi-   6
nates the truth of this drama—the spot-news shot or the propaganda pose? Will Clinton-Reno Justice be remembered for the happy reunion or by the brutal excess of police power that brought it about?

I've been among the majority who believed that, in the close   7
judgment between a father's custodial rights and a child's opportunity to live in a free society, the father had the edge. Let the courts decide, we thought; in due course, Mr. González would prevail and the rule of law be grudgingly obeyed.

But Reno, prodded by Clinton, who wanted to teach Cuban-   8
Americans a lesson, could not abide further challenge to executive fiats. When the lawyer Craig turned down the final compromise that had been agreed to by Elián's relatives in Miami, she caved in to the pressure and sent in the troops.

In so doing, she made three mistakes that discredited her office,   9
disgusted the fair-minded, and demeaned the United States.

Mistake 1: *I am the law.* No executive officials can arrogate to   10
themselves the notion that they are "the law"; they merely execute

laws passed by legislatures and interpreted by courts. The genius of the American system is that the individual can with impunity fight the federal government in federal courts and in Congress. In this case, the Clinton administration circumvented a federal appeals court decision that encouraged the relatives' case; instead, the can't-wait enforcers took the law into their own heavy hands.

Mistake 2: *Treating Elián as a hostage.* When hostages are endangered, the government can trick the terrorists by stringing them along and then striking in the dead of night with overwhelming force. Wrongly construing Elián to be a hostage, Reno talked with the relatives' lawyers on the phone, supposedly negotiating, even as her agents in body armor smashed down the door.   11

But Elián was no hostage; nobody was harming him or threatening anybody's life. In this civil case, lawyers for the boy's loving relatives were disputing the Immigration Service's demands in a court of law. For Reno to claim "intelligence" (from the F.B.I.?) that the Cuban-Americans' arguably legal defiance was backed up with hidden weapons—and therefore that she was urgently required to launch a preemptive assault by a score of our most ferocious-looking agents—is ludicrous. Clinton Justice plainly lost its head.   12

Mistake 3: *In the dead of night, nobody would see.* Clinton may have realized that by pressing Reno to smash into a peaceful citizen's home in darkness to search and seize, the only visible injury would be to the spirit of the Fourth Amendment. He counted, as usual, on not getting caught in the act. That was the crowning mistake: A photographer showed up to record the nation's shame.   13

Vocabulary/Using a Dictionary

1. "The first photo was shot by Alan Diaz of the Associated Press, who will presumably provide its reporters with full details surrounding the politically *dismaying* spot-news photo," Safire writes in paragraph 3. Explain the author's statement in your own words.

2. What does Safire mean by *cajoling* (para. 4)? To whom does he refer as having *cajoled* someone?

3. What is a "*preemptive* assault" (para. 12)? Why was Attorney General Janet Reno forced to launch one?

Responding to Words in Context

1. What is the difference between *objective* and *subjective* points of view, as in paragraph 3 where Safire writes, "The news organization is *objective;* we'll believe its report"? Explain your answers.

2. In paragraph 8, Safire remarks: "Reno, *prodded* by Clinton, who wanted to teach Cuban Americans a lesson, could not abide further challenge to executive fiats." What does the word *prodded* mean? In your own words, restate the previous statement.

Discussing Main Point and Meaning

1. What is suggested by Safire's brief analysis of the two photographs in paragraphs 3–6? Which of the two photographs do you think the author favors? What, specifically, makes you think so?

2. Safire explains that Janet Reno "made three mistakes that discredited her office" (para. 9). According to the author, what were these mistakes? How did they discredit her office?

3. To what does the title, "In the Dead of Night," refer? What associations does it call up? What might the title imply about Safire's essay?

Examining Sentences, Paragraphs, and Organization

1. What are the topic sentences of paragraphs 3 and 11? Why do you think so?

2. What supporting evidence does the author give for his generalized conclusion "a photographer showed up to record the nation's shame" (para. 13)?

Thinking Critically

1. What tone does Safire take in the essay? What was your reaction to this tone?

2. "I've been among the majority who believed that, in the close judgment between a father's custodial rights and a child's opportunity to live in a free society, the father had the edge," decrees the author in paragraph 7. Do you agree with Safire that a father's

custodial rights are more important than a child's opportunity to live in a free society?

In-Class Writing Activities

1. The Fourth Amendment to the United States Constitution states: "The right of the people to be secure in their persons, houses, papers, and effects, against unreasonable search and seizures, shall not be violated, no Warrants shall issue, but upon probable cause, supported by Oath or affirmation, and particularly describing the place to be searched, and the persons or things to be seized." Based on Safire's essay, write a brief essay agreeing or disagreeing with Safire's assertion in paragraph 13 that Attorney General Janet Reno violated this amendment to the Constitution. Are the two pictures evidence enough to support your conclusion?

2. The news media have been the target of much negative criticism in recent years. On the contrary, Safire comments on the reliability of the news in paragraph 3: "The first photo was shot by Alan Diaz of the Associated Press.... *The news organization is objective; we'll believe its report.*" Freewrite about the reliability of information from the news media, agreeing or disagreeing with Safire's claim.

LINDSAY COHEN

A Tale of Two Images

[THE DAILY NORTHWESTERN, NORTHWESTERN UNIVERSITY/May 3, 2000]

Before You Read

How much force is "too much" force when the U.S. military is involved in domestic situations? Think about the way the U.S. government has handled recent governmental police actions. Did it use excessive force? Do you think it is right for the government to use any force on its own people? Is it necessary?

Words to Learn

inception (para. 1): the act of beginning; start (n.)

inundated (para. 1): covered with (or as with) a flood (v.)

conjure (para. 3): to summon; to call to mind (v.)

reiterates (para. 4): repeats; says or does again (v.)

efficacy (para. 4): power to produce effects or intended results (n.)

brandishing (para. 6): shaking or exhibiting in a menacing way (v.)

expletive (para. 6): an oath or exclamation (n.)

vilified (para. 6): described in abusive or slanderous language about or of; defiance (v.)

You can't escape the disturbing photos. From their inception 1
early Saturday morning, they inundated every conceivable corner of
the media, beginning first with television, then traveling onto the Internet, and ending finally on the front pages of newspapers and
magazines throughout the country and the world.

LINDSAY COHEN *(b. 1979) was a junior at Northwestern University when
she was inspired to write about the "sudden clash of political powers" during
the Elián case. Cohen is a double major in communication studies and English and is a reporter and weekly columnist for the* Daily Northwestern.

The images depict a frightened young boy, taken from his Miami   2
relatives as the sun rose on another Florida morning. A squad of
heavily armed federal agents, firing pepper spray and using a battering ram to get beyond gates surrounding the house where he stayed,
entered the home to whisk young Elián away to meet his father.
Hardly a positive image.

It is a picture, however, that does conjure heated emotions on   3
both sides of the battle over Elián. On the one hand, protesters, outraged at the forceful siege, flung rocks at
the van that carried the child from his
You can't escape the   family's home. Mere hours later they held
disturbing photos.   signs with the frightened boy's image and
questioned with captions and words the
actions of the U.S. government.

But it is also a picture that tells a different tale, one that reiterates   4
the efficacy of the U.S. Constitution. The other message accompany-
ing the snapshot, though unwritten, reinforces the notion that our
government can and will use force to uphold the law. The image of
agents using arms and aggression to rescue Elián fortifies the fact that
Attorney General Janet Reno and her team were, indeed, exercising
and enforcing the full extent of U.S. law.

For five tiring months, Elián's Miami relatives dodged this law,   5
playing not by the rules but rather on public opinion. They relied on
both the words of prominent Hispanics and the work of the media to
build a case to keep the boy in their custody. As negotiations stalled
with federal agents, the protests in front of their Miami home turned
into a street circus and rumors mounted of defensive measures that
protesters would take should the Feds use force to apprehend Elián.

Who, then, will argue that the early-morning invasion decreased   6
the likelihood of injury to both federal agents and protesters? Who,
then, can uphold that the agents did not need to arm themselves, for
fear they could be "hurt," as Elián's cousin Marisleysis had warned?
Who, then, will question that in the face of such circumstances, the
government's forceful raid was not a necessity? Those brandishing
Elián's picture and shouting expletives on Saturday morning probably would. Those who declined to go to work this past Tuesday, in
protest of the raid, might. And those who vilified Reno for her choice
of actions would undoubtedly raise such questions.

There is only one answer: that all stories have two sides. In the   7
case of last Saturday's raid, it proves, rather, a tale of two images.
While most people will certainly remember the picture of an alarmed
Elián when they recall the occasion, what they will soon forget is that

a mere few hours later, the young boy was photographed smiling in the arms of his father. Reunited at last with his dad, Elián showed signs of a promising future.

Thus, we must understand and defend the choices that Reno   8
made to take Elián safely from the home of his Miami relatives. Braving harsh criticism that will no doubt follow for months to come, she and others used the force — and they did so justifiably.

Vocabulary / Using a Dictionary

1. Commenting upon the "Miami raid" picture, Cohen states, "It is also a picture that tells a different tale, one that reiterates the efficacy of the U.S. Constitution" (para. 4). Describe what Cohen means in your own words.

2. Look up *inundate* in a dictionary (para. 1). From what language does it come? From what word does *inundate* originate?

3. What does Cohen mean when she refers to "those who *vilified* Reno for her choice of actions" (para. 6)? What other words share the same root as *vilified*?

Responding to Words in Context

1. Elián's Miami relatives "relied on both the words of *prominent* Hispanics and the work of the media to build a case to keep the boy in their custody," says Cohen in paragraph 5. What does the word *prominent* mean? Can you think of some synonyms for the word?

2. In paragraph 3 the author explains that protesters were "outraged at the forceful *siege*" (para. 3) and "flung rocks at the van that carried the child from his family's home" (para. 3). What do you think a *siege* is?

Discussing Main Point and Meaning

1. When discussing the first ("Miami raid") photograph, Cohen comments that the picture tells two tales (paras. 2–4). What are those two tales?

2. To the question "Who, then, will argue that . . . the government's forceful raid was not a necessity?" (para. 6), what answer does Cohen give?

3. In paragraph 7, the author reminds us "most people will certainly remember the picture of an alarmed Elián when they recall the occasion." Yet what, argues Cohen, will people soon forget?

Examining Sentences, Paragraphs, and Organization

1. What is the purpose of the barrage of questions asked in paragraph 6? Why does the author use this rhetorical method?
2. If Cohen is trying to convince the reader that Janet Reno's show of force in Miami was justified, then why does she use paragraph 2 to paint such an appalling picture of the seizure of Elián by federal agents ("Hardly a positive image")?
3. Compare and contrast the tone of the opening and closing paragraphs of Cohen's essay. Consider the opinions presented, and the information provided.

Thinking Critically

1. Does Cohen's essay help convince you that Attorney General Janet Reno's show of force in Miami was justified? Even if you disagree with Cohen's conclusion, which of her examples do you find most convincing?
2. "While most people will certainly remember the picture of an alarmed Elián when they recall the occasion, what they will soon forget is that . . . the young boy was photographed smiling in the arms of his father," surmises Cohen in paragraph 7. Do you agree with the author, that the picture of a smiling Elián will be an image that people will soon forget?

In-Class Writing Activities

1. The phrase "Elián is a hero" has been uttered in media channels throughout America. Is Elián a hero? What constitutes heroism? In a brief essay, reflect and write about these questions.
2. In Cohen's "A Tale of Two Images," she states that "all stories have two sides" (para. 7). In the case of the April 22, 2000, raid, the author comments that there was "a tale of two images" (para. 7). In your personal experience, have you ever been involved in an important situation in which there were two differ-

ent opinions, or two different stories to tell? In a freewrite, explain the situation and the two resulting convictions.

CARMEN CERRA

Poison Ink

[IOWA STATE DAILY, IOWA STATE UNIVERSITY / April 24, 2000]

Before You Read

How do the media and the government interact? Have you ever felt that the media control too much popular opinion in the United States? Have you ever known anyone who has had a strong opinion swayed by the media? Have you ever felt that the media have limited power over our government?

CARMEN CERRA *(b. 1973) is a student at Iowa State University, where he studies biological and premedical illustration. "The cartoon was against the press," Cerra says. "My editor said I was attacking myself since I am part of the press." Cerra is a cartoonist for the* Iowa State Daily, *where he has worked since 1997.*

Responding to Words in Context

1. Emblazoned on the helmet of the soldier is the word *press*. In this situation, what does that word mean? What does it suggest about the soldier?

2. What is the definition of the word *media?* How does it relate to the definition of the word *press?*

Discussing Main Point and Meaning

1. State briefly what comment you think the artist is making about North American culture.

2. Compare and contrast the original "Miami raid" photograph with Carmen Cerra's cartoon. What are the major similarities? The major differences?

3. Why does the artist replace the officer's gun with a camera? What idea is Cerra trying to express?

Thinking Critically

1. In choosing to *satirize* (to use irony, sarcasm, or ridicule in exposing vice or folly) the "Miami raid" photograph, the artist acknowledges the importance of the image. Could you look at a newspaper or television news report at the time of the raid and avoid this photo? Why was the photograph so important to U.S. society?

2. Do you agree with the comment that Cerra is trying to make about North American culture? Do you feel that the cartoon makes a valid point, or is the use of satire off base?

In-Class Writing Activities

1. Place both the Miami raid photograph and Cerra's cartoon in front of you. Freewrite about the similarities and differences between the two pictures, stating comparisons and contrasts, ideas, concepts, and conclusions you reach from your observations.

2. Write a brief essay about the importance of the Elián event in the annals of history. In the essay, relate not only how you think the event will affect history, but also whether or not it is an important success/defeat for democracy. Will the incident be recorded in history books?

Discussing the Unit

Suggested Topic for Discussion

The selections in this unit deal with how Americans regard the Elián González incident. Whether it is laissez-faire (William Safire), critical (William Saletan), pro-military (Lindsay Cohen), or antimedia (Carmen Cerra), each author's or artist's interpretation of the event is different. If you could write an article about the Miami raid, what opinion would you state? How is your opinion affected by the media presentation of the event?

Preparing for Class Discussion

1. How do you think Lindsay Cohen might respond to William Safire's comment that President Clinton injured "the spirit of the Fourth Amendment" when pressuring Janet Reno into seizing Elián?

2. What do you think all three authors' reactions would be to cartoonist Carmen Cerra's depiction of "Poison Ink"? Explain your answers.

From Discussion to Writing

1. American historian Henry Adams wrote in 1906: "Images are not arguments, rarely even lead to proof, but the mind craves them, and, of late more than ever, the keenest experimenters find twenty images better than one, especially if contradictory; since the human mind has already learned to deal in contradictions."

   Relating this quote to the three essays and one cartoon you've looked at in this unit, write an essay explicating (explaining) Adams's quote. Begin by explaining, in your own words, what you think the historian means, and then what you think all four contributors' opinions are on Adams's subject.

2. Write a brief essay about the community in which you grew up. How do you think the Elián González incident affected the lives in that community? What members do you think would rally for the welfare of young Elián? What members would give support to Janet Reno and her military siege?

3. Pretend you are the U.S. attorney general. Besides using the essays provided to you in this unit, research a few more articles about the Elián incident. Describe how you, as attorney general, would have handled the situation. Conclude your paper by agreeing or disagreeing with the steps that were actually taken.

Topics for Cross-Cultural Discussion

1. How do you think other governments would have handled the Elián incident? Would they have sent the boy back to his native country immediately? Or would they have embraced the child and refused to return him to his home?

2. What is the relationship between government and other countries' media? Do the media create propaganda in support of the government? Do the media have the right to criticize it?

2

Our Body Image—How Early Does It Begin?

Are you content with the way you look? Opinion polls show that most Americans are not and that females are generally less content with their appearance than males. As individual self-esteem seems increasingly dependent on body image, many young people go to extreme measures to alter their looks—with drugs, radical diets, and cosmetic surgery.

Recent investigations into the importance of body image have shown that it plays a large role in childhood development as well. It is not merely an adolescent issue that begins with dating and the emergence of sexual self-consciousness. For example, the photographer Wendy Ewald discovered the childhood significance of body image when she originated a Literacy through Photography project in the Durham, North Carolina, public schools. In this unit's first selection, "The Best Part of Me," she offers a sample of how third, fourth, and fifth graders responded when asked to "choose the part of their body they liked best or that explained the most about them." She was "startled" by what the students revealed.

Though they may not be personally aware of body image issues, even toddlers—as the next selection shows—are subjected to measurements (especially height) that put them into physical competition with others. In "A Verbal Way to Stand Tall," Eric Nagourney reflects on why men and women are surprisingly more "inclined to overstate their height than to understate their weight."

The final selection of this unit examines the role played by mass media and popular culture in the formation of body image. University of Nebraska columnist Lesley Owusu believes that very young children are bombarded with unrealistic physical images, such as Barbie dolls and supermodels, that exert a powerful influence on their evolving self-image and self-esteem. Are we, as Owusu suggests, allowing popular culture to dictate to us what we must look like?

WENDY EWALD

The Best Part of Me

[DOUBLETAKE/Winter 1999]

Before You Read

Are the children you know happy with their bodies? Are they proud of what their bodies can do? Do they like being unique or do they wish they looked like someone else? How did you feel about your body when you were a kid?

Words to Learn

measly: contemptibly small; meager (adj.)
regard: consider; look at (v.)
composition: arrangement of artistic parts to form a unified whole (n.)
allude: make an indirect reference to something (v.)

WENDY EWALD (b. 1951) *is a senior research associate at the Center for International Studies and Documentary Studies at Duke University. Ewald is passionate about working with children, as is showcased in her latest book,* Secret Games: Wendy Ewald's Collaboration with Children, 1969–1999 *(2000), and a forthcoming children's book,* The Best Part of Me, *which is based on this article.*

My eyes are brown and black.
Big and round.
I see lots of colors around.
I see me I see you.
I like my eyes I should not be
surprised. I see your eyes I see my eyes.
I know my eyes can see with in me.
Without eyes you couldn't see not one
tree. you couldn't see.
Not one eye you couldn't buy.

The eye is good the eye is mad when
you are mad it can seem very

sad.

Denysa Elliott

My back ~~parts~~ by: Beverly Benton
parts of my body
I pick. my back becouse iD I did't have
my back then I ~~am~~
coun't move becous every
thang ~~carts~~ counts on my back
And I put my ~~hair~~
in the picther becouse
I like my hair I can
put barets in my hair
a I can brad it
My mom brads my
hair alot she says
I am her little
~~barse~~ barbie' my hair
is longe than my
short Sleve shirt.

By: Beverly
    Benton

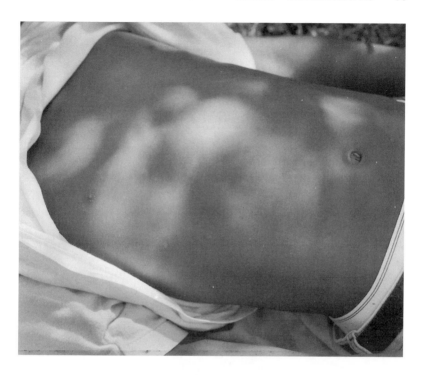

My name is Antwaune
Mims. This is my chest
I got my abs from my
dad. It is me in the sun-
light looking at the sky
thinking about What is in
the sky and where Will
~~I~~ go to rest.

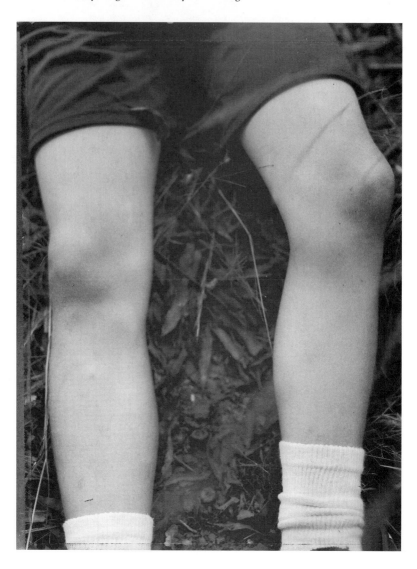

MY WONDERFUL LEGS! By Andrew Legge

Legs, Legs, you carry me a long way,
You hold me up when I'm out to play.
Legs, Legs, you're so strong,
So that I'm able to run very long.
You get very tired when I rollerblade
But you still go on,
That's how strong you are made.
You don't get hurt very easily,
I just hate when people call
you measly.

"The Best Part of Me" is one of several projects I developed in collaboration with teachers and students in the Durham public schools as part of Literacy through Photography, a program I originated to use photography as a starting point for writing.

Over the past few years, photography has become increasingly interested in the human body and in issues that arise when portraying children. I became curious to know how the children themselves regarded their bodies. In working as an artist and a teacher, I often ask people to create self-portraits in writing or photographs. Many times I've heard children describe themselves and their kinships with others in terms of parts of their bodies — "I have Mom's eyes," one of my students from Kentucky told me. "They're real little."

> *Over the past few years, photography has become increasingly interested in the human body and in issues that arise when portraying children.*

I asked each of the students in Ms. Lord's third-, fourth-, and fifth-grade class at Club Boulevard Elementary School to choose the part of their body they liked best or that explained the most about them. Then, using a view camera so I could focus as closely as I needed to, I took a Polaroid picture of each child. The child and I then looked at the photograph together and discussed changes in composition or background that might reflect the child's vision of him- or herself. Once we were satisfied with the image, the child took it back into the classroom and wrote about it.

I decided to make a book of the photographs and writings for an exhibition and asked the students to help me design and title it. When we looked at the assembled pictures and text, I was startled by how revealing they were about the individual students and about how the different cultural groups conceived of and thought about their bodies. Beverly Benton chose her back and her hair and likened herself to a Barbie doll. Antwaune Mims asked me to photograph his chest from above while he lay on the grass thinking about where he'll go when he dies.

Vocabulary/Using a Dictionary

1. *Regard* can be a noun as well as a verb. Write a sentence that uses the noun form of the word. Refer to a dictionary if necessary.

2. Using the definition in question 1, explain what Ewald means when she refers to the *composition* of a photograph.

3. What is the noun form of *allude*? Look it up in the dictionary and provide a definition. How do the two definitions relate?

Responding to Words in Context

1. For each of the students' writing, make a list of all the adjectives the students use to describe their body parts. What contradictions are implied, if any? What do you make of the students' word choices?

2. Within the children's own writing, locate all the instances of words with negative connotations. How do the children use these words? Why are they included in an essay titled "The Best Part of Me"?

Discussing Main Point and Meaning

1. Why did Ewald want these photos to be accompanied by the written words of her subjects? What does the writing add to the overall effect of the piece?

2. How do the photos/words of Beverly Benton and Antwaune Mims compare? How do they contrast?

3. What do these children's voices say to you about their body images and self-perceptions? Use examples from their text when providing your answer.

Examining Sentences, Paragraphs, and Organization

1. Donyea Elliott writes, "I know my eyes can see with in me." What do you think this sentence means?

2. Does the overall structure of this photographic essay seem to be based on a particular logic? Look at the way the body parts and descriptions build off of each other and see if you can discover any organizing principle(s).

Thinking Critically

1. Who do you imagine the audience of this piece to be? Who do you think it would "speak to" most effectively? Is there anyone you think might have trouble understanding its purpose or message? Explain your answer.

2.   Do you think it was fair of Wendy Ewald to ask these young people to evaluate their bodies so publicly? Why or why not?

In-Class Writing Activities

1.   Pick the least favorite part of your body and write about it as if it *were* a favorite. For example, if you dislike a crooked tooth, you might emphasize its unique character. Or if you have a knee that's been prone to injury, you might explain that it helps to remind you to take good care of yourself. When you finish, explain whether or not the exercise made you feel better about that part of your body.

2.   Imagine Ewald's project being done with adults. What do you think would be different about the writing? How do you think adults view their bodies as compared to children? Pick one example to rewrite from an adult perspective.

ERIC NAGOURNEY

A Verbal Way to Stand Tall

[THE NEW YORK TIMES MAGAZINE/June 4, 2000]

Before You Read

Do you think about your height often? Do you wish you could change it? Is height as important to one's body image as weight? Why or why not?

ERIC NAGOURNEY (b. 1959) *has been an editor and writer at the* New York Times *since 1998. Nagourney feels that, as demonstrated in his piece, he has grown professionally at the* New York Times, *if in no other way.*

Words to Learn

paradoxically (para. 2): inexplicably; in a contradictory way (adv.)

stature (para. 2): natural height of a human or animal in an upright position (n.)

tool (para. 4): to drive or travel around in a vehicle (v.)

skewed (para. 7): distorted or biased in meaning or effect (adj.)

prevarication (para. 11): lie, untruth (n.)

psychosocial (para. 12): related to the mental processes of those belonging to a society (adj.)

postulated (para. 12): assumed; taken for granted (v.)

ingrained (para. 13): deep-rooted (adj.)

complicity (para. 16): state of being an accomplice (n.)

Some months back, I took my two-and-a-half-year-old son to the pediatrician for a checkup and got some unexpected news: He had shrunk half an inch from his previous visit. 1

No cause for alarm here. The explanation was simple enough: For the first time, Clement had been measured standing up, not lying down fidgeting on the crinkly paper that covered the examination table. With this one giant leap into toddlerhood, he had, paradoxically, shrunk a bit in stature. 2

No big deal. Except that my son is already on the short end of the height spectrum—something of a family trait, if truth be told—and he could really use that half inch. 3

So in the admittedly unlikely event that the question of size comes up among his pals as they tool around the sandbox, I will not be surprised if he lies, reclaiming that stolen half inch and maybe even adding on another for good measure. 4

After all, Clement would be in good company. A study appearing this month in the American Statistical Association Proceedings reports that many Americans appear to lie about their height. Not weight or age, though they lie about that, too. Height. 5

How do we know this? 6

Because researchers at St. Louis University were curious about the accuracy of the self-reported data used in many health studies and decided to do a little comparison. The term refers to personal information gathered from people who volunteer it to researchers without benefit of physical exams. If the data is inaccurate, the results of the surveys can be skewed. 7

William D. Hart, the nutrition and dietetics professor who led 8 the study, compared the heights and weights reported by subjects in one survey with figures from another in which people were examined. He and his colleagues took self-reported data offered by more than six thousand people who participated in the National Health Interview Surveys from 1988 to 1994, and put them up against actual measurements from the more than five hundred thousand people examined in the National Health and Nutrition Examination.

The researchers found that many people fudged their weight— not a complete surprise. But they were not prepared for the number of people who seem to have volunteered inaccurate information about their height.   9

From ages twenty to eighty-four, men and women exaggerated. Indeed, more people were inclined to overstate their height than to understate their weight.   10

> *Indeed, more people were inclined to overstate their height than to understate their weight.*

For health experts, the main cause of concern is not the prevarication itself but something perhaps more serious. If the researchers are right, Americans, already among the most obese people in the world, could be in worse shape than previously thought.   11

The researchers did not offer any theories for the misrepresentation. "Psychosocial explanations can be postulated but not confirmed with this data," they wrote.   12

You don't need a psychosociologist, however, to understand why Americans would want to be taller. Height is often equated with power, wealth, and even intelligence, said Jennifer F. Taylor, a clinical psychologist at Harvard University's McLean Hospital. "It's something that's culturally ingrained from very early on," she said.   13

Just consider the sight of two schoolchildren, back to back, trying to see who is taller—with one or both sneaking onto tiptoes. Even in politics, presidential candidates who are taller are often considered to have an edge over their opponents.   14

Where psychosociology might come in handy is in explaining why people would believe they could get away with lying about height. If you decide to shave ten pounds off your weight, who can be sure? If you say you're five years younger, who is going to argue?   15

But asking others to believe you are a couple of inches taller than you are, when they need only compare your stature with theirs, is another matter entirely. It requires not just an absence of skepticism on   16 their part but actual complicity. It's the kind of thing that could happen only if everybody were lying about height.

Of course, another explanation is that many people don't really know their own height, some experts say. There are few occasions in adulthood when it is taken. And in the end, it may simply be that people are engaging not so much in deceit as in wishful thinking.   17

Consider: My position is that I am 5 feet 4 inches. My wife labors under the mistaken impression that she is 5 feet 4½ inches—which is physically impossible, of course, because she is about 2 inches taller than I am. (Want more proof she's wrong? The other day, after I told him how tall I was, my brother declared that he was 5 feet 5. And yet he is shorter than my wife.)   18

Of course, lying is such an ugly word. It is true that the last time I was measured by a doctor, my height was not recorded as 5 feet 4. But maybe they got it wrong. It would not be surprising, since they measured me when I was standing up.   19

Vocabulary / Using a Dictionary

1. What does Nagourney mean by *tool* in paragraph 4?

2. "For health experts, the main cause of concern is not the prevarication itself but something perhaps more serious," remarks Nagourney in paragraph 11. What does he mean by *prevarication* here? Use the word in a sentence of your own.

3. How is it different for the researchers quoted in paragraph 12 to use the term *psychosocial* rather than *psychological* or *social*?

Responding to Words in Context

1. "The researchers found that many people fudged their weight," the author writes (para. 9). What does the word *fudged* mean here? Consider the other meanings of *fudged*.

2. What is the "self-reported data" referred to by the author in paragraphs 7 and 8?

Discussing Main Point and Meaning

1. How does the author explain the fact that his two-and-a-half-year-old son seemed to have shrunk from one doctor's visit to the next?

2. Why would researchers want to compare "self-reported data" with "actual" data (para. 8), according to this article?

3. Lying about one's height "requires not just an absence of skepticism on [the part of others] but actual complicity," Nagourney writes (para. 16). What does he mean by this?

4. What is the general purpose of this article? Is it descriptive, informative, argumentative, or some combination of the three? How do you know?

Examining Sentences, Paragraphs, and Organization

1. Nagourney begins this article with an anecdote about his young son and ends it with one about his wife. How does beginning and ending on a personal note change the reader's understanding of the essay as a whole? Do you think this structure is effective?

2. In paragraph 5, the author writes: "A study appearing this month in the American Statistical Association Proceedings reports that many Americans appear to lie about their height. Not weight or age, though they lie about that, too. Height." Why does Nagourney go to such lengths to emphasize this point?

3. Paragraph 15 once again compares lying about one's height to lying about weight or age. What is the author's purpose in making this comparison?

Thinking Critically

1. Why does Nagourney use the anecdote of his wife arguing that she is shorter than her actual height? Doesn't this weaken his general point that people pretend to be taller than they really are?

2. Can you expand on Nagourney's claim that society rewards the tall? Give some examples of how we value height and reject shortness.

In-Class Writing Activities

1. *Short-change, shortcoming, shorthanded, shortage,* and *short end of the stick* are some expressions that contain pejorative connotations of shortness. There are almost no expressions that use *tall* with the same negativity (*tall tale* and *tall order,* perhaps). Write an essay that attempts to explain *why* people associate height

with success and shortness with the lack of success. Use whatever cultural knowledge you have to rationalize why we think tall is better than short.

2. Is the topic of height significant in your family? Is it important to you? Do you wish you were taller or shorter? Write a few paragraphs about what your height has meant to you in your life.

LESLEY OWUSU

Weighty Issues

[DAILY NEBRASKAN, UNIVERSITY OF NEBRASKA–LINCOLN / February 1, 2000]

Before You Read

How common are eating disorders and cosmetic surgery in your school? Do you think they're on the rise? If so, why? Do the media play a role?

Words to Learn

continuum (para. 5): a range in which no parts can be fully distinguished from the whole (n.)

proportions (para. 5): size; extent; dimensions (n.)

halo (para. 5): an aura of majesty or glory surrounding a person regarded with reverence or awe (n.)

LESLEY OWUSU *(b. 1978) was a senior at the University of Nebraska–Lincoln when she wrote this essay. "I wanted to reach out to my peers and community and really touch them and impact them," Owusu says about her piece. She is a broadcast journalism major, with minors in history, English, and communication studies.*

Now, more than ever, it doesn't matter who you are but what   1
you look like.

Janet was just twenty-five years old. She had a great job and   2
seemed happy. She committed suicide. In her suicide note she wrote
that she felt "un-pretty" and that no man ever loved her. Amy was
just fifteen when hospitalized for eating disorders. She suffered from
both anorexia and bulimia. She lost more than one hundred pounds
in two months. Both victims battled problems with their body image
and physical appearance.

"Oh, I'm too fat." "My butt is too big and my breasts too   3
small." "I hate my body and I feel ugly." "I want to be beautiful."
The number of men and women who feel these things about themselves is increasing dramatically.

I can identify two main categories of body-image problems: addi-   4
tive versus subtractive. Those who enhance their appearance through
cosmetic surgery fall into the additive group; those who hope to improve their looks through starvation belong to the subtractive category. Both groups have two things in common: They are never satisfied and they are always obsessed.

Eating disorders afflict as many as five to ten million women and   5
one million men in the United States. One out of four female college
students suffers from an eating disorder. But why? Carri Kirby, a University of Nebraska mental health counselor, says that body image
and eating disorders are continuum addictions in which individuals
seek to discover their identities. The idea that we should look a certain
way and possess a certain shape is instilled in us at a very early age.
Young girls not only play with Barbie dolls that display impossible,
even comical, proportions, but they are also bombarded with images
of supermodels. These images leave an indelible mental imprint of
what society believes a female body should look like. Kirby adds that
there is a halo effect to body image as well: "We immediately identify
physical attractiveness to mean success and happiness."

The media can be blamed for contributing to various body-image   6
illnesses. We cannot walk into a bookstore without being exposed to
perfect male and female bodies on the covers of magazines. We see
such images every day — in commercials, billboards, on television,
and in movies. These images continually remind women and young
girls that if you want to be happy you must be beautiful, and if you
want to be beautiful you must be thin.

This ideal may be the main objective of the fashion, cosmetic,   7
diet, fitness, and plastic surgery industries who stand to make millions

from body-image anxiety. But does it work for us? Are women who lose weight in order to be toothpick thin really happy? Are women who have had breast implants really happy? What truly defines a person? Is it his or her physical appearance or is it character? Beauty is supposed to be "skin deep." But we can all be beautiful inside.

> Beauty is supposed to be "skin deep."

People are killing themselves for unrealistic physical standards dictated by our popular culture. We need to be made more aware of this issue. To be celebrity-thin is not to be beautiful nor happy. It can also be unattractive. Individuals who are obsessed with their bodies are only causing damage to themselves and their loved ones. But as long as the media maintain their message that "thin is in," then the medical and psychological problems our society faces will continue to grow.

8

Vocabulary/Using a Dictionary

1. What does Owusu mean by the terms *additive* and *subtractive* in paragraph 4?

2. How does *continuum* (para. 5) relate to the verb *continue?*

3. *Halo* (para. 5) comes from the Greek for "disk of the sun or the moon." Why do you think the usage has evolved to include the meaning Owusu intends?

Responding to Words in Context

1. Examine the use of the word *un-pretty* in paragraph 2. What does it mean? Why or how is it different from *ugly?*

2. In paragraph 7, the author uses the word *toothpick* to describe the "image of perfection" today's women are trying to achieve. What do you make of this word? Is it an exaggerated metaphor? If so, why do you think the author chose it?

Discussing Main Point and Meaning

1. Do you think the purpose of this essay is to change the behavior or the thinking of its readers? Cite examples from the essay to explain your answer.

2. What connection does Owusu make between eating disorders and self-esteem?

3. According to Owusu, what exactly is the problem? What are the causes of the problem? Cite specific examples from the essay to explain your answer.

Examining Sentences, Paragraphs, and Organization

1. Examine the quotes featured in paragraph 3. What purpose do they serve?

2. Pick out the specific examples that Owusu uses throughout her essay. How do they change as the essay progresses?

3. What is the function of the concluding paragraph? How does it tie together some of the issues raised in the body of the essay?

Thinking Critically

1. In paragraphs 6–8, Owusu blames the media for the problem of eating disorders in girls and women. However, some might say the media merely mirror the trends of their viewers, giving the people what they want. What do you think?

2. In paragraph 5, Owusu refers to national statistics on eating disorders, suggesting that the numbers are alarmingly large. But Americans in general are getting bigger with every generation. Do you think there is an important connection to be made between the rise of eating disorders and the rise of obesity rates in our society?

In-Class Writing Activities

1. Describe a healthy body, in your own words. Must a healthy body be an athletic body? What do you think a healthy body is to an eighty-year-old? To a cancer patient? A nutritionist? An expectant mother?

2. How many times during the course of a day do you evaluate how you look? List them in a narrative describing a normal day for you. In what situations and for what reasons do you think about how you might look to others? Try to be exhaustive in your list. When you are finished, examine the list. Which self-evaluations

are unnecessary? Which serve an important purpose? How much time do you think you use up in the course of a day thinking about or attending to your looks?

Discussing the Unit

Suggested Topic for Discussion

This unit presents one familiar and two novel perspectives on the ubiquitous body-image issue. Student Lesley Owusu covers the recognizable terrain of eating disorders and cosmetic surgery, examining their similar effect on women's self-esteem. But Wendy Ewald and Eric Nagourney take up children's body images and height anxiety, respectively, proving that we continue to add new verses to the old standard. How do these new approaches complicate your understanding of the issue? Do eating disorders and cosmetic surgery seem more poignant when placed in context with the innocent celebrations of the body that Ewald's essay presents? Or do they seem more exasperating when juxtaposed with the silly way we fib about our height?

Preparing for Class Discussion

1. All three of the selections in this unit are related in some degree to the ways in which children are socialized to perceive themselves physically. How did you feel about your body when you were a small child? How have your perceptions changed of what your body is and should be? What would you change in the way you perceived your body as a child? What would you change in the way you perceive your body now?

2. Studies have shown that the more conventionally attractive a person is, the more likely she is to get hired or promoted by an employer, the more likely it is that someone will stop to offer roadside assistance if her car is broken down, and the more likely it is that she will be sympathetically treated by a jury. How do you think this kind of "lookism" compares to sexism or racism as a type of discrimination? How much do you think personality traits are related to looks?

From Discussion to Writing

1. Compare and contrast these three selections with respect to their perspectives. Ewald is an artist and educator, Owusu is a student, and Nagourney is a journalist. How do you think each of their occupations influences the way they examine the topic of body image? Is there one perspective of the three that most resonates with you? Explain.

2. How do you know the difference between beauty and ugliness? For example, what principles make you sure that a rose is more beautiful than a tin can? That a tiger is more beautiful than a fly? Write an essay in which you attempt to articulate your standards of beauty. Draw from the texts in this unit for support or to disagree with them.

Topics for Cross-Cultural Discussion

1. Discuss the topic of body image as it relates to your native culture. What is prized in a body? What is scorned? Are the ideals very different or similar to those in the United States? If they are different, how do you explain that? If they are similar, why do you think that is so?

2. Do you think the American standard of beauty is beginning to influence the rest of the world because of its predominance in the media? Or is it possible that other standards are beginning to gain some exposure? Explain your answer by using specific examples and referring to the texts in this unit.

3

Are Gender Differences Real?

It's commonly observed that girls and boys display different types of behavior from early childhood on. At play, for example, boys tend to be more aggressive and competitive, while girls generally are more social and accommodating. What psychologists are deeply interested in finding out, however, is whether these differences are mostly biological and genetic or are primarily a result of cultural conditioning. If our society expects boys to be more aggressive, one argument goes, they will automatically become so. In this chapter several writers address the issue of gender differences as they surface in various activities.

In "What's the Difference between Boys and Girls?" Deborah Blum, an authority on gender identity, examines preschoolers at play as she attempts to classify behavior that seems to originate in basic body chemistry from behavior that appears to be culturally influenced. Do these childhood differences carry over into adulthood? In "Are Men's Fingers Faster?" Edward Cohn takes a critical look at one of the nation's most popular game shows and wonders what role gender differences play in establishing a contestant base that consists almost entirely of white males: Do men have a greater stake in trivia? Penelope Scambly Schott gently points out in her very brief "Report on the Difference between Men and Women" how subtle gender distinctions can surprisingly emerge in long-term relationships.

The chapter concludes with opposing views, as two students, Steve Dalton and Rachael Cowley, debate one of the most stereotypical issues relating to gender differences: Do men or women make better drivers?

DEBORAH BLUM

What's the Difference between Boys and Girls?

[LIFE/July 1999]

Before You Read

Thinking back to your baby pictures, do you recall whether your parents dressed you in an all-blue outfit (for boys) or an all-pink outfit (for girls)? If so, why do you think they did this? Do you think it may have affected your "gender identity"? Do you believe that men and women have distinctly different preferences due to their gender? Preferences in sports? Academics? Social activities? Are these preferences adopted because of the rules of society or because of innate sexual characteristics?

Words to Learn

arsenal (para. 2): a place for storing weapons (n.)

phallic (para. 2): of, like, or relating to a representation of the penis (adj.)

neuroscientist (para. 9): a specialist in science who studies the nervous system (n.)

analogous (para. 9): similar in certain respects (adj.)

testosterone (para. 11): a male, steroid, sex hormone (n.)

provocative (para. 15): provoking or intending to provoke (adj.)

in utero (para. 16): in the uterus; unborn (n.)

exuberant (para. 17): luxuriant; growing (adj.)

rambunctious (para. 20): wild, disorderly, unruly (adj.)

continuum (para. 21): a continuous whole (n.)

DEBORAH BLUM *(b. 1954), a journalist and nonfiction writer, is the author of many works on ecology and environmental science. She is the recipient of numerous awards, including the Pulitzer Prize for her book* The Monkey Wars *(1994) on the issues of using primates in medical and psychological testing. Her most recent book is* Sex on the Brain: The Biological Differences between Men and Women *(1997).*

My four-year-old son asked for a Barbie this year. His blue eyes   1
were hopeful, his small face angelic. His mother was suspicious.

Between this child and his older brother, our house is a Toys R   2
Us warehouse of heavily muscled action figures, dinosaurs with
jagged teeth, light-up swords, and leaking water pistols. Complaint is
constant—Oh, Mom, you're no fun—over my refusal to buy more
additions to the arsenal. My older son at one point began to see
weapons in household objects the way
adults dream up phallic symbols. "Shoot
her with the toothbrush," he once shouted
to a companion as they chased the cat
around the house.

*When is biology the
primary influence?
Where does culture
overtake it, and at what
point, in the startling
fluid landscape of
human behavior, does
one alter the other?*

"Why do you want the Barbie, honey?"   3
I asked.

"I wanna chop her head off."   4

There I was again, standing at the   5
edge of the great gender divide, the place
and the moment where one becomes absolutely sure that the opposite sex is, in
fact, opposite. I know of no way for
women of my generation, raised to believe in gender neutrality, to
reach this edge faster than through trying to raise children.

"I did not do this," a friend insisted on the day her son started   6
carefully biting his toast into the shape of a gun. "I think my daughter has a pink gene," a British journalist confided recently, as she confessed that her daughter has not only a Barbie collection but all the
matched plastic purses and tiny high-heeled shoes. I don't think in
pastels myself. I think jungle-green, blood-red. Most of all, I think
there's a reason—a reasonable biology—to the differences we see in
little boys and girls, men and women, males and females.

We are, I hope, moving past the old politically correct notion that   7
we are pure culture, that children are born blank slates to be influenced—or, worse, manipulated—by the adults around them. There's
a straightforward reason why we are a male-female species: Reproduc-
tively, it works. We are all born with bodies designed to be the same
(breathe, circulate blood) and to be different (produce sperm, produce
eggs, produce milk, produce none). There's an internal biology—
structural and behavioral—that supports those differences. It's not all
of who we are, but it's a part. When is biology the primary influence?
Where does culture overtake it, and at what point, in the startling fluid
landscape of human behavior, does one alter the other?

One of my favorite illustrations of the way culture fine-tunes us   8
for gender roles has to do with the Barbie versus Godzilla effect. It
turns out that lots of little boys ask for dolls and other so-called girl
toys. They aren't encouraged though; parents really hesitate to buy
their children "gender inappropriate" toys. In a study involving almost 300 children, researchers found that if little boys asked for a
soldier equipped with battle cannons for their birthday, they got it
some 70 percent of the time. If they asked for a Barbie doll, or any of
her plastic peers, the success rate was 40 percent or less. Can you
think of a child who wouldn't figure out in, oh, a day, how to work
that system?

Marc Breedlove, a neuroscientist at the University of California,   9
Berkeley, points out that splitting apart biology and culture is analogous to splitting hairs. But scientists try to separate the strands anyway, exhaustively exploring early development. A few ambitious scientists have even looked for prebirth differences, arguing that it's
difficult to slap too much cultural attitude onto a fetus. It turns out
that boy fetuses are a little more active, more restless, than girl fetuses. And in the first year after birth, toy preferences already seem
distinct: Boy infants rapidly engage with more mechanical or structural toys; little girls of a few months gravitate toward toys with
faces, toys that can be cuddled.

The world of play—the toys we gravitate to, how we play with   10
them, how we play in general—has now become serious business to
scientists. Today's hottest theory of play is that it's a practice run at
the challenges of adult life. Through games, the experts tell us, we
learn the art of measuring the competition, how to win and lose
gracefully (we hope), which leads pretty directly into how to build
friendships. In scientific terms, we learn socialization.

"Play offers a non–life-threatening way of asserting yourself,"   11
says Christine Drea, a researcher. "By playing, you learn skills of
managing competition and aggression." We are a social species. We
find isolation destructive, and we establish patterns of childhood play
that reflect adult social structures. In humans, our patterns tend to
conform to our chemistry: Human males are likely to produce seven
to ten times more testosterone, for example, than females. . . . And
so, you would correctly predict, little boys tend to be more rough-
and-tumble than little girls. That's true, in fact, for the entire realm of
primates (monkeys, apes, man).

Back in the late 1970s, Robert Goy, a psychologist at the Univer-   12
sity of Wisconsin, first documented that young male monkeys consis-

tently played much more roughly than juvenile females. Goy then went on to show that if you manipulate testosterone level—raising it in females, cutting it off in males—you reverse those effects, creating sweet little boy monkeys and rough-and-tumble girls. We don't experiment with human development this way, obviously. But there are naturally occurring genetic variations that make closely comparable points. As mentioned earlier, human males circulate higher levels of testosterone. There's a well-known exception, however, called congenital adrenal hyperplasia (CAH), in which a baby girl's adrenal gland inadvertently boosts testosterone levels. Researchers have found that CAH girls, in general, prefer trucks and cars and aggressive play. That doesn't mean they don't join in more traditional girl games with friends—but if left to choose, they prefer to play on the rowdy side of the street.

Higher testosterone levels are also responsible for another characteristic: competitiveness. In fact, testosterone is almost predictable in this regard. It shoots up before a competition; that's been measured in everything from chess matches to soccer games to courtroom battles to brawls. It stays up if you win, drops if you lose. Its role, scientists think, is to get you up and running and right on the competitive edge. 13

Even in preschool, boys and girls fall into very different play patterns. Boys tend to gather in larger, competitive groups. They play games that have clear winners and losers and bluster through them, boasting about their skills. Girls, early on, gather in small groups, playing theatrical games that don't feature hierarchy or winners. One study of children aged three to four found they were already resolving conflict in separate ways—boys resorting to threats, girls negotiating verbally and often reaching a compromise. 14

There are some provocative new insights into that verbal difference. Recently, researchers at Emory University have found that little female monkeys are much quicker to pick up "verbal" skills than little boy monkeys. Sound familiar? The small female monkeys do more contact calling (cooing affectionately) than their male counterparts. And it appears, again, that this is related to their mothers' prenatal hormones. Some very preliminary tests suggest that females exposed to androgens early in their fetal development become more like male monkeys: They are less likely to use language to express themselves. 15

In humans, too, we look for natural biological variations. In general, girls have sharper hearing than boys—the tiny hair cells that register sound waves vibrate more forcefully. These are ears tuned for 16 intense communication. (The rare exception tends to be in boy-girl twin pairs. Those girls are more likely to have ears built a little more like their brothers'—less active hair cells, notched-down response. Researchers looking at this suspect a higher exposure to androgens in utero.) There's something about the biology of the egg-producing sex that seems to demand more acute communication abilities.

Of course, there's a whole range of personalities and behaviors   17
that don't fall into any of the obvious stereotypes. What about tomboys, those exuberant girls who prefer softball to tea parties? What about the affectionate sweetness of little boys, who—away from the battle zone of their friends and brothers—turn out to be surprisingly cuddly and clingy? What about the female stiff, the chatty male, and so on, into infinity? The quick answer: Sex differences are group differences, overall patterns.

The complex of genes and hormones and neurotransmitters and   18
internal chemistry that may influence our behaviors varies from person to person and is designed to be flexible. There's nothing in average, everyday biology that forbids either the truck-loving girl or the boy who likes to play house, the aggressive, competitive adult woman, or the nurturing, stay-at-home man. Human biology makes room for every possible type of personality and sexuality in the range between those stereotypes.

And finally, the way we behave can actually influence our biol-   19
ogy. The link between testosterone and competition makes this point perfectly. Yes, corporate lawyers tend to have higher testosterone levels than ministers. But there's a chicken-or-egg aspect to this. Is the lawyer someone born with a high testosterone level? Or is it the profession that pushed it up? Or some combination of both? It's worth noting that the parallel works in men and in women; women in competitive jobs have more testosterone; men who stay home with their children have less.

Nothing in biology labels behaviors as right or wrong, normal or   20
abnormal. Any stereotypes we impose on children—and, by extension, adults—are purely cultural, not biological. For example: Little boys are noisy and rambunctious; we tend to equate that with being emotionally tough. But what science actually tells us is the exact opposite. Little boys, we're learning, need a lot of emotional support. One revealing study of children of depressed and withdrawn mothers, done at U.C. Berkeley, found that a lack of affection actually lowered the IQ of little boys. Laura Allen, a neuroscientist at the University of

California, Los Angeles, explains it like this: "I think boys need more one-on-one attention. I think affection may change the sex hormone level in the brain, which then affects brain development." Both the Berkeley study and a more recent federal daycare study find a different pattern in girls. They're emotionally sturdier—I think most of us have already figured this out—and their healthy development seems most harmed by being restricted. It's confinement that seems to drive down IQ in our daughters.

What's the real difference between boys and girls? More, and less, than we thought. With rare exceptions, the anatomy of gender is straightforward, separate. But the chemistry of gender is more complex. It's a continuum, I think, and we can each find a place within the wide band of "normal." What's more, we can change our place. And we can influence our children's places—not by force but by guidance. 21

And so, if you're wondering, I did not buy my son the doll. I'm too grown up these days to approve of dismembering pricey toys. I did let him pick out a scaled-down Barbie, instead of a toy car, in one of those fast-food kid's meal promotions. It turned out to be cream and gold in appearance, annoyingly indestructible, and he lost interest. These days, he likes to make books and draw pictures of blood-dripping dinosaurs. Me? I pass him the red crayons. 22

Vocabulary/Using a Dictionary

1. In paragraph 9 of Blum's essay, neuroscientist Marc Breedlove explains: "splitting apart biology and culture is *analogous* to splitting hairs." What is meant by the use of the word *analogous*? What word does *analogous* derive from? What is the origin of this word?

2. The definition of the word *provocative* (para. 15) reads "provoking or intending to provoke." What does it mean when you "intend to provoke" someone or something?

3. Blum expresses the opinion that "the chemistry of gender is more complex. It's a *continuum*, I think ..." (para. 21). What do you think the author means when she expresses this idea? What word does *continuum* look similar to? Do these words share the same root?

Responding to Words in Context

1. Blum states in paragraph 5: "I know of no way for women in my generation, raised to believe in *gender neutrality,* to reach this edge faster than through trying to raise children." In this context, what do you think *gender neutrality* means?

2. Further on in her essay, Blum explains: "parents really hesitate to buy their children *'gender inappropriate'* toys" (para. 8). What do you think *gender inappropriate* means? Give some examples that would help describe this term.

3. In her description of preschool girls' play patterns, Blum observes: "Girls, early on, gather in small groups, playing theatrical games that don't feature *hierarchy* or winners" (para. 14). By looking at this observation, what do you think the word *hierarchy* might mean?

Discussing Main Point and Meaning

1. In response to her son's wanting to chop the head off of a Barbie doll, Blum states: "There I was again, standing at the edge of a great gender divide, the place and the moment where one becomes absolutely sure that the opposite sex is, in fact, opposite" (para. 5). Explain, in your own words, what Blum is trying to express.

2. In paragraph 7, Blum states the *thesis* (or main idea/purpose) of her essay. What is her thesis? Why would she find this idea to be curious?

3. What is the "Barbie versus Godzilla effect"? (para. 8).

4. Why has childhood playtime "now become serious business to scientists"? (para. 10).

Examining Sentences, Paragraphs, and Organization

1. From the very first paragraph the reader gets a feel for what the author is going to discuss in her essay. Looking at paragraph 1, explain how the reader could discern what the topic of Blum's essay might be.

2. In the middle of Blum's essay (paragraphs 8–16), she uses examples supported by testimony given from various researchers and scientists. List a few of the many examples these people provide,

and assess whether or not they make the author's argument more valid.

3. In the final few lines of her essay, Blum concludes: "These days, he [her son] likes to make books and draw pictures of blood-dripping dinosaurs. Me? I pass him the red crayons" (para. 22). Explain how this is less an obvious and direct concluding statement than it is an implied suggestion of the author's intent. Do you think it is an effective conclusion to the essay?

Thinking Critically

1. Does Blum's essay seem overly technical, supported with too much scientific evidence, or is it the proper mix of personal narrative experience and researched data? Explain your answer.

2. Do you agree with Blum encouraging her son's masculine and rambunctious behavior (such as letting him choose a scaled-down Barbie to dismember, and passing him a crayon in support of his drawing "blood-dripping dinosaurs" [para. 22])?

In-Class Writing Activities

1. "Swapping toys may not change the basic differences in the ways the genders approach play. Little boys may tear apart their dress-up clothes, and little girls may find a way to interact collaboratively with toy cars," says *Life* magazine. In a brief essay, agree or disagree with this statement, basing your conclusions on what you've read in Blum's piece, and on your own experiences.

2. Freewrite about your preschool and elementary years. How much do you think society influenced your gender-based choices? Now, a more difficult question: How many of your choices do you think were made biologically?

EDWARD COHN

Are Men's Fingers Faster?

[AMERICAN PROSPECT / April 24, 2000]

Before You Read

Think about gender differences you see on TV, especially game shows. Is there a difference between those shows dominated by women winners and those by men? Why do you think this is so? Can you think of any other area of entertainment that has noticeable gender differences, both in participation and outcome? What about sports? Literature?

Words to Learn

monologue (para. 1): a prolonged talk by a single speaker (n.)

demographically (para. 3): as relating to the vital statistics of a population (adv.)

grande dame (para. 4): a usually dignified elderly lady (n.)

sublimated (para. 5): impulses redirected to socially constructive ends (adj.)

dynamic (para. 7): a force producing change (n.)

atypical (para. 8): not characteristic; abnormal (adj.)

anecdotal (para. 9): based on reports or observation; unscientific (adj.)

postulates (para. 9): claims, presupposes (v.)

discomfiting (para. 10): disconcerting; frustrating (v.)

chagrin (para. 10): feeling of embarrassment because one has been disappointed (n.)

throes (para. 15): spasms or pangs of pain (n.)

Edward Cohn (b. 1976) is a 1999 graduate of Swarthmore College and has been a staff writer at American Prospect *since then. He will soon enter a graduate program in history at the University of Chicago.*

"Can anyone explain this to me?" Regis Philbin asked his *Who* 1
Wants to Be a Millionaire audience of thirty million one evening in
February. "Why is it that nearly all of our contestants are white men?
I'm a white man, so you know I have nothing against them, but come
on. . . . We would really like a little more diversity!" He ended his
monologue with an appeal to women and minorities. "So here's the
challenge," he said. "Everyone out there who has thought about
being on the show—who isn't a white male—dial that 800 number,
and let's get into the game."

Who Wants to Be a Millionaire, of course, has been a runaway 2
hit since ABC imported it from Britain last August. . . . The show begins with a lineup of ten contestants, who race to answer a "fastest
finger" question in the speediest time; the winner then heads to the
"hot seat," where he—or, occasionally, she—is asked a series of
multiple-choice questions worth from $100 to $1 million apiece. *Millionaire*'s producers pride themselves on the program's open contestant selection process, in which callers to an 800 number try out by
answering timed multiple-choice questions. Much of the show's success derives from its democratic appeal (and its easy, field-leveling
questions): Anyone can come home a winner.

Anyone, that is, who's white and male. As of this writing, 147 3
men have sat in the "hot seat," compared to only 21 women; two
men, and no women, have won a million dollars; 38 men have won
at least $125,000, compared to only three women. "The program
looks like a '50s game show in more ways than one," says Robert
Thompson, the director of Syracuse University's Center for the Study
of Popular Television. And Michael Davies, the show's executive producer, admits that the gender gap bothers him, and has considered
changes in the show to make the contestants more demographically
representative of the country.

That may be harder than it sounds because the quiz show gender 4
gap isn't unique to *Millionaire. Jeopardy!,* for example, the grande
dame of TV quiz shows, is dominated by men: 80 of the show's top
100 contestants have been male, and only one woman has won *Jeopardy!*'s year-end "tournament of champions" in the sixteen-year history of the show. And NBC's *Twenty One* and Fox's *Greed,* which
aim to copy *Millionaire*'s success, have succeeded in featuring more
diverse contestants only by selecting competitors through casting
them, not via a blind test.

Theories abound for why men dominate these shows. Men, some 5
say, are more competitive and aggressive; women, more nurturing.

Men, say others, pursue trivia as a form of adolescent one-upmanship; women have the sense to concentrate on more productive things. A *Washington Post* article even suggested that men's love of trivia was "fueled by the same sublimated aggression and status competition born on the playground."

Another possible explanation is that the questions are somehow 6
biased toward men. Critics point to the high number of sports questions, which may favor males; the show's producers reply that *Millionaire* has a diverse team of question writers and that an equal number of questions could be said to favor women.

Could the gap derive from the multiple-choice telephone quiz 7
used to decide who goes on the show and the "fastest finger" question that decides who competes for the money? Possibly. In one sense, after all, TV quiz shows are more a test of finger reflexes than a real test of knowledge, and many people suspect that men are better than women at delivering rapid-fire responses to trivia questions. Robert Schaeffer, the director of public education at the National Center for Fair and Open Testing (FairTest), uses the literature on standardized tests to support his argument that this type of questioning puts women at a distinct disadvantage. "Fast-paced multiple-choice games with an emphasis on strategic guessing favor a style that is associated with whites and males in our society," he says. The College Board's Advanced Placement exams, for instance, typically include two types of questions: multiple choice and constructed response (involving essays, diagrams, and other more detailed answers). Boys tend to outscore girls on the multiple-choice questions, but "the gender gap narrows, disappears, or reverses," Schaeffer says, when it comes to constructive-response exercises. The reasons for this aren't entirely clear, but, Schaeffer argues, the same dynamic helps men outperform women on *Millionaire*'s qualifying questions.

The show's producers dispute this explanation. "There is no evi- 8
dence that women are any slower than men at the 'fastest finger,'" Davies said at a January press conference. One woman, Shannon McGehee, has logged the best time ever on a "fastest finger" question; another holds the record for the fastest time during a pregame rehearsal. But these women were atypical—they had already made it through two rounds of similar questions. *On average,* men tend to outperform women on speed-based questions—and that may explain the quiz show gender gap.

But why should men have "faster fingers"? One theory holds that 9
the men who make it to the show are simply more determined. Anec-

dotal evidence suggests that there is a class of hypercompetitive men determined to appear on the show—and willing to call back repeatedly in order to do so. Several men have beaten the odds and appeared on the show twice, and one contestant told Rosie O'Donnell that he had called the toll-free number forty or fifty times before getting on. Another theory postulates that *Millionaire* (and game shows in general) appeal to a distinctive subspecies of the American male, the sci-fi geek, for whom the show's space-age special effects and video-game-like "fast finger" are comfortably familiar.

But *Millionaire*'s gender gap may not just be a quirk of game   10
show culture. Here's a discomfiting fact: Males dominate nearly every competition based on the recall of knowledge, at whatever age level, whether or not speed is a factor. Consider the National Geographic Bee, an annual geography competition for children in grades four through eight. The competition begins at over 15,000 elementary and middle schools, each of which crowns a school champion; each school champion then takes a written exam; the high scorers on the exam head to the state finals; finally, fifty-five state and territorial winners travel to Washington, D.C., to compete for the grand prize,

> *Males dominate nearly every competition based on the recall of knowledge, at whatever age level, whether or not speed is a factor.*

a $25,000 scholarship. But to the chagrin of the event's sponsor, the National Geographic Society, boys outnumber girls at every level of the competition, with the gender gap increasing at each step along the ladder. Over the bee's eleven-year history, in fact, only one girl has won, and every year, at least fifty of the fifty-five national finalists have been boys.

Puzzled by this, the National Geographic Society commissioned a   11
study by two Penn State researchers, geography professor Roger Downs and psychologist Lynn Liben. Their report found that boys and girls entered the bee in roughly equal numbers; that the competitors most likely to succeed were those who loved geography—not those who wanted to win for winning's sake; that the fear of competing in public did not harm the performance of girls; and that boys tended to have slightly better spatial skills and a greater interest in maps. In short, Downs and Liben found that the gender gap in bee winners is probably based on "small, but real" differences in how much boys and girls know about geography.

Look at similar competitions, and the pattern repeats itself. Every   12
spring the nation's capital plays host to a series of national academic

competitions for elementary- and middle-school students, on topics ranging from spelling and geography to math and civics, but only the National Spelling Bee—the contest with the least emphasis on the recall of knowledge—fields roughly equal numbers of boys and girls. The same is true of the high school and college quiz bowl circuits, where a similarly commanding majority of the competitors are men.

Part of the explanation for the gender gap at competitions for   13
younger children presumably lies in the realm of education policy. Many critics argue, for instance, that schools shortchange girls, subtly encouraging boys to act assertively and to dominate classroom discussions. This in turn establishes a series of self-reinforcing assumptions: When girls see boys winning geography bees or trivia contests, they're less likely to join the high school quiz team or try out for *Who Wants to Be a Millionaire* later on.

Nevertheless, women have recently begun to appear on *Million-*   14
aire in greater numbers, perhaps because of the show's appeal for diversity. In the month following Regis's plea, in fact, roughly 40 percent of the contestants in the "hot seat" were women. This may just be a temporary blip—and only three of these contestants earned as much as $125,000—but it may be a sign that a little recruitment has helped *Millionaire* buck the trend.

Whatever its origins, the most interesting thing about the quiz   15
show gender gap could be that it had been so widely noticed and discussed. Maybe this isn't surprising. When your coworkers keep asking you, "Is that your final answer?" and your grandmother is offering you lifelines, you know America is in the throes of a pop culture phenomenon that will, for a while, be Topic A of conversation. But given the persistence of more significant gender gaps—in wages, in executive positions, and in a number of other areas—that go generally undiscussed in the popular culture, it's striking how much attention is being lavished on a differential that is, ultimately, trivial.

Vocabulary / Using a Dictionary

1. When analyzing Regis Philbin's comments on *Who Wants to Be a Millionaire*, Cohn describes the host's appeal as being a *mono-logue*. What is a *monologue*? Break the word into parts. What other words contain those parts?

2. "One woman, Shannon McGehee, has logged the best time ever on a 'fastest finger' question; another holds the record for the

fastest time during a pregame rehearsal. But these women were *atypical*—they had already made it through two rounds of similar questions," explains the author in paragraph 8. Think of some synonyms for the word *atypical*. How do the word parts combine to create its meaning? What is the root of the word?

3. In paragraph 10, Cohn states: "Here's a *discomfiting* fact: Males dominate nearly every competition based on the recall of knowledge, at whatever age level, whether or not speed is a factor." What is the difference between the words *discomfiting* and *discomforting*? Explain.

Responding to Words in Context

1. "Much of the show's success [of *Who Wants to Be a Millionaire*] derives from its democratic appeal (and its easy, *field-leveling* questions): Anyone can come home a winner," comments Cohn in paragraph 2. What does the expression *field-leveling* mean?

2. What does the author mean when he relates, "Men . . . pursue trivia as a form of adolescent *one-upmanship*; women have the sense to concentrate on more productive things" (para. 5). What is *one-upmanship*?

3. At the end of his essay, Cohn comments about the nature of analyzing gender gaps on television game shows, concluding that "it's striking how much attention is being lavished on a *differential* that is, ultimately, trivial" (para. 15). To what is the author referring? What is a differential?

Discussing Main Point and Meaning

1. What problem does the author find with the fact that anyone who goes on *Who Wants to Be a Millionaire* "can come home a winner"?

2. State two theories from Cohn's article that may possibly explain why men might have "faster fingers" than women.

3. How does Cohn explain the "gender gap at competitions for younger children" (para. 13)? Why is this a problem?

4. According to the author, what is "the most interesting thing about the quiz show gender gap" (para. 15)? Why does Cohn

take issue with this fact? What does he consider to be more important?

Examining Sentences, Paragraphs, and Organization

1. What is the thesis (main idea) of Cohn's essay? Where can it be found? Explain your answers.
2. A transition sentence connects one idea to another. Locate several examples of transition sentences in Cohn's essay. Explain what ideas they connect and how.
3. What topic is the first half of Cohn's essay organized around? The second half? Why do you think he has used this strategy?

Thinking Critically

1. In his conclusion, Cohn states that "given the persistence of more significant gender gaps [than that of television quiz shows]—in wages, in executive positions, and in a number of other areas— that go generally undiscussed in the popular culture, it's striking how much attention is being lavished on a differential that is, ultimately, trivial" (para. 15). However, Cohn spends fifteen paragraphs discussing this so-called trivial differential, which indicates that he considers it more than just "trivial." What reasons might Cohn have for writing this essay? How might this strategy be considered effective?

In-Class Writing Assignments

1. Make a list of pros and cons, agreeing and disagreeing with Cohn's explanation of the gender gap in *Who Wants to Be a Millionaire*. After you have a substantial list of points on either side of the argument, write an essay arguing one way or the other, carefully addressing each of the opposing points.
2. In paragraph 15, Cohn mentions wages, executive positions, and "a number of other areas" in which gender gaps exist. What other areas is Cohn referring to? In what other areas of life do you see a gender gap? Choose one area that Cohn does not specifically mention, and discuss the gender gap, outlining its symptoms and explaining its causes. Be sure to cite ample evidence as you write.

PENELOPE SCAMBLY SCHOTT

Report on the Difference between Men and Women

[FOURTH GENRE/Fall 1999]

Before You Read

Try picturing yourself many years into a relationship (or marriage).
How do you imagine you would feel? Comfortable? Passionate?
Bored? Can you think of some of the characteristics of a couple that
has been married for a long time?

Words to Learn

preliminary (para. 3): something coming before or leading up to the main
   action (n.)
convulses (para. 4): shakes or disturbs violently; agitates (v.)
enormous (para. 5): huge; vast (adj.)

After thirteen years and twenty-seven days of marriage, my hus-   1
band turns to me and asks, "How come we never have lemonade?"
He pauses. "That kind that comes frozen in a can?"

It's not like he's never been to the grocery store or I haven't   2
asked him regularly if there's anything he'd like me to pick up, anything special he's in the mood for.

So on the twenty-eighth day of our fourteenth year of marriage, I   3
go to the store and buy lemonade, that kind that comes frozen in the
can. At the checkout, I push the frozen pale yellow cylinder onto the

*PENELOPE SCAMBLY SCHOTT (b. 1942) is convinced that men and women
are different species and that only perpetual optimism brings them together.
She publishes poetry and teaches college correspondence courses for adults.
Schott's book-length poem* Penelope: The Story of the Half-Scalped Woman
(1999) tells the true story of an early New Jersey settler.

conveyer belt and look into the eyes of the middle-aged woman who is ringing up my groceries. Without preliminary, I announce, "After all the time we've been married, my husband just asked me yesterday, out of the blue, 'How come we never have lemonade?'"

> *Neither of us needs to say another word.*

She looks back at me. The edges of her mouth flicker in and out. First the whole bottom of her face and then her shoulders begin to tremble. She convulses into giggling. Neither of us needs to say another word.   4

I go home, unbag, defrost the can, mix up his lemonade in a tall jar, shake it well, and put it in the refrigerator, front and center on the top shelf where even he can't miss it. When he comes in from work and starts browsing for something to drink, I say, "I bought lemonade today. It's right here in the front," and I point to it. He pours an enormous glass.   5

I wonder what else he secretly wants.   6

Vocabulary / Using a Dictionary

1. Schott uses the phrase "without *preliminary*" in paragraph 3. What does she mean?

2. The middle-aged woman who rings up the author's groceries "*convulses* into giggling" after Schott's announcement (para. 4). Describe this giggling.

3. In your own words, what does the word *enormous* mean (para. 5)? As a follow-up exercise, go to your dictionary and find the archaic (ancient; old-fashioned; outdated) meaning of the word. How would this archaic definition change the meaning of *enormous* in Schott's sentence "He pours an *enormous* glass"?

Responding to Words in Context

1. Schott describes the checkout woman as *middle-aged* (para. 3). What do you think she means by this?

2. In paragraph 3, Schott's frozen can of lemonade travels on a *conveyer belt*. What verb does the compound noun *conveyer belt* come from? What is the definition of that word?

Discussing Main Point and Meaning

1. According to the author, what is the implied difference between men and women? What does her essay "report" about this difference?

2. In Schott's essay, why is it important that the checkout worker be a middle-aged woman?

3. Why does the author conclude the essay with the statement: "I wonder what else he secretly wants" (para. 6)?

Examining Sentences, Paragraphs, and Organization

1. Why is it important that the first sentences of paragraphs 1 and 3 both begin with Schott describing the number of years and days she has been married? Are these two topic sentences effective?

2. Paragraph 4 of Schott's essay provides the reader with the checkout woman's response to the author's statement, "After all the time we've been married, my husband just asked me yesterday, out of the blue, 'How come we never have lemonade?'" How does this testimony add credence (believability; credentials) to Schott's "report"?

3. Schott's essay is organized around conversations and responses/reactions to those conversations. Describe how the events are ordered in the essay. Is this method effective?

Thinking Critically

1. Note that Schott's title uses the word *difference,* not the plural *differences.* Why do you think she emphasized the singular?

2. Do you find that Schott's "Report on the Difference between Men and Women" is a little biased? Is her essay an unfair report on the relationship of men and women, or an accurate one? Explain.

In-Class Writing Activities

1. Have you (or someone close to you) ever been involved in a situation like Schott's, which shows a distinct difference between men and women? Write a brief essay describing the experience.

2. Communication between two people is of paramount importance to a relationship. Further, it is often remarked that the number-one quality interviewers look for in potential employees is the ability to communicate effectively, as it aids in running a successful business. Freewrite for a few minutes about how you think people can better develop their communication skills (in marriage, around friends, at the workplace, etc.).

OPPOSING VIEWS

King or Queen of the Road?

Before You Read

How often have you heard that women are bad drivers or that men are too proud to ask for directions? Have you seen examples of these stereotypes? Have you seen (or experienced) examples that contradict these stereotypes?

Words to Learn [Dalton]

barreling (para. 1): traveling or driving very fast (v.)
yakking (para. 4): talking senselessly and steadily (v.)

Words to Learn [Cowley]

juvenile (para. 1): characteristic of or suitable for young people (adj.)
obnoxious (para. 1): extremely objectionable or offensive (adj.)
audible (para. 5): loud enough to be heard (adj.)
utterly (para. 5): completely; in the greatest degree (adv.)

STEVE DALTON

The Mirror Is Not for Makeup

[THE SPECTRUM, KANSAS CITY METROPOLITAN COMMUNITY COLLEGE/
December 8, 1999]

There are so many bad things about women drivers, I don't   1
know where to start. I guess I will get the ball rolling by talking
about one of my biggest pet peeves. Why do women have to wait
until they are in the car and barreling down the highway at sixty
miles an hour before they decide it is time to put on their makeup?

Is there a law that I don't know about that says women have to   2
do their makeup in the car because the bathroom isn't good enough
for them? I don't know if anyone has ever informed women, but the
mirror in the car is not a makeup mirror. The mirror is used for looking at other cars and pedestrians. So please do us all a favor and do
your makeup before you leave the house.

The next order of business for the men should be to find out   3
whose brilliant idea it was for women to have a phone in the car. This
has disaster written all over it. Everyone knows that women can't even
walk and chew gum at the same time, so how in the hell are they
going to drive and talk on the phone? Why is it that every time you
are sitting at a red light the woman in front of you thinks this is a
good time to make a phone call? "HELLO LADY. THE LIGHT IS
GREEN, GET OFF THE PHONE AND GO!" I really think we need
to outlaw women using their cell phones while they drive.

Another accident waiting to happen is when you get two women   4
in the same car together. How many times have you seen two women
just yakking away and the driver isn't paying attention to where she
is going? There is either one of two things that happens when two
women get in the car together. One: The women are talking and the

---

*Steve Dalton (b. 1970) recently received his associate's degree from
Penn Valley Community College, where he developed the idea for a debate
between a "pig-headed guy" and a "sensitive woman." "It's supposed to be
funny," Dalton says. "I wanted to express the inner-macho-pig-guy in me."*

driver doesn't see the stop sign in front of her, so she runs it. Two: The two women are talking and at the last minute the driver realizes there is her turn, so she stops really quick in front of you and you almost rear-end her. So women please pay more attention to your driving and, for the love of God, use your turn signals—they aren't there for decoration.

> *The mirror is not a makeup mirror.*

I know all the women out there are yelling at   5
me and saying, "Women are better drivers than guys." If women were better drivers than men, why do guys drive on dates? Why don't women ever tell the guy, I will come pick you up? Why are almost all truck drivers guys? Why is it when a woman is going to move and she rents a U-Haul van, she always calls a guy to drive it for her? When was the last time you watched a woman win the Indy 500 or Daytona 500? All of these questions just go to prove why guys are the kings of the road.

RACHAEL COWLEY

Women Stop for Directions

[THE SPECTRUM, KANSAS CITY METROPOLITAN COMMUNITY COLLEGE/ December 8, 1999]

Women make better drivers than men for so many reasons, yet   1
we take all the flack about being horrible drivers. Why is that, do you suppose? Wouldn't you think that competing at who has better driving abilities is juvenile and pointless? If you ask me, men crack their obnoxious jokes because they have some sort of inferiority complex. They know that women are superior drivers but have too much

---

RACHAEL COWLEY *(b. 1977) was a junior at Park University, in Kansas City, Missouri, when she wrote this piece for the Kansas City Metropolitan Community College* Spectrum. *Cowley says the piece was an exercise to try to "learn the journalistic style," and she hopes to continue in a career in journalism.*

testosterone running through their veins to admit the truth—women are queens of the road.

Unlike men, women stop for directions when they have no clue   2
as to where they are going. We don't drive around for hours pointlessly wasting a tank of gas only to find ourselves stranded and heading in the wrong direction. Have you ever been in the car with a man who is lost? He tells you to shut up when you even begin to open your mouth because he is a "human compass" and knows exactly what he's doing. And every five minutes or so he takes a turn going forty-five miles per hour, smashing your face against the window, or recklessly cuts across four lanes of traffic only to find out he's made another wrong turn. If he would have simply stopped and asked directions in the first place, he wouldn't have found himself kissing someone else's bumper at a stoplight.

> *Unlike men, women stop for directions.*

Why is it that men continually think they're driving in a competi-   3
tive race? If they are stopped at a red light, they rev their engines the entire time, and the instant the light changes to green they take off squealing their tires. This is annoying and dangerous. What if there was a car or pedestrian that missed its own red light and snuck out into the road? Guys, if you're doing this because you think it's cool or attracts women, you're wrong. It makes us more nervous than anything and it's very uncool and unsafe.

Speeding is what men do best on the road. Traffic is not a race. It   4
isn't a competition as to who reaches their destination first, or who can turn corners the fastest, or who gets the most speeding and reckless driving tickets. There is a reason why men get more speeding tickets than women. Not because we flirt to get out of tickets but only because we don't get pulled over as frequently. We don't speed. We have more intelligence than senselessly to put our own lives as well as the lives of others in danger.

My largest issue with male drivers is how a majority of them   5
drive with one hand on the wheel and the other hand doing only God knows what. The seat is reclined as far back as possible, and they're banging their heads to loud obnoxious music cranked way beyond a necessary audible level. How can anyone possibly be able to maneuver a vehicle safely while driving in this manner? How did they even get their licenses in the first place? You don't ever see women driving like that. In my opinion, any man seen driving in this manner should be reported to the proper authorities, have his license revoked, and

serve jail time not only for driving dangerously but also for looking utterly ridiculous.

I feel that the above evidence more than proves my point that women are not only better drivers but also safer drivers than men. We definitely rule the road. Oh, and men, if you want to continue bashing women for being bad drivers, bring it on. We know you're insecure, or else you wouldn't be wasting your valuable time cracking jokes about the ones you may choose to spend the rest of your days with.

6

Vocabulary / Using a Dictionary

1. Dalton states in paragraph 1 of his essay: "I guess I will get the ball rolling by talking about one of my biggest *pet peeves*. Why do women have to wait until they are in the car and barreling down the highway at sixty miles an hour before they decide it is time to put on their makeup?" What is a *pet peeve*? Can you think of *your* pet peeves?

2. "I really think we need to *outlaw* women using their cell phones while they drive," comments Dalton in paragraph 3. In this context, what does the word *outlaw* mean? What are some other meanings for the word *outlaw*?

3. In paragraph 5, Cowley remarks, "In my opinion, any man seen driving in this manner should be reported to the proper authorities, have his license revoked, and serve jail time not only for driving dangerously but also for looking *utterly* ridiculous." How does someone look "*utterly* ridiculous"? What are some synonyms for the word *utterly*?

Responding to Words in Context

1. Before proceeding to his second example of why "there are so many bad things about women drivers" (para. 1), Dalton writes the words: "*The next order of business*" (para. 3). What does this expression mean?

2. In Cowley's first paragraph, the author comments: "Women make better drivers than men for so many reasons, yet we *take all the flack* about being horrible drivers." What does the author suggest when she uses the phrase *take all the flack*?

3. "If you ask me, men crack their obnoxious jokes because they have some sort of inferiority complex," hypothesizes Cowley in paragraph 1. In your own words, explain what the author is suggesting with her idea.

Discussing Main Point and Meaning

1. What is one of Dalton's biggest pet peeves? Why does this bother him? Explain your answer.

2. According to Dalton, what happens when "you get two women in the same car together" (para. 4)?

3. In Cowley's essay, she describes the difference between how women and men obtain directions when they are driving. What is the difference?

4. What is Cowley's "largest issue with male drivers" (para. 5)? Why does this bother her? Explain your answer.

Examining Sentences, Paragraphs, and Organization

1. Pick out one transitional statement from each of the two student articles. Explain why each of these is a transitional statement.

2. Compare and contrast the concluding paragraphs of the two student articles. Which conclusion do you think is more effective? Why? Explain your answer.

3. Do either of the two student writers provide statistics to support his or her opinions/generalizations? Does this influence your reading of the essays? Do you still feel strongly in support of one author over the other?

Thinking Critically

1. In his conclusion, Dalton subjects the reader to a battery of questions: "Why don't women ever tell the guy, I will come pick you up? Why are almost all truck drivers guys? Why is it when a woman is going to move and she rents a U-Haul van, she always calls a guy to drive it for her? When was the last time you watched a woman win the Indy 500 or Daytona 500?" (para. 5). Do these rhetorical questions help to convince you that the author's point is valid? Explain your answer.

2. Twice in her essay, Cowley ruminates about men cracking "obnoxious jokes" about female drivers because of a masculine inferiority complex. She feels that men are insecure, or else they wouldn't be wasting their valuable free time cracking jokes "about the ones you may choose to spend the rest of your days with" (para. 6). Do you agree with Cowley's point of view? Are most men prejudiced against female drivers?

In-Class Writing Activities

1. Describe some of your earliest experiences with driving, concentrating on what treatment you received by your instructor. Did you get preferential treatment as a boy or girl? Were you taught by a man or woman? What role do you think gender played (if any) in your learning how to drive?

2. Recently, SUVs have become very popular as methods of transportation in America, with women purchasing these vehicles more often than men. It is suggested that women buy these because they feel safer and more secure on the streets if they are driving something "tank-like." Do men typically buy certain types of cars? Do women prefer different types? Why? What controls these tastes and preferences? Freewrite your answers, which you can base on your personal experiences.

Discussing the Unit

Suggested Topic for Discussion

Do you think differences between men and women are biological and genetic, or a result of cultural conditioning? Are men more aggressive than women? What other behavior do you think is culturally influenced? Biologically influenced? If American society expects men to be more aggressive, and women to be more passive, will they automatically become so?

Preparing for Class Discussion

1. Are you familiar with any organizations or programs on your campus that encourage discussions about gender relations? If so,

how effective do you think they are? If you aren't familiar with any such programs, what kind of gender issues do you *think* should be dealt with in discussion groups? Provide reasons to support your answers.

2. The United States is a country that appears to be growing more enlightened every year, but gender biases still persist: Americans can't seem to eliminate their prejudices. Do you foresee a day when gender differences no longer matter? How do you think your children will regard gender differences?

From Discussion to Writing

1. In each of the five essays you've read in this unit, the authors take a different *tone:* their particular style or manner of expression in speaking or writing is different. Compare and contrast their differences in tone.

2. How might Deborah Blum and Penelope Scambly Schott respond to Edward Cohn's conclusion: "given the persistence of more significant gender gaps—in wages, in executive positions, and in a number of other areas—that go generally undiscussed in the popular culture, it's striking how much attention is being lavished on a differential [the quiz show gender gap] that is, ultimately, trivial" (para. 15)? Write an essay discussing how you think they would respond to Cohn's statement.

3. Compose a dialogue among the five authors in this unit discussing the reality or illusion of gender differences. When using a dialogue format, be sure to identify the speaker of each line and to use the language and tone of voice appropriate to each of the authors.

Topics for Cross-Cultural Discussion

1. How do gender differences in your homeland differ from those in the United States? What are the different roles that men and women play in your country? Explain your answers.

2. How are women encouraged to act in your culture? Are men encouraged to act any differently? Who educates and influences the way children in your culture are "supposed" to act?

4

How Important Is
Ethnic Identity?

How important is ethnic heritage to our sense of personal identity? Aren't we all separate individuals first—with our own complicated histories—and members of groups second? And if we belong to more than one ethnic group—if our identities are "mixed"—is it necessary to choose one as more authentic than the others? These questions have been part of the process of becoming an American ever since the founding of the nation, but today, with a growing immigrant population that is skeptical of assimilation, this issue has become one of the most hotly debated topics of our time.

This unit explores three common attitudes toward multiethnic identity in America. Standing at a busy rotary in Saigon, Quang Bao suddenly realizes in "My Unhoming" that his true identity will never be purely Vietnamese nor purely American. But Bao's realization is exactly the sort that troubles Travis Weigel, a Kansas State political science major, who worries that America is in the process of losing its own common identity: "The United States," he argues, "has become little more than a conglomeration of separate and different social groups." In "The People in Me," Robin D. G. Kelley questions the very idea of a national common identity by proposing a "polycultural," as opposed to a "multicultural," perspective. We need, she believes, to see the "world as One—a tiny little globe where people and cultures are always on the move, where nothing stays still no matter how many times we name it." The unit concludes with an advertisement protesting the recent imprisonment of a Chinese American for espionage.

QUANG BAO

My Unhoming

[A. MAGAZINE/February–March 2000]

Before You Read

Have you or would you like to visit the land of your ancestors? What do you think you might find out about yourself if you did? With whom do you have more in common: the other students in your school, or your great-grandparents?

Words to Learn

rotary (para. 1): a traffic circle often with several entrances and exits (n.)
dilemma (para. 6): a situation requiring a choice between two equally persuasive alternatives; a predicament without an apparent solution (n.)
undeniably (para. 6): unquestionably; irrefutably (adv.)

On the last day of my trip back to Vietnam, I felt sentimental, standing at the main rotary in Saigon on Dong Khoi Boulevard, watching the motorcycles, taxis, bicycles, and pedestrians. The four-week trip had had its disappointments—obsess about a place long enough and it will always fall short of your expectations. But it was also beautiful, wondrous, and life-changing.

I amused myself watching a woman transport a refrigerator on the back of her scooter, a cyclo driver pedaling a baby water buffalo in the passenger seat, and two young boys running through the confusion, one piggy-back on the other. I felt joy at seeing Vietnamese people doing Vietnamese things. Throughout my trip, they had been

1

2

QUANG BAO (b. 1969) is managing editor of The Asian American Writer's Workshop. He is the coeditor of Take Out: Queer Writing from Asian Pacific America (AAWW) and has been published in The Threepenny Review, the Boston Globe, and the New York Times.

the ones watching me. In the role of the "other," the rich, lucky American, I told relatives and strangers about my life in the U.S. At times, I felt foolish because I don't speak Vietnamese well. I also have First World habits that felt out of place at dinner tables and throughout the countryside. I couldn't even imagine navigating that rotary.

Suddenly, in the swirl of traffic, a man without legs and only   3
one arm tugged at the hem of my pants, holding up his palm for money. The inside of his horrible hand was bloody and scarred, and I pictured him belly-flat on his skateboard, wheeling himself and begging throughout the city. He didn't wait for me to respond, simply pushing on into the traffic, making it across without harm and disappearing.

Once I leave this corner,   In that instant, I burst into tears.   4

I will never be   I thought: *Once I leave this corner, I*   5
will never be Vietnamese again. It was a

Vietnamese again.   strange revelation, brought on by the sensation of feeling totally disregarded by the crowds that passed me by. As refreshingly easy as it was to be Vietnamese in Vietnam, I felt like the punch line to a joke: What do you call a boy who leaves Vietnam at age six, who can't read, write, or speak his birth language, and who lives in America? *Not Vietnamese.*

I have in me only six years of Vietnamese-ness, and I was sad-   6
dened by the realization that it would never grow further, no matter how many trips back I made. The next morning, I realized that an internal dilemma had fallen away. "Vietnamese American" is a new construct, but it is undeniably who I am. The rest of my life stretched out ahead.

I boarded the plane for home.   7

Vocabulary / Using a Dictionary

1. How is the word *wondrous* used in paragraph 1? List a few synonyms and antonyms for the word.

2. A *dilemma* by definition has no apparent solution. What is Bao's *dilemma* (para. 6), and what happens to it?

3. What is the root word of *undeniably* (para. 6)? What does that root mean? Write a sentence about Bao's predicament, using that word.

Responding to Words in Context

1. In paragraph 2, Bao calls himself "the 'other.'" What does he mean by this? Why does he put the word *other* in quotation marks?

2. What does Bao mean when he uses the term *punch line* in paragraph 5?

3. What does the title word *unhoming* mean?

Discussing Main Point and Meaning

1. Does the author feel more or less like a Vietnamese at the end of his trip? How do you know? Point to examples in the text that support your answer.

2. Why does Bao burst into tears in paragraph 4? Why does he tell you about this moment? What conclusions about this experience can you draw from his behavior?

3. "*Once I leave this corner, I will never be Vietnamese again,*" Bao writes (para. 5). What does he mean by this? How does he know this to be true?

4. Why do you think the author went to Vietnam? Do you think he accomplished what he had originally set out to accomplish by going back? Explain.

Examining Sentences, Paragraphs, and Organization

1. Why do you think Bao begins by describing his *last day* in Vietnam? Why not begin with the first day? What effect does his starting this way have on the reader?

2. Describe the general effect of paragraph 2. What is the purpose of the paragraph? What is its tone?

3. There are two one-sentence paragraphs in this essay (4 and 7). Why do these sentences stand alone? Do they have a special purpose? Do they have any relationship to each other?

Thinking Critically

1. Do you think the author was naive to believe that Vietnam would be "home" to him? Why do you think that someone who

has lived in the United States from age six would feel the need to travel to a country that has, over the years, become foreign to him?

2. How do you think that the people of Vietnam received the author? Do you think that his reception there might have influenced his realization that he was *"Not Vietnamese"* (para. 5)? Or do you think this was a more internal journey for the author?

In-Class Writing Activities

1. In a short essay, describe an experience of feeling "out of place" in a situation you had thought would feel natural to you. How did you resolve your discomfort?

2. Write an essay about the gains and sacrifices that come from emigration to another country. Is more gained or lost? Is it more important to be accepted socially by the new culture than to accept the new society internally? Does assimilating to the new culture make it impossible to ever feel once again comfortable in the old culture?

TRAVIS WEIGEL

America's Identity Crisis

[KANSAS STATE COLLEGIAN, KANSAS STATE UNIVERSITY / February 4, 2000]

Before You Read

Can one be both American *and* Italian (or Korean or Haitian or Ukrainian)? What is American identity if not a mixture of all cultures? Do we need a unified ethnic identity in America, or can we find strength in diversity?

Words to Learn

patriotism (para. 2): love and support of one's country (n.)

prissy (para. 3): finicky; unnecessarily careful or prudish (adj.)

noxious (para. 3): harmful to health; injurious (adj.)

chokehold (para. 3): restriction of the throat, neck, or breath through physical restraint (n.)

conglomeration (para. 7): a collection of miscellaneous things (n.)

fragile (para. 7): easily broken (adj.)

mosaic (para. 7): a design made from small pieces of tile set in mortar or cement (n.)

proximity (para. 7): nearness (n.)

"I pledge allegiance to the flag of the United States of America and to the republic for which it stands. One nation under God, indivisible, with liberty and justice for all."   1

For those of you who might have forgotten, those are the words to the Pledge of Allegiance. Unfortunately, some people have not recited these words since elementary school, if at all, because of the   2

TRAVIS WEIGEL (b. 1979) was a first-year student at Kansas State University when he tackled the subject of American identity for the Collegian. *A Kansas State University Leadership Scholar, Weigel expects to receive a B.S. in political science in 2003.*

political incorrectness of the word God.[1] Many others simply do not possess the patriotism required to recite it, largely because of the absence of a uniform American identity.

Political correctness, in theory, means giving people their space   3 and encouraging a range of opinions and lifestyles. In practice, however, it means continually alternating between prissy self-censorship and cultural bum-kissing. Regrettably, political correctness—as well as affirmative action—has become an invaluable tool used in the war against inequality and differentiation. Sadly, political correctness has caused differentiation to spread like a noxious weed that now has a chokehold on our society.

> We call ourselves Americans, but the truth is most of us do not know what it means to be an American.

But what is differentiation, anyway?   4 According to *Merriam-Webster's Collegiate Dictionary, differentiation* is the development from the one to the many. Instead of focusing on what the members of a particular group might have in common, it focuses upon what they do not. Put simply, differentiation is dividing a given society based upon social issues such as religion, race, or ethnicity.

An unfortunate side effect of differentiation is that it often causes   5 a lack of unity among the members within a given society to develop. This problem is aggravated by the excessive use of political correctness and the reverse-discriminatory habits of affirmative action.

In the United States, this lethal combination has resulted in the   6 creation of a uniquely American terminology. This new terminology combines the ethnic origin of an individual with that of being American. As a result, we now have terms such as African-American, Japanese-American, and Mexican-American. These new terms not only have made the already visible social divisions within our society even more apparent, but they also have resulted in the loss of a common American identity.

Without a common American identity, the United States has become little more than a conglomeration of separate and different social   7 groups. As each group becomes more and more self-sufficient, more ties are broken with the rest of society, resulting in self-segregation. As fewer and fewer threads remain to hold together our increasingly fragile society, the less we look like a patchwork quilt and the more

---

[1]To read more about this issue, see Unit 11.

we begin to look like a mosaic, held together only by our proximity to one another.

Somehow I do not believe this current movement is what our founding fathers meant by forming "a more perfect Union." By separating and segregating ourselves from one another based solely upon our ancestry, we no longer can consider ourselves "We the People of the United States" because there is no "we." Sadly, the only time we seem to set aside our differences and come together as one unanimous voice is in times of extreme crisis, such as during Operation Desert Storm or the bombing of the Alfred P. Murrah Federal Building.   8

We call ourselves Americans, but the truth is most of us do not know what it means to be an American. We get so wrapped up in our insignificant daily lives that we forget just how lucky and how much better off we are by just being here. Every year, thousands of people come to the United States yearning to breathe free as we do, and every single one of them is more than honored to be called an American. Shouldn't we?   9

Vocabulary/Using a Dictionary

1. The root of the word *patriotism* (para. 2) is from the Latin word for *father*. What do you think is the relationship between "patriots" and "fathers"?

2. How does the word *noxious* relate to the more familiar word *obnoxious*? What is the meaning of the prefix? How does the addition of the prefix change the meaning?

3. What does the author mean by *proximity* in paragraph 7? How does this word relate to the word *approximate*?

Responding to Words in Context

1. Why does the author cite a dictionary definition for the word *differentiation* in paragraph 4?

2. What is the "lethal" combination Weigel refers to in paragraph 6? How does his use of this word differ from other meanings the word has?

Discussing Main Point and Meaning

1. What is causing the problem of *differentiation* in North American culture, according to the author?

2. When Weigel says that Americans look less like a "patchwork quilt" and more "like a mosaic" (para. 7), what do you think he means by that? How are those two images different?

3. How would you characterize the main goal of this essay? What do you think Weigel wants done about the problem he presents?

Examining Sentences, Paragraphs, and Organization

1. In paragraph 3, Weigel suggests that "political correctness" is a combination of "prissy self-censorship and cultural bum-kissing." What is the tone of that sentence? Why do you think the author uses this tone? Does the author's tone have the desired effect on you, the reader?

2. Examine paragraph 4, where Weigel provides a dictionary definition for a word and then expands on that definition. How close in meaning are the two definitions? What is the purpose of this paragraph?

3. What is the purpose of referring to the Pledge of Allegiance in paragraph 1, and alluding to the U.S. Constitution in paragraph 8? How do these historical references provide a frame or structure for this essay?

Thinking Critically

1. In paragraph 9, the author suggests that Americans should be "honored" to call themselves just that (without adding the elements that divide us, such as those mentioned in paragraph 6). Do you agree that Americans should be "honored" to have been born in America? Do you feel that to be patriotic one must adhere to a common culture? Can't Americans be at once diverse *and* unified?

2. Weigel's argument is primarily an argument about language. He objects to the hyphenated labels that describe the various backgrounds of Americans, he criticizes the fact that many students no longer recite the Pledge of Allegiance, and he holds up the words of the Constitution as evidence that society has changed

for the worse. Is language as powerful as Weigel suggests? Are the real instances of both discrimination *and* belonging more important, in your opinion, than the language we use to describe those differences?

In-Class Writing Activities

1. Describe the level of *political correctness* at the school you attend. Do you feel unfairly restricted in your speech? Do you think such restrictions hurt the unity and spirit of the campus? Give examples of any restrictions of which you are aware.

2. In a brief essay, argue for or against the recitation of the Pledge of Allegiance in public schools.

ROBIN D. G. KELLEY

The People in Me

[COLORLINES / Winter 1999]

Before You Read

Do you wish for people to recognize your ethnicity when they meet you? How relevant do you think it is to your identity? How much does it play a part in your associations with others?

ROBIN D. G. KELLEY (b. 1962) is a professor of history and Africana studies at New York University. His most recent book, Yo' Mama's DisFunktional! Fighting the Culture Wars in Urban America (1997), was selected one of the top ten books of 1998 by the Village Voice. Kelley has written and edited several books, including the forthcoming Misterioso: In Search of Thelonious Monk, and his essays have appeared in The Nation, the New York Times Magazine, African Studies Review, and the Boston Review.

Words to Learn

exotics (para. 2): intriguing because of their foreignness (n.)

patois (para. 2): nonstandard dialect (n.)

enigmas (para. 2): something inexplicable or puzzling (n.)

demure (para. 3): reserved, modest (adj.)

scoundrel (para. 4): villain (n.)

reifies (para. 5): solidifies; makes real (v.)

hybrid (para. 7): of mixed origins (adj.)

émigrés (para. 8): immigrants (n.)

dynamism (para. 11): a process characterized by energy in motion (n.)

"So, what are you?" I don't know how many times people have asked me that. "Are you Puerto Rican? Dominican? Indian or something? You must be mixed." My stock answer has rarely changed: "My mom is from Jamaica but grew up in New York, and my father was from North Carolina but grew up in Boston. Both black."   1

My family has lived with "the question" for as long as I can remember. We're "exotics," all cursed with "good hair" and strange accents—we don't sound like we from da Souf or the Norwth, and don't have that West Coast–by-way-of-Texas Calabama thang going on. The only one with the real West Indian singsong vibe is my grandmother, who looks even more East Indian than my sisters. Whatever Jamaican patois my mom possessed was pummeled out of her by cruel preteens who never had sensitivity seminars in diversity. The result for us was a nondescript way of talking, walking, and being that made us not black enough, not white enough—just a bunch of not-quite-nappy-headed enigmas.   2

My mother never fit the "black momma" media image. A beautiful, demure, light brown woman, she didn't drink, smoke, curse, or say things like "Lawd Jesus" or "hallelujah," nor did she cook chitlins or gumbo. A vegetarian, she played the harmonium (a foot-pumped miniature organ), spoke softly with textbook diction, meditated, followed the teachings of Paramahansa Yogananda, and had wild hair like Chaka Khan.[1] She burned incense in our tiny Harlem apartment, sometimes walked the streets barefoot, and, when she could afford it, cooked foods from the East.   3

To this day, my big sister gets misidentified for Pakistani or Bengali or Ethiopian. (Of course, changing her name from Sheral Anne   4

---

[1]*Chaka Khan:* Popular black soul singer of the '70s and '80s.

Kelley to Makani Themba has not helped.) Not long ago, an Oakland cab driver, apparently a Sikh who had immigrated from India, treated my sister like dirt until he discovered that she was not a "scoundrel from Sri Lanka," but a common black American. Talk about ironic: How often are black women spared indignities *because* they are African American? "What are you?" dogged my little brother more than any of us. He came out looking just like his father, who was white. In the black communities of Los Angeles and Pasadena, my baby bro' had to fight his way into blackness, usually winning only when he invited his friends to the house. When he got tired of this, he became what people thought he was—a cool white boy. Today he lives in Tokyo, speaks fluent Japanese, and is happily married to a Japanese woman (who is actually Korean passing as Japanese!). He stands as the perfect example of our mulattoness: a black boy trapped in a white body who speaks English with a slight Japanese accent and has a son who will spend his life confronting "the question."

Although folk had trouble naming us, we were never blanks or   5 aliens in a "black world." We were and are "polycultural," and I'm talking about all peoples in the Western world. It is not skin, hair, walk, or talk that renders black people so diverse. Rather, it is the fact that most of them are products of different "cultures"—living cultures, not dead ones. These cultures live in and through us every day, with almost no self-consciousness about hierarchy or meaning. "Polycultural" works better than "multicultural," which implies that cultures are fixed, discrete entities that exist side by side—a kind of zoological approach to culture. Such a view obscures power relations, but often reifies race and gender differences.

Black people were polycultural from the get-go. Most of our an-   6 cestors came to these shores not as Africans, but as Ibo, Yoruba, Hausa, Kongo, Bambara, Mende, Mandingo, and so on. Some of our ancestors came as Spanish, Portuguese, French, Dutch, Irish, English, Italian. And more than a few of us, in North America as well as in the Caribbean and Latin America, have Asian and Native American roots.

Our lines of biological descent are about as pure as O. J.'s blood   7 sample, and our cultural lines of descent are about as mixed up as a pot of gumbo. What we know as "black culture" has always been fluid and hybrid. In Harlem in the late 1960s and 1970s, Nehru suits were as popular—and as "black"—as dashikis, and martial arts films placed Bruce Lee among a pantheon of black heroes that included Walt Frazier of the New York Knicks and Richard Rountree, who played John Shaft in blaxploitation cinema. How do we understand the zoot suit—or the conk—without the pachuco culture of Mexican American youth, or low riders in black communities without Chicanos? How can we discuss black visual artists in the interwar years without reference to the Mexican muralists, or the radical graphics tradition dating back to the late nineteenth century, or the Latin American artists influenced by surrealism?

Vague notions of "Eastern" religion and philosophy, as well as a variety of Orientalist assumptions, were far more important to the formation of the Lost-Found Nation of Islam than anything coming out of Africa. And Rastafarians drew many of their ideas from South Asians, from vegetarianism to marijuana, which was introduced into Jamaica by Indians. Major black movements like Garveyism and the African Blood Brotherhood are also the products of global developments. We won't understand these movements until we see them as part of a dialogue with Irish nationalists from the Easter Rebellion, Russian and Jewish émigrés from the 1905 and 1917 revolutions, and Asian socialists like India's M. N. Roy and Japan's Sen Katayama.

> *All of us are inheritors of European, African, Native American, and Asian pasts, even if we can't exactly trace our bloodlines to these continents.*

Indeed, I'm not sure we can even limit ourselves to Earth. How do we make sense of musicians Sun Ra, George Clinton, and Lee "Scratch" Perry or, for that matter, the Nation of Islam, when we consider the fact that space travel and notions of intergalactic exchange constitute a key source of their ideas?

So-called "mixed race" children are not the only ones with a claim to multiple heritages. All of us are inheritors of European, African, Native American, and Asian pasts, even if we can't exactly trace our bloodlines to these continents.

To some people that's a dangerous concept. Too many Europeans don't want to acknowledge that Africans helped create so-called Western civilization, that they are both indebted to and descendants of those they enslaved. They don't want to see the world as One—a tiny little globe where people and cultures are always on the move, where nothing stays still no matter how many times we name it. To acknowledge our polycultural heritage and cultural dynamism is not to give up our black identity. It does mean expanding our definition of blackness, taking our history more seriously, and looking at the rich diversity within us with new eyes.

So next time you see me, don't ask where I'm from or what I am,   12
unless you're ready to sit through a long-ass lecture. As singer/song-
writer Abbey Lincoln once put it, "I've got some people in me."

Vocabulary/Using a Dictionary

1. Why does Kelley put *exotics* in quotation marks in paragraph 2?

2. Reread paragraph 7. How does the author illustrate his claim
   that black culture has always been *hybrid?* What different origins
   does he cite as contributing to this *hybrid* culture?

3. *Dynamite* shares the same root as *dynamism* (para. 11). Explore
   the ways in which you think the author might be suggesting that
   black American culture is explosive in its dynamism.

Responding to Words in Context

1. Why does Kelley specifically use the phrase *baby bro'* in paragraph 4 to describe his little brother? What effect does this description have on the reader?

2. In paragraph 7, you'll find the slang word *blaxploitation.* What
   do you think it means?

3. Kelley says in paragraph 5 that "'polycultural' works better than
   'multicultural.'" What is the difference between the two prefixes
   (*poly* and *multi*)? Use a dictionary if necessary. (It might help to
   think of other words that share these prefixes.)

Discussing Main Point and Meaning

1. What is the question this author lives with? Do you live with it
   yourself? How much does it matter to you? How much do you
   think it matters to the author?

2. This essay draws on several historical and cultural examples.
   Pick one that you recognize and explain how it supports the author's main idea.

3. Describe Kelley's tone of voice. How does he feel about this subject matter? Is he amused, curious, frustrated, bitter, or all of
   these things? How can you tell?

4. How does this article complicate or add to what you understand
   diversity to be? Explain your answer.

Examining Sentences, Paragraphs, and Organization

1. Kelley begins and ends his essay with quotes. What effect does this have? How is the end quote related to the beginning quote?

2. Examine paragraph 3, where the author describes his mother. How does the picture of this woman develop over the course of the paragraph?

3. In paragraph 8, Kelley mentions a number of historical and cultural events, people, and organizations. What does this paragraph tell you about the author? What does it tell you about his relationship to this subject matter?

4. What would you say is the eventual argument of this essay? How does the author use his personal story to make a more general point about society?

Thinking Critically

1. Kelley's diction is formal and informal, academic and slang-filled. Does this inconsistency hurt his writing? Would you use this style in your own writing? Why or why not?

2. Do you think that the author has contempt for the people who ask him what ethnicity he is or where he is from? Are they the same people to whom this essay is addressed? Does this author strike you as someone who is very concerned with what others think of him? How do you know?

In-Class Writing Activities

1. Kelley writes, "So-called 'mixed race' children are not the only ones with a claim to multiple heritages. All of us are inheritors of European, African, Native American, and Asian pasts, even if we can't exactly trace our bloodlines to these continents" (para. 10). Write a brief essay that tries to articulate what this means. What things do you think are a part of that "inheritance"? Try to avoid naming only concrete things like food, songs, or fashions. Include memories, ideas, and cultural debates as well.

2. Try to list and explain "the people in [you]," to borrow Abbey Lincoln's words (para. 12). What stories would you have to tell, what people would you have to describe, what cultural influences would you have to cite to explain "what you are"?

CHINESE FOR AFFIRMATIVE ACTION

[2000]

Before You Read

This advertisement may require some background. Dr. Wen Ho Lee, a Taiwan-born, naturalized U.S. citizen, was arrested in December 1999 and charged with violating the federal Espionage Act by acting as a spy for China and removing secret nuclear files from computers at the Los Alamos (New Mexico) weapons lab. Lee was held without bail in solitary confinement at a federal prison for nine months until he was released in September 2000. Lee agreed to plead guilty to one of the many felony violations he was charged with and the FBI dropped its case, though Lee must still explain his mishandling of classified information. Approving of the plea agreement, a federal judge said that the government "embarrassed this entire nation."

Do you think that the U.S. government may be reacting harshly against Lee because of his ethnic identity? In other words, that he is essentially "charged with being ethnic Chinese"? Consider what information you would need to know in order to make an informed decision about Lee's guilt or innocence.

Words to Learn

languishing (para. 1): lingering, undergoing neglect (v.)

espionage (para. 2): government use of spies to discover military or political secrets (n.)

allegation (para. 2): in law, an assertion of a criminal act that remains to be proven (n.)

indicted (para. 4): in law, charged with an offense or crime (v.)

affidavit (para. 7): in law, written declaration made before an authorized official (n.)

Charged with being ethnic Chinese.

WHY IS American scientist Dr. Wen Ho Lee still languishing in prison?

He is not charged with espionage. Early news leaks to the contrary, the FBI cleared Dr. Lee of sharing warhead information with any foreign government. Today, the sole allegation is that Dr. Wen Ho Lee downloaded data onto computer disks at Los Alamos.

The data was unclassified when he downloaded it. The government classified it as "secret" only after his dismissal.

Ex-CIA director John Deutch allegedly downloaded classified information into his home computers. Other Los Alamos staffers apparently misplaced hard drives with classified information. None has been criminally indicted or is in custody. Dr. Lee alone faces criminal charges — the only person ever charged under the Atomic Energy Act.

Dr. Lee has been separated from his family for eight months.

The 60-year-old Taiwan-born American scientist, employed at Los Alamos for two decades, has been held in solitary confinement in a federal prison, without bail, for eight months. Contact with his family is restricted and monitored. He is shackled hand and foot on the rare occasions he is taken from his cell. Why?

The chief of Los Alamos counterintelligence says that Dr. Lee was singled out for investigation because of his "ethnicity."

The search warrant for his home was obtained on the U.S. Attorney's affidavit that Dr. Lee is "overseas ethnic Chinese."

Charged with being ethnic Chinese, how can he prove his innocence? And why, of all Americans, should he be forced to?

Professional organizations protesting Dr. Lee's treatment:

American Association for the Advancement of Science

American Physical Society

Asian Pacific Americans in Higher Education

Association of Asian American Studies

Committee of Concerned Scientists

New York Academy of Sciences

Caught up in a classic witch hunt built on racist stereotypes and racial profiling, Dr. Lee faces life in prison because of domestic politics, not international intrigue. The 1950's-style nuclear security hysteria whipped up in Congress last year made Dr. Lee the scapegoat because he is ethnic Chinese, and for that reason alone.

It should chill us all that our government is still persecuting Dr. Lee and bankrupting his family long after any basis for prosecution has evaporated.

As Chinese-Americans — as Americans — we demand justice.

Drop all charges. Free Dr. Wen Ho Lee now.

Chinese for Affirmative Action

Chinese for Affirmative Action, 17 Walter U. Lum Place, San Francisco, California 94108
To learn more, please visit www.caasf.org.

Vocabulary/Using a Dictionary

1. Look up *languish* in a dictionary. What range of meanings does it have? Do all of them apply to the term as used in the advertisement?

2. Look up the various meanings of the complex verb *to charge* in a dictionary. What main meaning does it have as used in the ad's headline?

Responding to Words in Context

1. Note all of the specific legal terms used in the advertising text. How many can you identify? Do you think all of these words are readily understood by the general public? Which ones confuse you? Why do you think the writer of the ad used these words?

2. Why do you think the U.S. attorney's affidavit mentioned in paragraph 7 identifies Lee as "overseas ethnic Chinese"? Do you think the identification is intended to be racist? What reasons would the authorities have to use this expression?

Discussing Main Point and Meaning

1. What is the primary purpose of the advertisement? What does it want Americans to know? What action does it want Americans to take? To whom is the advertisement addressed?

2. What is a "classic witch hunt"? In what sense is Lee a "scapegoat," as reported in paragraph 9? Who made him one, and why?

Examining Details, Imagery, and Design

1. What is the effect of the photograph? Why do you think the designer inserted it tilted? Would it have been more persuasive to use a photo of Dr. Lee at work in his Los Alamos lab? Why or why not?

2. What is the effect of listing along the side the professional organizations protesting Dr. Lee's treatment? Do you know what these organizations are? Do you think the general public is familiar with them? Do you know for certain whether they believe he is innocent?

Thinking Critically

1. Note the headline and its repetition in paragraphs 7 and 8. Do you think Dr. Lee has actually been "charged with being ethnic

Chinese"? That is, that among the criminal acts Lee is accused of one of them is specifically his being "Chinese"? Review closely paragraphs 6–8, and discuss the logical connections between each paragraph.

2. Does the advertisement persuade you fully that Dr. Lee is innocent? Is that its primary intention? Would you feel comfortable joining a protest to free Dr. Lee based solely on the information provided by the advertisement? Why or why not? What additional information would you like to see?

In-Class Writing Activities

1. Do you believe that people are sometimes singled out for allegedly committing crimes because of their race or ethnic identity? In a few paragraphs, freewrite your thoughts about this practice. You might also compare this ad with "Driving While Black" on p. 204.

2. Consider the persuasive effect of the photograph used in the ad supporting Dr. Lee. What effect is it meant to have? Freewrite a few paragraphs in which you discuss the way depiction of family is often used by the media to create positive images of an individual.

Discussing the Unit

Suggested Topic for Discussion

To a certain extent, all of the authors in this unit need to come to grips with ethnic identity in order to live with themselves. Are you unsettled by questions of ethnicity? Do you feel "unhomed," as Quang Bao does? Are you in "crisis," as Weigel suggests all Americans are? Or do you feel fortified by the complexity and persistence of your identity(ies)?

Preparing for Class Discussion

1. What does it mean to have an "ethnic identity" as an American? Is there such a thing as a unified "American culture"? How would you characterize it?

2. Two of these authors are struggling with their own personal identities; the third is interested in collective identity. Explain how these two things are connected.

From Discussion to Writing

1. Compose a dialogue between Robin D. G. Kelley and Travis Weigel. Keep in mind that both authors refer to historical events and ideas, and both authors attempt to discover what it means to be "American" to some extent. Begin the dialogue by having each of the authors answer the question, "What is an American?"

2. Write a short story from the point of view of Quang Bao. Describe his experiences as a six-year-old spending his first weeks in America. How would his reactions be similar to or different from his adult reactions to Vietnam?

3. Drawing on the texts for comparison, write an essay that describes what you think to be your ethnic identity.

Topics for Cross-Cultural Discussion

1. How important are ethnic self-definitions in other cultures? Do people worry too much about defining themselves? Do you think the American debates about these issues are more liberating or confining to personal identity than in other places?

2. Ethnicity, race, culture, heritage, nationality, and ancestry are often used interchangeably in American English. Do other languages have more or fewer words to describe one's origins? Are the words as interchangeable in another language, or do they have more distinct uses?

5

Do Words Matter?

Do the words we use in everyday conversation matter? How? Does it make any difference whether we say we "love" ice cream, whether we come out and say we're sorry, or what our vehicles are called? In this chapter we will look at how certain words can oversimplify reality, create hostile or comfortable environments, and help advertisers sell us products we probably don't need.

Because *love* is perhaps "the most overused word in the English language," Camille DeAngelis, a student at New York University, believes it is easily undervalued and its power "diluted by eons of misuse." In "Pondering 'Love,'" she argues that before using the word we should first contemplate its enormous complexity. Two other powerful words in the English language are "I'm sorry." Yet, why do women find these words easier to say than men do? An expert in linguistics, Deborah Tannen examines that issue in "Contrite Makes Right," an essay that demonstrates the power of apologies in both personal and international relationships. The final essay of the chapter takes a look at the powerful language of marketing. "What's in a name?" asks Jack Hitt in "The Hidden Life of SUVs," as he wonders why so many Americans are so easily persuaded to buy superexpensive vehicles with names like "Durango," "Cherokee," "Blazer," "Pathfinder," "Explorer," "Mountaineer," and "Yukon." Who are all these rich new pioneers? he asks. And what wilderness are they attempting to conquer?

CAMILLE DeANGELIS

Pondering "Love"

[WASHINGTON SQUARE NEWS, NEW YORK UNIVERSITY/October 26, 1999]

Before You Read

Can you define the word *love?* Are you in love now? Have you ever been in love with someone? Many poets and artists have tried to express their ideas of love in words or pictures. Try to describe the emotion you feel (have felt) in words. Can you? How is the emotion of love different from contentment, warmth, happiness, or affection?

Words to Learn

eons (para. 2): extremely long, indefinite periods of time (n.)
unrequited (para. 6): not returned or reciprocated (v.)
trite (para. 7): no longer having freshness, originality, or novelty (adj.)
inherent (para. 7): existing in someone or something as a natural and inseparable quality (adj.)

"Love" is the most overused word in the English language. I say   1
I love Chunky Monkey ice cream. I love the Muppets and poetry and
any song U2 has ever written. I love New York. But rarely do I consider the meaning of the word I use so liberally.

"Love" is a word whose power has been diluted by eons of mis-   2
use. I'm not sure I'm ready to see my own reflection in the things and
people I profess to love, because I'm not at all confident I really do
love them. It's a dirty or worthless word for some. Others hold it as

CAMILLE DeANGELIS (b. 1980) was "in one of those 'question everything'
modes" when she wrote this piece as a freshman for New York University's
Washington Square News. *DeAngelis is busy writing a travel guide titled*
Hanging Out in Ireland, *scheduled for publication in 2001, and she expects
to graduate in 2002.*

completely sacred and pure and refuse to waste it on musical artists or Ben & Jerry or even on people they merely like.

But most of us really are confused about the true meaning of the word, whether or not we realize it. It doesn't help that you run into it wherever you go: "Love" in pop songs on the radio, "love" in movies, and "love" on television. Love poetry ranges from the romantic (like Byron: "She walks in beauty, like the night / Of cloudless climes and starry skies . . . A heart whose love is innocent!") to the angst-ridden (like Plath: "I should have loved a thunderbird instead; / At least when spring comes they roar back again").   3

So, what *is* love? The most fascinating, and frustrating, aspect of that question is that there is no simple answer. Any dictionary definition is horribly unsatisfactory. Love is much more than "warm attachment" or "strong affection." True love, I think, ought to last. But can the love of which those poets write be the one that so often does not last? Is love unconditional?   4

I can say for sure, however, that love is not logical. The goal in the pursuit of logic is absolute truth and even perfection, neither of which is compatible with love. Should rational thought win out over romance, any relationship in question would surely fade as quickly as it had begun.   5

The actress Katharine Hepburn's thoughts on the matter are certainly thought-provoking. "Love has nothing to do with what you are expecting to get — only with what you are expecting to give — which is everything." But what if I give everything and receive nothing in return? Can that possibly be love, however "unrequited"? When Sheryl Crow sings that "need is love, and love is need," is she singing about dependency, or is love really based on necessity? One definition states that if you truly love someone, you find you simply cannot live without them. But I consider myself an independent being. I don't need anyone in order to function. Does that make me incapable of love? Perhaps a more refined definition would be that "love" is wanting (but not needing) the other person in your life for always, because ideally I want to be a much better person for having known him.   6

So what if it doesn't work out? You pick yourself up, dust yourself off, and think about anything but romance until someone else comes along who inspires you to try again. Most people believe that even if a relationship doesn't last, it still could have been love. I'm not so sure. A Chinese proverb states that if you love someone, let them go. If they return to you, it was meant to be. If they don't, their love   7 was never yours to begin with. This, too, is trite, but its inherent truth is undeniable.

> Perhaps to use the word love in terms of any college relationship is absurd.

Perhaps to use the word *love* in terms 8 of any college relationship is absurd. There can be no promises and no plans, because so often plans and promises go unfulfilled. We hang on when we ought to let go. In the end only one thing can be certain: We enter into relationships and risk loving someone because all of the joy and the agony leads us to a greater sense of self. "Love" can never be completely defined; ultimately the only definition that matters is your own. I'd like to suggest, however, that the next time you choose to use the word, you contemplate first all the profoundly marvelous possibilities that it contains.

Vocabulary / Using a Dictionary

1. In paragraph 6, DeAngelis mentions love that is *unrequited*. What does *unrequited* mean? What other words share the same root? How do these words relate to *unrequited*?

2. In paragraph 7, DeAngelis comments: "This, too, is *trite*, but its inherent truth is undeniable." What does the author mean by her use of the word *trite*? What is the origin of the word *trite*?

3. "The next time you choose to use the word, you *contemplate* first all the profoundly marvelous possibilities that it contains," suggests the author in paragraph 8. What does it mean, to *contemplate*? Can you use the word in a sentence?

Responding to Words in Context

1. "Love poetry ranges from the romantic (like Byron . . .) to the *angst-ridden* (like Plath: 'I should have loved a thunderbird instead;/at least when spring comes they roar back again')," comments DeAngelis in paragraph 3. What do you think *angst-ridden* means? Have you ever felt this way?

2. DeAngelis suggests that "a more *refined* definition [of love] would be that 'love' is wanting (but not needing) the other person in your life for always" (para. 6). What is a *refined* definition? What does it mean when something (or someone) is *refined*?

3. In the conclusion to her essay, DeAngelis suggests that the next time we use the word *love*, we "contemplate first all the profoundly *marvelous* possibilities that it contains" (para. 8). What does the adjective *marvelous* mean? What other word does *marvelous* suggest? What is the meaning of that word?

Discussing Main Point and Meaning

1. Why does DeAngelis comment that "most of us really are confused about the true meaning of the word [*love*]" (para. 3)?
2. How does DeAngelis respond to the question "So, what is love?" (para. 4)?
3. If DeAngelis were in love, could she live without that person? Is she incapable of love? State the author's "refined definition" of love and how it applies to her.
4. All things considered, in the end what is the one thing that can be certain when it comes to love, according to DeAngelis?

Examining Sentences, Paragraphs, and Organization

1. What is the topic sentence of paragraph 3? Why do you think so? Paragraph 4? Why?
2. Examine the quote from Katharine Hepburn in paragraph 6. How do the actress's comments about *getting* and *giving* love relate to DeAngelis's argument?
3. DeAngelis's essay (and most other essays) are organized so that they lead the reader toward a conclusion that the author hopes will urge the reader to action. The author tries to persuade the reader to act upon an idea, to perform a task, and so on. What is DeAngelis trying to persuade the reader to do?

Thinking Critically

1. Do you agree with DeAngelis that "most of us really are confused about the true meaning of the word [*love*], whether or not we realize it" (para. 3)? Are you confused about love? Just some aspects of it? Do you love anyone unconditionally?
2. "So what if it [love] doesn't work out? You pick yourself up, dust yourself off, and think about anything but romance until someone else comes along to inspire you to try again," suggests DeAngelis in

paragraph 8. Is this advice you can take? Do you find it easy for someone to "dust themselves off" after a break-up?

In-Class Writing Activities

1. DeAngelis concludes, in paragraph 8, that "perhaps to use the word *love* in terms of any college relationship is absurd. There can be no promises and no plans, because so often plans and promises go unfulfilled. We hang on when we ought to let go. In the end, only one thing can be certain: We enter into relationships and risk loving someone because all of the joy and the agony leads us to a greater sense of self." Briefly freewrite your thoughts about the author's conclusion, perhaps discussing your own experiences with the subject.

2. *Webster's New World Dictionary of the American Language* gives many different definitions for the word *love:* "(1) a deep and tender feeling of affection for or attachment or devotion to a person or persons; (2) a feeling of brotherhood and goodwill toward other people; (3) a strong liking for or interest in something; (4) a strong, usually passionate, affection of one person for another, based in part on sexual attraction." After reviewing these definitions, and delving into your own experience, construct a working definition of the word *love*. Feel free to consult another dictionary to help you refine your definition. As a follow-up to this exercise, explain how and why you chose your definition.

DEBORAH TANNEN

Contrite Makes Right

[CIVILIZATION/April–May 1999]

Before You Read

Have you ever been in a situation where you have had to utter the words "I'm sorry"? How did you feel after the apology? Has someone expressed regret to you? How did their apology make you feel? Is it easy for you to say you are sorry? Difficult? Why?

Words to Learn

schisms (para. 1): splits, divisions, conflicts (n.)

bevy (para. 2): a group, flock, or collection (n.)

conventionalized (para. 2): conformed to accepted standards (v.)

contrition (para. 3): regretfulness, remorse (n.)

empathize (para. 4): to undergo the projection of one's personality into another's feelings (v.)

attuned (para. 6): brought into harmony or agreement (v.)

litigious (para. 10): given to carrying on lawsuits (adj.)

precarious (para. 10): uncertain; insecure (adj.)*veritable* (para. 11): actual; real; genuine (adj.)

veritable (para. 11): actual; real; genuine (adj.)

philanthropic (para. 12): charitable; benevolent; humane (adj.)

facile (para. 13): not hard to do or achieve; easy (adj.)

discourse (para. 14): communication of ideas, information, and so on, especially by talking; conversation (n.)

contentiousness (para. 14): belligerence; hostility (n.)

DEBORAH TANNEN *(b. 1945) is University Professor of Linguistics at Georgetown University. In her research Tannen focuses on the different ways men and women communicate—and the difficulties of communicating across gender. Her most recent publications include* Talking from 9 to 5: Women and Men in the Workplace *(1995) and* The Argument Culture: Moving from Debate to Dialogue *(1998).*

Apologies are powerful. They resolve conflicts without violence, repair schisms between nations, allow governments to acknowledge the suffering of their citizens, and restore equilibrium to personal relationships. They are an effective way to restore trust and gain respect. They can be a sign of strength: proof that the apologizer has the self-confidence to admit a mistake.

Apologies, like so many other communication strategies, begin at home. They are one of a bevy of what some linguists call speech acts and are used to keep relationships on track. Each cultural group has its own customs with regard to conversational formalities, including conventionalized means of repairing disruptions.

> *If apologies are so effective in repairing disruptions, why do some people, especially many men, resist them?*

In the American context, there is ample evidence that women are more inclined to offer expressions of contrition than men. One woman, for example, told me that her husband's resistance to apologizing makes their disputes go on and on. Once, after he forgot to give her a particularly important telephone message, she couldn't get over her anger, not because he had forgotten (she realized anyone can make a mistake), but because he didn't apologize. "Had I done something like that," she said, "I would have fallen all over myself saying how sorry I was. . . . I felt as though he didn't care." When I asked her husband for his side of the story, he said apologizing would not have repaired the damage. "So what good does it do?" he wondered.

The good it does is cement the relationship. By saying he was sorry—and saying it as if he meant it—he would have conveyed that he felt bad about letting her down. Not saying anything sent the opposite message: It implied that he didn't care. Showing that you empathize provides the element of contrition, remorse, or repentance that is central to apologies—as does the promise to make amends and not repeat the offense. In the absence of these, why should the wife trust her husband not to do it again?

If apologies are so effective in repairing disruptions, why do some people, especially many men, resist them? In my work on women and men talking, the theme that runs through many of the differences I observe is this: Women tend to focus more on the question, "Is this conversation bringing us closer or pushing us further apart?" Men, on the other hand, tend to focus more on the question, "Is this conversation putting me in a one-up or a one-down position?"

These contrasting sensitivities explain our tendency to view   6
apologies differently. For most women, they are to be embraced because they reinforce connections, but many men are attuned to the
symbolic power of an apology to advertise defeat. Like a wolf baring
its neck or a dog rolling over on its back, an apologizer is taking a
one-down position. And the socialization of boys teaches them to
avoid that posture, as it could be exploited by an opponent in the
future.

This fear is well founded, as some people use the apology as a   7
way to humiliate an adversary. This explains, I believe, the disparity
between the responses of the average person and those of many journalists and politicians to the apologies President Clinton offered after
his relationship with Monica Lewinsky came to light.[1] Polls indicated
that a majority of American citizens was satisfied with the president's
initial statement, in which he admitted fault ("It was wrong") and
promised to make amends ("I must put it right"). But those who were
not satisfied demanded that he offer a better apology, like street
toughs insisting that an adversary who lost a fight publicly humiliate
himself.

However, among men—and even in the quintessentially mas-   8
culine world of the military—the ability to admit fault can be a sign
of strength. In 1975, the ship of Navy Commander Jeremy "Mike"
Boorda scraped bottom, destroying its sonar dome. This accident
could have ended his career. But Admiral Isaac Kidd, the officer to
whom the report was sent, cut short the investigation because Boorda
took responsibility. "There were no ifs, ands, or buts about it," Kidd
said of Boorda's report. "It was just what you hoped a person of un-
questioned integrity would write." Boorda went on to become an admiral and Chief of Naval Operations.

Apologies can be equally powerful in day-to-day situations, at   9
home and at work. One company manager told me that they were
magic bullets. When he admitted to subordinates that he had made a
mistake and then expressed remorse, they not only forgave him but
became even more loyal. Conversely, when I asked people what most
frustrated them in their work lives, co-workers' refusing to admit
fault was a frequent answer.

Given the importance of taking responsibility for the results of   10
our actions, it is distressing when the litigious nature of our society

[1]See the Editor's Supplement following this selection for the text of the apology.

prevents us from doing so. We are, for example, instructed by lawyers and auto insurance companies never to admit fault—or say we're sorry—following automobile accidents, since this may put us in a precarious legal position. This stance makes sense but takes a toll spiritually.

The power of apologies as a display of caring lies at the heart of the veritable avalanche of them that we are now seeing in the public sphere. Governments, for instance, can demonstrate that they care about a group that was wronged, such as when the United States apologized in 1997 to African American men who were denied treatment for syphilis as part of a 40-year medical experiment that began in the 1930s.

Offering an apology to another country is an effective way to lay the groundwork for future cooperation. In the late 1990s, the Czech Republic remained the only European nation with which Germany had not reached a settlement providing restitution for Nazi persecution during World War II. Germany refused to pay Czech victims until the Czechs formally apologized for their postwar expulsion of ethnic Germans from the Sudetenland. In the interest of receiving both reparations and Germany's support for inclusion in NATO, the Czech government offered the apology in 1997 (despite the opposition of many of its citizens). The gamble paid off, as Germany responded by setting up a philanthropic fund for the benefit of the Czechs, and this year both NATO and the European Union have invited the Czech Republic to join their ranks.

Sometimes it may seem that a nation or group tries to purchase forgiveness with a facile apology. It is absurd—even grotesque—for the leaders of the Khmer Rouge to offer the people of Cambodia brief regrets and immediately suggest that they let bygones be bygones. The statement is woefully inadequate in light of the massive slaughter and suffering the Khmer Rouge caused while it was in power. Furthermore, by taking the initiative in suggesting the past be laid to rest, they seem to be forgiving themselves—something that it is not the offender's place to do.

The rising popularity of apologies reflects a transformation in the ethics underlying public discourse. Linguist Robin Lakoff, in her book *Talking Power,* suggests that the United States is becoming a camaraderie culture: Witness our greater informality, including our widespread use of first names to address each other, she writes. In addition, our ever more frequent use of apologies may be a corrective to what I have called the argument culture, which is marked by the increasing contentiousness of public discourse and has, in turn, led to demands for civility.

As nations discover the possibilities and limits of the peacemaking power of apologies, couples too must find ways to accommodate differing points of view. I have learned to pay attention to the ways my husband adjusts his behavior, even in situations where he resists apologizing. For his part, he has learned how easy it is to get me to drop a grievance by uttering the magic words of apology. This makes me wonder whether translators would have had an easier time if Erich Segal had written, "Love means being able to say you're sorry, and say it as if you mean it, and say what you're going to do to make amends." 15

Vocabulary/Using a Dictionary

1. "Showing that you *empathize* provides the element of contrition, remorse, or repentance that is central to apologies," states Tannen in paragraph 4. What does it mean when you *empathize?* Think of some synonyms for the word. What other words share the root of *empathy?*

2. When discussing the inclination for Americans to engage in lawsuits, Tannen comments: "We are . . . instructed by lawyers . . . never to admit fault—or say we're sorry—following automobile accidents, since this may put us in a *precarious* legal position" (para. 10). What does the word *precarious* suggest about our legal positions? What are the origins of the word?

3. After the Czech Republic apologized to Germany for their postwar expulsion of ethnic Germans from Sudetenland, Germany responded "by setting up a *philanthropic* fund for the benefit of the Czechs" (para. 12). What is the meaning of *philanthropic?* Looking at this definition, how would you define a *philanthropist?*

Responding to Words in Context

1. Throughout Tannen's essay she mentions the word *apology.* What are the origins of the word?

2. When discussing apologies in the workplace, Tannen speaks of a company manager who told her that he had "admitted to *subor-*

dinates that he had made a mistake and then expressed remorse" (para. 9). What is a *subordinate?* Can you think of other words that may mean the same thing?

3. In Tannen's title *"Contrite* Makes Right," the author makes use of the word *contrite.* In paragraph 3, Tannen comments: "Women are more inclined to offer expressions of *contrition* than men." In paragraph 4, the author asserts: "Showing that you empathize provides the element of *contrition,* remorse, or repentance that is central to apologies." How are these words different?

Discussing Main Point and Meaning

1. In paragraph 3, Tannen relates a story about a husband and wife discussing the usefulness of apologies. The husband believes that apologizing (for not telling his wife she received an important phone call) wouldn't have repaired the damage he caused. He closed the conversation by stating: "So what good does it [apologizing] do?" How would Tannen answer his question?

2. According to Tannen, do men and women view apologies differently? Why or why not? Explain.

3. Give a few examples of the "veritable avalanche" of apologies that "we are now seeing in the public sphere" (para. 11).

4. What does Tannen suggest when she quotes linguist Robin Lakoff, who refers to the United States as having a "camaraderie culture"? Explain your answer.

Examining Sentences, Paragraphs, and Organization

1. If you read the first four sentences of the essay and then stopped without looking at the rest of the composition, how would you feel about the writer? Why does she use these sentences as an introduction?

2. Does Tannen's essay make use of effective examples and illustrations to support her main idea, that "Contrite Makes Right"?

3. In her conclusion, Tannen comments about her husband: "For his part, he has learned how easy it is to get me to drop a grievance by uttering the magic words of apology." How does this logically link with the introduction of her essay, where she states: "Apologies are powerful. . . . They can be a sign of strength:

proof that the apologizer has the self-confidence to admit a mistake" (para. 1)?

Thinking Critically

1. "In the American context, there is ample evidence that women are more inclined to offer expressions of contrition than men," states Tannen in paragraph 3. Does Tannen herself offer *ample evidence* in "Contrite Makes Right" to prove her point? Discuss your examples.

2. Do you agree with linguist Robin Lakoff that the United States is becoming a *camaraderie culture*: a "friendship" culture marked by greater informality, a widespread use of first names, and a more frequent use of apologies? Think of several examples from your own experience that support or dispute this claim.

In-Class Writing Activities

1. Tannen closes her essay by modifying a well-known quote from Erich Segal: "Love means being able to say you're sorry, and say it as if you mean it, and say what you're going to do to make amends" (para. 15). Briefly freewrite about whether you think this is an adequate definition of the word *love*. Do you agree or disagree with the quote? Why or why not?

2. In a short essay write about a time you *gave* or *received* a very important apology. In your essay discuss the situation: the people involved, the wrong that was committed, how the apology was given, and how the person felt after the apology was delivered. Be sure to try to capture the situation as realistically as possible and discuss the particular benefits and consequences of the apology.

3. Most people use the expressions "I'm sorry" and "I apologize" interchangeably. Yet consider them carefully for a few moments. Do they mean the same thing? What are we saying when we say "I'm sorry"? What do we say when we say "I apologize." Can we say "I'm sorry" without making an apology? Can we say "I apologize" without feeling sorry? Write a short essay in which you compare and contrast the significance of these two powerful expressions.

Editor's Supplement

Following is the full text of President Clinton's apology regarding his relationship with Monica Lewinsky to which Deborah Tannen refers in her essay, "Contrite Makes Right":

Good evening.   1

This afternoon in this room, from this chair, I testified before the   2
Office of Independent Counsel and the grand jury.

I answered their questions truthfully, including questions about my   3
private life, questions no American citizen would ever want to answer.

Still, I must take complete responsibility for all my actions, both   4
public and private. And that is why I am speaking to you tonight.

As you know, in a deposition in January, I was asked questions   5
about my relationship with Monica Lewinsky. While my answers
were legally accurate, I did not volunteer information.

Indeed, I did have a relationship with Ms. Lewinsky that was not   6
appropriate. In fact, it was wrong. It constituted a critical lapse in
judgment and a personal failure on my part for which I am solely and
completely responsible.

But I told the grand jury today, and I say to you now, that at no   7
time did I ask anyone to lie, to hide or destroy evidence, or to take
any other unlawful action.

I know that my public comments and my silence about this mat-   8
ter gave a false impression. I misled people, including even my wife. I
deeply regret that.

I can only tell you I was motivated by many factors. First, by a   9
desire to protect myself from the embarrassment of my own conduct.

I was also very concerned about protecting my family. The fact   10
that these questions were being asked in a politically inspired lawsuit,
which has since been dismissed, was a consideration, too.

In addition, I had real and serious concerns about an independent   11
counsel investigation that began with private business dealings
twenty years ago, dealings, I might add, about which an independent
federal agency found no evidence of any wrongdoing by me or my
wife over two years ago.

The independent counsel investigation moved on to my staff and   12
friends, then into my private life. And now the investigation itself is
under investigation.

This has gone on too long, cost too much, and hurt too many in-   13
nocent people.

Now, this matter is between me, the two people I love most—my   14
wife and our daughter—and our God. I must put it right, and I am
prepared to do whatever it takes to do so.

Nothing is more important to me personally. But it is private,   15
and I intend to reclaim my family life for my family. It's nobody's
business but ours.

Even presidents have private lives. It is time to stop the pursuit of   16
personal destruction and the prying into private lives and get on with
our national life.

Our country has been distracted by this matter for too long, and   17
I take my responsibility for my part in all of this. That is all I can do.

Now it is time—in fact, it is past time—to move on.   18

We have important work to do—real opportunities to seize, real   19
problems to solve, real security matters to face.

And so tonight, I ask you to turn away from the spectacle of the   20
past seven months, to repair the fabric of our national discourse, and
to return our attention to all the challenges and all the promise of the
next American century.

Thank you for watching. And good night.   21

JACK HITT

The Hidden Life of SUVs

[MOTHER JONES / July–August 1999]

Before You Read

Do you know someone who owns a sport utility vehicle? Do you have one in your family? Comment on how you think drivers of these vehicles feel. Do you desire one yourself? Why? What is the "American" allure of SUVs?

Words to Learn

displacing (para. 3): moving from a usual place (v.)

savvy (para. 4): shrewd or discerning (adj.)

touts (para. 5): praises or recommends highly (v.)

inexorable (para. 7): that cannot be checked; unrelenting (adj.)

cowcatcher (para. 7): a frame on the front of a vehicle to remove objects in its path (n.)

ersatz (para. 10): substitute; a word suggesting inferior quality (n.)

enunciation (para. 10): clear pronunciation (n.)

gentry (para. 14): people of high social standing (n.)

archetype (para. 19): a perfect example of a group (n.)

lulls (para. 19): calms or soothes (v.)

alpha state (para. 19): a state of relaxation and removal from sensory awareness (n.)

scuttling (para. 21): running or moving quickly (v.)

bourgeoisie (para. 22): middle class (n.)

bull-market (para. 22): having a successful stock market, indicating a strong economy (adj.)

JACK HITT (b. 1957) is a contributing writer for the New York Times, Harper's *magazine, and National Public Radio. His knowledge of preferred modes of travel may have informed his book* Off the Road: A Modern-Day Walk down the Ancient Pilgrim's Route in Spain *(1994).*

What's in a name? What do you make of a passenger vehicle   1
called a Bronco?

Or one dubbed a Cherokee? How about a Wrangler? Are they   2
just chrome-plated expressions of sublimated testosterone flooding
the highways? Check out the herd that grazes the average car lot
these days: Blazer, Tracker, Yukon, Navigator, Tahoe, Range Rover,
Explorer, Mountaineer, Denali, Expedition, Discovery, Bravada. Besides signaling that we're not Civic or Galant, they indicate there's
something else going on here.

These are, of course, all names of sport utility vehicles, the   3
miracle that has resurrected Motown. Think back to the dark days of
the previous decade when the Japanese auto industry had nearly
buried Detroit. In 1981, only a relative handful of four-wheel-drives
traveled the road, and the phrase "sport utility vehicle" hadn't entered the language. Today, they number more than 14 million, and
that figure is growing fast. If you include pickups and vans, then
quasi trucks now constitute about half of all the vehicles sold in
America. Half. They're rapidly displacing cars on the highways of
our new unbraking economy.

Go to any car lot and jawbone with a salesman, and you'll find   4
that big is once again better. Any savvy dealer (clutching his copy of
Zig Ziglar's *Ziglar on Selling*) will try to talk you up to one of the latest behemoths, which have bloated to such Brobdingnagian[1] dimensions as to have entered the realm of the absurd.

Ford, in fact, has unveiled a new monster, the Excursion, due to   5
hit the showrooms before the millennium. With a corporate straight
face, its literature touts as selling points that the Excursion is "less
than 7 feet tall . . . and less than 20 feet long" and is "more fuel efficient . . . than two average full-size sedans."

These Big Berthas have even spawned new vocabulary words.   6
The biggest of the big, for instance, can no longer fit comfortably in a
standard-size garage or the average parking space. So salesmen will
often sell you on one of the "smaller" SUVs by praising its "garage-
ability."

What, then, explains the inexorable advance of these giant SUVs   7
into our lives? Why do we want cars that are, in fact, high-clearance
trucks with four-wheel drive, an optional winch, and what amounts
to a cowcatcher?

---

[1]*Brobdingnagian:* Gigantic; the term derives from *Brobdingnag,* the land of giants in
Jonathan Swift's *Gulliver's Travels* (1726).

The answer, in part, lies in the vehicles themselves. Cars are not 8
fickle fashions. They are the most expensive and visible purchases in
an economy drenched in matters of status and tricked out with hidden meanings.

Some people will tell you that the shift from car to truck can be 9
explained simply: We Americans are getting, um, bigger in the beam.
We aren't comfortable in those Camrys, so we trade up to a vehicle
we can sit in without feeling scrunched. Here's a new buzzword for
Ziglar disciples: fatassability.

But I think the key is found not so much in their size or expense 10
(although both keep ballooning) but in those ersatz Western names.
The other day, I saw an acquaintance of mine in a boxy steed called a
Durango. Say it out loud for me: "Durango." Can you get the syl-
lables off your tongue without irony? In the post-*Seinfeld* era, can
anyone say Durango without giving it an Elaine Benes enunciation at
every syllable? Doo-RANG-Go.

The true irony comes from the fact that this thoroughly market- 11
researched word no longer has any core meaning. No one comprehends its denotation (Colorado town) but only its vague connotations
(rugged individualism, mastery over the wilderness, cowboy en-
durance). The word does not pin down meaning so much as conjure
up images.

These names are only the end product of the intense buyer- 12
profiling that the car companies and the marketing firms continu-
ously carry out. By the time they make it to the lot, these cars are
streamlined Frankensteinian concoctions of our private anxieties and
desires. We consumers don't so much shop for one of these SUVs as
they shop for us.

A typical focus-group study might be one like the "cluster analy- 13
sis" conducted by college students for Washington, D.C.–area car
dealers in 1994 and reported in *Marketing Tools*. The analysts coor-
dinated numerous databases, mail surveys, and census information to
profile the typical "Bill and Barb Blazers," whose consumer appre-
hensions can shift from block to block, but can be pinpointed down
to the four-digit appendix on the old zip code.

Each Bill and Barb then got tagged as "Young Suburbia" or 14
"Blue-Collar Nursery" or "Urban Gentry." Translation, respectively:
"college-educated, upwardly mobile white" or "middle-class, small-
town" or "educated black" people. The students next identified what
images spoke to the underlying appeal of an SUV for each group
(prestige, child space, weekend leisure). Then they developed targeted

ads to run in the media most favored by each group: the *Wall Street Journal, National Geographic,* Black Entertainment Television.

Many of the ads they developed were directed at women. For example, the one meant for upscale homeowners depicted a "woman architect standing next to her four-door [Blazer] at a Washington-area construction site" and "conveyed her professional leadership in a city with one of the highest rates of labor force participation for women."

Sport utility vehicles are quickly becoming women's cars. In fact, current statistics show that 40 percent of all SUV sales are to women, and the proportion is growing. (More men, on the other hand, are buying bigger, tougher pickup trucks.) But one wonders what's going on in the mind of that female architect or that soccer mom, high above the world in her soundproof, tinted-glass SUV, chatting on her cellular phone as she steers her mobile fortress down the street.

> *What do you make of a passenger vehicle called a Bronco? Or one dubbed a Cherokee?*

When GMC decided to launch the Denali (an SUV named for the Alaskan mountain), the auto-trade papers discussed the subtleties of that outdoorsy name: Even though most buyers "will never venture into territory any less trampled than the local country club parking lot," wrote Ward's *Auto World,* "the important goal of the Denali marketing hype is to plant the image in customers' minds that they can conquer rugged terrain. The metaphor of Alaska is particularly apt because SUVs, especially the larger of the species, depend on the myth that we have new frontiers yet to pave. Perhaps we're trying to tame a different kind of wilderness. Indeed, in an age of gated communities the SUV is the perfect transportation shelter to protect us from fears both real and imagined."

In one focus group, female drivers confessed they hesitated even to exit the interstate "because they are afraid of what they are going to find on some surface streets."

G. Clotaire Rapaille, a French medical anthropologist and student of the consumer mind, practices a more advanced marketing technique called "archetype research." In one session he has consumers lie on the floor and lulls them into a relaxed alpha state with soothing music. Then he asks them to free-associate from images of different vehicle designs and write stories about what they hoped the design would become. Overwhelmingly, Rapaille told the *Wall Street Journal,* his participants had the same reaction: "It's a jungle out there. It's Mad Max. People want to kill me, rape me. Give me a big thing like a tank."

More and more, SUVs give us that tanklike security, and part of the feeling derives from their literal altitude. Down there is the old working class, the new peasants who haven't figured out how to snatch a six-figure income out of our roaring economy—the little people who don't own a single Fidelity fund. There's a brutal Darwinian selection at work: They huddle down in their wretched Escorts and their Metros—not merely because they are poor but because they deserve to be.

These are the new savages: people who drive cars. They scrape   21
and fetch about in their tiny compacts, scuttling along on surface streets. But above it all, in their gleaming, skyscraping vehicles, is the new high society—the ambitious, the exurban pioneers, the downtown frontiersmen.

It's been said that the most distinctive feature of the American   22
character is that we continually define ourselves as pilgrims facing a new frontier. In their darkest hearts, the members of the new-money bourgeoisie have convinced themselves that we live in an unforgiving wilderness of marauders and brutes. The hidden meaning of our new conveyances can be found right on the surface. Once upon a time, Trailblazers, Explorers, and Trackers tamed the Wild West. Now, through the sorcery of focus groups, the bull-market gentry have brought the Pathfinders and Mountaineers back into their lives in the belief that they need to conquer the savage land one more time.

Vocabulary / Using a Dictionary

1. What does the word *touts* (para. 5) suggest about the literature regarding the Ford Excursion?

2. In paragraph 7, the author questions the desirability of SUVs by stating, "Why do we want cars . . . with four-wheel drive, an optional winch, and what amounts to a *cowcatcher?*" What is a cowcatcher? Where do you think the name of the word originally came from? What does the author suggest by using it?

3. G. Clotaire Rapaille, a French medical anthropologist, practices a marketing technique called *archetype* research (para. 19). What type of research do you think this is?

Responding to Words in Context

1. When reviewing the market-researched word *Durango,* Hitt comments: "No one comprehends its *denotation* (Colorado town) but only its vague *connotations*" (para. 11). What is the difference between *denotation* and *connotation*?

2. Briefly discuss the definitions of a few of the following names that Hitt lists for SUVs: Bronco, Cherokee, Wrangler, Blazer, Tracker, Yukon, Navigator, Tahoe, Range Rover, Explorer, Mountaineer, and so on. What do these words suggest?

Discussing Main Point and Meaning

1. According to the essay, what do SUVs (and their names) reveal about the lives of Americans—financially and emotionally?

2. One of the most important lines of Hitt's essay states: "We consumers don't so much shop for one of these SUVs as they shop for us" (para. 12). What does the author imply by this statement?

3. In paragraphs 20 and 21, the author describes a class conflict occurring on the roads of North America. Based on what Hitt presents in his essay, can you articulate this possible conflict?

Examining Sentences, Paragraphs, and Organization

1. What is the topic sentence of paragraph 16? How do you know?

2. Do you think Hitt's essay would be as effective if the first paragraph (beginning: "What's in a name?") were put at the end of the essay? Do you think the article would be as thought provoking? Why or why not?

3. A paragraph is *unified* when all its sentences clarify or help support the main idea. Unity is lost if a paragraph strays from the topic by including sentences unrelated to the main idea. Keeping this definition of *unity* in mind, does paragraph 10 have unity?

4. Who do you think is Hitt's audience? To whom is he speaking? Explain your answer.

Thinking Critically

1. Do you agree with the author's statement that "SUVs give us that tanklike security, and part of the feeling derives from their literal altitude. Down there is the old working class, the new peasants who haven't figured out how to snatch a six-figure income out of our roaring economy. . . . There's a brutal Darwinian selection at work" (para. 20)? Do people who own SUVs fit the part of the

bourgeoisie? Do people who don't own SUVs fit the part of the peasants?

2. Hitt concludes his essay by stating: "Now, through the sorcery of focus groups, the bull-market gentry have brought the Pathfinders and Mountaineers back into their lives in the belief that they need to conquer the savage land one more time" (para. 22). To whom is the author referring (*"their* lives . . . *they* need . . ."*)? Do you agree with this statement?

In-Class Writing Activities

1. The author quotes an article in paragraph 17: "Perhaps we're trying to tame a different kind of wilderness. Indeed, in an age of gated communities the SUV is the perfect *transportation shelter* to protect us from fears both real and imagined." Brainstorm some ideas about what you think is being suggested about the security of modern American life.

2. Do you drive a motor vehicle? List some names of vehicles that you (or someone you know) have (has) driven. What is the name of a vehicle supposed to do? Does the name always fully describe the way the vehicle functions? What is the purpose of researchers coming up with vehicle names? In a brief essay, discuss these questions using examples from your own life.

Discussing the Unit

Suggested Topic for Discussion

How important is it that "we think before we speak"? When you are engaged in conversation, do you find that you think before you speak, or do words just "come out" of your mouth? Do you believe that thinking before speaking is an admirable quality? Do you choose your words carefully? What kind of power is there in choosing the right words?

Preparing for Class Discussion

1. Words are, in some cases, expressions of language and culture: Are you familiar with any groups or organizations on your cam-

pus that encourage discussions about language and culture? If so, how important do you think they are to students? If you aren't familiar with any such organizations, what kinds of languages and cultures do you think should be represented in these groups? Provide reasons to support your answers.

2. The United States is a country that seems to have a number of different dialects and distinct slang expressions within the American language. Have you ever used a regional dialect or slang term that would be considered different from "normal American language"? Do you think this is an expression of your identity? Explain.

From Discussion to Writing

1. Sigmund Freud (1856–1939), the famous psychoanalyst, once said: "In psychoanalytic treatment nothing happens but an exchange of words between the patient and the physician. . . . Words and magic were in the beginning one and the same thing, and even today words contain much of their magical power. By words one can give to another the greatest happiness or bring about utter despair. . . . Words call forth emotion and are universally the means by which we influence our fellow creatures. Therefore let us not despise the use of words in psycho-therapy." Write a brief essay analyzing Freud's quote, agreeing or disagreeing with his view of the power of words. Cite examples from the essays in the chapter to support your ideas.

2. Each of the three authors in this unit has discussed the power that words possess. In "Contrite Makes Right," Deborah Tannen writes about the effectiveness and rising popularity of spoken apologies. Camille DeAngelis ponders the profundity of love in her essay, trying to glean the true meaning of the "most overused word in the English language." Finally, in "The Hidden Life of SUVs," Jack Hitt reveals the deeper meaning behind the names of sport utility vehicles. In a short essay, discuss, compare, and contrast how each author views the power of words, and explain how important they feel words are, specifically in the lives of average Americans.

Topics for Cross-Cultural Discussion

1. Are people in other cultures familiar with words and languages from cultures other than their own? Are they familiar with American words and the English language? How do people from other cultures view North Americans? What relationship does this have to language?

2. Are there any words or phrases from your language that Americans would be familiar with? How well does your language translate into American English? Was it difficult for you to become familiar with the English language? What gave you the most trouble? What gave you the least amount of problems?

6

Who Should Our Heroes Be?

A common characteristic of young people is their need for heroes or role models—individuals whose talents they admire and whose careers they hope to imitate. Some find their heroes on baseball fields and basketball courts; others look for them in movies and popular entertainment; and still others locate them in classrooms, courtrooms, boardrooms, or books.

Yet do role models need to be celebrities or prominent people we may never know or even see in person? Isn't it possible to find our heroes closer to our homes and communities? In this unit, three selections provide an unusual array of personal heroes. When Newsweek.com solicited essays from readers about "Family Heroes," Jim Tella contributed "Sipping Coffee," a brief celebration of his mother, who has become an enormous asset in the life he lives as a gay man. Community activists may not be known outside of their neighborhoods, but University of Kansas junior Breeze Luetke-Stahlman suggests that young people could do worse than find their heroes among them. In "Real People Make Real Role Models," she writes, "One activist can make a difference, and that is the kind of person we should all strive to emulate." This unit concludes with "Unsung Heroes," a short essay by the noted historian Howard Zinn, who calls into question our habit of making "slave holders, Indian-killers, and militarists the heroes of our history books." Zinn reminds us: "Our country is full of heroic people who are not presidents or military leaders or

Wall Street wizards, but who are doing something to keep alive the spirit of resistance to injustice and war."

JIM TELLA

Sipping Coffee

[NEWSWEEK.COM / November 5, 1999]

Before You Read

How important is it for us to find heroism within our own families? Can you think of instances where your parents or siblings (or other family members) behaved heroically or became role models for you?

Words to Learn

invincible (para. 2): unconquerable (adj.)
alter egos (para. 3): other sides of oneself; second selves (n.)
psyche (para. 3): the soul or spirit, as distinguished from the body (n.)

My mother is my hero times two. Yet until I was an adult, I saw   1
neither the strength nor the courage that exists within her.

When I was a child, my heroes were always found in the pages of   2
my comic books; the Fantastic Four, the Avengers, the Adventures of Superman. And while most boys my age wanted to be Captain America, I dreamed of being the Scarlet Witch. As long as the comic books remained open and the comforting figure of my mother sat at the kitchen table reading the latest edition of the *Boston Herald,* I was

---

JIM TELLA wrote this piece in response to a call for articles concerning role models. The piece was published on Newsweek.com, a Web site that has since merged with MSNBC.

invincible. But childhood ends quickly, heroes stay within the ink-colored pages, and I wondered if my mother would grow tired and leave.

The superheroes had alter egos. The Scarlet Witch was also 3 Wanda, but despite a strong resemblance, none of the other characters ever noticed they were the same person. Was it simply because Wanda wasn't wearing a red hat and suit or because the writers decided to make it so? Perhaps it was because people only see what they want to see. I empathized with her divided psyche and the failure of others to notice.

When I was a child, my heroes were always found in the pages of my comic books.

Since then I have realized that it takes 4 time, knowledge, and a willingness to learn and share before you discover the person within the person.

I still remember the day I told my 5 mother. A coming-out story I'd found in the Glad Day Bookstore, *Are You Still My Mother?*, was beside my bed. As she walked into my apartment, I thought about how awful I was to turn her world upside down. I stumbled over the words, and when I finally spit them out, they burned my tongue. I watched her turn into a rubber band in my arms. It seemed as if I'd transferred all the pain of my childhood onto her with one single sentence. She cried for hours and the tissues I kept by the couch disappeared in minutes.

She took the book with her when she left my apartment, and I 6 expected the worst. But the next day she returned with a list of more than twenty questions for me to answer. And so began my mother's education and the shifting of a relationship that has flourished to new levels over the past ten years.

My mother doesn't belong to PFLAG, nor does she march in gay 7 pride parades with signs declaring how proud she is of her gay son. Instead, when she visits, she sits with every one of my friends and calls them her sons (or at times, her daughters, depending on the time of year and the outfits they've decided to wear for the evening). When I joined the ranks of drag queens and began performing in small nightclubs, she was the loudest in the crowd. My music would start and I would become Barbra Streisand or Shirley Bassey. Then I'd look up and see my mother jumping to her feet and cheering. It is a memory that is forever etched into my mind.

"Are you his mother?" someone behind her asked that night as 8 she screamed my name. "Yes, I am," she replied. Giving her a bear hug, the man kissed her on the lips. "You look so proud! Good for you!"

The baby books could never have prepared my mother for all of 9 the ways she has seen me grow. And I, in turn, have watched a different kind of hero, one who does not need to rescue me every time I'm in danger, but only has to be who she is: my mother. Without her, I would have been lost—perhaps becoming a runaway, a junkie on the streets, or a kid who escaped childhood by escaping life. If I hadn't felt confident during my youth that she would be there to catch me and lift me up, I wouldn't be here today.

Today, as I climb the stairs to my old house, she is still there. 10 Quietly sipping her coffee and reading her paper. With one silent smile she conveys every ounce of pride she feels. And I know if she wants to, she can make a helluva lot of noise.

Vocabulary / Using a Dictionary

1. Tella uses the word *invincible* (para. 2) in the context of a childhood spent reading comic books. In what other contexts can you imagine using the word *invincible?* What does it say about this type of childhood?

2. Look up *ego* in the dictionary. What does it mean? Describe the relationship you perceive there to be between the *ego* and the *alter ego.*

3. In classical mythology, the maiden Psyche is the lover of Eros (the god of love and son of beauty, Aphrodite). She was thought to be the personification of the soul. Try to explain the definition of the word *psyche* as we use it today in the context of this classical role.

Responding to Words in Context

1. Tella refers to a *coming-out story* in paragraph 5. Had you heard this expression before? What is your understanding of the term?

2. "Since then I have realized that it takes time, knowledge, and a willingness to learn and share before you discover the person within the person." This statement in paragraph 4 serves as a transition between Tella's discussion about comic book characters

and his mother's reaction to the news that he is gay. To what "person" does this statement refer?

Discussing Main Point and Meaning

1. Examine the story of the Scarlet Witch in paragraph 3 of Tella's article. Why does he allude specifically to this comic book character?

2. Tella explains in paragraph 7 that his mother doesn't belong to any organized support groups for the parents or friends of gay individuals. How does he recognize his mother's support and admiration without such evidence?

3. Can you provide the definition of *hero* you think Tella is employing in this essay?

4. What do you make of the title of this piece, *Sipping Coffee?*

Examining Sentences, Paragraphs, and Organization

1. "I stumbled over the words, and when I finally spit them out, they burned my tongue" (paragraph 5). Identify all of the metaphors in this sentence.

2. Discuss the central topic of the concluding paragraph. What image and/or idea does Tella want the reader to take with him or her after reading his article?

3. Where do you find the thesis of this essay? Is it explicitly or implicitly stated?

Thinking Critically

1. Do you think that Tella's mother is a hero? Isn't it a parent's responsibility to love her son? Has she done anything special?

2. Are there any connections to be made between Tella's love of comic books and his drag performances? Why do you think he includes discussions about both of these interests?

In-Class Writing Activities

1. Has anyone ever stood up for you publicly in a difficult situation? Try to think of a time where you, like Tella, were grateful

for another person's courageous support. Describe the incident in a one-page essay.

2. Who were your childhood make-believe heroes? Did you read comic books? Watch cartoons? Have a favorite video game or book? Write an essay about a fictional hero you identified with as a child. Do you still see parts of yourself in those characters or have you, like Tella, moved on to new characters?

BREEZE LUETKE-STAHLMAN

Real People Make Real Role Models

[THE DAILY KANSAN, THE UNIVERSITY OF KANSAS/February 7, 2000]

Before You Read

Who are your heroes and role models? Are they real people in your life, historical figures, celebrities, or mythical characters? Do you think kids should have role models in their communities, or can they do just as well with their parents and favorite action figures?

Words to Learn

heritage (para. 4): legacy; tradition; inheritance (n.)
blockade (para. 7): to close off an area to traffic and/or communication, especially to hostile parties or organizations (v.)

Breeze Luetke-Stahlman (b. 1978) has been an activist all her life. A junior majoring in both economics and American studies at the University of Kansas when she wrote this piece, she is optimistic about her life as an activist: "I consider myself an organizer and find my network of incredible people around the world to be my greatest resource," she says.

When was the last time you asked a child who his or her role   1
model was? When was the last time you asked yourself?

Unfortunately, many of today's youth will answer this question   2
with a fictional character, one born in the world of television. No
thanks to mass media, today's youth often are not encouraged to see
real people and their incredible gifts to a community, or strive to be
like them.

But with a little effort, role models can be seen and pointed out,   3
and it's possible that communities can again have youth who look up
to those around them.

A community is defined in *Webster's* dictionary as "a social   4
group whose members live in a specific locality, share government,
and have a common heritage."

I work a lot with youth and often discuss this idea. The definition   5
I use is: "A community is made up of people who live in the same
place or have things in common." Let's keep things simple.

The people who strive to make the environment in which this   6
community lives and functions a better place are activists. I usually
say: An activist is a person who challenges the way things are now in
the world in order to make the earth and their communities, or someone else's community, better. I think too many people have given the
label "activist" too narrow of a definition. Consequently, people are
scared of the word, but really, many of these same people are activists
themselves.

There are many ways of going about challenging the way things   7
are now. On one hand, you could blockade the doors of the conference center where the World Trade Organization is scheduled to
meet, demanding that the people whose lives will be influenced by the
decisions have representation. On the other hand, you could write a
letter to the editor and help educate the readers, your fellow community members, about the fact that you would appreciate having bike
lanes on some of the major roads in Lawrence because you would feel
a lot safer if they were there.

Last year I wrote for a publication that ran my column once a   8
month. It was called "Just for Kids," and it sought to persuade nine-
to twelve-year-old youths to view men and women who are active in
their communities as role models. While my column was geared toward youth, the publication was not specifically targeted at that age
group, and with each column I wrote, I hoped people of all ages
would be inspired.

I didn't think of the column idea on my own. I had received a   9 phone call one day from my aunt, who was calling to ask if I knew anything about Julia "Butterfly" Hill, a tree-sitter in California. Hill had been up in a 300-foot-tall redwood tree since Dec. 10, 1997, protesting the logging of old growth forest. My nine-year-old cousin had read an article about Hill and had become fascinated with her. She wanted to write Hill a letter, and not sure of where to get that information, my aunt had called me, the "activist" of the family.

> One person can make a difference, and it is these people who we should all strive to be like.

After passing on the information and 10 talking to my cousin on the phone, encouraging her interest, I thought a lot about how excited she had become about the interesting life of this twenty-four-year-old woman. I then thought of all the other amazing people I knew and knew of, and how their stories might spark that same enthusiasm in another child. The column was born.

I hope writing it was only my beginning. I want to influence 11 people to talk to each other, and especially to youth, about the real people they admire. There are so many individuals who are changing their communities for the better, simply by trying to make their own lives better, more fulfilling and happy. Often they are doing so instead of trying to meet the goals American society instructs us to: Make money, be beautiful, and buy things.

One person can make a difference, and it is these people who we 12 should all strive to be like. Luckily, they are all around us, present in every community. We just have to find them and give them the recognition they deserve.

Vocabulary / Using a Dictionary

1. How does the word *heritage* (para. 4) function in the author's definition of *community*?

2. *Blockade* (para. 7) is related in its root to the Latin for *ambush* (ambuscade). Do you know what an ambush is? How is it similar to or different from a blockade?

3. Examine Luetke-Stahlman's definition of *community* in paragraph 5. How is it different from the dictionary definition she supplies in paragraph 4?

Responding to Words in Context

1. What does Luetke-Stahlman think an *activist* is? Give some examples of people you know who could be called activists under this definition.

2. "American society instructs us to: Make money, be beautiful, and buy things," the author writes (para. 11). What do you think she means by "American society"? You? Everyone? And who is "us"?

Discussing Main Point and Meaning

1. Does Luetke-Stahlman have an identifiable purpose? What is it?

2. Who is the audience for this essay? How is it different from other audiences for whom the author has written in the past?

3. Why does this essay emphasize the definition of terms so much?

4. What does the author reveal about herself in this essay? What kind of person do you think she is? How would you characterize her tone of voice?

Examining Sentences, Paragraphs, and Organization

1. This essay opens by questioning the reader. Are these questions meant to be answered, or are they examples of *rhetorical questions* (questions the author intends to answer or already knows the answer to)?

2. Why does Luetke-Stahlman quote from a dictionary? Have you ever used this technique in your writing? Why or why not?

3. Paragraphs 8–10 present a personal anecdote. What is the story Luetke-Stahlman presents in those paragraphs, and why is it located in the second half of the essay? Do you find it effective?

Thinking Critically

1. In paragraph 6, the author argues that the word *activist* has "too narrow of a definition" in the minds of most people. Do you agree? Don't you think a person who goes to jail for a cause, or devotes a lifetime to helping others, is more of an activist than a person who writes a letter to the editor, or sends a yearly dona-

tion to a campaign? Does the narrower definition "scare" people away from any kind of activism, as Luetke-Stahlman suggests?

2. "There are so many individuals who are changing their communities for the better, simply by trying to make their own lives better, more fulfilling and happy," Luetke-Stahlman writes in paragraph 11. Does the author mean to suggest that making one's own life better is the desired result of activism? What do you think about that possible connotation?

In-Class Writing Activities

1. What issue would you like to get active about: The environment? Discrimination? Violence? Education? Write a letter to the editor of your campus paper or your local newspaper calling your readers' attention to an issue you care deeply about.

2. Write an essay similar to Luetke-Stahlman's that grapples with the definition of something that most people take for granted. You could choose a role as she does: father, teacher, president; or you could choose a concept: respect, beauty, intelligence, and so on. Please provide as many specific details and examples of your definition as possible.

HOWARD ZINN

Unsung Heroes

[THE PROGRESSIVE/June 2000]

Before You Read

Is history, as some say, "written by the winners"? If so, what happens to the stories of everyone else? What happens to the heroism of those who don't make the headlines? Why are national heroes so important?

Words to Learn

emulate (para. 3): strive to equal or excel; imitate (v.)

bondholders (para. 3): owners of bonds (investments or savings) (n.)

speculators (para. 3): those who buy and sell for great profit (n.)

levied (paras. 6 and 24): having imposed or collected a tax (v.)

guerrilla (para. 8): characteristic of revolutionary military organiza-

tions fighting unconventionally against an established power (adj.)

pantheon (para. 12): memorial to gods (n.)

covert (para. 14): secret; concealed (adj.)

dissent (para. 18): refuse to accept the doctrines of an established position or institution (v.)

martial (para. 18): related to war or the military (adj.)

A high school student recently confronted me: "I read in your   1
book *A People's History of the United States* about the massacres of
Indians, the long history of racism, the persistence of poverty in the
richest country in the world, the senseless wars. How can I keep from
being thoroughly alienated and depressed?"

*HOWARD ZINN (b. 1922) is a historian, author, playwright, and professor
emeritus of political science at Boston University. Zinn has authored many
books of essays, plays, and articles, some of which have appeared in* Harper's
magazine, The Nation, The New Republic, *and* The Progressive. *Zinn is perhaps best known for his revolutionary work* A People's History of the United
States *(1990).*

It's a question I've heard many times before. Another question 2 often put to me by students is: Don't we need our national idols? You are taking down all our national heroes—the Founding Fathers, Andrew Jackson, Abraham Lincoln, Theodore Roosevelt, Woodrow Wilson, John F. Kennedy.

Granted, it is good to have historical figures we can admire and 3 emulate. But why hold up as models the fifty-five rich white men who drafted the Constitution as a way of establishing a government that would protect the interests of their class—slaveholders, merchants, bondholders, land speculators?

Why not recall the humanitarianism of William Penn, an early 4 colonist who made peace with the Delaware Indians instead of warring on them, as other colonial leaders were doing?

Why not John Woolman, who, in the years before the Revolu- 5 tion, refused to pay taxes to support the British wars, and who spoke out against slavery?

Why not Captain Daniel Shays, veteran of the Revolutionary 6 War, who led a revolt of poor farmers in Western Massachusetts against the oppressive taxes levied by the rich who controlled the Massachusetts legislature?

Why go along with the hero-worship, so universal in our history 7 textbooks, of Andrew Jackson, the slave-owner, the killer of Indians? Jackson was the architect of the Trail of Tears, which resulted in the deaths of four thousand of sixteen thousand Cherokees who were kicked off their land in Georgia and sent into exile in Oklahoma.

Why not replace him as national icon with John Ross, a Chero- 8 kee chief who resisted the dispossession of his people, and whose wife died on the Trail of Tears? Or the Seminole leader Osceola, imprisoned and finally killed for leading a guerrilla campaign against the removal of the Indians?

And while we're at it, should not the Lincoln Memorial be joined 9 by a memorial to Frederick Douglass, who better represented the struggle against slavery? It was that crusade of black and white abolitionists, growing into a great national movement, that pushed a reluctant Lincoln into finally issuing a half-hearted Emancipation Proclamation, and persuaded Congress to pass the Thirteenth, Fourteenth, and Fifteenth amendments.

Take another presidential hero, Theodore Roosevelt, who is al- 10 ways near the top of the tiresome lists of Our Greatest Presidents. There he is on Mount Rushmore, as a permanent reminder of our historical amnesia about his racism, his militarism, his love of war.

Why not replace him as hero—granted, removing him from   11
Mount Rushmore will take some doing—with Mark Twain? Roosevelt, remember, had congratulated an American general who in
1906 ordered the massacre of six hundred men, women, and children
on a Philippine island. As vice president of the Anti-Imperialist
League, Twain denounced this and continued to point out the cruelties committed in the Philippine war under the slogan "My country,
right or wrong."

As for Woodrow Wilson, another honored figure in the pantheon   12
of American liberalism, shouldn't we remind his admirers that he insisted on racial segregation in federal buildings, that he bombarded
the Mexican coast, sent an occupation army into Haiti and the Dominican Republic, brought our country into the hell of World War I,
and put anti-war protesters in prison?

Should we not bring forward as a national hero Emma Goldman,   13
one of those Wilson sent to prison, or Helen Keller, who fearlessly
spoke out against the war?

And enough worship of John F. Kennedy, a Cold Warrior who   14
began the covert war in Indochina, went along with the planned invasion of Cuba, and was slow to act against racial segregation in the
South.

Should we not replace the portraits of our presidents, which too   15
often take up all the space on our classroom walls, with the likenesses
of grassroots heroes like Fannie Lou Hamer, the Mississippi share-
cropper? Mrs. Hamer was evicted from her farm and tortured in
prison after she joined the civil rights movement, but she became an
eloquent voice for freedom. Or with Ella Baker, whose wise counsel
and support guided the young black people in the Student Nonviolent
Coordinating Committee, the militant edge of the civil rights movement in the Deep South?

In the year 1992, the quincentennial of the arrival of Columbus   16
in this hemisphere, there were meetings all over the country to celebrate him, but also, for the first time, to challenge the customary ex-
altation of the Great Discoverer. I was at a symposium in New Jersey
where I pointed to the terrible crimes against the indigenous people
of Hispaniola committed by Columbus and his fellow Spaniards. Afterward, the other man on the platform, who was chairman of the
New Jersey Columbus Day celebration, said to me: "You don't understand—we Italian Americans need our heroes." Yes, I understood
the desire for heroes, I said, but why choose a murderer and kidnap-

per for such an honor? Why not choose Joe DiMaggio, or Toscanini, or Fiorello LaGuardia, or Sacco and Vanzetti? (The man was not persuaded.)

The same misguided values that have made slaveholders, Indian-   17
killers, and militarists the heroes of our history books still operate today. We have heard Senator John McCain, Republican of Arizona, repeatedly referred to as a war hero. Yes, we must sympathize with McCain's ordeal as a war prisoner in Vietnam, where he endured cruelties. But must we call someone a hero who participated in the invasion of a far-off country and dropped bombs on men, women, and children?

> *The same misguided values that have made slaveholders, Indian-killers, and militarists the heroes of our history books still operate today.*

I came across only one voice in the   18
mainstream press daring to dissent from the general admiration for McCain—that of the poet, novelist, and *Boston Globe* columnist James Carroll. Carroll contrasted the heroism of McCain, the warrior, to that of Philip Berrigan, who has gone to prison dozens of times for protesting the war in Vietnam and the dangerous nuclear arsenal maintained by our government. Carroll wrote: "Berrigan, in jail, is the truly free man, while McCain remains imprisoned in an unexamined sense of martial honor."

Our country is full of heroic people who are not presidents or   19
military leaders or Wall Street wizards, but who are doing something to keep alive the spirit of resistance to injustice and war.

I think of Kathy Kelly and all those other people from Voices in   20
the Wilderness who, in defiance of federal law, have traveled to Iraq more than a dozen times to bring food and medicine to people suffering under the U.S.-imposed sanctions.

I think also of the thousands of students on more than one hun-   21
dred college campuses across the country who are protesting their universities' connection with sweatshop-produced apparel.

I think of the four McDonald sisters in Minneapolis, all nuns,   22
who have gone to jail repeatedly for protesting against the Alliant Corporation's production of land mines.

I think, too, of the thousands of people who have traveled to Fort   23
Benning, Georgia, to demand the closing of the murderous School of the Americas.

I think of the West Coast Longshoremen who participated in an   24
eight-hour work stoppage to protest the death sentence levied against
Mumia Abu-Jamal.

And so many more.   25

We all know individuals—most of them unsung, unrecognized—   26
who have, often in the most modest ways, spoken out or acted on
their beliefs for a more egalitarian, more just, peace-loving society.

To ward off alienation and gloom, it is only necessary to remem-   27
ber the unremembered heroes of the past, and to look around us for
the unnoticed heroes of the present.

Vocabulary / Using a Dictionary

1. How do you think the word *grassroots* (para. 15) has come to
   have its present meaning?
2. What is the meaning of *dissent* (para. 18)? What is its most logical antonym?
3. What do you think it means to be in a state of *martial law,* given
   the definition of "martial" on page 130?

Responding to Words in Context

1. Zinn uses the word *architect* to describe Andrew Jackson's role
   in the Trail of Tears (para. 7). How is the word normally used?
   What does the author intend it to mean here?
2. What does Zinn mean when he refers to *historical amnesia* in
   paragraph 10?

Discussing Main Point and Meaning

1. Where is the thesis statement of this essay?
2. In paragraph 9, Zinn refers to the Emancipation Proclamation as
   "half-hearted"; in paragraph 10, he refers to the lists of "Our
   Greatest Presidents" as "tiresome." How would you characterize
   the tone of this essay?
3. Explain Zinn's position on "war heroes." Look to paragraphs 17
   and 18 for help.
4. How do the remarks of the high school student who confronted
   the author in paragraph 1 inspire Zinn's essay? Do you think the

student would be satisfied with Zinn's answer to his question in the final paragraph?

Examining Sentences, Paragraphs, and Organization

1. There are many questions posed to the reader in this article. How does the accumulation of questions affect you as a reader?
2. Describe the function of the Columbus Day anecdote in paragraph 16. What does this discussion contribute to Zinn's overall point?
3. In what ways are paragraphs 20–24 like a speech?

Thinking Critically

1. Do you agree with Zinn that we are looking to the wrong heroes? He points out the flaws of many of the most established of American heroes: Might not some of the substitutes he suggests also have flaws?
2. Is it possible that we should have no heroes? Is not their value merely symbolic? Why do you think people look up so much to these idealized icons? Would we be better off if we did not look to these "larger than life" figures for hope and inspiration, and instead looked to ourselves?

In-Class Writing Activities

1. Write a descriptive essay about someone you perceive to be a hero whom others might not know. Perhaps someone in your community saved an old couple from a burning building, or stopped an attempted assault in a shopping mall. Or maybe you have an aunt who has cared for her sick son around the clock for his whole life. Be sure to provide your definition of hero in the context of your description.
2. Write a short essay that attempts to articulate a compromise between Zinn's view of heroism and the views he criticizes. Can you accommodate both the antiwar, prolabor view of Zinn with the capitalistic nationalism (and militarism) of his adversaries?

Discussing the Unit

Suggested Topic for Discussion

Would you rather be a hero, or a role model? Is there a difference? Two of the essays in this unit—by Jim Tella and Breeze Luetke-Stahlman—seem to suggest that to be a role model in today's times *is* to be equated with being a hero. In addition, another essay—by Howard Zinn—asks us to replace our militarily triumphant heroes with those more focused on social 'fights,' suggesting an entirely new definition of hero. How do you define *hero?* Under whose description in this unit would you like to be named a hero?

Preparing for Class Discussion

1. Both Luetke-Stahlman and Zinn are interested in presenting social and political heroes to readers who may be unfamiliar with them. Tella, on the other hand, has in mind a very personal hero. How do you think these authors would respond to each other's ideas?

2. Are role models and heroes the same thing? Is one more important than the other? Which terms do these authors prefer? Why do you think they choose the terms they do?

From Discussion to Writing

1. Compare and contrast Jim Tella's mother, Julia "Butterfly" Hill (the tree-sitter mentioned in Breeze Luetke-Stahlman's essay), and Kathy Kelly or the McDonald sisters (from Howard Zinn's article). What characteristics do they share as heroes? In what ways do they differ?

2. Consider the Hollywood version of heroism. Bruce Willis plays John McClane in the famous *Die Hard* series; Mel Gibson plays Martin Riggs in the equally popular and violent *Lethal Weapon* series. Tom Hanks immortalizes a hapless happy-go-lucky brand of heroism in *Forrest Gump;* Dustin Hoffman's autistic portrayal of *Rain Man* won him an Oscar. And who can forget the romancing, gadget-wielding wonder himself—007, James Bond? Must Hollywood heroes be either murderers or idiot savants to pass muster with the American public? Are there other kinds of

Hollywood heroes? Write an essay in which you attempt to define the Hollywood hero. Provide examples from movies you've seen in recent years.

Topics for Cross-Cultural Discussion

1. Are heroes important in your culture? Who are some of the most significant? How do they compare to mainstream American heroes?

2. How important do you think it is for children and young adults to have heroes and role models? Do you think local community heroes and family members are more important to children than the bigger historical figures who are immortalized in schools, literature, music, and art?

7

Today's Choices — How Do We Decide What to Do?

As adults, we are continually faced with serious choices and moral decisions. Should I lie about why a term paper is late? So what if I'm the designated driver, a few beers won't make any difference. Nobody saw me back into that car, so should I bother to leave the driver a note? Would another driver do the same for me? Hardly a day goes by in which we are not confronted with the necessity of making tough decisions; some of these may be ethically trivial but others can have mortal consequences.

This unit looks at three tough decisions, each of which is especially relevant to today's America. In "A Gun to My Head," an anonymous medical student wonders whether she should put her life and career at risk by learning how to perform abortions. Her conclusion: "It seems cowardly to let fear stop me from acting on what I believe." This individual medical student's fears are given concrete form in an advertisement from the National Abortion Federation against "anti-choice violence."

If we are living comfortably, do we have a moral obligation to do whatever we can to alleviate the enormous suffering caused by world poverty? In "The Singer Solution to World Poverty," the philosopher Peter Singer, called by the *New York Times* "perhaps the world's most controversial ethicist," poses a few tough hypothetical choices that go directly to the heart of human moral conduct. On a more personal note, Brenda Neff, a Central Missouri State columnist, ponders an issue that has become extremely important to young people: Should couples first try living together before making the decision to marry?

ANONYMOUS, AS TOLD TO SARA CORBETT

A Gun to My Head

[ESQUIRE/February 1999]

Before You Read

What happens when the laws of the state conflict with the laws of some religions? How far should antiabortion protesters be allowed to take their protests? What do you make of the doctor who wants to be able to perform abortions and deliver babies?

Words to Learn

aneurysm (para. 3): an abnormal, blood-filled dilation of a blood vessel (n.)

hemorrhaging (para. 3): bleeding excessively (adj.)

anesthetic (para. 9): an agent that causes unconsciousness or insensitivity to pain (n.)

discreetly (para. 10): modestly and respectfully (adv.)

SARA CORBETT (b. 1968) *is the author of* Venus to the Hoop (1997), *a book about the gold-medal-winning 1996 Olympic team. Her work has appeared in* Esquire, *the* New York Times Magazine, *and* Outside. *"'A Gun to My Head' came about one night shortly after Dr. Barnett Slepian, a doctor in New York, had been killed—shot in front of his children—by an antiabortion protestor," says Corbett. "I had just spent some time with a friend who was finishing medical school and . . . I thought it would be interesting to look at abortion from the point of view of somebody who wrestles with the issue in a very real way."*

butyric acid (para. 18): an acid with
  a noxious odor often used by
  antiabortion protesters (n.)

I saw my first abortion about six months ago, in the summer. It   1
was in a clinic that didn't look like a clinic — an old white clapboard
on a busy street in a city about an hour from where I live. You'd
think it was a regular home, except for the intercom and tiny video
camera on the front porch. You say your name into the intercom and
then hold a picture ID up to the camera for proof, and then you're
buzzed in. Inside, there's a wide staircase and big couches for the
women to sit on; there's fresh coffee and soft rugs on the floor. Outside, there are protesters. Five or six people in lawn chairs, mostly
older men who look quite at home. All that's missing is a hibachi and
their wives.

The doctor I was with kind of chuckled about them. He'd look   2
out the window and say, "Oh, we got Bob here today" or "Looks
like Roger's back." The doctor didn't wear a bulletproof vest or anything, though I noticed he parked his car way down the street instead
of in front of the clinic. I had to walk past the protesters only once
myself, and they didn't say a thing to me — I'm not sure why. One of
them waved a leaflet, but I ignored it. It was intimidating just to have
them there. I remember thinking, Could I really do this every day?
Aren't these the kind of people who'd want to kill me?

The first woman having an abortion that day was a college stu-   3
dent, a sophomore or so, blond and nervous and not very different
from the person I used to be seven years ago. Right now, I'm in my
fourth year of medical school, and next year I'll start my residency in
OB/GYN. In three and a half years of school, I have watched doctors
replace heart valves and kidneys. I've seen ruptured aortic aneurysms
and hemorrhaging livers and colons riddled with cancer. I've been
bled on, vomited on, peed on. I've spent time with a six-year-old
who'd attempted suicide, an emphysema patient trying to sneak out
for a smoke, a car-crash victim whom I had to stitch up after he'd already died. I've seen uteruses come out and feet get amputated, and,
once, I helped remove an infected tumor that was big and bloody and
nearly the size of my head. Through all of this, though, in three and a
half years of textbooks and hospital rounds, before that day last summer, I had never seen an abortion. This wasn't my choice. It's simply
how it is. Abortion, despite being one of the most common surgical

procedures among women in this country, is not talked about, not taught, not even debated in most medical schools.

I could give you the statistics. I could explain that we have sixty **4** million women of childbearing age in the United States and yet only about two thousand providers willing to do abortions; many of the practitioners are gray-haired and ready to retire. I could note that nine out of ten OB/GYN residencies don't require abortion training, and half of the chief residents in the field have never even performed one. I could recite some of the legislation Congress has passed to make abortions harder to come by. I could name the doctors who've been shot—Dr. Gunn, Dr. Britton, Dr. Slepian—or tell some of the stories I've heard about protesters loosening the lug nuts on doctors' car tires or taping up WANTED signs with doctors' faces on them.

> *That morning in the clinic, I hadn't really decided yet which direction I was headed.*

I could tell you that there are very **5** good reasons to become a doctor who provides abortions and that there are more reasons to become a doctor who doesn't.

That morning in the clinic, I hadn't really decided yet which di- **6** rection I was headed. This may sound funny, but I was excited to be there. I hoped that being there would help me make up my mind—not about abortion but about *me* and abortion, about what kind of doctor I'll be. I'd signed up to spend a day at the clinic with this doctor, a gray-haired, soft-spoken man who leaves his private practice once a week to come here, sometimes to perform fifteen or twenty abortions in a day.

The women who arrive for their appointments do their paper- **7** work before meeting with a counselor and seeing a short video on the procedure. Then they change into long nightshirts, putting their clothes in a little basket. They're allowed to keep their underwear on until they get upstairs. Everything else goes in the basket, which they carry with them.

I felt nervous for the sophomore, or maybe I felt kind of sorry for **8** her. She came into the procedure room, took off her underwear, and put it in her basket. She was emotional but acting brave. Her boyfriend was sitting down in the waiting room. Her parents, she said, didn't know.

The doctor listened to her heart and lungs. He asked me to size **9** her uterus, to measure how far along in the pregnancy she was. She was at about eleven weeks. Had she been a week more pregnant, we would've had to turn her away and send her to the nearest hospital that does second-trimester abortions — a two-hour drive and another week's wait for an appointment. Next, the doctor gave her two shots of lidocaine, a local anesthetic, one on either side of the cervix. Then he used dilators — long, thin surgical tools of increasing width — to coax open what's called the cervical os, the doorway to the uterus.

There were five of us in the room: me, the doc, his technician, and one of the staff counselors, who was holding the patient's hand and saying encouraging things. The patient was lying on the examining table, her feet in stirrups. The doctor sat at her feet with a tray of instruments on his lap, a bright lamp to his left, and, on the other side, the vacuum machine, a two-foot-by-two-foot box covered, not very discreetly, with a green surgical cloth.

They say the noise is the worst part, and I suppose that's true. The doctor inserted the vacuum tube — called the cannula — and turned on the machine. First, it just hummed, and then the doctor lifted his thumb from a valve on the tube to start the suction. Have you ever had a dentist suction the saliva out of your mouth? The noise was like that — not loud, not particularly ugly, just . . . suction. And in thirty seconds, maybe forty-five, it was over. The machine was off, the cannula came out, the doctor did one last check with a curette — a tool used to scrape clean the uterine walls — and the sophomore started to breathe more deeply. It was time to inspect the products.

In medicine, they're called the products of conception. They get evacuated into a large glass beaker, and the technician goes into a screened-off area in the procedure room and strains out the liquid, and then you have to look — to make sure it all came out. I went behind the screen with the doctor, and I looked down at the beaker. I don't know what I expected from that moment, exactly, but here's what I saw: a rib cage, an arm. Tiny things, just pieces, less than an inch long and transparent. A lot of pink floaty tissue, like the plants you put in a fishbowl. Was this life? To me, no.

I know I can't convince anyone that what I believe is absolutely right and what they believe is absolutely wrong. But more than anything, I think of abortion as personal. That woman, the college girl — I couldn't know anything of her life, her circumstances. I couldn't say whether she was right to terminate her pregnancy. And neither could the protesters outside, nor could a bunch of congressmen.

I won't say she was happy when it was over, but she did seem relieved and a bit tired. She was wrapped in warm blankets and led to the recovery room, where she could lie down, have a cup of tea and some cookies, visit with her boyfriend. She had been on the examining table less than ten minutes altogether. In another hour, she'd be allowed to put her clothes on and go—out the door and past the protesters and back to her own life.

Everything didn't change for me, spending time in the clinic. But it did confirm what I guess I already knew: It seems cowardly to let fear stop me from acting on what I believe. In a few months, I will have a medical degree, and I will use it to help women have healthier reproductive lives. This includes providing abortions. I've decided I'd be wrong not to. But it scares me.   15

A few weeks ago, I was on the phone with a classmate. I mentioned that I'd seen an abortion last summer, and he said, "Oh, are you into that?" I said, "*Into it?* No." But I told him I'd decided to make abortions part of my practice someday, and it came out that he's on the antichoice side, and we argued for a long time. I found out, too, that one of my cousins is a protester. I can accept that about her, but will she accept that I may be the one pushing past her to get to the clinic door? I don't know. It bothers me that my classmates and I can talk about every medical issue under the sun, but we seldom talk about abortion. It bothers me that when I go to learn the procedure during my residency next year, I'll have to do it as an elective in my spare time—which is to say, in addition to the eighty-hour workweeks.   16

It bothers me that in making abortions a part of my practice, they could take it over. With so few abortion providers out there, that sometimes happens. You get labeled an abortion doctor, and people forget that you are an obstetrician, too. I want to deliver babies. I imagine it'll be the best part of my job.   17

Someday, I will need to sit my children down and explain all this to them. And I will also try to explain the risks of what I've chosen to do, why butyric acid and hit lists and snipers will probably always be, at least theoretically, a part of our lives.   18

Vocabulary / Using a Dictionary

1. The verb form of *anesthetic* (para. 9)—*anesthetize*—is sometimes used to describe a dulling of the senses or emotions. Describe a context in which a person might be anesthetized in this way.

2. *Hemo,* one part of the word *hemorrhage,* comes from the Greek for blood. What does *rrhage* mean?

3. *Discreetly* (para. 10) comes, ultimately, from the Latin *discernere,* meaning to separate. What do you think is being "separated" when one behaves "discreetly"?

Responding to Words in Context

1. Why does the author refer to a *hibachi* (a small grill) in paragraph 1? How does it affect your understanding of the men in the lawn chairs?

2. When the author's classmate asks her if she is "into" abortion, what do you think he means? Why does the author question this word choice?

Discussing Main Point and Meaning

1. What relation does the title, "A Gun to My Head," have to the main idea of this article? What are all of the implications of that title?

2. The author tells the story of a college student whose abortion she witnessed. Why do you think she puts a face to this issue? Why does she include such details as the girl's hair color, her waiting boyfriend, the basket she is given for her clothes, and her visible relief after the procedure is over?

3. In paragraph 15, the author realizes that, to a certain extent, she had already known what her choice would be before she visited the abortion clinic. Why then do you think she frames the article as an exploration or decision-making process? Why does she wait so long to reveal what she had known almost from the start?

Examining Sentences, Paragraphs, and Organization

1. What effect do you think the first words of this article, "I saw my first abortion about six months ago," are meant to have on the reader?

2. In paragraph 3, the narrator lists a number of the sights she has seen as a medical student, including hemorrhaging, amputations, and bloody tumors. Why does she use a listing technique here?

How does the list build up to the point she makes at the end of the paragraph?

3. In paragraph 4, every sentence begins with the phrase "I could," which suggests an implicit follow-up: "but I won't." There is one more use of the phrase in paragraph 5. What is the effect of this repetition, and how does it contribute to the overall point?

4. In paragraph 17, the writer mentions that she very much wants to deliver babies, and that she imagines it will be "the best part of" her job. Why do you think she takes the time to say this at the end of her essay? Similarly, why does she focus on her own future children in the final paragraph?

Thinking Critically

1. Do you think that additional examples of women wanting or needing abortions would help or hurt the author's purpose here? Does the one college student make abortion seem necessary or frivolous, in your opinion? Would statistics about unwanted babies, abused children, or families in poverty be more or less persuasive to you than the anecdote provided? Explain your answer.

2. Why does the author describe the abortion procedure in such great detail? Doesn't this detract from her position somewhat?

In-Class Writing Activities

1. This is a two-part assignment. First, write a letter from the point of view of the protesters outside the clinic, appealing to the medical student to make a different choice than she does. Try to use the kind of calm tone and measured approach of the writer herself rather than being too emotional. Second, write a letter from the girl receiving the abortion to the protesters outside, trying to explain her choice to terminate her pregnancy. In both cases, be careful not to parody (to make fun of) the letter writers.

2. Choose one of the subtopics of this essay to develop further: medical school training, harassment of and violence against abortion providers, or the small number of abortion providers in the United States. Write an essay in which you express your opinion on one of these issues, quoting from the article if appropriate.

NATIONAL ABORTION FEDERATION

[1999]

Before You Read

With the advances in medicine in the past few years, do you believe that abortions are safer than they were ten years ago? What is your stand on abortion? Are you pro-life or pro-choice? How do you feel about someone who does not share your view on abortion? Do we have the right to freedom of choice regarding this topic?

Responding to Words in Context

1. What does the word *abortion* mean? What is the origin of the word?

2. "Every year, physicians face *harassment,* death threats, and even physical violence," states the advertisement in paragraph 1. What is harassment? What does it mean to harass someone?

Discussing Main Point and Meaning

1. What is an "unfortunate reality for many abortion providers" today (para. 3), according to the NAF?

2. According to the advertisement by the NAF, is abortion safe? Is it safer than childbirth?

3. How does the NAF regard the character of doctors who provide women with abortions? What choice have these doctors made?

4. According to the advertisement, for what reason would you contact the NAF?

Examining Details, Imagery, and Design

1. The words *Our doctors* and *safe* are the largest in the advertisement. What is suggested by pairing them this way? To what audience might this be targeted?

2. What is the significance of using a female doctor in the ad?

Thinking Critically

1. What impression did the title of the advertisement suggest upon your first reading? Do you agree with this title: "Our doctors have learned everything there is to know about making abortion safe"?

2. Should we afford more protection to doctors and physicians that provide women with abortions? Are these terrible facts that "since 1993, seven people have died as a result of anti-choice violence" and that "every year, physicians face harassment, death threats, and even physical violence" (para. 1)?

In-Class Writing Activities

1. Pretend that a woman you know has confided to you that she is thinking about having an abortion: She has asked your opinion. Write her a short letter encouraging or discouraging her choice. Keep in mind that this is a very sensitive matter, and that your opinion is of great importance to her making a decision.

2. Discuss the community you grew up in. How do you think your community would react to the National Abortion Federation's advertisement? What people would support the ad? What people would oppose it? Based on these answers, would you consider your community enlightened? Write a short essay discussing these issues.

PETER SINGER

The Singer Solution to World Poverty

[THE NEW YORK TIMES MAGAZINE/September 5, 1999]

Before You Read

Do you donate to charities? Why or why not? Do you think everyone should? If charity could solve the problem of world hunger, then why do so many people avoid giving?

PETER SINGER *(b. 1946) is an Australian-born philosopher and bioethicist. His book* Animal Liberation *(1975) is a classic text of the animal rights movement. Singer's most recent book is titled* How Are We to Live? *(1993), and he has recently joined the faculty at Princeton University's Center for Human Values.*

Words to Learn

incongruity (para. 5): something inconsistent or inharmonious (n.)

ingenious (para. 6): exceptionally clever; brilliant (adj.)

paraphrase (para. 6): a restatement of a text in different words (n.)

atrocities (para. 13): monstrous behaviors, conditions, or acts (n.)

hurtle (para. 14): rushing uncontrollably (v.)

hypothetical (para. 16): based on a theory; uncertain (adj.)

farcical (para. 16): absurd; wholly improbable (adj.)

altruistic (para. 23): selfless; concerned for the welfare of others (adj.)

arduous (para. 23): strenuous; full of hardships (adj.)

In the Brazilian film *Central Station*, Dora is a retired schoolteacher who makes ends meet by sitting at the station writing letters for illiterate people. Suddenly she has an opportunity to pocket $1,000. All she has to do is persuade a homeless nine-year-old boy to follow her to an address she has been given. (She is told he will be adopted by wealthy foreigners.) She delivers the boy, gets the money, spends some of it on a television set, and settles down to enjoy her new acquisition. Her neighbor spoils the fun, however, by telling her that the boy was too old to be adopted—he will be killed and his organs sold for transplantation. Perhaps Dora knew this all along, but after her neighbor's plain speaking, she spends a troubled night. In the morning Dora resolves to take the boy back.   1

Suppose Dora had told her neighbor that it is a tough world, other people have nice new TVs too, and if selling the kid is the only way she can get one, well, he was only a street kid. She would then have become, in the eyes of the audience, a monster. She redeems herself only by being prepared to bear considerable risks to save the boy.   2

At the end of the movie, in cinemas in the affluent nations of the world, people who would have been quick to condemn Dora if she had not rescued the boy go home to places far more comfortable than her apartment. In fact, the average family in the United States spends almost one-third of its income on things that are no more necessary to them than Dora's new TV was to her. Going out to nice restaurants, buying new clothes because the old ones are no longer stylish, vacationing at beach resorts—so much of our income is spent on things not essential to the preservation of our lives and health. Donated to one of a number of charitable agencies, that money could mean the difference between life and death for children in need.   3

All of which raises a question: In the end, what is the ethical   4
distinction between a Brazilian who sells a homeless child to organ
peddlers and an American who already has a TV and upgrades to a
better one—knowing that the money could be donated to an organization that would use it to save the lives of kids in need?

Of course, there are several differences between the two situa-   5
tions that could support different moral judgments about them. For
one thing, to be able to consign a child to death when he is standing
right in front of you takes a chilling kind of heartlessness; it is much
easier to ignore an appeal for money to help children you will never
meet. Yet for a utilitarian philosopher like myself—that is, one who
judges whether acts are right or wrong by their consequences—if the
upshot of the American's failure to donate the money is that one
more kid dies on the streets of a Brazilian city, then it is, in some
sense, just as bad as selling the kid to the organ peddlers. But one
doesn't need to embrace my utilitarian ethic to see that, at the very
least, there is a troubling incongruity in being so quick to condemn
Dora for taking the child to the organ peddlers while, at the same
time, not regarding the American consumer's behavior as raising a serious moral issue.

In his 1996 book, *Living High and Letting Die,* the New York   6
University philosopher Peter Unger presented an ingenious series of
imaginary examples designed to probe our intuitions about whether
it is wrong to live well without giving substantial amounts of money
to help people who are hungry, malnourished, or dying from easily
treatable illnesses like diarrhea. Here's my paraphrase of one of these
examples:

Bob is close to retirement. He has invested most of his savings in   7
a very rare and valuable old car, a Bugatti, which he has not been
able to insure. The Bugatti is his pride and joy. In addition to the
pleasure he gets from driving and caring for his car, Bob knows that
its rising market value means that he will always be able to sell it and
live comfortably after retirement. One day when Bob is out for a
drive, he parks the Bugatti near the end of a railway siding and goes
for a walk up the track. As he does so, he sees that a runaway train,
with no one aboard, is running down the railway track. Looking far-
ther down the track, he sees the small figure of a child very likely to
be killed by the runaway train. He can't stop the train and the child is
too far away to warn of the danger, but he can throw a switch that
will divert the train down the siding where his Bugatti is parked.
Then nobody will be killed—but the train will destroy his Bugatti.

Thinking of his joy in owning the car and the financial security it represents, Bob decides not to throw the switch. The child is killed. For many years to come, Bob enjoys owning his Bugatti and the financial security it represents.

Bob's conduct, most of us will immediately respond, was gravely   8
wrong. Unger agrees. But then he reminds us that we, too, have opportunities to save the lives of children. We can give to organizations like Unicef or Oxfam America. How much would we have to give one of these organizations to have a high probability of saving the life of a child threatened by easily preventable diseases? (I do not believe that children are more worth saving than adults, but since no one can argue that children have brought their poverty on themselves, focusing on them simplifies the issues.) Unger called up some experts and used the information they provided to offer some plausible estimates that include the cost of raising money, administrative expenses, and the cost of delivering aid where it is most needed. By his calculation, $200 in donations would help a sickly two-year-old transform into a healthy six-year-old—offering safe passage through childhood's most dangerous years. To show how practical philosophical argument can be, Unger even tells his readers that they can easily donate funds by using their credit card and calling one of these toll-free numbers: (800) 367-5437 for Unicef; (800) 693-2687 for Oxfam America.

Now you, too, have the information you need to save a child's   9
life. How should you judge yourself if you don't do it? Think again about Bob and his Bugatti. Unlike Dora, Bob did not have to look into the eyes of the child he was sacrificing for his own material comfort. The child was a complete stranger to him and too far away to relate to in an intimate, personal way. Unlike Dora, too, he did not mislead the child or initiate the chain of events imperiling him. In all these respects, Bob's situation resembles that of people able but unwilling to donate to overseas aid and differs from Dora's situation.

If you still think that it was very wrong of Bob not to throw the   10
switch that would have diverted the train and saved the child's life, then it is hard to see how you could deny that it is also very wrong not to send money to one of the organizations listed above. Unless, that is, there is some morally important difference between the two situations that I have overlooked.

Is it the practical uncertainties about whether aid will really reach   11
the people who need it? Nobody who knows the world of overseas aid can doubt that such uncertainties exist. But Unger's figure of $200 to save a child's life was reached after he had made conservative

assumptions about the proportion of the money donated that will actually reach its target.

One genuine difference between Bob and those who can afford to   12
donate to overseas aid organizations but don't is that only Bob can
save the child on the tracks, whereas there are hundreds of millions of
people who can give $200 to overseas aid organizations. The problem
is that most of them aren't doing it. Does this mean that it is all right
for you not to do it?

Suppose that there were more owners of priceless vintage cars—   13
Carol, Dave, Emma, Fred and so on, down to Ziggy—all in exactly
the same situation as Bob, with their own siding and their own
switch, all sacrificing the child in order to preserve their own cherished car. Would that make it all right for Bob to do the same? To
answer this question affirmatively is to endorse follow-the-crowd
ethics—the kind of ethics that led many Germans to look away when
the Nazi atrocities were being committed. We do not excuse them because others were behaving no better.

We seem to lack a sound basis for drawing a clear moral line be-   14
tween Bob's situation and that of any reader of this article with $200
to spare who does not donate it to an overseas aid agency. These
readers seem to be acting at least as badly as Bob was acting when he
chose to let the runaway train hurtle toward the unsuspecting child.
In the light of this conclusion, I trust that many readers will reach for
the phone and donate that $200. Perhaps you should do it before
reading further.

Now that you have distinguished yourself morally from people   15
who put their vintage cars ahead of a child's life, how about treating
yourself and your partner to dinner at your favorite restaurant? But
wait. The money you will spend at the restaurant could also help save
the lives of children overseas! True, you weren't planning to blow
$200 tonight, but if you were to give up dining out just for one
month, you would easily save that amount. And what is one month's
dining out, compared to a child's life? There's the rub. Since there are
a lot of desperately needy children in the world, there will always be
another child whose life you could save for another $200. Are you
therefore obliged to keep giving until you have nothing left? At what
point can you stop?

Hypothetical examples can easily become farcical. Consider Bob.   16
How far past losing the Bugatti should he go? Imagine that Bob had
got his foot stuck in the track of the siding, and if he diverted the
train, then before it rammed the car it would also amputate his big

toe. Should he still throw the switch? What if it would amputate his foot? His entire leg?

As absurd as the Bugatti scenario gets when pushed to extremes, the point it raises is a serious one: Only when the sacrifices become very significant indeed would most people be prepared to say that Bob does nothing wrong when he decides not to throw the switch. Of course, most people could be wrong; we can't decide moral issues by taking opinion polls. But consider for yourself the level of sacrifice that you would demand of Bob, and then think about how much money you would have to give away in order to make a sacrifice that is roughly equal to that. It's almost certainly much, much more than $200. For most middle-class Americans, it could easily be more like $200,000.   17

Isn't it counterproductive to ask people to do so much? Don't we run the risk that many will shrug their shoulders and say that morality, so conceived, is fine for saints but not for them? I accept that we are unlikely to see, in the near or even medium-term future, a world in which it is normal for wealthy Americans to give the bulk of their wealth to strangers. When it comes to praising or blaming people for what they do, we tend to use a standard that is relative to some conception of normal behavior. Comfortably off Americans who give, say, 10 percent of their income to overseas aid organizations are so far ahead of most of their equally comfortable fellow citizens that I wouldn't go out of my way to chastise them for not doing more. Nevertheless, they should be doing much more, and they are in no position to criticize Bob for failing to make the much greater sacrifice of his Bugatti.   18

At this point various objections may crop up. Someone may say: "If every citizen living in the affluent nations contributed his or her share I wouldn't have to make such a drastic sacrifice, because long before such levels were reached, the resources would have been there to save the lives of all those children dying from lack of food or medical care. So why should I give more than my fair share?" Another, related objection is that the government ought to increase its overseas aid allocations, since that would spread the burden more equitably across all taxpayers.   19

Yet the question of how much we ought to give is a matter to be decided in the real world—and that, sadly, is a world in which we know that most people do not, and in the immediate future will not, give substantial amounts to overseas aid agencies. We know, too, that at least in the next year, the United States government is not going to meet even the very modest United Nations–recommended target of 0.7 percent of gross national product; at the moment it lags   20 far below that, at 0.09 percent, not even half of Japan's 0.22 percent or a tenth of Denmark's 0.97 percent. Thus, we know that the money we can give beyond that theoretical "fair share" is still going to save lives that would otherwise be lost. While the idea that no one need do more than his or her fair share is a powerful one, should it prevail if we know that others are not doing their fair share and that children will die preventable deaths unless we do more than our fair share? That would be taking fairness too far.

That's right: I'm saying that you shouldn't buy that new car, take that cruise, redecorate the house, or get that pricey new suit. After all, a $1,000 suit could save five children's lives.

21 Thus, this ground for limiting how much we ought to give also fails. In the world as it is now, I can see no escape from the conclusion that each one of us with wealth surplus to his or her essential needs should be giving most of it to help people suffering from poverty so dire as to be life-threatening. That's right: I'm saying that you shouldn't buy that new car, take that cruise, redecorate the house, or get that pricey new suit. After all, a $1,000 suit could save five children's lives.

22 So how does my philosophy break down in dollars and cents? An American household with an income of $50,000 spends around $30,000 annually on necessities, according to the Conference Board, a nonprofit economic research organization. Therefore, for a household bringing in $50,000 a year, donations to help the world's poor should be as close as possible to $20,000. The $30,000 required for necessities holds for higher incomes as well. So a household making $100,000 could cut a yearly check for $70,000. Again, the formula is simple: Whatever money you're spending on luxuries, not necessities, should be given away.

23 Now, evolutionary psychologists tell us that human nature just isn't sufficiently altruistic to make it plausible that many people will sacrifice so much for strangers. On the facts of human nature, they might be right, but they would be wrong to draw a moral conclusion from those facts. If it is the case that we ought to do things that, predictably, most of us won't do, then let's face that fact head-on. Then, if we value the life of a child more than going to fancy restaurants, the next time we dine out we will know that we could have done something better with our money. If that makes living a morally decent life extremely arduous, well, then that is the way things are. If we don't do it, then we should at least know that we are failing to live a morally decent life—not because it is good to wallow in guilt

but because knowing where we should be going is the first step toward heading in that direction.

When Bob first grasped the dilemma that faced him as he stood   24
by that railway switch, he must have thought how extraordinarily unlucky he was to be placed in a situation in which he must choose between the life of an innocent child and the sacrifice of most of his savings. But he was not unlucky at all. We are all in that situation.

Vocabulary/Using a Dictionary

1. *Para* has many meanings. Look it up in your dictionary and try to find the meaning that fits for its use in *paraphrase* (para. 6). Also, look up *paragraph, paradigm,* and *parallel.* How do their meanings compare to the meaning of paraphrase?

2. How is the word *obliged* (para. 15) similar to or different from *obligated?*

3. Look up the word *farce,* the noun form of *farcical* (para. 16). What does it mean?

Responding to Words in Context

1. In paragraph 5, Singer defines a *utilitarian philosopher* as someone who "judges whether acts are right or wrong by their consequences." What consequences, specifically, do you think he refers to here? Can you think of other utilitarian positions one might take in today's society?

2. The first sentence in paragraph 16 reads, "Hypothetical examples can easily become farcical." What does Singer mean by this?

Discussing Main Point and Meaning

1. What do you think is the main goal of this essay? Is it to inform the reader about a problem? To criticize someone or something? Or to persuade the reader to do something? Explain your answer.

2. This is an essay filled with numbers—percentages, dollar amounts, phone numbers. What effect do all of these numbers have on the reader? How do they contribute to Singer's main purpose?

3. In paragraph 23, Singer refers to "evolutionary psychologists" who argue that human beings are naturally selfish. How does he rebut that claim?

Examining Sentences, Paragraphs, and Organization

1. Singer borrows Peter Unger's tactic of listing the phone numbers for Unicef and Oxfam America for the reader (para. 8). Describe the first two sentences in paragraph 9 and show how they build off of this information.

2. Why does this essay open with a description of a movie plot, followed by a description of a hypothetical scenario (paras. 1–7)?

3. What is the topic of the final paragraph? Where in the paragraph does the topic sentence fall?

Thinking Critically

1. In paragraph 18, Singer questions his own argument when he asks, "Isn't it counterproductive to ask people to do so much?" Are you satisfied with the answer he provides? Or do you think that his argument is counterproductive in asking for such immediate and unusual results?

2. Singer focuses quite specifically on America's obligations to the poor of the world. Why? Do you think this is fair? Does it matter that Singer himself is not American?

In-Class Writing Activities

1. Try to create a hypothetical scenario similar to Peter Unger's example of Bob and his Bugatti. Imagine a situation that presents a difficult moral dilemma, and describe it in detail. Then explain what you think would be the "moral" response to the dilemma you describe.

2. What do you think is the proper attitude to have toward charitable giving? Should we make the kinds of sacrifices Singer suggests? Is there a place to draw the line? Doesn't someone who works hard for a living have a right to enjoy herself? How can you reconcile the extreme wealth of some people with the extreme poverty of others? Who is ultimately responsible for the poorest people of the world? Write a short essay that presents your opinion on these issues.

BRENDA NEFF

Living Together

[MULESKINNER.ORG, CENTRAL MISSOURI STATE UNIVERSITY/January 19, 1999]

Before You Read

Should people live together before marriage? Why do some people think it's wrong? Is living together a good way to "test drive" a potential marriage, or is it the lazy way out of committing for life?

Words to Learn

taboo (para. 1): something prohibited by social custom (n.)
surface (para. 4): emerge after a period of concealment (v.)
inappropriate (para. 6): improper (adj.)

Love can't conquer all. So, before couples tie the knot, they should 1
know what they're getting into. The taboo against couples living together before marriage is decreasing, and more and more people are
saying "I do" after they've spent months, or even years, living together.

As much as a person loves another, he or she never really 2
knows what happens behind closed doors unless he or she is standing on the other side. While some people view living together before marriage as immoral, couples are actually expanding the
boundaries of their relationship by moving in together. For example, the division of household responsibilities can be a major
issue for newlyweds. By living together, couples can solve imbal-

BRENDA NEFF *(b. 1979) was a senior at Central Missouri State University
when she wrote this piece for the Central Missouri State University* Muleskinner Online. *Neff has received more feedback about this article than any
other she has written, perhaps, she feels, because "students appreciated reading a positive view of a situation that people usually expect to be kept quiet."
Neff received a B.S. in journalism and political science in May 2000.*

ances in the distribution of those responsibilities before someone realizes he or she has married a lazy bum.

This may seem like a small point, but how many women—and men—are out there who never thought they would be the only ones cooking, washing dishes, vacuuming, mopping, scrubbing, disinfecting, cleaning laundry, dusting, etc.?   3

One of the largest problems in marriages is the "m" word: money. If couples live together before marriage, they learn one another's saving and spending styles. By sharing expenses, people learn not only how each person controls the purse strings but how to discuss finance matters with each other. It's important for couples to figure out budget priorities before they are married, and this is difficult to do unless a person has been sharing expenses with his or her partner. If couples don't have their financial issues in order, they are bound to surface, causing trouble in the marriage.   4

> *Even though two people love each other and enjoy spending time together, the real question is, Can you live together?*

It's also difficult to know someone intimately without living with him or her. A special bond forms between people who share their living space, their personal belongings, and their lives together. Some things you just don't know until you've lived with someone.   5

While some people believe living together before marriage is inappropriate, like most everything else in this country, it is a choice that everyone should respect. Living together can be a positive experience that will later reenforce a marriage, but it can also be something that ends a relationship. But if a relationship is going to end, it's better people discover the hard truth before they marry. Even though two people love each other and enjoy spending time together, the real question is, Can you live together? People might want to find out before they make the serious decision to marry.   6

Vocabulary / Using a Dictionary

1. What is the root of *surface*? How do the noun and its root forms relate to each other? What does the prefix mean?

2. *Inappropriate* (para. 6) comes from the same root as *proper*: the Latin word *proprius,* meaning "one's own" or "for the individual."

How do you think this original meaning developed into the common connotation of *correctness* we use today?

3. Explain what you perceive to be the difference between *immoral* (para. 2) and *inappropriate* (para. 6).

Responding to Words in Context

1. Why does Neff call money "the 'm' word"? What effect does her doing so have on the reader?

2. What does Neff mean when she says couples ought to know "how each person controls the purse strings"?

Discussing Main Point and Meaning

1. "Love can't conquer all" is Neff's opening line. What does she mean? How does this sentence introduce her main point?

2. What point does the author make about household responsibilities in paragraph 2?

3. "A special bond forms between people who share their living space, their personal belongings, and their lives together. Some things you just don't know until you've lived with someone" (para. 5). What things do you think Neff thinks people learn by living together (besides each other's cleaning and spending habits)? What do you think Neff means by a "special bond"?

Examining Sentences, Paragraphs, and Organization

1. Take another look at the following sentence: "This may seem like a small point, but how many women — and men — are out there who never thought they would be the only ones cooking, washing dishes, vacuuming, mopping, scrubbing, disinfecting, cleaning laundry, dusting, etc.?" (para. 3). How does the structure of the sentence contribute to the meaning?

2. What does Neff think about the possibility that living together can end a relationship?

3. A title generally presents a preview of, or an indirect reference to, the main idea in an essay. How does the title of this essay relate to the author's main point?

Thinking Critically

1. Do you agree that "Love can't conquer all"? Explain your position.
2. Some would argue that couples who live together and break up do so because they were not committed enough to their relationships in the first place (that is, because they did not marry). How might Neff respond to this argument?

In-Class Writing Activities

1. Write a short essay defining marriage. Note how many of the details you include are also true (or at least potentially true) of a couple living together.
2. Did most of the married (or divorced) couples you know live together first? Try to generate a small amount of data to hold up to Neff's theory. Write a short summary of your findings, explaining whether or not they support Neff's ideas.

Discussing the Unit

Suggested Topic for Discussion

Would you endanger your life for a cause? Would you give up the luxuries you've worked for to feed the bottomless pit of world hunger? Do you feel the need to marry and live in a traditional way because that's what society finds appropriate? Think about *how* you know right from wrong. Does your morality come from experience the way the anonymous doctor and Peter Singer's morality does? Or do you work off of or against the morality set up for you by society, as does Brenda Neff?

Preparing for Class Discussion

1. All of the issues discussed in this unit present very personal perspectives on issues that affect society as a whole. If morality is the measure of good and evil, then which do you think is more important — doing what's right for society in general, or doing what seems most correct to oneself? How do we reconcile these two competing interests in making moral decisions ourselves?

2. Peter Singer attempts to call his readers to action, and Brenda Neff attempts to challenge her readers' perceptions and persuade them to accede to her thinking. How do you think the author of "A Gun to My Head" wants to affect the thinking of her readers? How are her intentions similar to or different from the other authors' intentions?

From Discussion to Writing

1. Which of these three essays do you think deals with the most important moral issue we face today? In an essay of your own, describe that issue as you see it, drawing on the selection itself for support where needed.

2. "A Gun to My Head" is in large part interested in the ways morality and the law interact. Using any of these essays as a springboard for your discussion, write an essay about the relationship between morality and the law.

3. You are the principal of a high school and you have decided to create a new required course for all students called "Morality 101." What are the issues you would include in this course? How would you organize the course? Write an essay describing the course and its goals.

Topics for Cross-Cultural Discussion

1. How do poor nations perceive the responsibility of affluent nations with respect to charity and foreign aid programs? How do affluent nations perceive their responsibility? Think of some particular examples you have read about.

2. Various countries have population policies that either restrict or promote reproduction. Based on your knowledge of other cultures outside the United States, do you think the issue of abortion is primarily a moral, political, economic, or religious issue?

8

The Future — What Can We Expect?

Although technology is changing rapidly, will the much-hyped "new millennium" also lead to surprising changes in society and human behavior? Will transformations in science result in transformations in social consciousness? By 2050, say, will Americans be living in ways we cannot now imagine, or will everyday life remain pretty much the way it is now?

This chapter offers three forecasts of what the future may hold in store. In "Will Women Still Need Men?" the noted *Time* magazine columnist Barbara Ehrenreich wonders whether this "could be the century when the sexes go their separate ways." She predicts "three possible scenarios" based on how biological sciences and changing social customs may profoundly alter traditional views of marriage, family, and community.

Will the new century also see major changes in racial classification? With rising rates of intermarriage, increasing immigration, and the erosion of many racial barriers, will whites become a minority in the United States? Will race cease to matter? In "The Colors of Race," Ellis Cose directly confronts these issues. He finds reasons to be both optimistic and cautious about the so-called end of race.

Our glimpse into the future concludes with speculation about the direction of scientific research. In "The Next Frontier," Brandon Eckenrode, a student at Western Illinois University, believes it's time to pull back on research that studies the world around us and begin to focus on what's inside us. The great scientific endeavor of the next century should be, he argues, the exploration of the human brain.

The unit concludes with an advertisement that sees U.S. immigration policy as a threat to a sustainable future.

BARBARA EHRENREICH

Will Women Still Need Men?

[TIME/February 21, 2000]

Before You Read

With advances in bio-research and cloning, will we need the opposite sex to survive in the twenty-first century? Will males and females become more or less dependent on one another in the future? Will you see a real separation of the sexes in your or your children's lifetimes?

Words to Learn

amicable (para. 3): peaceable; friendly (adj.)

placidly (para. 4): meekly; gently (adv.)

brothels (para. 6): whorehouses (n.)

tactile (para. 7): tangible; perceptible by touch (adj.)

churn (para. 9): to stir or agitate (v.)

coercion (para. 10): compulsion; intimidation (n.)

betrothals (para. 11): promises or contracts for a future marriage (n.)

ineluctably (para. 11): inevitably (adv.)

restigmatize (para. 12): to mark again, in infamous terms (adj.)

Barbara Ehrenreich (b. 1941) is a writer, novelist, and activist. Her works have appeared in many publications, including Mother Jones, Harper's *magazine,* The Nation, *and* Time. *Ehrenreich's most recent book is* The Snarling Citizen *(1995), and she has won several awards, including the National Magazine Award for Excellence in Reporting (1980) and a Guggenheim Fellowship (1987–88).*

subversive (para. 12): rebellious;
    revolutionary (adj.)
paradigm (para. 14): standard, pat-
    tern, archetype (n.)

unbohemian (para. 14): conven-
    tional, not wandering, conformist
    (adj.)

This could be the century when the sexes go their separate ways. 1
Sure, we've hung in there together for about a thousand millenniums
so far—through hunting-gathering, agriculture, and heavy industry—
but what choice did we have? For most of human existence, if you
wanted to make a living, raise children, or even have a roaring good
time now and then, you had to get the cooperation of the other sex.

What's new about the future, and potentially more challenging to 2
our species than Martian colonization or silicon brain implants, is
that the partnership between the sexes is
becoming entirely voluntary. We can decide to stick together—or we can finally
say, "Sayonara, other sex!" For the first
time in human history and prehistory
combined, the choice will be ours.

> *This could be the*
> *century when the sexes*
> *go their separate ways.*

I predict three possible scenarios, 3
starting with the Big Divorce. Somewhere around 2025, people will
pick a gender equivalent of the Mason-Dixon Line[1] and sort themselves out accordingly. In Guy Land the men will be free to spend
their evenings staging belching contests and watching old Howard
Stern tapes. In Gal Land the women will all be fat and happy, and no
one will bother to shave her legs. Aside from a few initial border
clashes, the separation will for the most part be amicable. At least the
"battle of the sexes," insofar as anyone can remember it, will be removed from the kitchens and bedrooms of America and into the UN.

And why not? If the monosexual way of life were counter to 4
human nature, men wouldn't have spent so much of the past millennium dodging women by enlisting in armies, monasteries, and all-male

---

[1]*Mason-Dixon Line:* The popular name for the boundary between Maryland and
Pennsylvania. It is so called because it was surveyed (1763–1767) by two British as-
tronomers, Charles Mason and Jeremiah Dixon, to settle a boundary dispute between
the two colonies. The term *Mason-Dixon Line* was later used to designate the line that
divided the free states from the slave states during the congressional debates over the
Missouri Compromise in 1820. The term is still used sometimes to mean the boundary
between the North and the South.

guilds and professions. Up until the past half-century, women only fantasized about their version of the same: a utopia like the one described by nineteenth-century feminist Charlotte Perkins Gilman, where women would lead placidly sexless lives and reproduce by parthenogenesis.[2] But a real separation began to look feasible about fifty years ago. With the invention of TV dinners and drip-dry shirts, for the first time the average man became capable of feeding and dressing himself. Sensing their increasing dispensability on the home front, and tired of picking up dropped socks, women rushed into the work force. They haven't achieved full economic independence by any means (women still earn only 75 percent of what men do), but more and more of them are realizing that ancient female dream—a room, or better yet, a condo of their own.

The truly species-shaking change is coming from the new technologies of reproduction. Up until now, if you wanted to reproduce, you not only had to fraternize with a member of the other sex for at least a few minutes, but you also ran a 50 percent risk that any resulting baby would turn out be a member of the foreign sex. No more. Thanks to in vitro fertilization, we can have babies without having sex. And with the latest techniques of sex selection, we can have babies of whatever sex we want.   5

Obviously women, with their built-in baby incubators, will have the advantage in a monosexual future. They just have to pack up a good supply of frozen semen, a truckload of turkey basters, and go their own way. But men will be catching up. For one thing, until now, frozen-and-thawed ova have been tricky to fertilize because their outer membrane gets too hard. But a new technique called intracytoplasmic sperm injection makes frozen ova fully fertilizable, and so now Guy Land can have its ovum banks. As for the incubation problem, a few years ago feminist writer Gena Corea offered the seemingly paranoid suggestion that men might eventually keep just a few women around in "reproductive brothels," gestating on demand. A guy will pick an ovum for attractive qualities like smart, tall, and allergy-free, then have it inserted into some faceless surrogate mother employed as a reproductive slave.   6

What about sex, though, meaning the experience, not the category? Chances are, we will be having sex with machines, mostly computers. Even today you can buy interactive CD-ROMs like Virtual Valerie, and there's talk of full-body, virtual-reality sex in which the   7

---

[2]*Parthenogenesis:* Reproduction by development of an unfertilized gamete (mature male or female cell) that especially occurs among lower plants and invertebrate animals.

pleasure seeker wears a specially fitted suit—very specially fitted—
allowing for tactile as well as audiovisual sensation. If that sounds
farfetched, consider the fact that cyber-innovation is currently in the
hands of social skills–challenged geeks who couldn't hope to get a
date without flashing their Internet stock options.

Still, there's a reason why the Big Divorce scenario isn't likely to   8
work out, even by Y3K: We love each other, we males and females—
madly, sporadically, intermittently, to be sure—but at least enough
to keep us pair bonding furiously, even when there's no obvious
hardheaded reason to do so. Hence, despite predictions of the immi-
nent "breakdown of the family," the divorce rate leveled off in the
1990s, and the average couple is still hopeful or deluded enough to
invest about $20,000 in their first wedding. True, fewer people are
marrying: 88 percent of Americans have married at least once, down
from 94 percent in 1988. But the difference is largely made up by
couples who set up housekeeping without the blessing of the state.
And an astounding 16 percent of the population has been married
three times—which shows a remarkable commitment to, if nothing
else, the institution of marriage.

The question for the new century is, Do we love each other   9
enough—enough, that is, to sustain the old pair-bonded way of life?
Many experts see the glass half empty: Cohabitation may be replac-
ing marriage, but it's even less likely to last. Hearts are routinely broken and children's lives disrupted as we churn, ever starry-eyed, from
one relationship to the next. Even liberal icons like Hillary Rodham
Clinton and Harvard Afro-American studies professor Cornel West
have been heard muttering about the need to limit the ease and accessibility of divorce.

Hence, perhaps, Scenario B: Seeing that the old economic and bi-   10
ological pressures to marry don't work anymore, people will decide
to replace them with new forms of coercion. Divorce will be outlawed, along with abortion and possibly contraception. Extramarital
hanky-panky will be punishable with shunning or, in the more hard-
line jurisdictions, stoning. There will still be sex, and probably plenty
of it inside marriage, thanks to what will be known as Chemically As-
sisted Monogamy: Viagra for men and Viagra-like drugs for women,
such as apomorphine and Estratest (both are being tested right now),
to reignite the spark long after familiarity has threatened to extin-
guish it. Naturally, prescriptions will be available only upon presentation of a valid marriage license.

It couldn't happen here, even in a thousand years? Already, a   11
growing "marriage movement," including groups like the Promise

Keepers, is working to make divorce lawyers as rare as elevator operators. Since 1997, Louisiana and Arizona have been offering ultra-tight "covenant marriages," which can be dissolved only in the case of infidelity, abuse, or felony conviction, and similar measures have been introduced in seventeen other states. As for the age-old problem of premarital fooling around, some extremely conservative Christian activists have launched a movement to halt the dangerous practice of dating and replace it with parent-supervised betrothals leading swiftly and ineluctably to the altar.

But Scenario B has a lot going against it too. The 1998 impeach-   12
ment fiasco showed just how hard it will be to restigmatize extramarital sex. Sure, we think adultery is a bad thing, just not bad enough to disqualify anyone from ruling the world. Meanwhile, there have been few takers for covenant marriages, showing that most people like to keep their options open. Tulane University sociologist Laura Sanchez speculates that the ultimate effect of covenant marriages may be to open up the subversive possibility of diversifying the institution of marriage—with different types for different folks, including, perhaps someday, even gay folks.

Which brings us to the third big scenario. This is the diversity op-   13
tion, arising from the realization that the one-size-fits-all model of marriage may have been one of the biggest sources of tension between the sexes all along—based as it is on the wildly unrealistic expectation that a single spouse can meet one's needs for a lover, friend, co-parent, financial partner, reliably, 24-7. Instead there will be renewable marriages, which get re-evaluated every five to seven years, after which they can be revised, recelebrated, or dissolved with no, or at least fewer, hard feelings. There will be unions between people who don't live together full-time but do want to share a home base. And of course there will always be plenty of people who live together but don't want to make a big deal out of it. Already, thanks to the gay-rights movement, more than six hundred corporations and other employers offer domestic-partner benefits, a sixty-fold increase since 1990.

And the children? The real paradigm shift will come when we   14
stop trying to base our entire society on the wavering sexual connection between individuals. Romantic love ebbs and surges unaccountably; it's the bond between parents and children that has to remain rocklike year after year. Putting children first would mean that adults would make a contract—not to live together or sleep together but to take joint responsibility for a child or an elderly adult. Some of these arrangements will look very much like today's marriages, with a heterosexual couple undertaking the care of their biological children.

Others will look like nothing we've seen before, at least not in suburban America, especially since there's no natural limit on the number of contracting caretakers. A group of people—male, female, gay, straight—will unite in their responsibility for the children they bear or acquire through the local Artificial Reproduction Center. Heather may routinely have two mommies, or at least a whole bunch of resident aunts—which is, of course, more or less how things have been for eons in such distinctly unbohemian settings as the tribal village.

So how will things play out this century and beyond? Just so you will be prepared, here's my timeline: 15

Between 2000 and 2339: Geographical diversity prevails. The Southeast and a large swath of the Rockies will go for Scenario B (early marriage, no divorce). Oregon, California, and New York will offer renewable marriages, and a few states will go monosexual, as in Scenario A. But because of the 1996 Defense of Marriage Act, each state is entitled to recognize only the kinds of "marriages" it approves of, so you will need a "marriage visa" to travel across the country, at least if you intend to share a motel room. 16

Between 2340 and 2387: NATO will be forced to intervene in the Custody Wars that break out between the Polygamous Republic of Utah and the Free Love Zone of the Central Southwest. A huge refugee crisis will develop when singles are ethnically cleansed from the Christian Nation of Idaho. Florida will be partitioned into divorce-free and marriage-free zones. 17

In 2786: The new President's Inauguration will be attended by all five members of the mixed-sex, multiracial commune that raised her. She will establish sizable tax reductions for couples or groups of any size that create stable households for their children and other dependents. Peace will break out. 18

And in 2999: A scholar of ancient history will discover these words penned by a gay writer named Fenton Johnson back in 1996: "The mystery of love and life and death is really grander and more glorious than human beings can grasp, much less legislate." He will put this sentence onto a bumper sticker. The message will spread. We will realize that the sexes can't live without each other, but neither can they be joined at the hip. We will grow up. 19

Vocabulary / Using a Dictionary

1. What does it mean to get along *amicably* (para. 3) with someone? What are some synonyms for the word?

2. In paragraph 11, Ehrenreich states that "some extremely conservative Christian activists have launched a movement to halt the dangerous practice of dating and replace it with parent-supervised *betrothals* leading swiftly and *ineluctably* to the altar." What does the author mean? Translate what Ehrenreich is saying. What effect does it have to use those words?

3. Ehrenreich refers to the tribal village as being *unbohemian* (para. 14). What does the word mean? How is it different from the word *bohemian?* Give some examples of things or persons who might be called bohemian.

Responding to Words in Context

1. "With the invention of TV dinners and drip-dry shirts, for the first time the average man became capable of feeding and dressing himself. Sensing their increasing *dispensability* on the home front, and tired of picking up dropped socks, women rushed into the work force," states the author (para. 4). What do you think the word *dispensability* means? How is it related to the word *dispense?*

2. In paragraph 8, Ehrenreich comments that "we love each other, we males and females—madly, *sporadically, intermittently,* to be sure—but at least enough to keep us pair bonding furiously, even when there's no obvious hardheaded reason to do so." Explain what the author is trying to say, in your own words.

3. What do you think a *covenant* is? In paragraph 11, the author states: "Since 1997, Louisiana and Arizona have been offering ultratight *covenant marriages,* which can be dissolved only in the case of infidelity, abuse, or felony conviction" (para. 11). What do you think a *covenant marriage* is?

Discussing Main Point and Meaning

1. In paragraph 2, Ehrenreich explains that "partnership between the sexes is becoming entirely voluntary. We can decide to stick together—or we can finally say, 'Sayonara . . .' . . . the choice will be ours." From this reasoning, the author predicts that there will be three possible scenarios in which the sexes will engage. What are these scenarios? Briefly explain each of them.

2. According to the author, who will have the advantage in a mono-sexual future? Men or women? Why?

3. What is Ehrenreich's response to *the* question for the new century: "Do we love each other enough . . . to sustain the old pair-bonded way of life?" (para. 9). How does she think we should address this problem?

4. Briefly outline how Ehrenreich thinks the sexes will fare in this century and beyond. Use the timeline she has constructed to illustrate your answer.

Examining Sentences, Paragraphs, and Organization

1. In paragraph 3, Ehrenreich writes: "In Guy Land the men will be free to spend their evenings staging belching contests and watching old Howard Stern tapes. In Gal Land the women will all be fat and happy, and no one will bother to shave her legs." In these two sentences, how is the author's point of view revealed?

2. How would you characterize the tone of this piece? Is there a change in the tone between the first paragraph and the last one? If so, how would you characterize the change?

3. Where do you think the conclusion to Ehrenreich's essay starts? Explain your answer.

Thinking Critically

1. In her discussion of *in vitro* fertilization (fertilization occurring outside the human body and in an artificial environment), Ehrenreich acts as an advocate, mentioning that "up until now, if you wanted to reproduce, you . . . had to fraternize with a member of the other sex for at least a few minutes. . . . Thanks to in vitro fertilization, we can have babies without having sex" (para. 5). Describe the author's view of in vitro fertilization. Do you agree? How do you feel about reproduction without having relations with a member of the opposite sex?

2. In paragraph 7, the author states: "Today you can buy interactive CD-ROMs like Virtual Valerie, and there's talk of full-body, virtual-reality sex . . . allowing for tactile as well as audio-visual sensation. If that sounds farfetched, consider the fact that cyber-innovation is currently in the hands of social skills–challenged geeks who couldn't hope to get a date without flashing their In-

ternet stock options." Describe the author's attitude toward these cyber-innovations. How does she feel about the creators of virtual reality and cyber-sex?

In-Class Writing Activities

1. Make two lists—things that you think the average man needs to be happy, and things that you think the average woman needs to be happy. In your list include bare necessities and more esoteric (obscure) possessions. Compare and contrast the items on the two lists.

2. In paragraph 19, Ehrenreich quotes Fenton Johnson as saying: "The mystery of love and life and death is really grander and more glorious than human beings can grasp, much less legislate." Write a brief essay including your current reaction to the quote, and conclude the assignment by answering how you might feel about the statement in twenty or thirty years.

ELLIS COSE

The Colors of Race

[NEWSWEEK/January 1, 2000]

Before You Read

Is intermarriage rising in the United States? Are racial barriers eroding? Is the United States more tolerant than ever? Do you think we will ever arrive at a "majority-minority" in the future? Will interracial marriage be more possible and easier in the future?

Words to Learn

apartheid (para. 1): official policy of racial segregation (n.)

substantive (para. 2): permanent; enduring (adj.)

stigmatized (para. 2): branded with a mark of shame (v.)

bemusement (para. 4): a state of confusion (n.)

albeit (para. 5): even though (conj.)

cohorts (para. 6): a band or group (n.)

demographic (para. 8): referring to the statistical characteristics of a population (adj.)

circumscribed (para. 10): to constrict the range of (v.)

disparities (para. 10): differences (n.)

ELLIS COSE (b. 1951) has been contributing editor for Newsweek *since 1993. His latest book,* Color-Blind: Seeing Beyond Race in a Race-Obsessed World *(1997), has been excerpted in* Newsweek. *Cose shared a National Association of Black Journalists' Award with three colleagues for the March 1997* Newsweek *cover package "Black Like Who?"*

The United States closed the nineteenth century declaring—in   1
Plessy v. Ferguson[1]—that rigid segregation was the natural order. It
was a time when W. E. B. Du Bois[2] despaired that America would
ever get beyond its homespun apartheid. "The problem of the twentieth century is the problem of the color line—the relation of the
darker to the lighter races of men," he famously pronounced in 1903.
Americans have not proved Du Bois wrong. Still, the country enters
the millennium self-consciously striving to be a more tolerant place.
The new century will not see the end of race—the dawning of an era
when skin color is of no consequence—but it will see a further erosion of racial walls. And it will see America struggling to make sense
of shifting racial classifications.

Already, Americans are changing—in ways both substantive and   2
superficial—to conform to the new, more egalitarian, ideal. Nazis
may still march, but they are inevitably outnumbered by counterpro-
testers. Aryan Nation kooks may still kill; but, if caught, they are imprisoned, stigmatized, and scorned. Racial purity is not as prized as it
once was. People who call themselves white proudly acknowledge
Latino and Native American roots. A small number even acknowledge some black ancestry. And interracial romance, once outlawed
and condemned, now openly blooms.

Between 1960 and 1992 the number of interracially married cou-   3
ples multiplied more than seven times over. Black-white unions are
still not the norm, accounting for only 20 percent of interracial marriages, but the marriage color line has all but dissolved between
Asians and whites. In America, more children are born to white-
Japanese couples than to parents who are both of Japanese ancestry.
Then there are Hispanics, who are projected to become America's
second largest racial-ethnic group (after whites) by 2010. Latinos
may consider themselves white, black, American Indian, Asian, or Pacific Islander—or deem themselves none of the above. It is not unusual in Latin America for people who don't consider themselves
black to speak of a grandparent who is. Whatever they call themselves, the presence of an ever-growing number of multiracials or

[1]*Plessy v. Ferguson:* The 1892 Supreme Court case pitting Homer Plessy, a thirty-year-
old, one-eighth-black shoemaker, against John Howard Ferguson, a Massachusetts
lawyer. Ultimately the Court ruled against Plessy and decided that public places (restrooms, buses, trains, etc.) could in effect be "separate but equal." This was supposedly
to benefit both the black and white "races."
[2]*W. E. B. Du Bois* (1868–1963): A leading African American author and intellectual
whose classic collection of essays, *The Souls of Black Folk,* appeared in 1903.

mestizos[3] is forcing Americans to relinquish the notion that everyone can be put in a single racial box. The Census Bureau, acknowledging that reality, will allow people to be counted in more than one racial category during next year's census.

When Tiger Woods revealed in 1997 that he thought of himself as "Cablinasian"—a mixture of Caucasian, black, Indian, and Asian—when growing up, he was greeted with bemusement, even hostility. In fact, very few black Americans are just black. If people with "black blood" can now be white or at least not black, what becomes of the concept of passing? Passing, after all, implies a denial of one's authentic ancestry to be accepted as a member of another race. But what happens when the definition of the other race changes enough to accommodate formerly forbidden ancestries? And what happens to the very notion of racism in a society where race has lost much of its meaning?

> **Status and privilege are still connected to lighter skin.**

The rise of the mixed-race—or *café au lait*—society has led some to predict the end of distinctions based on ethnicity, racial appearance, or ancestry. That seems unlikely. Even in Brazil, where racial mixing is accepted, even celebrated, color coding has not lost its sting. Status and privilege are still connected to lighter skin. Racial distinctions, albeit mutable and imprecise, are constantly made. In the emerging U.S. mestizo future, some people will still be whiter than others—and if the Latin America experience is any guide, they will have an advantage.

But what happens when whites become a minority? According to U.S. Census projections, by 2030 non-Hispanic whites may constitute fewer than half of those in the United States under the age of eighteen. A few decades after that, minorities, as now defined, will be in the majority. But common sense says the much-anticipated "majority-minority" future will never arrive. For one thing, such projections forecast the growth of ethnic cohorts as if racial intermingling will be insignificant, when it clearly will be anything but. And who is to say that a girl with one Asian grandparent, one Latino, and two who are white will consider herself Asian or Latino instead of white? Or that a boy with one black, one Argentine, and two Anglo grandparents will see himself as a "person of color"?

To complicate things even more, we have no idea what "majority

---

[3]*mestizos*: People born with both European and indigenous ancestors.

race" will mean a half century from now. If the past is any guide, groups who are not now counted in the "majority" will be. Earlier in this century, entry of Eastern and Southern Europeans was restricted because of their supposedly inferior racial stock. Now Romanians are considered as white as any other Europeans. By the middle of the twenty-first century, many of those whom the census projects to be Asian, Hispanic, or black may be considered white—or whatever the new term is for the majority. The racial hierarchy, in other words, will not be upended because "minorities" suddenly outnumber whites. Racial categories will change long before that day arrives.

But if demographic shifts will not bring about the end of race,   8
what will? The answer is that nothing will, not soon. Having established a more tolerant America is not the same as having established an America without racial assumptions and consequences. Even in today's United States, infant mortality among blacks is more than twice that for whites. Blacks suffer higher rates of cancer, have a lower life expectancy, and fare worse than whites on nearly every measure of health —including access to potentially lifesaving cancer surgery, according to an October report in the *New England Journal of Medicine*. Race also matters when it comes to educational opportunity. According to a study published by the Civil Rights Project at Harvard University, public-school segregation of blacks and Latinos is on the rise, in both cities and suburbs. And those increasingly black and Latino schools generally lack the resources of the typical white student's school.

So what does that mean for the future? It means understanding,   9
first of all, that the future is not a straightforward march from unenlightenment to paradise. When it comes to race, America has a habit of claiming victories it hasn't earned. And as evidenced by ethnic-cleansing campaigns in the Balkans and Rwanda and by ethno-religious conflict in Sri Lanka and in countless other points around the globe, intergroup tension is not a peculiarly American problem. It seems to simply be part of the human condition.

It would be wrong, though, to say that the future will be little   10
changed from the past, that Du Bois's bleak prophecy for the twentieth century will also define the new millennium. The color line is fraying all around us. The American future certainly will not be circumscribed by one long line with whites on one side and the "darker" races on the other; there will be many lines, and many camps, and few will be totally segregated. Disparities will remain. But with the rudest reminders of racism washed away, it will be a lot easier to tell ourselves that we finally have overcome.

Vocabulary/Using a Dictionary

1. What is the definition of the word *bemusement* (para. 4)? How is it different from *amusement*? What does each of the prefixes mean on its own?

2. In paragraph 6, Cose writes that "such projections forecast the growth of ethnic *cohorts* as if racial intermingling will be insignificant, when it clearly will be anything but." What does the word *cohorts* mean? Can you think of some synonyms for the word?

3. When commenting on the future of the American color line, the author remarks: "There will be many [color] lines, and many camps. . . . *Disparities* will remain" (para. 10). What is a *disparity?* What is *parity?* What does it mean when something is *disparate?*

Responding to Words in Context

1. "Latinos may consider themselves white, black, American Indian, Asian, or Pacific Islander—or *deem* themselves none of the above," comments Cose in paragraph 3. Looking at the word *deem* in this context, what do you think the word means? What may be some synonyms for the word?

2. In the conclusion to his essay, Cose states: "The color line is *fraying* all around us. The American future certainly will not be circumscribed by one long line with whites on one side and the 'darker' races on the other" (para. 10). What does the author mean in his use of the word *fraying?*

Discussing Main Point and Meaning

1. In Cose's essay, what did W. E. B. Du Bois feel was "the problem of the twentieth century" (para. 1)? Have Americans proved Du Bois wrong?

2. "The rise of the mixed-race—or *café au lait*—society has led some to predict the end of distinctions based on ethnicity, racial appearance, or ancestry," comments Cose in paragraph 5. What is Cose's take on this prediction?

3. What is the author's response to the question, "If demographic shifts will not bring about the end of race, what will?" (para. 8). Explain.

4. What does Cose predict for the future of race and racial issues in America?

Examining Sentences, Paragraphs, and Organization

1. What is gained by quoting W. E. B. Du Bois in the third sentence of Cose's essay? Is Cose showing off his learning, or is he trying to achieve some other effect?

2. What support does Cose give for his claim that "interracial romance, once outlawed and condemned, now openly blooms" (para. 2)? Do you think his support is feasible (suitable)?

3. Cose organizes the conclusion of his essay around a few questions found at the very beginning of his paragraphs: "But what happens when whites become a minority?" (para. 6), "But if demographic shifts will not bring about the end of race, what will?" (para. 8), and "So what does that mean for the future?" (para. 9). Why does the author make use of so many questions at the end of his essay? What useful purpose do these questions serve? How would you answer these questions?

Thinking Critically

1. "Racial purity is not as prized as it once was," claims Cose in paragraph 2. "People who call themselves white proudly acknowledge Latino and Native American roots. A small number even acknowledge some black ancestry." Do you agree with the author's statement? Thinking of your community at home, do you think Cose's opinion holds true?

2. In paragraph 8, the author states, "But if demographic shifts will not bring about the end of race, what will? The answer is that nothing will, not soon. Having established a more tolerant America is not the same as having established an America without racial assumptions and consequences." Do you agree with Cose, that nothing will bring about the end of race, at least not in the near future?

In-Class Writing Activities

1. In paragraph 1, Cose quotes W. E. B. Du Bois's despairing opinion of America's "homespun apartheid." Write a brief essay com-

menting on Du Bois's words, agreeing or disagreeing with the writer's opinion.

2. Freewrite some ideas about how you think your children's generation will view race and racism. How do you think race will fare in the next fifty years? Do you think we will see the end of the color line? Will you see a time when whites become a minority? Be sure to support your opinions with examples from everyday life or with evidence gathered from reading.

BRANDON ECKENRODE

The Next Frontier

[WESTERN COURIER ONLINE, WESTERN ILLINOIS UNIVERSITY/January 29, 2000]

Before You Read

Will the world be a better place in fifty years? How do you think your peers would answer this question? Are you a member of an optimistic or pessimistic generation? What do the facts of the matter say? How do you think Americans will fare in the future?

Words to Learn

frontier (para. 1): the farthermost limits of knowledge or achievement in a particular subject (n.)

dormant (para. 2): asleep; inactive (adj.)

BRANDON ECKENRODE *(b. 1978) was a junior at Western Illinois University when he became interested in the future of the human mind. Besides being an English major, Eckenrode is also a proud member of the Delta Chi fraternity.*

What will be the next frontier for the human race to explore? Generally, the answers given to this question are "outer space" or "the oceans." Yet both of these vast regions have been studied for years, and while we try to uncover the secrets of each, we may overlook another frontier much smaller and much closer to home: the human brain. Our brain is one object closer to us than anything else, but it remains distant and neglected. Any information that can be obtained about the brain will surely lead to a better understanding of human life—and of ourselves.

People should find it fascinating that parts of the brain lie dormant and have never been used by anyone. What mental functions or thought processes these unknown parts could unlock will be of enormous interest to future scientists. Whether they lead to new supplies of knowledge or they help us gain new insights into who we are, these discoveries would represent the breakthrough of the next millennium.

> *For many, it is hard to remember that the human race has not stopped evolving.*

For many, it is hard to remember that the human race has not stopped evolving. Since we have been at the top of the evolutionary ladder for so long, we have developed a superiority complex that prevents us from realizing that there is always the possibility of something or someone above us. I am not talking about a race of beings from the planet Krypton; I am speaking about people you see dragging themselves to class every morning. We have come a long way since the age of the caveman. What makes us think that we have now reached the apex of human possibility?

Who will be the ones to explore this new frontier? Who will be the next great thinkers of our era? History has always produced individuals who have expanded the boundaries of thought—Galileo, Beethoven, and Einstein are only a few of the all-time great intellectuals. The future great thinkers will probably be those who will make the landmark discoveries in the realm of the human mind. And it could be any one of us. While the world undergoes rapid technological progress, it may now be the time to rely on ourselves and put our trust in the vast potential that lies dormant within us.

Vocabulary / Using a Dictionary

1. What does Eckenrode mean when he says, "Parts of the brain lie *dormant*" (para. 2)? What other words share the same root?

Responding to Words in Context

1. In paragraph 3, Eckenrode writes: "For many, it is hard to remember that the human race has not stopped evolving." What does the author mean when he suggests that we are not done *evolving* yet? What is *evolution*?

2. "Since we have been on top of the evolutionary ladder for so long, we have developed a *superiority complex* that prevents us from realizing that there is always the possibility of something or someone above us," suggests the author in paragraph 3. What is a *superiority complex*? Describe how you think someone with a *superiority complex* would act.

Discussing Main Point and Meaning

1. According to the author, what are the two choices of frontiers that humankind has yet to unravel? Beside these two frontiers, what does Eckenrode describe as "closer to home" (para. 1)?

2. Why does Eckenrode place Einstein, Galileo, and Beethoven on the list of "all-time" greats (para. 4)? Who will be the next person(s) on that list?

3. While the world "undergoes rapid technological progress" (para. 4), what does the author feel that humans must rely on?

Examining Sentences, Paragraphs, and Organization

1. What is the topic sentence of paragraph 2? What makes this the topic sentence?

2. Who do you think is Eckenrode's audience for "The Next Frontier"? What do you think is the audience's level of education? How can you tell?

3. Eckenrode formulates an opinion with which he tries to *persuade* the reader throughout his essay. If his essay is one of *persuasion*, what is he trying to convince the reader that he or she ought to believe?

Thinking Critically

1. "For many, it is hard to remember that the human race has not stopped evolving," states Eckenrode in paragraph 3. Do you

agree with the author? Are we as human beings still evolving? Or have we reached the end of the evolutionary ladder? Are we progressing or regressing?

2.   The author mentions that there are three frontiers that humankind has yet to unravel — space, the ocean, and the human mind. Can you think of any more frontiers besides these three that humankind has yet to explore? Make sure to explain your answers.

In-Class Writing Activities

1.   "While the world undergoes rapid technological progress, it may now be the time to rely on ourselves and put our trust in the vast potential that lies dormant within us," observes Eckenrode in his conclusion (para. 4). What does he mean by "rapid technological progress"? Do you agree or disagree with the author? Why or why not? Write a short essay answering these three questions, citing specific examples to support your opinion.

2.   In paragraph 4, Eckenrode states: "History has always produced individuals who have expanded the boundaries of thought — Galileo, Beethoven, and Einstein. . . ." After this statement, the author hopes that there may be individuals in *our* age who will "make the landmark discoveries in the realm of the human mind." Do you know any of these people? Is it someone you know in your personal life? Is it some other figure? Do you believe that your generation will produce one of these figures? Freewrite an answer to these questions.

NEGATIVE POPULATION GROWTH

[1999]

Before You Read

Do you or others you know feel crowded on a daily basis? On campus? In town? Getting to and from school? Do you feel you need to compete for space and services because of increasingly crowded conditions? To what extent do you think this is a national or even a global problem? Reflect on your personal experiences—do you feel crowded? At home? School? In public places? In airports and on planes? Do you think this is a serious problem? Is it getting better or worse? Does it affect everyone's state of mind, causing impatience, anger, and hostile attitudes toward strangers?

Word to Learn

unsustainable (para. 2): incapable of being kept up or supported (adj.)

Vocabulary/Using a Dictionary

1. Look up the term *overwhelm* (para. 1) in a dictionary. What does the word suggest? Why do you think the writers of the ad copy used this term? In what contexts might this word commonly appear?

Responding to Words in Context

1. Why do you think the ad copy in paragraph 1 says, "Our suburban communities," and not simply, "Our suburbs"? Why the extra word? Is it merely redundant, or does the word *communities* contribute to the persuasive effect?

2. Why do you think the copy says in paragraph 2 "mass immigration" instead of just "immigration"? What does the word *mass* contribute to the ad's effect?

Discussing Main Point and Meaning

1. "Ask any of your neighbors . . ." The ad copy begins on a personal note. What kind of person is being addressed in the opening paragraph? Where is it assumed the person lives? Why do you think the ad does not illustrate its point with an image of a crowded city street?

2. What is the point of the road sign in the illustration? Do you think it's an official traffic sign? What does the sign suggest about the type of community that's endangered by overcrowding? Consider the sign carefully: Who do you imagine made it?

3. Does the ad copy appear more interested in the dangers of population growth as a result of birth rates or as a result of immigration rates? What reasons can you show for your answer?

Examining Details, Imagery, and Design

1. What does the ad's headline directly refer to? What is it asking the reader to "remember"? What conditions are we being asked to contrast?

2. Consider the movement of the ad's argument. What issue is addressed in the first paragraph of text? What sort of proof or

evidence is offered that suburbs are "overwhelmed by the demands of a larger population." If you read only the first paragraph, what might you blame for population growth?

3. What current issue is introduced in the second paragraph? What proof or evidence is offered to show that America will become unlivable in the near future if trends are not halted? How does the ad try to persuade you that the figures are reliable?

Thinking Critically

1. Whose interests are mostly being protected by the ad? Can you think of people or groups who will be inclined to agree with the ad? Is the ad trying to protect everyone's interest in a sustainable future? In what way does the ad associate the population issue with environmental concerns?

2. What image of America is the ad promoting? How is a sense of the past depicted verbally and visually? What is the most prominent word in the ad? In what sense does it have the impact of both a word and an image? Why do you think this design decision was made? How does that word support the general message of the ad?

In-Class Writing Activities

1. In two or three paragraphs, informally discuss your personal thoughts about overcrowding. Do you see it as a serious issue in your daily life? Or is it mainly something to worry about in the future?

2. Suppose you worked in the creative department of an ad agency and were asked by colleagues to comment on the ad. What would be your main objections? What would you suggest changing to make the ad more persuasive? What elements do you think work well?

Discussing the Unit

Suggested Topic for Discussion

All three of this unit's authors discuss the way North America will look in the future—in terms of race, gender, and intellectualism. Both Barbara Ehrenreich and Ellis Cose have optimistic conclusions to their essays on gender and race. Brandon Eckenrode's essay puts a positive spin on the subject in the hope that this generation of Americans may produce some great thinkers. Are you optimistic about the future of U.S. society? Do you give much thought to the future? Your future? In one year? Five years? Ten years or more?

Preparing for Class Discussion

1. How do you think Ellis Cose might respond to Barbara Ehrenreich's prediction, "In 2786: The new President's Inauguration will be attended by all five members of the mixed-sex, multiracial commune that raised her. . . . Peace will break out" (para. 18)?

2. How might Cose and Ehrenreich react to Brandon Eckenrode's statement: "Since we have been at the top of the evolutionary ladder for so long, we have developed a superiority complex. . . ." (para. 3)?

From Discussion to Writing

1. French mathematician and philosopher Blaise Pascal wrote in 1670: "The present is never our goal: the past and present our means: *the future alone is our goal.* Thus, we never live but we *hope* to live; and always *hoping* to be happy, it is inevitable that *we will never be so.*" Write an essay agreeing or disagreeing with what Pascal suggests in his statement, illustrating your opinion with examples from your life.

2. It has been commented that the youth of North America rarely think about the future. How do you feel about this accusation? Write an essay in which you discuss your view about the future in general and your future in particular, responding to this accusation.

3. We cannot live in America without being subject to science fiction movies and television shows such as *Star Wars* or *The X-Files.* Americans even have their own science fiction station:

the Sci-Fi Channel. Do you think that in the next fifty years some of the inventions/creations/vehicles/weapons from science fiction will be used in our everyday lives? Which ones? Write an essay describing at least two of these items, and explain why you think we will see them in the next fifty years.

Topics for Cross-Cultural Discussion

1. Are there any intellectual politicians/scholars/scientists in other countries pioneering their homelands into the future? How will that country fare in the next one hundred years? How will its progress affect the United States?

2. How are people in other countries you're familiar with educated to prepare for their futures? Is one group held more accountable for educating the young in these matters? Why?

9

Can We Resist Stereotypes?

Where do racial, ethnic, and gender stereotypes come from? Is it always wrong to base our behavior on stereotypes, or is some degree of stereotyping impossible to avoid? How do we know whether our perceptions of others are grounded in stereotypes or not? These are questions that everyone living in such a culturally diverse society as ours continually encounters.

If you saw two African American men holding hands in public, would you automatically assume they were homosexual? On a visit to South Africa, civil rights activist Bill Batson was surprised to see— as he says in his essay's title—that "In Africa, Men Hold Hands." He wonders whether this tradition could be imported to America and whether it might help eliminate the "macho posturing" that interferes with intimacy and sustains a culture of violence.

In a poor black Atlanta neighborhood, John Monczunski experiences a moment of fear that forces him to confront his own troublesome formation of stereotypes. "Am I paranoid, or prudent?" he asks himself in "Cornered."

As a young Filipino woman and a College of New Jersey student, Thea Palad has often found herself a victim of racial stereotyping. In "Fighting Stereotypes," while honestly acknowledging how difficult it is to abandon our prejudices, she finds a way to transform other people's "lack of tact" into an occasion to discover the value of her ethnic heritage. The unit concludes with an advertisement from the American Civil Liberties Union that attacks one of the uglier aspects of stereotyping—racial profiling.

BILL BATSON

In Africa, Men Hold Hands

[ESSENCE/December 1999]

Before You Read

Why are men allowed to be affectionate in some cultures but not others? Do you think it should be acceptable for men to hold hands or hug each other in public? Why or why not? Why is it acceptable in this culture for women to be affectionate but not men?

Words to Learn

squatter camp (para. 1): place where settlers have no legal claim to the land (n.)

apartheid (para. 1): official policy of racial segregation (n.)

corrugated (para. 1): ridged or wrinkled (adj.)

prospered (para. 5): to have been fortunate or successful; to have thrived (v.)

kinship (para. 7): state of being related by blood (n.)

unflinching (para. 7): showing no reaction (adj.)

familial (para. 8): pertaining to family (adj.)

veneer (para. 9): thin, hard sheet of coating, usually on furniture (n.)

evoke (para. 10): inspire; draw forth (v.)

It was my first time in a squatter camp in South Africa, so I   1
gladly took the hand of the elder as he led me along narrow unpaved
roads. My tour guide was intent on showing me the struggles the
poor were facing in the aftermath of apartheid. He led me past im-

BILL BATSON (b. 1963) *is assistant director of the New York Civil Liberties Union. For the past twenty years he has attempted to integrate his work as an artist and advocate through work as a community activist and political organizer from New York to South Africa. Batson is a contributing writer for* Essence *magazine,* Democratic Left, Cape Town Argus, *and* Sidelines Quarterly South African Journal, *among others.*

provised villas of corrugated metal and scrap wood, stopping to introduce the young children, covered in dirt from the lack of running water, to their first American visitor.

I had traveled to Africa when I was thirty-three years old, and like many young Black people, I was on a mission of discovery. For two years I would attend classes and work at a museum, while observing the growth of a new democracy. This guided tour was my first exposure to this land.

After about fifteen minutes, as the December heat of the Southern Hemisphere moistened my palms, I realized that my guide had not let go of my hand. I had been walking through an African village holding hands with a man.

In South Africa, it's common for men, young and old, to hold hands. This custom was difficult for me, as an African American from the land of the gangster pose, to comprehend at first. In my world, off the court, on the block, brothers didn't touch, and those who did were usually confined to liberated zones or the closet.

> *In my world, off the court, on the block, brothers didn't touch, and those who did were usually confined to liberated zones or the closet.*

I knew that to have a deeper experience, I would have to put aside the hype and stereotypes that many of us carry in our heads about Africa. And by doing so, I found out that African tradition is a magical thing. Each tradition carries a force through generations that has been responsible for the survival of a people under conditions that are virtually unparalleled in human history. Despite slavery, extermination campaigns, colonialism, and the outright theft of entire countries, the brothers and sisters have survived and even prospered in some places.

Confident of who they are, and caring deeply about the people who are around them, African men use their bodies, nonsexually, to express closeness and joy. I must admit that as I walked through the township with my hand being held by a male elder, surprisingly I did not feel foreign. I felt awkward because of this new attention, but not because of where I was, or for fear that I was out of place. In retrospect, I'd never felt so strong—so male.

A South African intern once tried to describe his relationship with someone to me. Finally, with some difficulty, he used a word foreign to his vocabulary: *cousin.* The closeness among people is like that of family. And I've found that there's an intense intimacy and kinship between families and extended groups who live together. That intimacy produces unflinching commitment in times of need or, in good times, the practice of men dancing together in celebration of a political or sporting victory.

Here in the United States, in a community beset with violence, in an environment of court involvement and victimization, intimacy even between blood brothers and sisters is extremely strained. On the male side, fear of intimacy can challenge our closest bonds. In Spike Lee's critically acclaimed *He Got Game,* Lee explores the relationship between a father and son. His characters twist and turn through some of the most obtuse and uptight gestures ever captured on film as they struggle to rekindle familial intimacy—a struggle true to life for too many brothers.

Could the lack of the affectionate hand of an elder man to lead a younger "brother" account for some of the aggression and violence in our communities, or explain our obsession with physical toughness? As a youth worker, I hesitated to encourage a touchy-feely approach, fearing that I might strip away the veneer of roughness that might keep a kid alive in the projects. But after living in Africa, I've begun to wonder if maybe it's that macho posturing that gets our kids killed.

It will be a long time before the sight of two African American men holding hands will do anything other than evoke homophobic slurs or uncomfortable stares. But maybe we can take lessons from overseas. They watch our Spike Lee movies in Africa, all right. And you just might find two brothers, holding hands as they exit, sharing their mixed reviews and wondering why, if we African Americans are so tough, we don't fight back against the "Man" who's coming down so hard on our communities. In Africa, many of those men holding hands were armed revolutionaries who overthrew the apartheid government. Maybe it's time we all tried a little "brotherly" tenderness.

Vocabulary / Using a Dictionary

1. Review the definition of *apartheid* (para. 1). What is the relationship between racism and apartheid? Between segregation and apartheid?

2. Do you know the adjective form of the verb *prosper* (para. 5)? If not, look it up in the dictionary. Provide the definition.

3. Use the word *evoke* (para. 10) in a sentence of your own.

Responding to Words in Context

1. What does Batson mean by the expression "gangster pose" in paragraph 4? For what image is this expression used to provide a contrast?

2. Describe Batson's interest in the word *cousin* (para. 7), used by an intern he encounters during his trip to South Africa.

3. What is meant by "the 'Man'" in paragraph 10?

Discussing Main Point and Meaning

1. How does Batson feel about holding hands with his tour guide in the African village they are visiting?

2. What connection is there between holding hands and masculinity, according to this essay? See paragraphs 6 and 10 for help.

3. What kind of argument about African American men does Batson begin to put forward in this essay?

4. What purpose does the reference to Spike Lee's *He Got Game* (para. 8) serve in this essay?

Examining Sentences, Paragraphs, and Organization

1. Where do you find the clearest articulation of Batson's main idea?

2. The last sentence of this essay is, "Maybe it's time we all tried a little 'brotherly' tenderness." What is Batson's point in this sentence? What does he suggest that "tenderness" could accomplish?

3. What is the organizing principle of this essay? In other words, is Batson's method chronological or in order of importance? From the simple to the complex or in some other way? Explain why you think Batson uses the organizing strategy you see.

Thinking Critically

1. Do you think that men in the United States try to act too "macho," as this essay suggests? On what evidence do you base your answer?

2. Is it possible that something as simple as handholding could change the culture of African American men? Or is this essay really about a larger set of social practices?

In-Class Writing Activities

1. Describe the physical and emotional relationships you observe among the men you know. Do they ever touch each other? Are they as close as "cousins"? Or do they seem to prohibit the expression of affection within their circles?

2. On a Boston subway in February 2000, a sixteen-year-old high school student from Morocco was molested, threatened with a knife, and beaten unconscious by a group of fellow students who had often seen her holding hands with her girlfriends at school. Write a short essay about how you think this girl would have been treated by other kids at your high school. Do friends ever hold hands, link arms, or kiss each other nonsexually where you're from? Why or why not? Do you think such behavior will ever be acceptable in U.S. high schools?

JOHN MONCZUNSKI

Cornered

[NOTRE DAME MAGAZINE/Spring 1999]

Before You Read

Do stereotypes sneak up on you despite your best intentions? Try to think of some specific examples of stereotypes that pop into your head without warning. Do some groups suffer from stereotyping more than others? If so, why? How can we learn to avoid stereotyping?

Words to Learn

strychnine (para. 1): a strong poison (n.)
prudent (para. 4): exercising good judgment (adj.)
paranoid (para. 6): unreasonably suspicious and mistrustful of others' intentions toward oneself (adj.)
edgy (para. 12): tense, nervous (adj.)

It was a poisonous thought, I now realize, that came to me as I set out on foot for downtown Atlanta. The hike would be easy, a breeze. Just walk down Auburn Street for ten or twelve blocks, turn right, and I'd be there, smack in the middle of Peachtree Center. But before I got very far the strychnine thought seeped through my body. *Maybe I'm in the wrong place at the wrong time.* There are consequences for that, you know.

The "wrong place/wrong time" idea first emerged earlier that morning as I gazed at the tomb of Martin Luther King Jr., who was

Jᴏʜɴ Mᴏɴᴄᴢᴜɴsᴋɪ *(b. 1947) is an associate editor of* Notre Dame Magazine. *He has received several awards for his feature writing, including the Gold Medal Award for Best Feature Article of the Year in 1997. This essay is an excerpt from Monczunski's forthcoming book,* Tale of the 'hound, *a chronicle of a month-long bus pilgrimage across the United States in search of the sacred.*

pierced by an assassin's bullet at the age of thirty-nine. My graveside meditation was colored by other events. Only days before in Jasper, Texas, a black man had been chained to a pickup truck and dragged to death by two white men. A few months earlier in Chicago, a black boy was knocked from his bicycle and brutally beaten by a group of white teenagers intent on "protecting" their neighborhood. Dr. King dreamed of a time when black and white children would join hands and walk as sisters and brothers. But for all the progress made, clearly we're not there yet. Such violence wounds us all, sometimes in ways of which we are unaware.

From King's grave I walk up Auburn Street through the poor   3
black neighborhood. Atlanta this Sunday seems as hot and deserted as when Sherman[1] tromped through town. Road tar bubbles and squeaks underfoot; hot air bounces off the pavement, rippling the city's spiky skyline like a funhouse mirror. The furnace sun has driven everyone inside except me. I trudge past silent churches and storefronts with no one in sight. The city is mine alone, or at least Auburn Street.

Like gunslingers at high noon we step relentlessly toward each other.

Then the spell breaks. Two blocks ahead a solitary figure   4
emerges from a building. He wheels around and begins walking toward me. When I see him my stomach knots. I am not sure if he is even aware of me, but I know I do not want to meet him. I decide on a tactical evasive maneuver and cross to the other side of the street. The man counters my move. Apparently he is intent on meeting me and he reestablishes our collision course. We mirror each other's movements all the while slicing the gap between us. His long-distance telegraphed intentions add to my unease. Am I paranoid or prudent?

I am, I think, a walking mugging-in-the-making. With my 35 mm   5
camera hanging around my neck, my backpack slung over my shoulder, and my shopping bag filled with T-shirts and souvenirs, I am one big bull's eye, an invitation for trouble. A stranger in a strange land. *"Rob me, why dontcha?"* my presence shouts. *Why didn't I take a cab? Let's get ready to rummmble! Lock and load.*

Maybe I *am* paranoid. Maybe it is just coincidence that he   6
switched sides of the street a step-and-a-half after I did. Maybe he just wanted to get out of the sun. But maybe not. There is, I realize,

[1]*Sherman:* Union General William Tecumseh Sherman burned Atlanta in his campaign to defeat the Confederacy in the U.S. Civil War.

no more shade here than there. Like gunslingers at high noon we step relentlessly toward each other. He has zeroed in like a slow-moving cruise missile and is intent to intercept. About a half-block away I see he is about forty, and wears a dirty, battered black baseball cap, a checkered long-sleeve shirt, and rumpled khaki pants. He also clutches something in one hand.

We are about to pass—maybe we won't even acknowledge each other—then he pivots and falls in step with me. What *is* he up to? What is this about? I look at him closely for any threatening moves, remembering the time I once was robbed at knifepoint at a deserted edge of Chicago's Loop. I have just broken the first commandment of big-city survival: "Thou shalt never make eye contact with a stranger." 7

"Afternoon," he says, an odd grin creasing his face. My eyes dart around to see if anyone will witness this encounter, but Auburn Street remains a people-free zone. "Hope you enjoyed your visit to the King Center," he gestures to the name printed on my shopping bag of "nonviolence" souvenirs. We continue walking in my direction and the man shoves a flier in my hand. He says, "My name's Brother Marvin and we're tryin' to raise some money for a demonstration to inspire the young people of Atlanta. We hope you could help out with a donation of whatever you could spare." 8

If nothing else this is a novel panhandling ploy. More imaginative than, "Hey mister, could you spare fifty cents for a cup of coffee?" I have my doubts, but I say, "Oh sure," and fish in my pocket for a dollar bill. There are several bills in my pocket, I know—a couple of singles, a twenty, and a ten. I'd rather he not know that I am carrying all that cash. I hope the bill my hand eventually pulls out is a single. I hand it over, relieved to see Washington's portrait on the crumpled green slip of paper. 9

Brother Marvin accepts my donation, but to my unease he doesn't go away. Stride for stride he sticks with me and I can tell from his pinched expression that the offering isn't satisfying. "Uhhh . . . we were lookin for a minimum of a two dollar donation," he says with an edge. 10

My eyes dart around again, but still we are alone. "Oh sure, okay," I reply as I fish again in my pocket for what I hope is the other single. I am uncertain what will happen next. If my hand dishes up the twenty, will he drop the panhandler persona and forcibly demand the rest of my stuff? I hand over another single. "Thank you kindly," Brother Marvin says. Before I can reply he has peeled off from our 11 two-man formation. He crosses the street and lopes away. A few seconds later I turn around, but by now he has vanished, melting back into one of the buildings.

The encounter leaves me oddly shaken. I wasn't robbed. At best I   12
had made a contribution to a worthy cause; at worst a contribution to the fund to replenish Brother Marvin's alcohol. But would I have been so edgy if Brother Marvin were white? Would he have sought me out so relentlessly if I were black? My answers, shaped by poison, trouble me.

Vocabulary / Using a Dictionary

1. What do you think it means to call someone a *prude*? List some other words that share the same root. How are they similar and different?

2. The word *edgy* (para. 12) comes out of the idiomatic, or slang, expression *on edge*. How do you think this expression relates to the more literal meaning of *edge*? Monczunski also describes Brother Marvin's voice as having "an edge" (para. 10). What does that mean? How does that expression relate to the other two?

3. *Paranoid* (para. 4) comes from the Greek for "beyond reason." Are the author's actions "beyond reason" in your opinion?

Responding to Words in Context

1. Look at the words in paragraph 4: *tactical evasive maneuver, counters, reestablishes,* and *collision course*. What do these words have in common? What sort of interaction do they suggest? How does this suggestion help to characterize the narrator?

2. Discuss the significance of the phrase *lock and load* in paragraph 5.

Discussing Main Point and Meaning

1. Why do you think the title of this article is "Cornered"? How does it relate to the general themes expressed in the text? Do you think it is an appropriate title? What other titles can you think of?

2. What is the purpose of this article? Is there an argument under the surface of the story? If so, what is it?

3. How would the story change if it were told from Brother Marvin's point of view?

Examining Sentences, Paragraphs, and Organization

1. How do the two incidents (which took place in Jasper and Chicago) described in paragraph 2 contribute to the author's purpose? Why does he discuss them before telling you his own story?

2. What does the author mean when he says that "there are consequences for that, you know" in paragraph 1? What is the "that" the sentence refers to—being in the wrong place or having a poisonous thought? Explore the ramifications of each possibility.

3. The use of *poison* in the first and last paragraphs emphasizes the sense that some external substance has caused the author's thinking. What is that substance? Is it external? Why does it frame the story so emphatically?

Thinking Critically

1. Do you think that the author learned anything from his experience? Do you think he would behave the same way in a similar situation as a result of this one? Explain your answer.

2. In paragraph 5, the author says his presence shouts, *"Rob me!"* Is this true? Do you think having a camera and souvenirs is so unusual? Since he is near a national monument (Martin Luther King Jr.'s tomb), do you think his presence is an "invitation to trouble," as he says? Or is it more likely a common sight? Why do you think he sees himself as being a "bull's eye"?

In-Class Writing Activities

1. Rewrite the story of Monczunski and Brother Marvin's exchange from Brother Marvin's point of view, and then again from the point of view of an outside observer. How does perspective determine the tone and detail of a story?

2. In a brief essay, discuss an encounter you have had with a stranger or an unfamiliar situation that unsettled you. Was your unease justified, or did it turn out to be based on "paranoia"?

THEA PALAD

Fighting Stereotypes

[THE CYBERSIGNAL, THE COLLEGE OF NEW JERSEY/January 24, 2000]

Before You Read

How do stereotypes affect relationships? How can a person learn to embrace her identity in the face of stereotyping?

Words to Learn

dumbstruck (para. 1): shocked into silence; unable to reply verbally (adj.)

consorted (para. 2): associated; kept company with (v.)

harbored (para. 3): kept nourished; protected (v.)

ubiquitous (para. 3): everywhere; omnipresent (adj.)

elusive (para. 3): avoiding one's grasp (physical or mental) (adj.)

alleged (para. 4): asserted but unproven (adj.)

gracious (para. 6): warmly courteous (adj.)

revere (para. 8): regard with awe (v.)

revel (para. 8): take great pleasure in something (v.)

pretense (para. 8): practiced false appearance (n.)

One day during my sophomore year of high school, a girl named Katie asked me, "How does your mother feel about your being in an interracial relationship?" For a moment, I was dumbstruck. *I* was in an interracial relationship? It had never occurred to me that others thought of me as, well, *different*. My skin was darker, sure. My hair was straighter than straight. My nose was small and flat. Yes, I was different.

1

THEA PALAD *(b. 1979) wrote this piece for the College of New Jersey's* CyberSignal *when she was a sophomore studying journalism. Palad's ultimate goal is to become a television news anchor. This essay is a result of her reassessment of her identity—"It's a terrible thing to be ashamed of who you are," she says.*

But it was difficult for me to comprehend how people today   2
could still focus on the shape of my eyes and the texture of my hair. I
mean, wasn't that politically incorrect? I spoke with no accent (outside of my New Jersey accent, of course). I dressed like everyone else.
I listened to the same music, watched the same television programs,
read the same books and magazines. All my friends were white.
Couldn't everyone see? I wasn't one of those "fresh off the boat"
students (FOBs, as we routinely called them)—kids who had just arrived from other countries and only con-
sorted with people of the same nationality. FOBs spoke in their native tongues in
the hallway between classes, and that an-
noyed everybody. Couldn't people see I
wasn't like that? No, people didn't see.

> But it was difficult for
> me to comprehend how
> people today could still
> focus on the shape of my
> eyes and the texture of
> my hair.

I suppose that my attitude towards   3
being a Filipino woman was never quite
healthy. When I was fresh off the boat myself at the age of five, I was quick to say,
"I'm not Filipino, I'm New York." It should be understood that in the
Philippines, everybody harbored the dream of going to America and
of one day becoming an American. People looked at you with a bit
more respect if you could speak English. The sight of my mom returning home from the States with packages full of American things threw
us kids into a frenzy. When I was younger, my cousins and I would
put clothespins on our noses, trying to get them to look more western.
In the Philippines, the American Dream was ubiquitous—and elusive.

Despite the fact that I was born and raised in the Philippines, I   4
would never have guessed that people saw me as different from my
Caucasian friends until that day during sophomore year. Earlier,
when I lived in a predominantly black community, I was the "white"
girl. So, of course, it really put me into a panic when Katie asked me
about my alleged interracial relationship.

Years later, I can't help but appreciate Katie's lack of tact and   5
disregard for political correctness. If it wasn't for her comment, I
would never have recognized that I was different, and I would never
have learned to celebrate that difference. Today, I consider being a
minority a blessing. Sure, there's the obvious stuff. You get special
opportunities for being a minority, like scholarships, jobs, intern-
ships, and you can be a part of interest groups. But there's the painful
part: the ethnic jokes, the stereotyping, the prejudices, the initial embarrassment of being a teenager and "different."

At twelve, it horrified me to no end that my friends would dis-   6
cover I ate rice three times a day. At seventeen, I was offended by the
man who interviewed me from Dartmouth, when he commended me
on how wonderfully I had acquired "his language." (Thirteen years in
a country will do that for you.) At eighteen, I encountered another
gracious individual while volunteering with a local Mobile Meals.
"Oh, you guys deliver?" I was asked in an elevator heading for the
eighth floor. I responded with, "Um, yeah, Meals on Wheels delivers."
"Oh, I thought you were from the Chinese food place," he said, getting off at the seventh floor. Recently, a cafeteria worker attempted to
speak to me in Korean; he assumed I was an exchange student.

Experiences like these make you stronger, force you to face your   7
heritage; it forces you to make a choice: accept it and defend it, or
deny it. I opted for the former. To do this, I have to fight stereotypes.
And it is difficult. Stereotypes exist for a reason, and prejudices die
hard. Some people assume that I'm good at math simply because I'm
Asian (or Pacific Islander, if you want to get technical). Some assume
I'm a bad driver. It's amazing how many people think that you're
predisposed to excel at certain things and be a failure at others simply
because of race. The color of my skin doesn't enhance my ability to
solve a differential equation. The texture of my hair doesn't deter me
from successfully switching lanes.

I suppose it would be an impossible objective, trying to convince   8
everyone to abandon their racial prejudices. And I'll be the first to
admit that I have yet to abandon my own. One thing is certain, however. I have learned to revere my heritage. I revel in the richness of
the blood that courses through my veins from the mother who gave
me my nose and the great-grandfather who gave me my smile. I have
learned to celebrate my history, and to refrain from hiding behind
fear or pretense. I will no longer allow the integrity of my background to be compromised by the ignorance of others. I'm not New
York. I'm Filipino.

Vocabulary / Using a Dictionary

1. The noun *harbor* means a protected place (often for boats). How
    does it relate to the verb form used in paragraph 3?

2. What does *ubiquitous* (para. 3) mean? Can you use it in a sen-
    tence of your own?

3. Can you think of any synonyms for *revere* (para. 8)?

Responding to Words in Context

1. What does Palad mean when she says that it's "politically incorrect" to remark on the physical differences of others (para. 2)?

2. Why do you suppose kids in the black community Palad lived in referred to her as the "'white' girl" (para. 4)?

3. What is the irony in Palad's being mistaken for a delivery person from a Chinese restaurant (para. 6)?

Discussing Main Point and Meaning

1. Why does Katie's question about interracial dating leave Palad "dumbstruck" (para. 1)? How does she come to be grateful for the girl's "lack of tact" (para. 5)?

2. Describe the significance of Palad's Dartmouth College interview.

3. What are the stereotypes of Asians or "Pacific Islanders" that Palad has to contend with? Do you know of others?

4. Describe what you perceive to be Palad's feelings about her looks throughout the essay.

Examining Sentences, Paragraphs, and Organization

1. Examine the contradiction in paragraph 5. How is the main point of the paragraph made through this contradiction?

2. Analyze the title of this essay. How does it set up the main theme?

3. How is this essay organized in general? Is the author narrating a story? Analyzing a problem? Comparing and contrasting two things? Explain your answer.

Thinking Critically

1. Palad and her friends referred to new immigrants to the United States as "FOBs," or "'fresh off the boat' students." Is this not an example of the very stereotyping Palad criticizes?

2. Palad's remark that "I'm not Filipino, I'm New York," changes eventually to "I'm not New York. I'm Filipino." Can't she be both? How do you refer to your ethnic background?

In-Class Writing Activities

1. Can you remember the first time you noticed that there were ethnic differences among your schoolmates and yourself? Describe your early lessons in ethnic difference or stereotyping.

2. What do you think the benefits and the drawbacks are to interracial dating and/or marriage? Write a short essay describing which aspects (positive or negative) you think outweigh the others.

AMERICAN CIVIL LIBERTIES UNION

[2000]

Before You Read

Would you think a police officer is more or less likely to pull over an automobile driver if he or she is black or white? Should dark skin color be a cause for suspicion, if someone is "driving a nice car"? Do you think there should be laws implemented that police officers must follow when pulling over a driver? Do police officers need to have a reason to pull you over?

Words to Learn

solely (para. 1): exclusively; only (adv.)

courier (para. 2): messenger; dispatch rider (n.)

humiliating (para. 2): shaming; disgracing; embarrassing (adj.)

manhandled (para. 2): pushed; shoved; jostled (v.)

civil liberties: freedom from governmental interference (as with the right of free speech) as guaranteed by the Bill of Rights (n.)

Let me ask you something... Should "Driving While Black" be a crime?

This is not a trick question. On highways all over this country, cars are being stopped by the police solely because of the driver's skin color. Dark skin color by itself is a cause for suspicion.

On I-95 if you're black and driving a nice car, you fit a so-called "drug courier profile." In one ACLU lawsuit challenging this practice, we found that of the millions of people who travel I-95, only 20 per cent are black. Yet, according to police statistics, about 70 per cent of those pulled over and searched are black. All over the country thousands of innocent people - including Members of Congress, prominent athletes and actors, lawyers, police officers, business leaders and their families - have been hauled out of their cars and subjected to humiliating roadside searches by police and drug-sniffing dogs. Some have been handcuffed and manhandled before being let go.

Thirty-five years ago, people were being lynched in this country because of the color of their skin. Obviously, legal and moral progress has been made since then. But is it enough?

Think about it.

Ira Glasser
Executive Director of the American Civil Liberties Union
125 Broad Street
New York, New York 10004
www.aclu.org

Vocabulary / Using a Dictionary

1. What is the definition of the word *courier?* What, then, would be a *drug courier?*

2. In paragraph 2, the advertisement states: "Some [innocent people] have been handcuffed and *manhandled* before being let go." What does *manhandled* mean in this context?

3. The advertisement you read was sponsored by the American Civil Liberties Union. What is the function of the ACLU?

Discussing Main Point and Meaning

1. What profile do you fit on I-95 if you're black and driving a nice car? What other statistics does the ACLU's advertisement offer the reader?

2. What was happening in our country thirty-five years ago? According to the advertisement, have we made legal and moral progress since then?

3. What is the purpose of the first line of the advertisement: "Let me ask you something . . . Should 'Driving While Black' be a crime?" What effect should it have on the reader?

Examining Details, Imagery, and Design

1. What effect does it create for this ad to have a primarily black background with white text, only broken by a white box with black text on the bottom of the page? Is this effect intentional?

2. The headline of the advertisement begins "Let me ask you something . . ." Who is speaking here? What could the writer have meant by using this technique?

Thinking Critically

1. The ACLU's advertisement states: "On highways all over this country, cars are being stopped by the police solely because of the driver's skin color. Dark skin color by itself is a cause for suspicion." Do you believe that this statement is true? Is this occurring "all over" America? Or is this statement too general?

2. After discussing the problems that America is encountering with "Driving While Black," the ACLU's advertisement compares this form of discrimination with lynching (mob execution without

legal sanction). Do you find the comparison between "Driving While Black" and lynching a bit extreme? Or is the ACLU justified in its evaluation?

In-Class Writing Activities

1. Have you ever been treated poorly based on the way you look? Were you wearing something that made you stand out? Were you acting in a certain way that you found appropriate, but someone else (perhaps an adult) found to be inappropriate? How did that make you feel? In a brief essay, describe a situation from your own life, and explain the feelings you had after reflecting upon that situation.

2. The beginning of the final paragraph of the ACLU's advertisement reads: "Thirty-five years ago, people were being lynched in this country because of the color of their skin. Obviously, legal and moral progress has been made since then. But is it enough?" In a freewrite, answer the final question asked by the ACLU. Is the legal and moral progress America has made in the last thirty-five years enough for us to be satisfied? Do we need more progress? How much progress has there been?

Discussing the Unit

Suggested Topic for Discussion

Does the title of this unit ask a sincere question or a rhetorical question to which everyone already knows the answer? Do you resist stereotypes? When you are in a new place, do you rely on superficial information to understand your own alienation? When you try to explain your own behavior, do you find you must do that *against* the prevailing social notions of who you are? Can we be forgiven these "accidents," or should we be working harder to undo these conditioned instincts? This unit brings many such questions to mind.

Preparing for Class Discussion

1. John Monczunski and Thea Palad both discuss the role that stereotyping plays in North American culture. Bill Batson is interested in ways of reversing the effects of stereotyping. Which do you think is a more important social concern: figuring out how

stereotypes develop, or finding antidotes to their effects? Explain
your answer.

2. The theme of personal insecurity plays an important role in each
of these pieces. Explain how stereotyping and insecurity are related, in your opinion.

From Discussion to Writing

1. Building on your answer to the previous question, and drawing
from these articles for evidence and illustration, write an essay
that tries to explain how a person's race can affect his or her self-
perception. How does something other people physically "see" in
you become something you mentally "see" in yourself?

2. Write a letter from the point of view of one of the unit's authors
to another one. Try to use the same tone and logical method
found in the author's article, and refer to incidents discussed in
the article if necessary.

3. Write an essay that attempts to define the relationship between
race and identity in the United States, using all three of these essays as evidence and illustration. What conclusions can you draw
about race in America that would incorporate the thinking of all
of these writers? Does the definition of "American" automatically have a racial component, or does American identity tran-
scend race? Is racial identity complicated by North American culture, or does race trump culture?

Topics for Cross-Cultural Discussion

1. How does race define social identity in other cultures? Does it
create boundaries, alliances, or conflicts? Does racial difference
seem to matter more or less in other countries than it does in the
United States?

2. Because Thea Palad immigrated to the United States from the
Philippines, she may have a different perspective on the American
"race question" than do other writers in this unit. What do you
think? Is it easier or harder to understand the importance of race
in American society when one has a connection to, or comes
from, another country?

10

Affirmative Action Programs — Are They Still Needed?

Affirmative action—selecting members of groups that traditionally have faced discrimination and providing them with educational and employment opportunities—has been a hotly contested policy since 1978, when the U.S. Supreme Court ruled in a landmark case that universities are entitled to consider race as a factor in admissions. Proponents of affirmative action argue that the program, though it may be imperfect, remains the only way to ensure that minorities are fairly represented in business, government, and education. Opponents, however, say that using race as a factor in deciding who receives educational and job opportunities can lead to "reverse discrimination" and other unfair policies. The student debate over affirmative action has intensified since California's passage of Proposition 209, which bans the use of race or ethnicity in the state's public college admissions. The controversial referendum was passed in November 1996 and went into effect in 1998.

Responding to the desire of colleges to admit more qualified African American, Hispanic, and low-income students, the Educational Testing Service (ETS) recently proposed an "affirmative action" program of its own that would deal with the disparity of SAT scores among various groups by offering colleges information that would help them adjust the scores depending on a number of significant background factors. Thus, a student from an educationally disadvantaged background who scores a combined 1000 on the SATs would be equivalent to a more privileged student who scores a 1200. The "adjustments," which ETS called a "Strivers" score, took some fourteen factors into account and were offered only as an option to colleges who might find them useful. ETS never implemented the plan, which nevertheless raised considerable controversy. One of the most illuminating debates on the merits of the idea was carried out in the pages of *The New Republic* by two prominent authorities on the topic of affirmative action. In "Should the SAT Account for Race?" Nathan Glazer and Abigail Thernstrom offer succinct opposing arguments in response to the ETS proposal.

Nowhere is the controversy over affirmative action more heated than on campuses where students — perhaps already affected by affirmative action programs when they applied to college — prepare for a job market where such policies may play a large role in determining their career opportunities. A perfect example of the way the controversy has played on campus can be found in opposing views from the University of Rochester's *Campus Times,* which asks, "What Should We Do about Affirmative Action?" Should we "End It," as Daniel Berkowitz argues in an opinion column, or "Keep It," as Anya Lakner recommends in an angry letter of response?

OPPOSING VIEWS

The End of Meritocracy: Should the SAT Account for Race?

Before You Read

The Educational Testing Service, known as ETS, the creator of the SAT (Scholastic Aptitude Test), recently proposed a plan to adjust a student's score based on socioeconomic background and race. Do you think the SATs should be adjusted in this way? Is this an effective method of aiding students who are at a disadvantage? Is this an effective way to promote affirmative action? Should it be the responsibility of those who create these tests to aid the disadvantaged students, or should it be the responsibility of the college admission boards?

Words to Learn [Glazer]

mollified (para. 2): soothed the temper of; pacified (v.)

benign (para. 4): good-natured; kindly (adj.)

berate (para 7): to scold or rebuke severely (v.)

subterfuge (para. 9): any plan, action, or device used to hide one's true objective (n.)

disproportionate (para. 10): not proportionate; not in proportion (adj.)

Words to Learn [Thernstrom]

demographic (para. 2): characteristic of a population (i.e., age, sex, etc.) (adj.)

obfuscating (para. 3): clouding over; obscuring (v.)

imprimatur (para. 4): license or permission to publish or print a book, article, and so on (n.)

preferential (para. 5): designated as receiving preference (adj.)

affluent (para. 8): wealthy (adj.)

matriculants (para. 10): persons who have enrolled (especially in a college or university) (n.)

leveling (para. 14): making even; well balanced (v.)

NATHAN GLAZER

Yes

[THE NEW REPUBLIC/September 27, 1999]

This month, the Educational Testing Service (ETS), creator and   1
marketer of the SAT—the most widely used test of academic ability
and the key measure that colleges and universities take into account

---

NATHAN GLAZER *(b. 1924) is professor emeritus at the Harvard Graduate School of Education and coeditor of* The Public Interest. *An authority on issues of race, immigration, urban development, and social policy, Glazer has been granted honorary degrees by a number of colleges and universities. He is also a contributing editor of* The New Republic.

when making admissions decisions — announced that it is developing a "Strivers" score, an adjustment of the SAT score to take into account a student's socioeconomic background and race, increasing the scores of those whose socioeconomic background or race is considered to put them at a disadvantage. Colleges and universities will be able to use the new Strivers score, if they wish, in making their admissions decisions. The ETS will offer institutions both a "race-blind" model, which includes only social, economic, and educational factors, and a model that also takes into account race — that is, whether the applicant is black, Hispanic, or Native American. ETS's chief competitor, the American College Testing Program, which produces a test used by many institutions instead of the SAT, will be developing a similar model.

Clearly, these developments are a response to the crumbling of   2
the legal support that colleges and universities have relied upon to justify the almost universal practice among selective institutions of giving some kind of preference to black and Hispanic students. And, just as surely, critics of racial preference in college admissions will not be mollified by the new Strivers score and other, similar new strategies. If the formula using race is factored into admissions decisions, the new procedure will be just as legally vulnerable as the existing formal or informal preferences for race that have been struck down by a federal appeals court ruling in a University of Texas case and are now being challenged in an important University of Michigan case. Nor, one would think, would the new approach survive in the courts of the states — California and Washington — where popular referenda have forbidden the states and their agencies, including colleges and universities, to take race into account when making admissions decisions.

And, if the Strivers score without the race factor is used, present   3
statistical patterns show that it will be less effective in identifying black students who may qualify for admission than the score that includes race as part of the formula. For race is indeed a factor in reducing test scores, independent of family wealth, education, and the other socioeconomic factors. It has a particularly strong independent effect in reducing scores for blacks, and, for most institutions, increasing the number of black students is a higher priority than increasing the number of Hispanic students.

What is most striking about the development of the Strivers score   4
is the evidence it gives us of the strength of the commitment to maintaining a higher number of black and Hispanic students in selective

institutions than would qualify on the basis of academic promise alone. It is not only the testing agencies that show this commitment. They are, after all, responding to their customers, the educational institutions, whose presidents and administrations universally support racial preference in admissions. They may call it "diversity," a softer and more benign term, but what diversity in practice means is more blacks than they would admit under admissions procedures that didn't take race into account. Writing in *National Review*, Stephan Thernstrom, a strong critic of racial preferences, informs us with disapproval that "[William] Bowen and [Derek] Bok argue [in their study of racial preference *The Shape of the River*] that administrators barred from using racial double-standards in admissions will elect to lower standards for all applicants so as to secure enough non-Asian minorities in the student body."

While this is not quite their position—it is, rather, that administrators will do what they can to maintain the number of black students even when legal bans on taking race into account exist—the fact is that it is not administrators alone who will do this in the effort to evade the clear effect of the elimination of race preference. The Texas legislature voted that the state university should consider the top 10 percent of the graduating class of every Texas high school eligible for the state university, a far more radical lowering of the standards for eligibility than any university administrator would have proposed.

Even more remarkably, the Regents of the University of California, who had earlier voted that race could not be taken into account in admissions decisions, have voted that the top 4 percent of the graduates of every California high school should be eligible for admissions to the state university system! The Texas and California actions both radically expand the number of black and Hispanic students eligible for the state universities, for in both states there are many high schools almost exclusively Hispanic and black in composition that would not be capable of producing students eligible for the top branches of the state university without the new policies.

The faculties of colleges and universities have not played much of a role in all this. Faculty members critical of racial preferences berate their colleagues for not speaking up—indeed, faculty members rarely speak up when a controversial issue does not affect them directly. But recent surveys show that the critics of racial preference will not get much support from university faculties. Although a recent survey of 34,000 faculty members conducted by the Higher Education Research Institute of the University of California at Los Angeles does not ask the racial preference question directly, it does ask whether "promoting diversity leads to the admission of too many underprepared students." Only 28 percent of respondents agreed. And 90.5 percent of respondents agreed with the following statement, admittedly not much more controversial than arguing the virtues of motherhood: "A racially/ethnically diverse student body enhances the educational experience of all students."

Thus college and university faculty and administrators, state   8
legislatures, and the ruling political bodies in charge of public universities all seem to have a commitment to maintaining the number of black and Hispanic students receiving higher education, and, bluntly, are willing to take evasive action to do it. They will use substitutes for race—and, if one substitute does not work, they will look for others. If focusing on applicants who live in a poor neighborhood doesn't help—perhaps there are too many Asians in one poor California neighborhood or another—they will try focusing on applicants who live in housing projects. One way or another, the commitment to enrolling more blacks than would qualify based on academic criteria alone will be pursued.

> *We are all, in principle, in favor of a race-blind society, and clearly that is an important principle, one that we all hope to realize in time.*

I believe this commitment, however cloaked in subterfuge it may   9
be, is a valid one. True, it has been clear from the beginning of affirmative action that the majority of the American population—and even a very substantial part of the black population—does not like the idea of making an individual's fate dependent on his or her race or ethnic background. We are all, in principle, in favor of a race-blind society, and clearly that is an important principle, one that we all hope to realize in time. But it has turned out that the use of strict race-blind admissions procedures will radically reduce the number of black students, and in lesser measure the number of Hispanic students, in the selective institutions of higher education—key institutions of our society. This can only serve to further divide non-Asian minorities and whites and to further postpone the day when we can achieve a truly race-blind, fully integrated society. And this is simply too high a price to pay for adhering to the principle of race-blind admissions today.

If, then, one accepts that admitting more non-Asian minorities   10
than would make the cut through academic criteria alone is a legiti-

mate goal, the Strivers score is not such a terrible way to achieve it. The new score, which is simply an adjustment of the actual SAT score, is based on the common observation that students from wealthier and more educated families, from well-to-do suburbs, from high schools with better students, and the like, will on average do better on the SAT than students from poorer and less-educated families and from worse high schools—the circumstances of a disproportionate number of minorities. It stands to reason that a student from a materially and educationally impoverished environment who does fairly well on the SAT and better than other students who come from a similar environment is probably stronger than the unadjusted score indicates. In the past, those colleges and universities whose admissions staffs and procedures permitted individual evaluation of applications took such factors into account informally. With the new Strivers score, they will have a statistical tool that includes no fewer than fourteen characteristics that are expected to affect SAT scores. It will, of course, be up to individual institutions to decide whether they want to make use of the Strivers adjustment, just as individual institutions now determine how much weight the SAT score should have in the admissions decision. Still, the Strivers score may make what was essentially an intuitive system more rational.

Of course, there's a strong possibility that it may not survive the inevitable legal challenges. It also remains to be seen just how effective the new approach will be at maintaining or increasing the number of black and Hispanic students in our colleges and universities. For instance, it's possible that the main effect may be instead to increase the number of Asians, in which case the effectiveness of the Strivers adjustment would undoubtedly be reviewed. 11

But even if the Strivers score approach does not succeed, its introduction has highlighted the need for institutions under legal attack to improve the informal and messy procedures that they have been using to raise their enrollment of minority students. Perhaps we can bury the overt emphasis on race while trying to reach the same objective; perhaps race can become the dirty little secret we are trying to take account of without directly saying so. Hypocrisy in the matter may be no minor gain. But it is clear that, for some time, if we are to maintain the appearance of being one nation when by many measures we are, in fact, two, a pure race-blind policy will be so strongly resisted that racial preference will by some means prevail. 12

ABIGAIL THERNSTROM

No

[THE NEW REPUBLIC/September 27, 1999]

The educational testing service (ETS) calls them "strivers." They could just as well be called the "but for" kids: kids who would have done better on their SATs *but for* . . . their racial or ethnic identities, their families' income, the quality of their schools, and so forth. Or so ETS believes. These and other circumstances call for college admissions officers to treat these students' scores differently than they otherwise would, the company suggests. Never mind that selective colleges already take such factors into account when weighing student applications. That inevitably subjective process is inadequate, ETS apparently believes. Schools with high admissions standards need further instruction and a tool to help read scores properly. "A combined score of 1000 on the SATs is not always a 1000," Anthony Carnevale, an ETS vice president who heads the Strivers project, has said. "When you look at a striver who gets a 1000, you're looking at someone who really performs at a 1200."

The students ETS has in mind are those who have done better than their demographic profile would predict. Carnevale suggests the low score is, in effect, a false negative, but ETS has evidently decided to leave the actual process of readjusting scores up to the schools themselves. It will provide the unadjusted score and a statistical formula that colleges can use to convert it to the Strivers number, should they so choose.

Or so it seems. In the wake of negative press, the company released an obfuscating memo denying any current "program or service based upon the Strivers research." But it did not rule out offering

ABIGAIL THERNSTROM *(b. 1936) is a senior fellow at the Manhattan Institute in New York and a member of the Massachusetts State Board of Education, a post to which she was appointed in 1995. She is currently working with her husband, Stephan Thernstrom, on a new book,* Getting the Answers Right: The Racial Gap in Academic Achievement and How to Close It.

a "program or service" once its final report is completed—in about two months. "Researchers" have been "studying the effect of considering additional background information" in order to "provide a richer context for candidates' scores," the memo explained. "ETS is committed to continuing a dialogue about fairness and equity in higher education."

That ongoing "dialogue" has largely been prompted, of course, 4 by the end of the use of racial preferences in admissions decisions in public higher education in Texas, California, and Washington state. Although University of Michigan President Lee Bollinger recently declared diversity to be "as vital as teaching Shakespeare or mathematics," the University of Michigan's own race-based admissions processes will soon be on trial in a federal district court. Suits against other elite colleges (all of which sort students on the basis of race and ethnicity) are sure to follow. But ETS may be riding to the schools' partial rescue with a formula that gives a pseudo-scientific imprimatur to setting lower SAT standards for "disadvantaged" students.

ETS broadens the definition of disadvantage beyond race and 5 ethnicity and is said to be working on two formulas. One will factor in race. The other will reportedly focus on only such variables as the employment status of the student's mother and the kinds of electrical appliances and number of books in the student's home, as reported— accurately or inaccurately—by the student. Thus, the University of California and the handful of other schools that are no longer allowed to make race-based admissions decisions will be able to use it. A formal acknowledgment that disadvantage comes in all colors and many forms would certainly be a step forward. But not a very big one. Expanding the universe of preferential admits does not solve the basic problem. ETS is simply adding more variables to a victimology index and reinforcing the already-too-widespread belief that demography is destiny. And once you start factoring in variables that lead to disadvantage, where do you stop? Should you take into account an applicant's birth order? Her relationship with her parents? The psychologists haven't even gotten into the act yet.

Of course, literally no one believes that SAT scores alone should 6 determine who gets into which schools. And, in fact, no college entirely ignores the "context" that ETS wants to stress. But does ETS really want high schools telling a black kid in the Bronx that no one expects him to do as well as the Vietnamese immigrant in his class? Should a teacher say to a white student from a low-income family,

"I'll count your C in math as an A. You come to the test with a disadvantage; I understand"?

Across the nation, states are getting serious about promoting   7
high academic standards in their elementary and secondary schools.
But, in Massachusetts and elsewhere, anti-testing voices have argued
that it is simply unfair to expect suburban
skills in urban schools with high concen-
Should a teacher say to a   trations of non-Asian minority kids.
white student from a   Teachers, critics say, are being asked to
low-income family, "I'll   achieve the impossible. Moreover, the Of-
count your C in math as   fice of Civil Rights in the U.S. Department
an A. You come to the   of Education has recently weighed in with
test with a disadvantage;   an attack on all high-stakes testing as po-
I understand"?   tentially discriminatory.

Without doubt, school is easier for   8
children who grow up in affluent and edu-
cated households. And yet, without tough tests and uniformly high
expectations, the academic performance of black and Hispanic children—which, on average, is woefully behind that of whites and
Asians—is unlikely to improve. ETS is proposing to send the worst
possible message to these kids: If you start out in life with less, we expect less of you—today, tomorrow, maybe forever. The die has been
cast. The fix is in.

The students who meet high academic expectations in the kinder-   9
garten-through-twelfth-grade years are likely to do well on the SATs,
and for most students those tests are excellent predictors of how they
will fare in college. As a consequence (as Carnevale surely knows), a
score of 1000 is simply not the same as 1200; the lower-scoring student is less academically prepared. Even a score of 1200 means a
rough academic ride for students at universities such as Princeton and
Stanford, where the median SAT score exceeds 1400.

If elite schools want to become nonselective, or if they want to   10
choose their matriculants randomly from the pool of applicants with
scores over, say, 1000, who could object on grounds of principle?
Needless to say, their fancy professors and devoted alumni might not
like the idea. The physics professor who is a Nobel laureate generally
wants to teach high-powered students, and the alumni like the prestige that accompanies highly selective admissions. A more random
system would let in plenty of strivers, but the schools themselves
would change. Students who were less prepared would require less

rigorous courses—unless the colleges suddenly became willing to flunk them out.

ETS is obviously trying to suggest otherwise. Strivers (by definition) have tried harder and thus can do as well as the kid with the much higher SAT, the testing service implies. The disadvantaged student with a score of 1000 will do just as well as the privileged one who got 1200. 11

Well, maybe, in some cases. But the notion rests on a questionable assumption—namely that a score of 1000, when it beats a racial or other group norm, represents extraordinary effort. That may not be the case. Perhaps the student from an impoverished family who seems to have beaten the SAT odds is simply good at taking standardized tests. Or perhaps her parents have intangible qualities that the ETS formula has failed to capture. It is even possible that she didn't try hard enough—that she is underperforming relative to her intellectual gifts. Her score may reflect academic talent, not hard work. In fact, if ETS is serious about finding the kids who really "strive," it might make much more sense to look at grade point averages, adjusted for the difficulty of the courses taken. Arguably, it is the student with a low SAT score but a high GPA who has demonstrated dedication and perseverance—true grit. 12

In addition, there is no evidence that students who outscore peers with the same demographic characteristics will experience exceptional intellectual growth in college. In general, for unknown reasons, black students, for instance, earn substantially lower grades in college than their SATs would lead us to predict. (This is one of the buried but depressing facts contained in William Bowen and Derek Bok's pro-affirmative-action book, *The Shape of the River*.) Another recent study, which focused on University of San Diego undergraduates, looked not only at blacks and Hispanics but also at the records of students who attended impoverished high schools, came from low-income families, or lived in neighborhoods with few college graduates. These disadvantaged youths also underperformed, by the measure of their SAT scores. 13

Most important, why should the measure of achievement be a group norm? Asians do better than whites on math SATs; should whites who outperform the white group norm be given special preference? Should a high-scoring Asian be rejected from MIT if she beats the non-Asian competition but scores lower than Asians in general? In fact, both Asians and Jews will suffer under any leveling scheme 14 that penalizes applicants who come from more prosperous and better-educated homes. These two groups are strikingly overrepresented on elite campuses today, precisely because they score so high on the SATs. Asians constitute only 4 percent of the population, but they represent almost a quarter of all students scoring above 750 on the math SATs, with the result that they make up nearly one-fifth of the student body at Harvard and a quarter or more at MIT and Cal Tech. It appears that the end of racial preferences in California has primarily benefited Asians.

ETS is perfectly right, of course, to say that race, ethnicity, and   15 socioeconomic status correlate with SAT scores. And SAT scores, the company should add, correlate with college performance. Instead of trafficking in group stereotypes, endlessly tinkering with scores, giving extra points for this or that sort of disadvantage, and pretending lower-scoring students are competitive when they are not, why not just educate the kids? Does ETS believe good schools are an impossible dream? Shame on it, if it does.

Vocabulary/Using a Dictionary

1. "I believe this commitment, however cloaked in *subterfuge* it may be, is a valid one," comments Glazer in paragraph 9. What does the word *subterfuge* mean in this context? What are the roots of the word? What is the word's origin?

2. What does it mean to give someone *preferential* treatment (Thernstrom, para. 5)? How is this word different from the words *preference* or *prefer*?

3. How does Glazer's use of the word *mollified* set the tone of the author's attitude toward "critics of racial preference in college admissions" (para. 2)?

Responding to Words in Context

1. What does the name "Strivers" imply about the students it is supposed to help? Think of some other names the adjusted SAT score could be given. How might these other names affect how Glazer and Thernstrom approach the issue?

2. In Thernstrom's essay, she argues: "Expanding the universe of preferential admits [admissions] does not solve the basic prob-

lem. ETS [the Educational Testing Service] is simply adding more variables to a *victimology* index and reinforcing the already-too-widespread belief that demography is destiny" (para. 5). Explain, in your own words, what the author means by these statements.

Discussing Main Point and Meaning

1. What point do you think Thernstrom is trying to make when she uses the following imaginary example in her essay: "Should a teacher say to a white student from a low-income family, 'I'll count your C in math as an A. You come to the test with a disadvantage; I understand'?" (para. 6). What is the tone of her comment?

2. In Glazer's essay, he comments that college and university faculty and administrators (state legislatures and ruling political bodies in charge of public universities) have a valid commitment ("however cloaked in subterfuge") to students (paras. 8 and 9). What is that commitment? Explain your answer.

3. Does Thernstrom conclude that the ETS is right to say that race, ethnicity, and socioeconomic status should correlate with SAT scores? More important, what opinion does the author bring to this conclusion?

4. Even if the Strivers score approach does not succeed, why does Glazer feel it is important enough to be commended?

Examining Sentences, Paragraphs, and Organization

1. Carefully examine the opening paragraphs of both Thernstrom and Glazer. Which of the two authors introduces their opinion in the first paragraph? Which of the two introductions seems more factual? Which is more persuasive? Why?

2. In the first sentence of paragraph 10, Glazer proclaims: "If, then, one accepts that admitting more non-Asian minorities than would make the cut through academic criteria alone is a legitimate goal, the Strivers score is not such a terrible way to achieve it." Do you believe that Glazer has provided enough evidence to support this substantial claim? Explain your answer using examples from the essay.

3. If the organization of Thernstrom's entire essay revolves around the strategy of *problem to solution,* what is the problem as stated by the author? What is the solution?

Thinking Critically

1. Glazer suggests that "there's a strong possibility that [the Strivers score] may not survive the inevitable legal challenges. It also remains to be seen just how effective the new approach will be at maintaining or increasing the number of black and Hispanic students in our colleges and universities" (para. 11). Does he offer an alternative solution to the Strivers score? If so, what is it?

2. One factor that will broaden the definition of disadvantaged students "beyond race and ethnicity," explains Thernstrom, "will reportedly focus on only such variables as the employment status of the student's mother and the kinds of electrical appliances and number of books in the student's home, as reported — accurately or inaccurately — by the student" (para. 5). Explain how Thernstrom's essay relies on suggestion to make her point understood. What suggestion is she making?

In-Class Writing Activities

1. Write a third essay based on the opposing views between Thernstrom and Glazer suggesting how they might join together in a compromise. Be sure to address the ways colleges, universities, and the Educational Testing Service might be persuaded to effect a solution to the problem of standardized testing (how it accounts for race).

2. Brainstorm a list of disadvantages that some students might have when attending school, college, or a university. After each disadvantage listed, offer a solution that would help to address it. As a follow-up activity, briefly freewrite a solution as to how we can help these students (besides adjusting standardized test scores) prepare for post–high school careers.

OPPOSING VIEWS

What Should We Do about Affirmative Action?

Before You Read

How do you feel about affirmative action? Have you ever benefited from it? Have you ever been adversely affected by it? Do you think affirmative action needs to be reformed? Do we still need affirmative action? Why or why not?

Words to Learn [Berkowitz]

respectively (para. 4): referring to two or more things, in the order named (adv.)

perpetuated (para. 4): caused to continue or be remembered (v.)

champion (para. 6): to fight for; defend; support (v.)

skews (para. 6): distorts; biases (v.)

mentoring (para. 7): advising or teaching someone wisely (v.)

Words to Learn [Lakner]

implementation (para. 1): the process of carrying something into full effect (n.)

pervasive (para. 1): diffused throughout (adj.)

contention (para. 1): strife, struggle, controversy, dispute, etc. (n.)

reside (para. 2): to dwell for a long time (v.)

determinant (para. 2): a thing or factor that defines or sets limits (n.)

aptitude (para. 2): capability; talent for (n.)

systematically (para. 5): orderly; methodically; regularly (adv.)

fabricated (para. 6): made; built; constructed (v.)

modification (para. 6): a partial or slight change in form (n.)

DANIEL BERKOWITZ

End It

[THE CAMPUS TIMES ONLINE, THE UNIVERSITY OF ROCHESTER/March 25, 1999]

When someone runs a race and loses, do the officials shorten the distance the athlete is expected to run next time? No. Instead we expect competitors to practice longer and harder to meet the challenge and overcome it. 1

In 1965, President Lyndon B. Johnson issued Executive Order 11246, known better by its household name, "affirmative action." Its purpose was to "take affirmative action to ensure that applicants are employed, and that employees are treated during employment, without regard to their race, creed, color, national origin [and a post-1967 revision, sex]," a noble purpose indeed. I can think of no better cause than equality. After all, our nation is founded on the belief that "All men are created equal." 2

But sometimes the best intentions don't produce the best results. Have thirty-four years of affirmative action brought us closer to that ultimate goal of total equality? They have not. 3

First, affirmative action lowers standards. Lowering standards never encourages people to improve, but instead reassures them that mediocre performance will get the job done. Statistics show that black students score an average of 110 points and 92 points lower than whites on the math and verbal sections of the SAT respectively, and on average black students have lower high school and college grades than whites. Such a trend is not corrected through affirma-tive action, but perpetuated. When you expect less of someone, you get less. 4

Second, affirmative action merely prolongs poor performance. Why not give minority students what they need when they need it: a 5

Daniel Berkowitz (b. 1977) was a senior at the University of Rochester, working toward a B.A. in political science, when he wrote this article. A brother of the Delta Upsilon fraternity, he is currently working for the Department of Defense.

true education. Letting students slip through the cracks with substandard scores and grades does the individual and society a disservice. It does not fix the problem, it merely passes the buck. Instead of providing minority students with the skills necessary to compete in today's job market, affirmative action allows us to ignore their shortcomings and overlook their inability to perform at the same level as their peers. How have we prepared these individuals for the day when the affirmative action crutch is not there to support them?

Third, affirmative action is an injustice to all those who truly 6 champion equality in this nation. The true victories won by minority students across the nation each day are negated by affirmative action. Affirmative action does not put us closer to equality, it just gives us the feeling that we are closer. Until we can be sure that every student who has succeeded has done so by living up to the same level expected of all students, we will never see true equality because we are not demanding it. We have tests and requirements for a reason—to separate those who are qualified from those who are not. Affirmative action skews those lines.

Most of us came to the University of Rochester because it has a 7 good academic reputation. That is in large part because the admission standards are higher and more is expected of high school students applying here. Is that wrong? Should we lower our standards so that more students can enjoy the education we are receiving? It may be cruel, but some people are not going to get into competitive colleges. We must remember a college education is a privilege and not a right. If affirmative action is not the solution, what is? Continued mentoring, after-school programs, and additional educational opportunities that truly prepare students for higher education are a definite step in the right direction. If we do have these programs, are students taking advantage of them? If they are not, do they deserve to succeed?

> *Affirmative action does not put us closer to equality, it just gives us the feeling that we are closer.*

It is also our responsibility as students to keep our institution in 8 check. We must demand that those minority students qualified to attend this university are not discouraged from attending based on the color of their skin. We must enter the workforce and look past skin color and ethnicity when interacting with or hiring others. I look forward to that day.

ANYA LAKNER

Keep It

[THE CAMPUS TIMES ONLINE, THE UNIVERSITY OF ROCHESTER/April 8, 1999]

I am writing in response to Daniel Berkowitz's opinion piece on   1
affirmative action. Berkowitz states that thirty-four years of affirmative action have not brought us President Lyndon B. Johnson's vision
of equality. What I say is that thirty-four years of the same ignorance
that he uses to defend his statement is what has prevented progress in
the direction of equality in our nation. I do believe that there are
major reforms needed in the implementation of affirmative action, so
as to prevent what is termed "reverse discrimination," for discrimination based on skin color or heritage should not come from a program
developed to prevent it. Yet, even with needed reform, I do believe
that affirmative action programs, properly crafted, continue to play
an important role in helping to reduce the pervasive discrimination
that still occurs to minorities. What I take into contention is how
Berkowitz states his argument.

Yes, on the average, black students score lower on their SATs   2
than white students. Why is this? The reality is that the majority of
blacks live in poorer, urban areas. Where are our nation's primary
schools crumbling? Which areas receive the least financial support?
Those same urban areas. Some of us were fortunate enough to have
the financial resources to enroll in special courses, pushing up our
SAT scores at least 200 points on the average. In which areas of our
nation do families of lower income reside? The urban areas. Thus,
cannot one possibly see a relationship between SAT scores and financial background? I find it inappropriate and ignorant of Berkowitz to
use SAT scores as a way to determining standards, when SAT scores

---

*ANYA LAKNER (b. 1978) says she responded to Daniel Berkowitz's piece
"because I felt it was misinformed and did not justify his position." A senior
studying political science when she responded, Anya now lives in Brooklyn,
New York, and hopes to become a human rights lawyer or professor of cultural politics.*

are skewed by financial and educational opportunity. Can something that is itself skewed be used as an honest determinant of standard aptitude?

No. Affirmative action does not promote or prolong poor performance. What a demeaning comment to make. By saying this, Berkowitz is belittling all of the hard work that minority students put into their courses. Getting into college is a free ride for very few, privileged individuals. The very fact that minority students hold onto and work toward their dreams of college, despite all the prejudice they face daily, is honorable. Also, once in college, all students are held to the same academic standards.

> *Some of us were fortunate enough to have the financial resources to enroll in special courses, pushing up our SAT scores at least 200 points on the average.*

I would also like to add that affirmative action not only protects the rights of ethnic minorities, but women as well. To prove the necessity of such programs, one must simply look at the Massachusetts Institute of Technology.

A *Newsweek* article (March 23, 1999) states that "female faculty at the Massachusetts Institute of Technology for years were systematically shortchanged in areas ranging from promotions and salaries to office space and access to research money, according to a report issued by the school." Without affirmative action, women would be trapped under the glass ceiling of the corporate ladder.

Discrimination is real. Minorities are trapped under a massive glass ceiling that has been fabricated by years of "old boy" networks. Affirmative action does need modification, but until individuals can be guaranteed equal protection and rights under the law, it must remain in existence.

Vocabulary / Using a Dictionary

1. Berkowitz states in paragraph 6, "Affirmative action is an injustice to all those who truly *champion* equality in this nation." What does he mean by his use of the word *champion*? What *else* can the word mean? From what language did the word originate?

2. "Continued *mentoring,* afterschool programs, and additional educational opportunities that truly prepare students for higher

education are a definite step in the right direction," comments Berkowitz in paragraph 7. What is *mentoring?* What is a *mentor?* Who was the first *mentor?*

3. In paragraph 6 of her essay, Lakner suggests, "Minorities are trapped under a glass ceiling that has been *fabricated* by years of 'old boy' networks." What does it mean when something is *fabricated?* How does this word relate to the word *fabric?*

Responding to Words in Context

1. "In 1965, President Lyndon B. Johnson issued Executive Order 11246, known better by its household name, 'affirmative action,'" states Berkowitz in paragraph 2. The author goes on to explain what the purpose of affirmative action is, yet does not define the term. What definition of *affirmative action* does the author assume?

2. In paragraph 5, Berkowitz argues that affirmative action "does not fix the problem, it merely *passes the buck.* Instead of providing minority students with the skills necessary to compete in today's job market, affirmative action allows us to ignore their shortcomings and overlook their inability to perform at the same level as their peers." What does the expression *passes the buck* mean? How do you think this expression came about?

3. In her conclusion, Anya Lakner comments: "Without affirmative action, women would be trapped under the *glass ceiling* of the corporate ladder." What is a *glass ceiling?* What does it mean to be trapped beneath one?

Discussing Main Point and Meaning

1. Does Daniel Berkowitz believe that thirty-four years of affirmative action have "brought us closer to that ultimate goal of total equality"? Give three brief examples from his essay that support his opinion.

2. According to Berkowitz, is college education a privilege? Does he believe that affirmative action is the solution to the problem of admission standards? If this is not the solution, then what does he suggest as an alternative?

3. Does Anya Lakner believe that affirmative action needs to be reformed? Why or why not? With what does she take issue in Daniel Berkowitz's editorial?

4. Outline how Lakner tries to refute each of the three supporting examples in Berkowitz's essay in order to disprove his argument.

Examining Sentences, Paragraphs, and Organization

1. What is the purpose of Daniel Berkowitz's opening statements — the first two full sentences of his essay?

2. Do you think that Anya Lakner's refutation (act of proving something false or wrong) of Daniel Berkowitz's argument is effective? Would you use her rhetorical method if you were to disagree with this essay? Why or why not?

3. Compare and contrast the tone of the two authors' final paragraphs.

Thinking Critically

1. Lakner argues: "Thirty-four years of the same ignorance that he [Berkowitz] uses to defend his statement is what has prevented progress in the direction of equality in our nation" (para. 1). Do you agree with Lakner that Berkowitz is ignorant? Are his thoughts (or those like his) impeding "progress in the direction of equality in our nation"?

2. In paragraph 3 of his essay, Daniel Berkowitz asks, "Have thirty-four years of affirmative action brought us closer to the ultimate goal of total equality?" Answer this question to the best of your ability.

In-Class Writing Activities

1. Upon addressing the University of Michigan on May 22, 1964, President Lyndon Baines Johnson said: "The Great Society rests on abundance and liberty for all. It demands an end to poverty and racial injustice to which we are totally committed in our time." Write an essay expressing whether you think Johnson's statement holds true for today's America. Are we totally committed to ending poverty and racial injustice *in our time*?

2. Put yourself in the place of the admissions officer of your college. Write up a list of qualities, abilities, and academic standards you would use for admitting students into your institution. On another sheet of paper, freewrite why you think these criteria are important.

Discussing the Unit

Suggested Topic for Discussion

The essays in this unit offer different opinions about the nature of public initiatives, such as affirmative action and "Strivers scores." In those selections, each author concerns him- or herself with whether equality should be publicly controlled. In your opinion, how much control should your national, state, or local governments exert to preserve equality? Should there be laws controlling equal opportunity, or should the idea of equality be controlled by an individual's own conscience?

Preparing for Class Discussion

1. The writers in this unit argue for the implementation or dissolution of the SAT Strivers score (Glazer and Thernstrom) or affirmative action (Berkowitz and Lakner). Each of the four articles in this unit was available to the reading public, whether in *The New Republic* or the University of Rochester's *Campus Times Online*. Have you ever considered that our constitution guarantees us the right to say what we want, whenever we please, as long as we do not injure another person? How do you feel about freedom of speech? Do you exercise this freedom?

2. All of the essays you've read in this unit focus on college admission: Both Strivers scores and affirmative action programs were developed to help disadvantaged students enter colleges they might not get into otherwise. Are these institutions, in your opinion, affected positively or negatively by such programs?

From Discussion to Writing

1. "We hold these truths to be sacred and undeniable: that all men are created *equal* and independent, that from that *equal* creation they derive rights inherent and inalienable, among which are the preservation of life and liberty, and the pursuit of happiness." This excerpt from the original draft of the Declaration of Independence defines each American's "inalienable" (something that may not be taken away or transferred) right. Write an essay comparing this draft with the final version, "We hold these truths to be self-evident, that all men are created equal, that they are endowed by their Creator with certain unalienable Rights, that among these are Life, Liberty, and the pursuit of Happiness." Discuss these excerpts as they relate to equality-enforcing public initiatives (such as Strivers scores and affirmative action).

2. In this unit, you've read essays on how equality can and cannot be achieved through public initiatives. Using the four essays as a model, write your own essay examining public initiatives such as Strivers scores or affirmative action. Do you feel such programs are necessary in our culture? Defend your position.

3. Compose a dialogue among the four authors in this unit concerning how each of them feels about the success of public programs that help to achieve equality. Try to avoid favoring your personal preference, and instead give each opinion equal weight.

Topics for Cross-Cultural Discussion

1. How is a person deemed to be "underprivileged" in other cultures? Are the qualities that determine this different from those in the United States?

2. What public programs exist in other cultures that provide equal opportunity for the disadvantaged? What do they do? Who are these programs for? Most important, are these programs under scrutiny by the people of those cultures?

11

God and the Constitution — Must They Be Separate?

The opening of the First Amendment of the Constitution declares that "Congress shall make no law respecting an establishment of religion, or prohibiting the free exercise thereof. . . ." The interpretation of the amendment has led to endless dispute, as it seems in one statement both to restrict religion as well as to guarantee its free expression. How far did the nation's founders want the restriction to apply? Clearly, they wanted to restrict Congress from selecting one religion, say Congregationalism, and making it the nation's established church. But did they intend that prayer should be prohibited in public school or that different religious symbols could not be exhibited in public?

A recent flurry over the First Amendment's famous Establishment Clause involved Ohio's state motto: "With God All Things Are Possible." After the American Civil Liberties Union challenged that the motto violated the First Amendment, an Ohio court agreed and prohibited its use. The decision, applauded by those who advocate a firm "wall of separation" between church and state, dismayed many, like columnist Jeff Jacoby, who argues in "Can We Use the G-Word?" that the expression is so general it specifies no particular religion: If Ohio's motto is prohibited, Jacoby suggests, then perhaps the government should remove "In God We Trust" from all of its currency and the "words 'under God' must be deleted from the Pledge of Allegiance." It's not only the American Civil Liberties Union, however, which serves as a First Amendment watchdog. The Anti-Defamation League as well, one of its advertisements maintains, is working hard "on local, state and Federal levels to keep both policy makers and the public aware of First Amendment violations. . . ."

The issue has also been a popular one on college campuses, as can be seen in the "opposing views" selections on whether the Ten Commandments should be displayed publicly as a way to discourage violent behavior. A staff editorial for *The Collegiate Times*, Virginia Polytechnic Institute's online student publication, argues that posting the Ten Commandments in public buildings is "clearly unconstitutional," while a Truman State College student, Andrea Hein, believes that the commandments have an important place in our culture and in no way violate the Constitution.

JEFF JACOBY

Can We Use the G-Word?

[THE BOSTON GLOBE/June 1, 2000]

Before You Read

In the schools you've attended, have you ever said a prayer with your class? Do you question the practice of prayer in schools? Does it have a place in public schools? Should religion have a place in the public sphere at all? And most important, who do you think should determine the rules about this situation?

JEFF JACOBY *(b. 1959) is a journalist at the* Boston Globe. *His column has been dubbed a "must-read," and Jacoby has been described as "the region's pre-eminent spokesman for Conservative Nation." In 1999, he became the first recipient of the Breindel Award for Excellence in Opinion Journalism, a major journalism prize. Mr. Jacoby and his wife live in Brookline, Massachusetts, with their son Caleb.*

Words to Learn

scourge (para. 1): severe critic (n.)

doctrines (para. 6): policies; principles; set of guidelines (n.)

particularistic (para. 7): devotion to one particular party, system, theory, and so on (adj.)

muster (para. 8): gathering; collecting; summoning (v.)

mammon (para. 9): wealth or gain regarded as an object of pursuit (n.)

omnipotence (para. 10): the state of having unlimited power (n.)

invocation (para. 11): chant, prayer (n.)

The American Civil Liberties Union has a well-deserved reputation as a scourge of religion in the public square.   1

When a judge in Alabama displayed the Ten Commandments in his courtroom, the ACLU filed suit to force their removal. When a church in Troy, Michigan, put a banner promoting the National Day of Prayer on the lawn of the civic center, the ACLU demanded that it be taken down. When the Sycamore School District in southern Ohio, anticipating a high number of absences, decided to cancel classes on Yom Kippur, the ACLU went to court to keep the schools open.   2

The ACLU has fought to stop town plows from clearing snow in church parking lots, to prevent Mothers Against Drunk Driving from putting up white crosses at the sites of fatal drunk-driving accidents, and, of course, to shoot down anything that smacks of organized prayer on public school grounds. But it is hard to see how the ACLU can possibly top its latest campaign: an assault on the motto of the State of Ohio.   3

In 1959, the Ohio Legislature adopted "With God All Things Are Possible" as the Buckeye[1] State's official motto. In 1996, then-Governor George Voinovich proposed that the motto be engraved in granite on a plaza at the Ohio State House. Whereupon the ACLU swung into action, arguing that the motto violates the Establishment Clause of the First Amendment and didn't belong on the State House plaza — or on anything else owned or created by the State of Ohio. A federal judge ruled for the state, but on April 25 a three-judge panel of the U.S. Court of Appeals for the Sixth Circuit reversed.   4

Because the words of the motto are a quotation from the New Testament — they are spoken by Jesus in the Book of Matthew — the judges found that they amount to "an endorsement of the Christian religion by   5

---

[1]*Buckeye:* A native inhabitant of Ohio; so called after the buckeye trees that grow there.

the State of Ohio." Indeed, they express "a uniquely Christian thought not shared by Jews and Moslems." As a result, the state has "effectively said to all who hear or see the words 'With God All Things Are Possible,' that Christianity is a preferred religion to the people of Ohio."

The ACLU was thrilled. "We are delighted with the ruling," said   6
the director of the Ohio Chapter, Christine Link. It "affirms the bedrock principle that the state cannot and should not choose between competing religious doctrines."

But is that what "With God All Things Are Possible" really does?   7
Could any sentiment be less particularistic? If Ohio's motto amounts to "a uniquely Christian thought" merely because the words are taken from the New Testament, then the motto that appears on all American coins and currency—"In God We Trust"—must be a uniquely Jewish thought, since it is adapted from the Hebrew bible ("In God I trust; I am not afraid"—Psalms 56:11).

The First Amendment is not an invitation to strip every hint of religious faith from the public sphere.

No, no, say the judges; the God on   8
the money is OK; it's only the other God, the God of Ohio's motto—the one who frowns on money—who doesn't pass constitutional muster. You think I am twisting the court's words? Listen:

"The god of the coin of the realm"—this is from Judge Merritt's   9
concurring opinion, in which Judge Cohn joined—"is not by any means the God of Matthew 19:21–26, who makes all things possible, a God who disapproves of mammon, and who through his son, Jesus Christ, reportedly threw the money changers out of the temple."

This is theological hooey. When Jesus said, "With God all things   10
are possible," he was echoing the words spoken by Job centuries earlier ("Then Job answered the Lord and said: I know that you can do all things, and that no purpose of yours can be hindered"—Job 42:1–2) and foreshadowing those of Mohammed centuries later ("Know you not that God is able to do all things?"—Koran, Sura 2:106). If the Court of Appeals and the ACLU truly imagine that the omnipotence of God is "a uniquely Christian thought not shared by Jews and Moslems," they are badly out of touch with the beliefs of most Americans.

Ohio's attorney general, Betty Montgomery, has appealed the   11
three-judge panel's ruling to the full Sixth Circuit. If necessary, she can also appeal to the U.S. Supreme Court—where, she pointedly

notes, each session begins with the invocation, "God save the United States and this honorable court."

The First Amendment is not an invitation to strip every hint of religious faith from the public sphere. If Ohio's motto is not allowed to stand, then the words "under God" must be deleted from the Pledge of Allegiance. Presidents must stop taking the oath of office on a bible. Congress must end the practice — which goes straight back to the Founders — of beginning each day's session with prayers led by an official chaplain. Is that what the ACLU wants? Maybe, but there are other views worth considering. This one, for instance: 12

"We have staked the future of all of our political institutions . . . upon the capacity of each and all of us to govern ourselves, to control ourselves, to sustain ourselves according to the Ten Commandments of God."   13

So wrote James Madison, the author of the First Amendment.   14

Vocabulary / Using a Dictionary

1. When commenting on the ruling of the state of Ohio, the ACLU remarked that it "affirms the bedrock principle that the state cannot and should not choose between competing religious *doctrines*" (para. 6). What is a *doctrine?* How is it related to the word *doctor?*

2. Jacoby mentions "the *omnipotence* of God" in paragraph 10. What is the *omnipotence* of God? What are the roots of the word? Explain how *omnipotence* is similar in meaning to *omniscient*.

Responding to Words in Context

1. "'The god of the coin of the realm' — this is from Judge Merritt's *concurring* opinion, in which Judge Cohn joined — 'is not by any means the God of Matthew 19:21–26, who makes all things possible . . .'" relates the author in paragraph 9. What does the author mean by his use of the word *concurring?* Think of some synonyms for the word.

2. Upon reflection of the judges' decision that the "God of Matthew" is different from the "God of the coin of the realm" (para. 9), the author replies: "This is theological *hooey*. . . . [the judges] are badly out of touch with the beliefs of most Americans" (para. 10). What is *hooey?* What does it mean in this context?

Discussing Main Point and Meaning

1. Give some examples of how the ACLU has earned a reputation as being a "scourge of religion in the public sphere" (para. 1).

2. Explain why, on April 25, 2000, a three-judge panel of the United States Court of Appeals reversed a federal judge's approval of the motto of the state of Ohio: "With God All Things Are Possible."

3. Why does Jacoby disagree with the ruling of the United States Court of Appeals? Explain his reasoning.

4. According to the author, what *should not* be the function of the First Amendment? If the ACLU effectively has Ohio's motto removed, what does Jacoby feel will sadly (and logically) follow?

Examining Sentences, Paragraphs, and Organization

1. Upon rereading the first sentence of Jacoby's essay, do you find that he presents a strong opinion about the American Civil Liberties Union? If so, what is this opinion, and how does it affect the readers' perception of the ACLU?

2. Does the content of the last paragraph effectively conclude Jacoby's argument? Why or why not?

3. Why does Jacoby wait until paragraph 7 of his essay to propose his argument of opposition to the ACLU? What is the effect of this organizational strategy?

Thinking Critically

1. Do you agree with Jacoby's implication in paragraph 10: "If the Court of Appeals and the ACLU truly imagine that the omnipotence of God is a 'uniquely Christian thought not shared by Jews and Moslems,' they are badly out of touch with the beliefs of most Americans," or is the author's case not worth pleading?

2. Do you agree with the logic behind Jacoby's conclusion, "If Ohio's motto is not allowed to stand, then the words 'under God' must be deleted from the Pledge of Allegiance. Presidents must stop taking the oath of office on a bible. Congress must end the practice . . . of beginning each day's session with prayers . . ." (para. 12)? Do you think the author's logic is sound, or are other areas of public displays of religion under threat?

In-Class Writing Activities

1. Amendment I of the Constitution begins: "Congress shall make no law respecting an establishment of religion, or prohibiting the free exercise thereof. . . ." How do you interpret this amendment? Freewrite in your own words what the First Amendment means to you.

2. Write an essay stating whether or not you believe religion should exist in the public arena. To help focus your writing, make sure to address the following questions: Do you feel that prayer is appropriate in public schools? Should the Ten Commandments be posted publicly? Should a chaplain be allowed to begin each day's session of Congress with a prayer? Should God and the Bible be left out of politics?

ANTI-DEFAMATION LEAGUE

[2000]

Before You Read

Do you know what the purpose of the separation of church and state is? How does it work? Do you think that it is effective in the United States? Does this separation allow for greater religious freedom? How important is freedom of religion to you? Do you exercise this right?

Words to Learn

flourish (sent. 1): to blossom; to grow vigorously (v.)
vitality (sent. 2): the power and strength to live or go on living (n.)
defamation (sent. 3): detraction, slander, libel, attacking or injuring the reputation or honor of by false or malicious statements (n.)

f Religious 1 freedom

is only as strong as

the wall

separating church and state.

For over 200 years, the separation of Church and State in America has allowed religions to flourish free from government interference. It is only by continuing to keep government out of religion and religion out of government that we can guarantee the continued vitality of religious freedom. That is why the Anti-Defamation League is working so hard on local, state and Federal levels to keep both policy makers and the public aware of First Amendment violations and to repair cracks in the wall. Call 1-800-295-0943 today for our free newsletter *Faith and Freedom: The Case for Church-State Separation*, or visit our Web site at www.adl.org for an online copy.

Howard P. Berkowitz, National Chairman, Abraham H. Foxman, National Director, Anti-Defamation League, 823 United Nations Plaza, New York, NY 10017

Vocabulary / Using a Dictionary

1. The first sentence of the advertisement reads: "The separation of Church and State in America has allowed religions to *flourish* free from government interference." In this context, what does the word *flourish* mean? What else does the word mean? What are the origins of *flourish*?

2. What is *vitality* (sent. 2)? What word do you think it comes from?

Responding to Words in Context

1. The Anti-Defamation League, which works hard "on local, state and Federal levels to keep both policy makers and the public aware of First Amendment violations" (sent. 3), posted the advertisement you've just read. In the context of this advertisement, what do you think anti-defamation means?

Discussing Main Point and Meaning

1. What does the separation of church and state in the United States allow? For how long have the church and state been separate in the United States?

2. Why does the Anti-Defamation League wish to continue to keep religion and government apart?

3. According to the advertisement, what does the Anti-Defamation League do?

Examining Sentences, Paragraphs, and Organization

1. Looking at the first line of the advertisement in large-size font that reads, "Religious freedom is only as strong as the wall separating church and state," which words in this line of the advertisement are most prominent? Why do you think they were enlarged?

2. What do you think the reader will find by following the advice given by the Anti-Defamation League in the final sentence of the advertisement?

Thinking Critically

1. Do you agree with the Anti-Defamation League that "for over 200 years, the separation of Church and State in America has allowed religions to flourish free from government interference" (sent. 1)? Do you ever think about why we have separation between church and state in the United States?

2. Would you support the Anti-Defamation League in its work "on local, state and Federal levels to keep both policy makers and the public aware of First Amendment violations and to repair cracks in the wall" (sent. 3)? Would you call them for a free newsletter or visit their Web site?

In-Class Writing Activities

1. Hugo L. Black (1886–1971), the late U.S. Supreme Court Justice, once said:

   "The 'establishment of religion' clause of the First Amendment means at least this: Neither a state nor the Federal Government can set up a church. Neither can pass laws which aid one religion, aid all religions, or prefer one religion over another.

   "The First Amendment has erected a wall between church and state. That wall must be kept high and impregnable. We could not approve the slightest breach."

   Freewrite a response to the second part of Black's quote: Why do you think Hugo feels that the wall between church and state must be "high and impregnable"? Why should the U.S. Supreme Court not approve "the slightest breach"?

OPPOSING VIEWS

Do the Ten Commandments Violate the First Amendment?

Before You Read

Whose responsibility is it to teach our children about morality? How important is the teaching of "morality" to the children in America's schools? Should morality be taught in school? Do students know the difference between right and wrong, or is this distinction gradually diminishing? Can the injection of religious doctrine (such as the Ten Commandments) in public schools help make classrooms safer for students?

Words to Learn [Editorial Board]

onslaught (para. 1): a violent, intense attack (adv.)

aberration (para. 2): a departure from what is right, true, correct (n.)

mandated (para. 2): assigned authoritative orders or commands (v.)

unwarranted (para. 2): not authorized or sanctioned (v.)

correlation (para. 3): degree of relative connection or correspondence (n.)

delinquent (para. 3): failing to do what duty requires (adj.)

explicitly (para. 6): plain to see; readily observable (adv.)

unequivocally (para. 6): plain, clear; not ambiguous (adv.)

quell (para. 7): put an end to; to quiet (v.)

Words to Learn [Hein]

ideals (para. 1): existing as ideas, models, or archetypes; consisting of ideas (n.)

Judaism (para. 2): the Jewish religion, a monotheistic religion based on the laws and teaching of the Holy Scripture and the Talmud (n.)

coveting (para. 4): wanting ardently; longing for with envy (v.)

Sabbath (para. 4): the seventh day of the week (Saturday), set aside by the Fourth Commandment for rest and worship and observed as such by Jews and some Christian sects (n.)

EDITORIAL BOARD

Yes

[COLLEGIATE TIMES, VIRGINIA POLYTECHNIC INSTITUTE/February 11, 2000]

The onslaught of a nationwide school violence epidemic in 1999   1
prompted many conservative lawmakers throughout the United
States to propose new measures to bring character and morality back
into the schools. Of these controversial propositions, the initiative
having the most applicable success has been the Ten Commandments
Legislation, a form of which was passed in February 2000 in an Indiana state house.

Unfortunately, the latest legal acceptance of this bill in Indiana is   2
not an aberration, as nine other states are currently on the verge of
passing similar proposals. Clearly, this latest offensive on the constitutionally mandated separation of church and state is unwarranted
and inappropriate, truly marking a low point in America's fight to
keep the nation's schools free from religious intrusions in any form.

This notion that somehow a rapid injection of mainstream reli-   3
gious beliefs and certain moral doctrines can make our country's
schools safer is an assertion that lacks not only reason, but also any
legitimate evidence to prove the plan's effectiveness. As to date, there
is no existence of any valid study indicating any correlation between
daily exposure to specific religious material, such as the Ten Commandments, and a subsequent reduction of violent attitudes and behavior in young adults. It would stand to reason that programs
proven to reduce these delinquent behaviors, specifically anger and
stress management seminars, would be a scientifically proven means
to increase school safety. Also, it would be more appropriate for a
public school environment and completely inoffensive to every student—no matter what one's religious beliefs.

Yet, these alternative strategies to solving this crisis are some-   4
thing conservative lawmakers do not want to take into consideration.
Therefore, as opposed to making guns harder to acquire with increased gun control legislation or fortifying existing school security
systems, these lawmakers opt instead to insert their own personal religious agendas.

It goes without saying that the display of any religious material in public schools and public buildings specifically violates the fundamental liberty defining separation of church and state. The excuse provided by supporters of the move, that these commandments are universal, is inherently biased and incorrect.

> *It goes without saying that the display of any religious material in public schools and public buildings specifically violates the fundamental liberty defining separation of church and state.*

While some of these codes are very basic and comprehensive, such as "You shall not kill" or "You shall not steal," others are explicitly religious. Particularly, "I am the Lord your God, who brought you out of the house of bondage. You shall have no other gods before me" is undeniably linked to religious beliefs, and is unequivocally Christian-oriented. This is not only insulting to members of other non-Christian religions, but to atheists as well. The promotion of these materials unconstitutionally interferes with every individual's freedom of religious belief. The state of Indiana has simply no right to officially endorse the primary symbols of one religion while simultaneously excluding others.

Putting aside the fact that this religious endorsement is clearly unconstitutional, it will not accomplish the purpose for which it is proposed. If enraged students or coworkers bring loaded firearms into a public building for the sole purpose of taking lives, the gentle reminder from a posted Ten Commandments sign is hardly going to quell their anger and return them to their senses. The assertion is as ridiculous as it is ineffective and unjust.

ANDREA HEIN

No

[NEW MEDIA INDEX, TRUMAN STATE UNIVERSITY / September 2, 1999]

We live in a nation afraid of the word *God* or any ideals stem-   1
ming from religion. The latest controversy surrounding religious
ideals grows out of the posting of the Ten Commandments in public
schools. What many fail to realize is that the Ten Commandments
have a place in our culture without violating the First Amendment.
The value of the Ten Commandments is not limited to religion. The
Commandments represent significant historical and cultural values.

Christianity has been an important part of Western cultural and   2
national development for almost 2,000 years. Judaism has influenced
the development of the Middle East for more than 4,000 years. As
part of the backbone of both religions, the Ten Commandments are
historically and culturally important.

So why are some people afraid to display such a valuable histori-   3
cal document? If schools are only posting the Ten Commandments,
the students' rights to freedom of religion are not being violated. Students have the choice to read or ignore them. More important, the
students retain the right to reject or accept the religious components
of the Ten Commandments.

The Commandments also serve a positive function—they repre-   4
sent morals important to our society. The ideals of not killing, steal-
ing, betraying, or coveting are all contained within the Ten Commandments. These are all ideals fundamental to our nation. Even the
commandments that make direct references to God contain universal
morals. They present the ideals of faithfulness and respect. The third
Commandment—remember the Sabbath day and keep it holy—is

*ANDREA HEIN (b. 1979) was a sophomore at Truman State University
when she wrote this piece for the Truman State University* New Media Index.
*Hein, who used to hate to write, says that the whole purpose of her writing is
"to make others aware of a certain viewpoint they may never have considered." She expects to graduate in 2001 with a B.A. in communication.*

not limited to observing days of worship. It can also serve as a reminder to take time for personal relaxation.

We have become so paranoid about anything having to do with   5
God or the mention of a god that we are
beginning to sell ourselves short. Instead
of discarding a document or ideal that
stems from a religious source, we need to
step back and evaluate the greater good it
serves. Perhaps if we did this more often,
documents like the Ten Commandments
would not run the risk of being obliter-
ated from our culture.

> *Students retain the right to reject or accept the religious components of the Ten Commandments.*

Vocabulary / Using a Dictionary

1. "As to date, there is no existence of any valid study indicating any
    correlation between daily exposure to specific religious material . . .
    and a subsequent reduction of violent attitudes and behavior in
    young adults," comments the Editorial Board in paragraph 3 of
    their essay. What does *correlation* mean? Can you think of some
    synonyms for the word?

2. In paragraph 3 of the article written by the Editorial Board, it is
    mentioned that "anger and stress management seminars" may be
    a "scientifically proven means to increase school safety" and re-
    duce "*delinquent* behavior." What is meant by *delinquent* behav-
    ior? Can you describe some different types of *delinquent* behav-
    ior?

3. In paragraph 4 of her essay, Andrea Hein comments: "The ideals
    of not killing, stealing, betraying, or *coveting* are all contained
    within the Ten Commandments." What does the word *covet*
    mean? Is *coveting* considered to be offensive behavior?

Responding to Words in Context

1. In paragraph 1 of their essay, the Editorial Board remarks that
    school violence is an *epidemic*. What comparison are they mak-
    ing? Why do you think they are making this comparison?

2. The Editorial Board does not trust the *assertion* that some people
    think a Ten Commandments sign is going to stop enraged stu-
    dents or coworkers from bringing a gun into a public building
    and opening fire on a crowd (para. 6): They feel that a posted

Ten Commandments sign is useless in preventing this situation. What is an *assertion?*

Discussing Main Point and Meaning

1. According to the Editorial Board of the *Collegiate Times,* what prompted conservative lawmakers to "propose new measures to bring character and morality back into the schools" (para. 1)? Which of these propositions has had the most success? How does the Editorial Board feel about this proposition?

2. Why does Hein feel that the Ten Commandments are historically and culturally important?

3. What other alternatives does the Editorial Board offer besides posting the Ten Commandments as a strategy to stop the "onslaught of a nationwide school violence epidemic" (para. 1)?

4. According to Hein, what positive functions do the Ten Commandments serve?

Examining Sentences, Paragraphs, and Organization

1. What is the topic sentence of paragraph 5 in Andrea Hein's essay? How do you know this is a topic sentence?

2. In the essay by the Editorial Board, note the divisions made between each paragraph in the essay. Hiding the numbers, try to divide the sentences into paragraphs by yourself. What are your criteria for judging where a new paragraph starts and an old paragraph ends?

3. In which paragraphs of their essays do Hein and the Editorial Board reveal their main ideas (theses)? What are their main ideas?

4. Where do you think the conclusion to the Editorial Board's essay starts? Explain your answer.

Thinking Critically

1. In paragraph 2 of the Editorial Board's essay, when speaking of the proposed "Ten Commandments Legislation," the authors state: "Clearly, this latest offensive on the constitutionally mandated separation of church and state is unwarranted and inappropriate, truly marking a low point in America's fight to keep the nation's schools free from religious intrusions in any form." Do you agree that the Ten Commandments legislation is a low

point in America's fight to keep public schools free from religion? Further, do you think the posting of the Ten Commandments in public schools will adversely affect the liberty of our children?

2. When discussing the Ten Commandments, the Editorial Board comments: "While some of these codes [of the Ten Commandments] are very basic and comprehensive, such as 'You shall not kill' or 'You shall not steal,' others are explicitly religious. Particularly, 'I am the Lord your God, who brought you out of the house of bondage. You shall have no other gods before me,' is undeniably linked to religious beliefs, and is *unequivocally Christian-oriented*" (para. 5). Are the Ten Commandments only oriented to the Christian faith, or do other faiths accept these laws? Do the commandments simply make a Christian claim?

In-Class Writing Activities

1. Andrea Hein suggests the following in paragraph 3 of her essay: "If schools are only posting the Ten Commandments, the students' rights to freedom of religion are not being violated. Students have the choice to read or ignore them. More important, the students retain the right to reject or accept the religious components of the Ten Commandments." Do you think younger students will read and ignore the Ten Commandments? Is this easy to do if they are posted in a public place every day? Do students feel that they have the right to accept or reject something that legislation has deemed worthy to post in public? Write an essay about how you think the Ten Commandments Legislation may affect elementary and high school students in America.

2. Looking at the list of the Ten Commandments, it appears they can be divided up into two parts: The first four commandments give our duty to God and religion, the last six, our duty to fellow human beings. The last six commandments read:

   Honor thy father and mother.

   Thou shalt not kill.

   Thou shalt not commit adultery.

   Thou shalt not steal.

   Thou shalt not bear false witness [lie] against thy neighbor.

   Write a brief essay discussing whether you think the last six commandments are of vital importance to the functioning of American society, and whether or not they should be implemented into public education programs. Do you think American students (eventual productive members of society) would benefit by following these last six commandments? Could we use the Ten Commandments in our schools?

Discussing the Unit

Suggested Topic for Discussion

In the past few years, there has been a drastic increase in school violence. Because of this, do you think prayer should be allowed in public schools? How about the posting of the Ten Commandments? There are over 1,500 religious denominations in America—is religion just too personal to let the government decide what prayers our children should be reciting in school?

Preparing for Class Discussion

1. In the mission statement posted on the homepage of the Anti-Defamation League, the goal of the league is as follows: "to stand up for the core values of America against those who seek to undermine them through word or deed." Do *you* think the First Amendment of the Bill of Rights (that government should be separate from religion) is a "core American value?" Why or why not?

2. The article by the Editorial Board of the *Collegiate Times* begins: "The onslaught of a nationwide school violence epidemic in 1999 prompted many conservative lawmakers throughout the United States to propose new measures to bring character and morality back into the schools." One of the controversial propositions offered was the Ten Commandments Legislation. After reading some of the views regarding the separation of church and state in this unit, what other suggestions would you have (besides the Ten Commandments Legislation) that could bring character and morality back to our public schools?

From Discussion to Writing

1. Pretend you are a public school teacher who has been asked to create a new course promoting morality, ethics, and character.

What would you call this class period? What issues would be discussed? How long would the period be? What texts would you use, if any?

2. Write an article like one of the three in this unit, discussing whether or not God and the Constitution must be separate. Use the three articles and the advertisement provided in this chapter when drafting your essay, and feel free to use the Internet or any other resource to support your ideas. Perhaps reviewing the First Amendment might be a good starting point for your essay. Also remember that it is up to you as an American to understand the Constitution. (If need be, propose an amendment to the First Amendment!)

3. In June 2000, when scientists announced that they had completed a map of the human genome, President Clinton remarked that "we are learning the language with which God created life." Do you think in saying this that he crossed the line that should separate church and state? Do you think, given the significance of his public role, that he made it acceptable for schools to teach Creationism as an alternative to evolution? What effect do you think it has on the public when elected officials introduce God into their pronouncements? Is there a double standard at work? Explain why you consider President Clinton's remark acceptable or unacceptable given the legal context of this unit.

Topics for Cross-Cultural Discussion

1. Does religion play a large role in the function of other cultures' governments? How about in the history of other countries? Does the government have any control over the religions in these cultures?

2. Do other countries have the same number of differing religions as the United States? What effect do you believe this variety has on those cultures?

12

Is the War on Drugs Worth Waging?

For years, America has waged a war on drugs designed to prevent the use and sale of certain drugs as well as the illegal smuggling of them into our country. But why is the sale and possession of some drugs—like crack, heroin, or marijuana—illegal, while few people seem troubled over the widespread promotion and distribution of beer, wine, and other alcoholic beverages? Is alcohol equivalent to other drugs? If so, should it be equally prohibited?

The chapter opens with an essay by someone with firsthand knowledge of the U.S. war on drugs. James E. Garcia, a journalist and publisher, served five years in jail for selling five grams of cocaine to a friend in 1979. In "War and Hypocrisy," Garcia argues that "America's War on Drugs is based on a hypocritical premise: a false distinction between the illegal drug user and the average beer drinker."

University of California columnist Adrian Haymond in "Can Legalization Solve America's Drug Problem?" also sees connections between drugs and alcohol: Why, he asks, should we assume the legalization of drugs would work any better in reducing crime and self-destruction than did the legalization of alcohol earlier in the century?

In "The Drug That Pretends It Isn't," the prominent *Newsweek* columnist Anna Quindlen agrees that "booze and beer are not the same as illegal drugs." "They're worse," she argues, wondering why alcohol doesn't come under the jurisdiction of our drug czar. The chapter concludes with two advertisements, one from Mothers Against Drunk Driving (MADD), an organization that for years has insisted on tougher alcohol legislation, and one from Common Sense for Drug Policy that advises jury members to "just say no" to prosecutors as a citizen's way to combat the "injustices of the war on drugs."

JAMES E. GARCIA

War and Hypocrisy

[THE TEXAS OBSERVER/January 21, 2000]

Before You Read

Is it hypocritical for us to drink alcohol and prohibit drug use? What is more important to you: Putting drug-related criminals behind bars, or preventing drug use and rehabilitating users?

Words to Learn

notwithstanding (para. 6): regardless of (prep.)

proxy (para. 9): substitute (adj.)

leftist (para. 9): revolutionary; antiestablishment (adj.)

cartels (para. 9): groups of independent organizations formed to regulate production and marketing of goods (n.)

collusion (para. 14): secret agreement for deceitful or fraudulent purposes (n.)

wholesalers (para. 14): those who sell in large quantities at a lower cost (n.)

JAMES E. GARCIA (b. 1959) is a veteran journalist. He has been a reporter, columnist, and editor. As a reporter and columnist, his articles have appeared in the Austin American-Statesman, the San Jose Mercury News, the Atlanta Journal–Constitution, the Dallas Morning News, Hispanic magazine, Mexico City News, and Latinolink.com. He is currently editor and publisher of Politico, a magazine of Latino culture and politics.

I knew why they had come. They were there to arrest me for sell- 1
ing five grams of cocaine, to a friend turned police informant. She
had turned me in to keep the cops from throwing her and her husband in prison and leaving their kids orphaned. I understood why
they did it and never blamed them.

Getting busted was my fault. I was the one who gave her the 2
drugs, while an undercover narcotics detective looked on. And I was
the one who, until that day, had been wasting my life as a small-time
drug peddler and big-time cocaine abuser.

I could have bought a good used car with the money I spent 3
snorting cocaine in 1979. I also could have shared in the early upbringing of my now nineteen-year-old son, if I hadn't spent nearly
five years locked up in the Indiana Department of Corrections.

I screwed up. I paid the price. I rebuilt my life. Since leaving an 4
Indiana state prison, I have worked as a newspaper reporter, columnist, editor, and publisher.

Fifteen years later, I think about the lessons I've learned. Most of 5
those lessons had to do with learning to appreciate my family and
friends. In the worst of times, they can be all you have. Perhaps the
most important lesson was the realization that if I care about the
world around me, then I should do what I can to help make it better.

I chose journalism because I believed that as a writer I could con- 6
tribute in some small way to the betterment of society. Our profession's low standing in recent polls notwithstanding, I still believe
that.

I tell you all this because I want to talk about the hypocrisy of 7
the War on Drugs. Over the course of the last twenty years, I have
concluded again and again that the government's escalating battle
to keep people from consuming illegal drugs has been a miserable
failure.

I thought about this as I watched last month's [Dec. 1999] tele- 8
vised news reports from the U.S.–Mexico border, about an alleged
mass gravesite that authorities think may be filled with the bodies of
informants and others killed by Mexican drug traffickers. As of early
January, few bodies had in fact been found—but the Mexican narcotraffickers are now among the most powerful in the world.

I think about the futility of the drug war when I read about the 9
U.S. government's efforts to fight a proxy war in Colombia by providing cash, training, and weapons for that government to use in its
efforts to defeat leftist rebels linked to international drug cartels.

And I think about our failed policy when I hear about young 10 people, many of them only children, who are willing to gun each other down on America's streets in crack cocaine turf battles.

The problem with the War on Drugs is that it demonizes an activity that our society also glorifies. We cannot fight a war that we perpetuate and promote.   11

You see, America's War on Drugs is based on a hypocritical premise: a false distinction between the illegal drug user and the average beer drinker. Alcohol is also a drug. Yet, we deny that, and instead advertise it as a magic potion for success and happiness. Sell someone a beer and they'll make a television sitcom glorifying your profession: remember *Cheers?* Sell someone a joint—and go to prison.   12

> *The problem with the War on Drugs is that it demonizes an activity that our society also glorifies. We cannot fight a war that we perpetuate and promote.*

The drug trade and the liquor industry exist for the same reason: People want a buzz, or simply to self-destruct. In either case, at the core, there is no distinction.   13

We have misidentified the enemy. Our generals tell us the enemy is the international drug profiteer in collusion with American wholesalers—including aimless punk kids in Indiana. They are wrong.   14

Our real enemy does not live in a guarded mansion, perched on the mountains of Colombia. The true enemy in this war is our own hypocrisy.   15

Our nation spent about $18 billion and arrested 1.5 million people implementing its national antidrug policy over the last year. Most of that money and manpower was wasted. Most of that would have been far better spent on drug and alcohol rehabilitation and prevention programs. I'm not even counting the billions spent annually to keep convicted nonviolent drug offenders in jail.   16

After New Year's Eve, after we watched the world's revelers tip their glasses to the New Millennium, we might also have thought about what's inside the glasses.   17

End the hypocrisy. End the war.   18

Vocabulary/Using a Dictionary

1. Explain the meaning of *hypocrisy* and Garcia's use of the term (para. 7). Provide some additional examples of hypocritical behavior or thinking.

2. The Latin root for the word *proxy* (para. 9) means "one who cares for." How do you think the word came to mean "substitute"?

3. Use the word *collusion* (para. 14), or its verb form *collude,* in a sentence of your own.

Responding to Words in Context

1. Explain what Garcia means by *narcotraffickers* (para. 8). What two words does he combine to form this word?

2. Why do you think Garcia and others so often refer to America's drug problem as a "war" (paras. 7, 11, 12, 18)? Do you think this is an appropriate metaphor?

Discussing Main Point and Meaning

1. Describe Garcia's response to his drug arrest and five-year term in an Indiana state prison.

2. Why did Garcia choose to become a journalist?

3. What is Garcia's position on the U.S. government's efforts to fight drug use? Provide examples from the text as evidence of your answer.

4. Garcia talks about "our enemy" in the "War on Drugs." Who or what does he perceive that enemy to be? How is his perception different from the government's?

Examining Sentences, Paragraphs, and Organization

1. "I've had a long time to think about this," Garcia's essay begins. Do you think this is an effective opening line? Why or why not?

2. Describe the function of paragraphs 8 through 10. How are they similar in content and structure? Why do you think they are grouped together?

3. In paragraph 11, the author writes: "The problem with the War on Drugs is that it demonizes an activity that our society also glorifies. We cannot fight a war that we perpetuate and promote." How does this paragraph set up the point Garcia goes on to make in paragraph 12? What central concept of Garcia's do the contrasts in paragraph 11 illustrate?

Thinking Critically

1. Garcia seems to accept the reasons why he was arrested and punished for selling and using drugs, and he was clearly able to rehabilitate himself—becoming a productive and successful member of society. Why, then, does he argue that the kinds of policies that punished him have been a "miserable failure" (para. 7)? Isn't there a contradiction in his position?

2. Do you agree with Garcia that America glorifies alcohol use? Explain your answer.

In-Class Writing Activities

1. Do you believe that drug activity and antidrug policies constitute a "war"? Who are the good guys, and who are the bad guys? What are the weapons used, and who are the innocent victims? Write an essay that expands on the application of this metaphor to the U.S. drug problem. Try to identify the various militaristic figures and strategies involved and, if possible, predict what the "postwar era" will be like.

2. Aside from war, what other metaphors might be used to describe the U.S. drug problem? Write an essay arguing for the application of your new metaphor. Be sure to explain exactly how the metaphor applies. Explore the ways in which thinking of the "drug war" in your new terms might change people's attitudes toward it.

ADRIAN HAYMOND

Can Legalization Solve America's Drug Problem?

[DAILY BRUIN ONLINE, UNIVERSITY OF CALIFORNIA, LOS ANGELES /
October 28, 1999]

Before You Read

What would happen if drugs, like alcohol, were legal? Would there be less drug-related crime? Would there be fewer addicts and drug deaths if drugs were regulated like alcohol is? Does regulation prevent alcohol-related crime and death?

Words to Learn

caches (para. 1): stores of goods (n.)

temperance (para. 4): abstinence from alcohol (n.)

voracious (para. 4): consuming; insatiable; greedy (adj.)

repeal (para. 4): official withdrawal (n.)

fermented (para. 4): chemical quality of being alcoholic (where yeast has acted upon sugar) (adj.)

cirrhosis (para. 10): disease of the liver preventing proper blood regulation (n.)

ADRIAN HAYMOND (b. 1963) wrote this essay as a senior at UCLA, pursuing a B.S. in business administration. He also received an earlier degree from UCLA, graduating in 1986 with a B.S. in physics. "I think we have concentrated an inordinate amount of energy debating the merits versus drawbacks of drug legalization," says Haymond. "In many instances, costs are not apparent to the average citizen; we must take all such factors into account."

One need only turn on the 11 o'clock news to determine   1
whether the "war on drugs" has been a success or a failure. Border
police and the FBI continue to nab ever-increasing caches of illegal
drugs, while our "tough on crime" policies haul thousands to jail on
drug trafficking and possession charges.

Yet, people young and old continue to purchase and consume   2
large amounts of drugs for a variety of reasons, ranging from medici-
nal to escapist. Even the most ardent drug enforcers have to admit
that the current offensive against drugs has been a dismal failure, because the government cannot prevent what people want to do merely
through laws (and their enforcement). But does this automatically
mean that drugs should be legalized?

We already have a case study to determine whether drug legaliza-   3
tion policies will be successful. America's struggles with alcohol provide a ready-made experiment in which the pros and cons of drug legalization can be measured in terms of lives affected and dollars
spent.

In the early portion of the twentieth century, our government re-   4
sponded to the demands of various temperance groups and prohibited the sale and distribution of alcoholic beverages. At about the
same time, organized crime gained power in cities such as Chicago
and New York. Since the general populace still had a voracious ap-
petite for alcohol, gangsters such as Al Capone made millions dealing
in this illicit trade. As their motive was to maximize profits regardless
of cost, the gangsters handled rivals in their own, intimate way—as
the "Valentine's Day Massacre" graphically showed. The violence
contributed to the eventual repeal of Prohibition laws, and America
enjoyed the products of fermented grapes, wheat, and barley once
more.

In 1999, we can see what more than a half century of legalized   5
alcohol use has done. Gangs do not shoot each other and innocent
bystanders for the right to sell beer and wine. No one has to sneak
into "speakeasies" in order to enjoy alcohol. Jails do not bust at the
seams due to arrests for alcohol possession and sales.

Our major brewing companies fund many of our sporting events   6
and account for an enormous amount of television revenue, helping
to support the majestic stadiums, arenas, and player-coaching salaries
that have skyrocketed in recent years. No one has to attack anyone to
get a beer; an alcoholic is more likely to beg for a dollar or so than
rob someone at gunpoint to obtain his or her "fix." And when was

the last time you heard of someone burglarizing a house to steal items for resale later just to obtain cheap wine?

But there are costs for the use of alcoholic beverages, and those costs are enormous. The National Highway Traffic Safety Administration reported that in 1998, 16,189 people in the United States were killed in crashes involving alcohol alone (not cocaine or speed, just alcohol), and 1,058,990 more were injured. Economically, this resulted in an estimated $45 billion just from the direct results of such accidents. Indirectly, $75 billion is estimated to be lost in reduced quality of life. With all the messages telling people to drink responsibly and to use a designated driver or taxi, it seems that people will do what they want to do, whether it may kill someone or not. Can we honestly say that those who use other drugs will act any more responsibly on the road than drunks?

7

> *We tell young people to stay off the bottle, but our social gatherings, athletic events, and media reek of irresponsible alcohol use.*

If one does not drive, there is still the danger of alcohol-induced violence. We know that alcohol acts as a depressant, suppressing inhibitions that otherwise prevent us from doing terrible things to others and to ourselves. The U.S. Department of Justice reported in 1998 that four out of every ten violent crimes involved alcohol. The victims of such crimes reported financial loss of more than $400 million, with the average victim experiencing out-of-pocket medical expenses of $1,500 an episode. More depressing is the fact that in two-thirds of violent crimes in which the perpetrator and victim know each other, alcohol is a contributing factor.

8

In spousal abuse cases, three out of every four incidents involved alcohol use by the offender. Knowing that other drugs stimulate (methamphetamine and cocaine), depress (barbiturates), impair (marijuana), or bend reality (heroin), are we playing with fire when suggesting that such items should be made legal (even under heavy restrictions)? Since drugs can be highly unpredictable in their effects on the human psyche, can we say with a straight face that there will be no increase in such crimes (and the resultant financial effects) with legalization?

9

The National Institute on Alcohol Abuse and Alcoholism states that in 1992, $18.8 billion was spent on health care services for alcohol problems, of which $13.2 billion was for alcohol-induced health

10

problems such as cirrhosis and trauma (due to falls, accidents, etc.). In addition, in the same year, 107,400 died as a result of alcohol use. Even if we assume that such numbers have dropped 25 percent (a hefty amount), one can see the costs are still staggering. We must remember that all drugs are lethal in sufficient amounts; are we willing to pay the costs of legalized abuse?

What do we want to show to the next generation? Already, we see   11
that "Just Say No" is a joke, in part because the messengers are hypocritical. Our high-profile celebrities make a mockery of efforts to stop drug use with well-documented plunges into addiction and abuse. We tell young people to stay off the bottle, but our social gatherings, athletic events, and media reek of irresponsible alcohol use. We're afraid to take the moralistic "high road" because of all the "skeletons" of drug abuse that bang around in our collective closets.

So, instead of changing strategy in the current war on drugs, we   12
either doggedly try the same old tactics that fail miserably or surrender unconditionally in the name of individual "rights." Well, what about the right of someone to drive without fear of sudden death via intoxicant? What about the baby doomed to painful life from drug-induced ailments? What about the spouse painted black, blue, and red by someone's fists, bat, or gun? Or the fan too scared to talk with a blustery drunk for fear of pulverization? Or of anyone paying higher car and health insurance rates?

A famous person once said, "Those who don't learn from history   13
are doomed to repeat it." In this situation, it would be doubly tragic, for "history" continues even today, instructing us on decisions of past generations. And yet once more, we're about to fail the final exam.

Vocabulary / Using a Dictionary

1. Can you think of an antonym for *escapism* (para. 2)?

2. "We know that alcohol acts as a depressant, suppressing inhibitions that otherwise prevent us from doing terrible things to others and ourselves" (para. 8). Rewrite or paraphrase this sentence in your own words, being particularly careful not to alter both the structure and word choice.

3. In paragraph 11, Haymond says that "our social gatherings, athletic events, and media *reek* of irresponsible alcohol use." What are the two possible meanings of *reek* in this sentence?

Responding to Words in Context

1. Can you guess what the *speakeasies* Haymond refers to are by examining the context in which they appear (para. 5)?

2. What do you make of the term *pulverization* (paragraph 12)? Why does Haymond use this word instead of using *a beating* or *physical abuse*?

Discussing Main Point and Meaning

1. What is the "case study" Haymond suggests we use in determining whether legalization of drugs could be effective?

2. Describe Haymond's feelings about the effects of legalized alcohol use.

3. What role do celebrities play in the problem of alcohol consumption, according to Haymond?

4. Do you think Haymond's primary goal is to argue against the legalization of drugs? Or is it to call for stricter laws about alcohol consumption?

Examining Sentences, Paragraphs, and Organization

1. Haymond opens this essay by saying, "One need only turn on the 11 o'clock news to determine whether the 'war on drugs' has been a success or a failure." What, according to the essay, is the answer?

2. Why does Haymond go into detail on the effects of Prohibition in paragraph 4?

3. Which of the various statistics Haymond refers to surprises you the most? Why?

4. Does Haymond make any concrete solutions as to how we should solve the problems he outlines? Are there any implied solutions (suggested but not directly stated)?

Thinking Critically

1. How much responsibility for alcohol and drug abuse can be placed on the users? How much can be placed on the makers and sellers of drugs and alcohol?

2. Do you think drug and alcohol use (and abuse) should be treated similarly? Why or why not?

In-Class Writing Activities

1. Compare and contrast the ways you see alcohol and drug use represented in the media. Provide examples where either is condoned or shunned. Which branches of the media do you think are most concerned with alcohol and drug use: the print media, television, movies, music, advertising, or the Internet? Explain your answer.

2. Write an essay from the point of view of someone whose life has been irrevocably changed by drug or alcohol use—a recovering addict, a mother who lost a child in a drunk driving accident, a former drug dealer paralyzed by a bullet wound, and so on. Imagine what you think this person would have to say about the way society promotes and/or fights alcohol and drug use.

ANNA QUINDLEN

The Drug That Pretends It Isn't

[NEWSWEEK/April 10, 2000]

Before You Read

Do you consider alcohol a drug? Are the consequences of addiction to alcohol as severe as the consequences of drug addiction? If so, who should be held responsible: the alcoholics themselves, the producers and sellers of alcohol, or the advertisers who promote the consumption of it?

Words to Learn

ganja (para. 2): Jamaican slang for marijuana (n.)
thronging (para. 2): crowding; gathering in; pressing on (v.)
purview (para. 5): range of function or power (n.)
czar (para. 5): autocrat; leader (n.)
wake (para. 6): aftermath (as in the movement of water behind a boat) (n.)
quantify (para. 6): to identify or express the quantity of something (v.)
excise tax (para. 7): tax on commodities—often tobacco or liquor (n.)
indelible (para. 8): permanent; unremovable (adj.)
ameliorate (para. 9): make better (v.)

ANNA QUINDLEN *(b. 1953) is the author of several books, including* Living Out Loud *(1988),* One True Thing *(1994), and* How Reading Changed My Life *(1998). She is also a journalist, and won a Pulitzer Prize for her* New York Times *column "Public and Private," which ran from 1977 to 1994. Her latest book is* A Short Guide to a Happy Life *(2000).*

Spring break in Jamaica, and the patios of the waterfront bars   1
are so packed that it seems the crowds of students must go tumbling
into the aquamarine sea, still clutching their glasses. Even at the airport one drunken young man with a peeling nose argues with a flight
attendant about whether he can bring his Red Stripe, kept cold in an
insulated sleeve, aboard the plane heading home.

The giggle about Jamaica for American visitors has always been   2
the availability of ganja; half the T shirts in the souvenir shops have
slogans about smoking grass. But the students thronging the streets of
Montego Bay seem more comfortable with their habitual drug of
choice: alcohol.

Whoops! Sorry! Not supposed to call alcohol a drug. Some of the   3
people who lead antidrug organizations don't like it because they fear
it dilutes the message about the "real"
drugs, heroin, cocaine and marijuana.

And it's true: Booze and Parents are offended by it; as they try to
beer are not the same figure out which vodka bottle came from
as illegal drugs. They're their party and which from their teen-
worse. ager's, they sigh and say, "Well, at least
it's not drugs." And naturally the lobby-
ists for the industry hate it. They're power
guys, these guys: The wine guy is George W's brother-in-law, the beer
guy meets regularly with House Majority Whip Tom DeLay. When
you lump a cocktail in with a joint, it makes them crazy.

And it's true: Booze and beer are not the same as illegal drugs.   4
They're worse. A policy-research group called Drug Strategies has
produced a report that calls alcohol "America's most pervasive drug
problem" and then goes on to document the claim. Alcohol-related
deaths outnumber deaths related to drugs four to one. Alcohol is a
factor in more than half of all domestic-violence and sexual-assault
cases. Between accidents, health problems, crime and lost productiv-
ity, researchers estimate alcohol abuse costs the economy $167 bil-
lion a year. In 1995 four out of every ten people on probation said
they were drinking when they committed a violent crime, while only
one in ten admitted using illicit drugs. Close your eyes and substitute
the word blah-blah for alcohol in any of those sentences, and you'd
have to conclude that an all-out war on blah-blah would result.

Yet when members of Congress tried to pass legislation that   5
would make alcohol part of the purview of the nation's drug czar the
measure failed. Mothers Against Drunk Driving faces opposition to
both its education programs and its public-service ads from principals

and parents who think illicit drugs should be given greater priority. The argument is this: Heroin, cocaine, and marijuana are harmful and against the law, but alcohol is used in moderation with no ill effects by many people.

Here's the counterargument: There are an enormous number of people who cannot and will never be able to drink in moderation. And what they leave in their wake is often more difficult to quantify than DWIs or date rapes. In his memoir, "A Drinking Life," Peter Hamill describes simply and eloquently the binges, the blackouts, the routine: "If I wrote a good column for the newspaper, I'd go to the bar and celebrate; if I wrote a poor column, I would drink away my regret. Then I'd go home, another dinner missed, another chance to play with the children gone, and in the morning, hung over, thick-tongued, and thick-fingered, I'd attempt through my disgust to make amends." Hamill and I used to drink, when we were younger, at a dark place down a short flight of stairs in the Village called the Lion's Head. There were book jackets covering the walls, jackets that I looked at with envy, books by the newspapermen and novelists who used to drink there. But then I got older, and when I passed the Head I sometimes thought of how many books had never been written at all because of the drinking.

Everyone has a friend/an uncle/a coworker/a spouse/a neighbor who drinks too much. A recent poll of 7,000 adults found that 82 percent said they'd even be willing to pay more for a drink if the money were used to combat alcohol abuse. New Mexico and Montana already use excise taxes on alcohol to pay for treatment programs. It's probably just coincidence that, as Drug Strategies reports, the average excise tax on beer is nineteen cents a gallon, while in Missouri and Wisconsin, homes to Anheuser-Busch and Miller, respectively, the tax is only six cents.

A wholesale uprising in Washington against Philip Morris, which owns Miller Brewing and was the largest donor of soft money to the Republicans in 1998, or against Seagram, which did the same for the Democrats in 1996, doesn't seem likely. Home schooling is in order, a harder sell even than to elected officials, since many parents prefer lessons that do not require self-examination. Talking about underage drinking and peer pressure lets them off the hook by suggesting that it's all about 16-year-olds with 6-packs. But the peer group is everywhere, from the frogs that croak "Bud" on commercials to those tiresome folks who behave as if wine were as important as books (it's not) to parents who drink to excess and teach an indelible life lesson.

Prohibition was cooked up to try to ameliorate the damage that   9
drinking does to daily life. It didn't work. But there is always self-
prohibition. It's not easy, since all the world's a speakeasy. "Not even
wine?" Hamill recalls he was asked at dinner parties after he stopped.
Of course children should not drink, and people who sell them alcohol should be prosecuted. Of course people should not drink and
drive, and those who do should be punished. But twenty-one is not a
magic number, and the living room is not necessarily a safe place.
There is a larger story that needs to be told, loud and clear, in homes
and schools and on commercials given as much prominence and paid
for in the same way as those that talk about the dangers of smack or
crack: that alcohol is a mind-altering, mood-altering drug, and that
lots of people should never start to drink at all. "I have no talent for
it," Hamill told friends. Just like that.

Vocabulary / Using a Dictionary

1. Why do you think Quindlen chooses the word *dilutes* (para. 3) to
   describe the process of what happens to the antidrug message
   when people call alcohol "a drug"?

2. Find the origin of the word *czar* in your dictionary. Why do you
   think the U.S. government has adopted it as a title for one of its
   administrative positions?

3. What is the meaning of *indelible* (para. 8)? What does Quindlen
   use the word to describe? Can you provide some additional examples of "indelible life lessons"?

Responding to Words to Context

1. Why does Quindlen suggest you substitute the word *blah-blah*
   for alcohol when looking at alcohol abuse statistics? What does
   this show?

2. Quindlen writes in paragraph 7, "Everyone has a friend/an uncle/
   a coworker/a spouse/a neighbor who drinks too much." Why
   doesn't she just say, "We all know someone who drinks too
   much"?

3. Based on her use of the term, how do you think Quindlen would
   define *peer pressure* (para. 8)?

Discussing Main Point and Meaning

1. Discuss Quindlen's use of the setting of Jamaica in the opening of this article. What is her purpose in using this setting?

2. Does it surprise you that 82 percent of surveyed adults said they would pay more for their drinks if it would help to combat alcohol abuse? Why do you think Quindlen cites this statistic?

3. Paraphrase Quindlen's point about "self-prohibition" (para. 9). (*Note:* a paraphrase is a restatement of text in approximately the same number of words.)

4. "I have no talent for [drinking]," Quindlen quotes Pete Hamill as saying (para. 9). What does Hamill mean by this?

Examining Sentences, Paragraphs, and Organization

1. "Well, at least it's not drugs" (para. 3), Quindlen quotes parents as saying about underage drinking. What does Quindlen think about this rationalization? How do you know?

2. How would you characterize the author's tone throughout this essay? Provide specific examples as evidence of your claim.

3. What is the excerpt quoted from Pete Hamill's *A Drinking Life* meant to illustrate? Is it an effective illustration?

4. "But twenty-one is not a magic number, and the living room is not necessarily a safe place" (para. 9). How does this sentence relate to the main claim of Quindlen's article?

Thinking Critically

1. The government regulates adult smoking behavior (prohibiting it in hospitals, airplanes, and other enclosed spaces) because smoking has proven harmful even to those who don't smoke. Why doesn't the government regulate adult drinking more if, as Quindlen argues, drinking has been proven harmful even to those who don't drink?

2. "Not even wine?" Pete Hamill was questioned repeatedly after he stopped drinking. How supportive do you think mainstream society is to nondrinkers? Do you think drinkers have any responsibility to support nondrinkers?

In-Class Writing Activities

1. How important is alcohol to the people you know? Can you imagine a wedding toast or a New Year's Eve party with only fake champagne? Nonalcoholic beer served at Superbowl parties? Celebrating your twenty-first birthday by doing shots of chocolate milk? Describe the role (or lack thereof) of alcohol in your social circle, and explain whether you feel it should be altered in some way.

2. Quindlen names the "Bud" frogs as an example of alcohol advertising that influences underage drinking. Citing as many examples as you can think of, describe the audience and goals of alcohol advertising as you perceive it.

MOTHERS AGAINST DRUNK DRIVING

[2000]

Before You Read

Have you ever been involved in an accident where someone you know drove drunk? How did you react to this? Is this something you think can be easily dismissed? Beside the legal aspects of driving drunk, have you been made aware of the serious repercussions of drunk driving?

Discussing Main Point and Meaning

1. In the opening line of MADD's advertisement, the statement reads: "Do You Really Want Jim, Johnnie, José or Jack Riding Shotgun With Him?" To what is this line referring? What effect do you think the picture of the young boy with this statement posted in front of him has on the reader?

2. In the first sentence of the full paragraph of the advertisement, the statement reads: "Not unless you want Joe Black tagging along for the ride." Explain what this line implies.

3. According to the advertisement, why should we talk to our children about the dangers of underage drunk driving? What does MADD further suggest at the end of their advertisement?

Examining Details, Imagery, and Design

1. The two main images in this advertisement are the young boy at the top of the page and the alcoholic drink in the middle. What does the placement of these images suggest?

2. Positioned just below the face of a smiling young boy, what does the question, "Do You Really Want Jim, Johnnie, José or Jack Riding Shotgun With Him?" suggest about the boy's safety?

Thinking Critically

1. "Soon, half of his friends won't just be hitting the streets, they'll be hitting the bottle as well" (sent. 2), states MADD's advertisement. Do you think that this statement is too dramatic? Do you think it is making an illogical assumption?

2. How effective do you think a parent calling the MADD hotline, or visiting the MADD Web site might be? Would you go to either of these sources to educate a child about the dangers of drunk driving and alcohol abuse?

3. Read the advertising copy carefully. How many puns can you find? How would you describe these puns? Given the seriousness of the issue, do you think the puns are appropriate? What effect do you think they are intended to have on parents who are the target of the ad? In your opinion, do they lighten or trivialize the issue or do they reinforce the message?

In-Class Writing Activities

1. Write an essay discussing how you would approach educating a group of young children about the dangers of drunk driving. What would your approach include? Lectures? Films? Testimony? Also try and consider what age group would be appropriate for your method.

2. Write a letter to a young person you know discussing the evils of drunk driving. Consider the sophistication of your language, the examples you use to illustrate your points, and the message that you are trying to deliver.

COMMON SENSE FOR DRUG POLICY

[2000]

Before You Read

Are American drug policies excessive? Are they overly harsh? Do you feel that America's "war on drugs" breeds injustice, or do you think that we need stricter laws regulating drug abuse in America? Has anyone you know been affected by drug laws that are too severe?

Words to Learn

essential (para. 1): necessary; vital; indispensable (adj.)

nullification (para. 1): invalidation; cancellation; abolishment (n.)

common law (para. 1): unwritten body of law developed in England, constituting the basis of the U.S. legal system (n.)

prosecutorial (para. 2): accusatory; examinatory (adj.)

excesses (para. 2): extremes; unrestrained behaviors (n.)

manifestly (para. 2): noticeably, clearly, obviously; distinctly (adv.)

legitimate (para. 2): lawful; rightful; legal (adj.)

Just Say Not Guilty?

The jury right to say "not guilty" is an essential safeguard against injustice. Jury nullification dates back to English common law and the founding of the United States.

☑ Jurors in early 19th-century America routinely refused to enforce the Alien and Sedition Act.

☑ Jurors in mid-19th-century America widely rejected the Fugitive Slave Act.

☑ Jurors in the early 20th-century America refused to enforce Alcohol Prohibition.

The injustices of the war on drugs have become obvious to many Americans. In cases where the law, the prosecutorial excesses, and the likely sentence seem manifestly unfair, jury nullification is a legitimate option.

For more information visit: www.csdp.org.
Common Sense for Drug Policy Kevin B. Zeese President   703-354-9050, 703-354-5695 (fax), info@csdp.org

Vocabulary / Using a Dictionary

1. "Jury *nullification* dates back to English common law . . ." states the third sentence of Common Sense for Drug Policy's advertisement. What does *nullification* mean? What word does *nullification* come from? What is the origin of this word?

2. What was *Prohibition?* What word does *prohibition* come from? What is the definition of that word?

3. The second paragraph of the advertisement reads: ". . . jury nullification is a *legitimate* option." Here, the word *legitimate* is being used as an adjective to describe the word *option*. Can the word *legitimate* also function as a verb? Explain.

Discussing Main Point and Meaning

1. What is *jury nullification* (para. 1)? Where does the idea of *jury nullification* come from?

2. What do you think a *prosecutorial excess* might be (para. 2)? How does it relate to America's war on drugs?

3. The title of the advertisement reads: "Just Say Not Guilty?" What does that title imply? Why would CSDP want that to be the title of their advertisement?

Examining Details, Imagery, and Design

1. What features of the advertisement make it look like a voting ballot? What do they suggest? How convincing is this design?

2. What does the headline, "Just Say Not Guilty?," implicitly refer to? Does this reference strengthen the advertisement's argument or weaken it? How?

Alien and Sedition Act(s): Four laws passed in 1798 by Congress in response to the threat of war with France. The laws lengthened the residency requirement for citizenship, empowered the president to expel dangerous aliens, and proscribed (banned) spoken or written criticism of the government.

Fugitive Slave Act: Passed by the government in 1793 and 1850, the law was intended to facilitate the recapture and extradition of runaway slaves and to commit the federal government to the legitimacy of slavery.

(Alcohol) Prohibition: The legal ban on the manufacture and sale of intoxicating drink; it became the Eighteenth Amendment in 1919.

Thinking Critically

1. According to the advertisement is the war on drugs just or unjust? Do you agree with this opinion? Explain your reasoning.

2. For what reason does CSDP's advertisement mention jurors' re-
   jecting and refusing to enforce the Alien and Sedition Act, the
   Fugitive Slave Act, and Alcohol Prohibition? What is CSDP hoping to convince the reader of?

In-Class Writing Activities

1. CSDP's advertisement states: "The injustices of the war on drugs
   have become obvious to many Americans" (para. 2). Do you
   think that the American legal system serves justice? Do you consider our legal system to be effective? Write a brief essay on this
   topic.

2. Clarence Darrow, a famous American lawyer, once said: "The
   litigants and their lawyers are supposed to want *justice,* but, in
   reality, there is no such thing as *justice,* either in or out of court.
   In fact, the word cannot be defined." Write an essay agreeing or
   disagreeing with Darrow's argument, supporting your claim with
   specific examples.

Discussing the Unit

Suggested Topic for Discussion

What kind of war are *you* waging against drugs? Do you feel any responsibility to think about how our drug laws affect drug use in America? And what about alcohol? This unit suggests we not only tolerate drug use but that we glorify it through our love/hate relationship with booze. Do you agree with the authors of this unit about that? If so, do you feel that drugs should be legalized or alcohol banned?

Preparing for Class Discussion

1. All three of these authors compare the drug trade with the alcohol industry to a certain degree. Do you think these comparisons are effective? Do you think one is more effective than the others?

2. Do you think drug and alcohol addiction are equally harmful? Do you think they should be treated the same way under the law? Why or why not?

From Discussion to Writing

1. A recent study by the Harvard School of Public Health found that the number of underage drinkers is increasing. Does this mean that the drinking age should be lowered? Or do we need new methods of preventing teens from drinking? Write a short essay describing your position.

2. If drug use were legal and regulated by the government, some say, much drug-related crime (theft, assault, murder) would decrease, addicts would not be too afraid or ashamed to get help, and the money usually spent on prosecution and incarceration of drug "criminals" could be used for prevention and rehabilitation programs so that drug abuse would actually decrease. Write a short essay either supporting or opposing this theory.

3. College students are famous for "binge drinking," a style of drinking that often leads to alcoholism in adulthood. Some say the reason for this is the low cost of alcohol in college drinking settings (at fraternity parties, happy hours, dorm socials, etc.).

Should alcohol be banned from your campus? Should the cost be more prohibitive? Write a letter to the editor of your campus newspaper about these issues, clearly defining your position on college drinking.

Topics for Cross-Cultural Discussion

1. How are regulations on drinking in other countries you're familiar with different from those in the United States?

2. Is there a "War on Drugs" in other countries? Should there be? How do you think your native country's perspective on the drug trade compares with that of the United States?

13

How Do We Define "Hate Crime"?

Do you think that violent behavior targeted at particular people because they happen to be members of a different race, or are gay or disabled, deserves the special designation of a "hate crime"? Should those who commit such crimes be subjected to greater penalties than other criminals? These questions, and many like them, have received enormous attention recently in the courts and media as legislators struggle with the issue of violent crime that also violates an individual's civil rights.

This chapter examines several different ways of viewing hate crimes. Such crimes not only depend on a certain type of victim but they also involve a particular kind of perpetrator. For noted feminist author Gloria Steinem in her essay "Supremacy Crimes," these perpetrators are usually, though not always, middle-class, white, heterosexual males. Interested more in establishing causation than blame, Steinem believes hate crimes are a result of a belief in a combination of male superiority and white supremacy.

In "Love and Hate in Laramie," however, Donna Minkowitz examines the murder of a young gay man, Matthew Shepard, who she feels was ritually slain by two impoverished young men who victimized Matthew as a way to escape their own victimization: "The left," she claims, "has never been particularly eager to examine the ways that class, victimhood, and violence are coded in the language of gender. . . ."

277

In the editorial "Hate Crime Laws Are Unnecessary," the editorial staff of *The Daily Universe* at Brigham Young University explores the idea of hate crime in itself and wonders whether such a designation doesn't lead to greater social polarization. Their position is challenged by Heather Summers, who attempts to show why hate crimes are more dangerous to communities than other criminal acts that do not single out special groups. Finally, an advertisement from Salon.com asks a question our "politically correct culture" may be reluctant to confront: "Why is it a hate crime when whites commit violence against blacks but not vice versa?"

GLORIA STEINEM

Supremacy Crimes

[MS./August–September 1999]

Before You Read

With the rise of hate crimes in the last few years, is there a necessity to define the people committing these crimes? Why? Is it safe to generalize about the motivation of these criminals? Has your institution experienced anything similar to what happened at Columbine High School? Think about how the media have handled these incidents and their perpetrators.

GLORIA STEINEM *(b. 1933) is an internationally renowned feminist and writer. She helped organize the* Women's Political Caucus *(1971) and was founding editor of* Ms. *magazine. Her books include* Outrageous Acts and Everyday Rebellions *(1983) and* Revolution from Within *(1992).*

Words to Learn

sadistic (para. 5): pleasure derived from inflicting pain on others (adj.)

disproportionately (para. 6): not in proportion (adv.)

hierarchy (para. 6): a group arranged in order of rank, grade, class, and so on (n.)

homophobic (para. 6): hating or fearing homosexuals or homosexuality (adj.)

causation (para. 8): the act of causing (n.)

biogenetic (para. 8): having to do with the biology of genetic structure (adj.)

desensitizes (para. 9): takes away the sensitivity of (v.)

affluence (para. 9): an abundance of riches; wealth (n.)

epithet (para. 15): a phrase used to characterize some person or thing, usually derogatory (n.)

propensity (para. 18): tendency, inclination (n.)

patriarchal (para. 18): of rule by males (adj.)

You've seen the ocean of television coverage, you've read the headlines: How to Spot a Troubled Kid, Twisted Teens, When Teens Fall Apart.

After the slaughter in Colorado that inspired those phrases, dozens of copycat threats were reported in the same generalized way: "Junior high students charged with conspiracy to kill students and teachers" (in Texas); "Five honor students overheard planning a June graduation bombing" (in New York); "More than 100 minor threats reported statewide" (in Pennsylvania). In response, the White House held an emergency strategy session titled "Children, Violence, and Responsibility." Nonetheless, another attack was soon reported: "Youth with 2 Guns Shoots 6 at Georgia School."

I don't know about you, but I've been talking back to the television set, waiting for someone to tell us the obvious: it's not "youth," "our children," or "our teens." It's our sons—and "our" can usually be read as "white," "middle class," and "heterosexual."

We know that hate crimes, violent and otherwise, are overwhelmingly committed by white men who are apparently straight. The same is true for an even higher percentage of impersonal, resentment-driven, mass killings like those in Colorado; the sort committed for no economic or rational gain except the need to say, "I'm superior because I can kill." Think of Charles Starkweather, who reported feeling powerful and serene after murdering ten women and men in the 1950s; or the shooter who climbed the University of Texas Tower in 1966, raining down death to gain celebrity. Think of the engineering student at the University of Montreal who resented females' ability to study that subject, and so shot to death 14 women students in 1989, while saying, "I'm against feminism." Think of nearly all those who have killed impersonally in the workplace, the post office, McDonald's.

White males—usually intelligent, middle class, and heterosexual, 5 or trying desperately to appear so—also account for virtually all the serial, sexually motivated, sadistic killings, those characterized by stalking, imprisoning, torturing, and "owning" victims in death. Think of Edmund Kemper, who began by killing animals, then murdered his grandparents, yet was released to sexually torture and dismember college students and other young women until he himself decided he "didn't want to kill *all* the coeds in the world." Or David Berkowitz, the Son of Sam, who murdered

> *We know that hate crimes, violent and otherwise, are overwhelmingly committed by white men who are apparently straight.*

some women in order to feel in control of *all* women. Or think of Ted Bundy, the charming, snobbish, young would-be lawyer who tortured and murdered as many as forty women, usually beautiful students who were symbols of the economic class he longed to join. As for John Wayne Gacy, he was obsessed with maintaining the public mask of masculinity, and so hid his homosexuality by killing and burying men and boys with whom he had had sex.

These "senseless" killings begin to seem less mysterious when you 6 consider that they were committed disproportionately by white, non-poor males, the group most likely to become hooked on the drug of superiority. It's a drug pushed by a male-dominant culture that presents dominance as a natural right; a racist hierarchy that falsely elevates whiteness; a materialist society that equates superiority with possessions, and a homophobic one that empowers only one form of sexuality.

As Elliott Leyton reports in *Hunting Humans: The Rise of the* 7 *Modern Multiple Murderer,* these killers see their behavior as "an appropriate—even 'manly'—response to the frustrations and disappointments that are a normal part of life." In other words, it's not their life experiences that are the problem, its's the impossible expectation of dominance to which they've become addicted.

This is not about blame. This is about causation. If anything, ending the massive cultural cover-up of supremacy crimes should make heroes out of boys and men who reject violence, especially those who reject the notion of superiority altogether. Even if one believes in a biogenetic component of male aggression, the very existence of gentle men proves that socialization can override it.   8

Nor is this about attributing such crimes to a single cause. Addiction to the drug of supremacy is not their only root, just the deepest and most ignored one. Additional reasons why this country has such a high rate of violence include the plentiful guns that make killing seem as unreal as a video game; male violence in the media that desensitizes viewers in much the same way that combat killers are desensitized in training; affluence that allows maximum access to violence-as-entertainment; a national history of genocide and slavery; the romanticizing of frontier violence and organized crime; not to mention extremes of wealth and poverty and the illusion that both are deserved.   9

But it is truly remarkable, given the relative reasons for anger at injustice in this country, that white, non-poor men have a near-monopoly on multiple killings of strangers, whether serial and sadistic or mass and random. How can we ignore this obvious fact? Others may kill to improve their own condition—in self-defense, or for money or drugs; to eliminate enemies; to declare turf in drive-by shootings; even for a jacket or a pair of sneakers—but white males addicted to supremacy kill even when it worsens their condition or ends in suicide.   10

Men of color and females are capable of serial and mass killing, and commit just enough to prove it. Think of Colin Ferguson, the crazed black man on the Long Island Railroad, or Wayne Williams, the young black man in Atlanta who kidnapped and killed black boys, apparently to conceal his homosexuality. Think of Aileen Carol Wuornos, the white prostitute in Florida who killed abusive johns "in self-defense," or Waneta Hoyt, the upstate New York woman who strangled her five infant children between 1965 and 1971, disguising their cause of death as sudden infant death syndrome. Such crimes are rare enough to leave a haunting refrain of disbelief as evoked in Pat Parker's poem "jonestown": "Black folks do not/Black folks do not/Black folks do not commit suicide." And yet they did.   11

Nonetheless, the proportion of serial killings that are not committed by white males is about the same as the proportion of anorexics who are not female. Yet we discuss the gender, race, and class   12 components of anorexia, but not the role of the same factors in producing epidemics among the powerful.

The reasons are buried deep in the culture, so invisible that only   13
by reversing our assumptions can we reveal them.

Suppose, for instance, that young black males—or any other   14
men of color—had carried out the slaughter in Colorado. Would the
media reports be so willing to describe the murderers as "our children"? Would there be so little discussion about the boys' race?
Would experts be calling the motive a mystery, or condemning the
high school cliques for making those young men feel like "outsiders"? Would there be the same empathy for parents who gave the
murderers luxurious homes, expensive cars, even rescued them from
brushes with the law? Would there be as much attention to generalized causes, such as the dangers of violent video games and recipes
for bombs on the Internet?

As for the victims, if racial identities had been reversed, would   15
racism remain so little discussed? In fact, the killers themselves said
they were targeting blacks and athletes. They used a racial epithet,
shot a black male student in the head, and then laughed over the fact
that they could see his brain. What if *that* had been reversed?

What if these two young murderers, who were called "fags" by   16
some of the jocks at Columbine High School, actually had been gay?
Would they have got the same sympathy for being gay-baited? What
if they had been lovers? Would we hear as little about their sexuality
as we now do, even though only their own homophobia could have
given the word *fag* such power to humiliate them?

Take one more leap of the imagination: Suppose these killings   17
had been planned and executed by young women—of any race, sexuality, or class. Would the media still be so disinterested in the role
played by gender-conditioning? Would journalists assume that female
murderers had suffered from being shut out of access to power in
high school, so much so that they were pushed beyond their limits?
What if dozens, even hundreds of young women around the country
had made imitative threats—as young men have done—expressing
admiration for a well-planned massacre and promising to do the
same? Would we be discussing their youth more than their gender, as
is the case so far with these male killers?

I think we begin to see that our national self-examination is ig-   18
noring something fundamental, precisely because it's like the air we
breathe: the while male factor, the middle-class and heterosexual
one, and the promise of superiority it carries. Yet this denial is self-

defeating—to say the least. We will never reduce the number of violent Americans, from bullies to killers, without challenging the assumptions on which masculinity is based: that males are superior to females, that they must find a place in a male hierarchy, and that the ability to dominate *someone* is so important that even a mere insult can justify lethal revenge. There are plenty of studies to support this view. As Dr. James Gilligan concluded in *Violence: Reflections on a National Epidemic,* "If humanity is to evolve beyond the propensity toward violence . . . then it can only do so by recognizing the extent to which the patriarchal code of honor and shame generates and obligates male violence."

I think the way out can only be found through a deeper reversal: Just as we as a society have begun to raise our daughters more like our sons—more like whole people—we must begin to raise our sons more like our daughters—that is, to value empathy as well as hierarchy; to measure success by other people's welfare as well as their own. 19

But first, we have to admit and name the truth about supremacy crimes. 20

Vocabulary/Using a Dictionary

1. In paragraph 6, the author states: "These 'senseless' killings begin to seem less mysterious when you consider that they were committed *disproportionately* by white, non-poor males. . . ." Break the word *disproportionately* into its component parts. What do its prefixes and suffixes mean? What is the meaning of the root?

2. Sentence four of paragraph 8 contains the word *biogenetic*. What does Steinem suggest by using it?

3. What does Dr. James Gilligan mean by the following statement (as quoted by Steinem): "'the *patriarchal* code of honor and shame generates and obligates [compels, requires] male violence'" (para. 18)?

Responding to Words in Context

1. The word *resent* is used twice in paragraph 4 ("The same is true for an even higher percentage of impersonal, *resentment*-driven, mass-killings . . ." and, "Think of the engineering student at the University of Montreal who *resented* females' ability to study

that subject"). Looking at the usage of the word in these two sentences, think of several synonyms for *resent*.

2. "Take one more leap of the imagination:" says Steinem in paragraph 17, "suppose these killings had been planned and executed by young women—of any race, sexuality, or class. Would the media still be so *disinterested* in the role played by gender-conditioning?" How is *disinterested* different from *uninterested*?

3. At the very end of her essay, Steinem concludes: "But first, we have to admit and name the truth about *supremacy crimes*" (para. 20). Can you summarize what the author might define as a *supremacy crime*?

Discussing Main Point and Meaning

1. In her essay, Steinem remarks: "This is not about blame. This is about causation" (para. 8). She goes on to state her ideas. What does the author suggest about her main point by this remark?

2. In paragraph 10, the author states that some people "may kill to improve their own condition—in self-defense, or for money or drugs; to eliminate enemies; to declare turf in drive-by shootings; even for a jacket or a pair of sneakers." How do these reasons contrast with the reasons behind "supremacy crimes"?

3. In paragraph 12, the author comments: "The proportion of serial killings that are not committed by white males is about the same as the proportion of anorexics who are not female. Yet we discuss the gender, race, and class components of anorexia, but not the role of the same factors in producing epidemics among the powerful." What does Steinem accomplish by making this comparison?

4. What, according to the author, can move America away from the increasingly large number of supremacy crimes? What does Steinem suggest?

Examining Sentences, Paragraphs, and Organization

1. What effect did the author's very first sentence have on you? What did you think Steinem was going to discuss in "Supremacy Crimes"? Examining the first sentence, were you surprised by how the author concluded the essay?

2. In paragraphs 4 and 5 the author repeats the phrase "think of" five different times ("Think of Charles Starkweather . . . ," "Think of the engineering student . . . ," "Think of nearly all those . . . ," and "Think of Edmund Kemper . . ."). Do you believe this is an effective rhetorical device? What do these words force the reader to do?

3. Why does Steinem begin some of her closing paragraphs by stating various suppositions? ("Suppose, for instance . . ." [para. 14], "What if . . ." [para. 16], and "Take one more leap of the imagination . . ." [para. 17].) What is her purpose?

Thinking Critically

1. Is "addiction to the drug of supremacy" the "deepest and most ignored" root of hate crimes? How do you know? What classifies it as an addiction?

2. In paragraphs 15–17, Steinem asks her readers to imagine several hypothetical situations, and suggests the results. Do you agree with her predictions about how the public and the media would react? What else might happen? How else might the participants be viewed?

In-Class Writing Activities

1. An open discussion of hate crimes often centers around the question of who, or what, is responsible. Is it television? The schools? The government? The patriarchy? The family? In an essay, address several possibilities, exploring their interrelationships. Be sure to address Steinem's hypothesis as a possibility.

2. If you were compelled to classify the characteristics of people committing supremacy crimes, what characteristics do you think they would possess? Disgruntled loner? Introvert? Extrovert? From a certain select group? Why? Write a brief essay discussing these points, and conclude by explaining whether or not you agree with the right to stereotype these people.

DONNA MINKOWITZ

Love and Hate in Laramie

[THE NATION/July 12, 1999]

Before You Read

Do we oversimplify the root causes of discrimination? Are hate crimes simply a result of racism, religious persecution, or homophobia? Or must there be a complex combination of factors at work? For example, how might homophobia and class distinctions be related?

Words to Learn

gentrified (para. 3): renovated to be inhabited by upper classes (adj.)

nymph (para. 5): beautiful female nature spirit (n.)

endemic (para. 8): prevalent among a particular group (adj.)

inculcated (para. 9): taught by forceful repetition (adj.)

reviled (para. 11): abused or denounced with harsh language (adj.)

crystal meth (para. 11): illegal drug stimulant (amphetamine) that can heighten or cause aggression (n.)

jacked (para. 20): robbed; fooled; lied to (from "car-jack" or "hijack") (adj.)

stead (para. 26): position usually occupied by another (n.)

DONNA MINKOWITZ *(b. 1964) is the author of the memoir* Ferocious Romance: What My Encounters with the Right Taught Me About Sex, God, and Fury *(1998), which won a Lambda Literary Award. Minkowitz writes for* Salon, The Nation, *and* New York Magazine. *She graduated from Yale in 1985.*

Comfort is easy to find in Laramie, if you're a yuppie like me. I feel like I am on vacation because luxury restaurants are so cheap here; my bed-and-breakfast is the nicest I have ever stayed in. By my standards, it is cheap: $57 a night.

And how does it feel to be a lesbian here? Fabulous. Annie Moore's is not only a Victorian filled with sensuous period furniture, it has a copy of *Rubyfruit Jungle* on the guest bookshelf. Lesbian and gay lovers stay in these sexy little rooms all the time, along with the University of Wyoming's most prestigious visitors. Sometimes the town's yups come to stay for the night just to feel well-off and taken care of. The charming innkeeper, Ann Acuff, who is straight, makes me feel at home by telling about the night she spent at a lesbian bar the last time she was in New York.

Matthew Shepard had much to love about living in Laramie, too; it is a town that caters to moneyed people of any sexual orientation. The guidebooks describe a place that "violates one's expectations of a Wyoming town" (a fascinating verb choice) because it is full of "flower shops, cafés, bookstores, vegetarian restaurants, bars that attract reggae or blues bands, and galleries filled with handcrafted items from all over the planet." In other words, it is very like my own beloved townlet, Park Slope, Brooklyn, which could be the model for gentrified progressive places everywhere. Well-off people move to Laramie by the score from out of state. ("When you buy a million-dollar home in Laramie, it's much, much bigger than a million-dollar home in California," observes Wende Barker, a local progressive politician.) The town is "an oasis of tolerance," says Jason Marsden, an openly gay reporter at the *Casper Star-Tribune*. "It's the only county in the state that can be counted on to vote Democratic," says Barker.

And it is full to bursting with scrumptious consumer goods. If I weren't here to write about an antigay torture-murder, I would be buying pottery at Earth, Wind, and Fire, pricing silver at Green Gold, acquiring delicate, feathery pastries at Jeffrey's Too. Matthew did. He spent money for fun, the way I often do; he bought fabulous clothes; he shelled out money for delightful items to improve his physical appearance in a way that straight men rarely feel entitled to do.

Of course, that's only one side of this story. When Russell Henderson and Aaron McKinney, both twenty-one years old, walked into the Fireside Lounge and encountered Matthew Shepard, they might have been looking at a wood nymph. I'm not going to say who was more oppressed, because all three of them can bear that label easily,

1

2

3

4

5

but their experience was each other's mirror image. When Russell's mother froze to death last January after staggering out of a bar, few people in town were surprised. Russell and his mom, a hotel maid, both lived in the part of Laramie that is home to many of the people who work at the boutiques, restaurants, hotels, and houses that the university people enjoy. The government doesn't even pave the streets there. It doesn't plow West Laramie when it snows; the falling-down trailers and junked cars can wait until it melts.

Recently, the City Council refused to appropriate taxpayer funds   6
to put up a deaf child crossing sign in front of a deaf child's home. "Next thing you know, there'll be a blind child wanting a sign," explained councilman E. G. Meyer. As it goes here with deaf children, so it goes here with busboys, manual laborers, cleaning women. On the gleaming streets of downtown, I get my boots shined by a seventy-year-old Hispanic man who tells me that he was always pushed off the streets for being Mexican, growing up here.

Actually, in this respect, too, Laramie is a lot like Park Slope,   7
where on a recent Friday morning scores of welfare recipients were tidying up Prospect Park for me as I got ready for my morning run. Pleasure, in both our towns, always seems to come at someone's expense. It's the way we were almost all taught about sex to begin with, as though men always hurt women by getting it, and we gradually learned the same lesson about delights of every kind. Russell and Aaron probably believe it more than most. Russell's late mother was the city's most famous battering victim, and he was severely battered by her boyfriends. Aaron's mother often locked him in a basement during his childhood, and as a result, perhaps, "his opinion of women has never been very high," according to a woman who knew him in high school. She remembers his girlfriend coming to school with black eyes.

Who's on top and who's on the bottom seems to be a matter of   8
enormous intensity in this city, perhaps even more than in the rest of America. The feminist movement has never been very strong here, and the incidence of rape and domestic violence against women and children is extraordinarily high. Last year, approximately one in twelve local women reported battering or sexual assault on herself or a child to Laramie's antiviolence project. That's shocking, considering that more than half of all rapes and battering cases are never reported at all. Most media coverage has attributed Shepard's murder to the supposed backwardness and endemic homophobia of rural people, inflaming the bitterness Laramieans have felt for years over the fact that the rest of the country sees them as dumb yokels. (The

uneducated and poor are especially despised here because of the sense that they contribute to that image.)

In fact, Laramie was the likeliest place in the state for an antigay 9 murder to happen, not because of its backwardness but because of its progressiveness and its pockets of wealth and poverty. Explaining why gets tricky, because we are in the realm of cultural memes[1] that bear only the slightest relation to reality. Comfort and voluptuousness (and, of course, consumerism) have been linked in the public mind with effeminacy and homosexuality for decades. Most antigay murders, in fact, aren't committed on the prairie but in liberal cities like New York and San Francisco, where the perception of gay privilege and boys' brutally inculcated fear of being feminine results in scores of antigay murders every year.

The left has never been particularly eager to examine the ways 10 that class, victimhood, and violence are coded in the language of gender, but examining this could help us understand why so many boys and men of all classes between the ages of fifteen and twenty-two are so worried about being on the bottom that they search gay-friendly neighborhoods for gay men to attack. Cultural dogma holds that men must demonstrate at every turn that they are not on the bottom, even if they actually are.

Laramie, the only college town in a state where a number of people 11 hunt for food, is obsessed with status, and Russell and Aaron were reviled for being "losers," dropouts, and poor. They were also addicted to crystal meth. Long ago, Russell had been an honors student and wanted badly to go to college, but instead he wound up as a roofer earning $12,000 a year. Aaron, for his part, saw himself as such a moron that when he won some money in an insurance settlement after his mother's death from a botched hysterectomy, he went out and bought an enormous necklace that displayed his nickname, "Dopey."

Almost no one in our society is comfortable seeing straight men 12 as victims, certainly not the men themselves. But until they do, men like Russell and Aaron will continue to prove their nonvictim status by attacking men like Matthew. And no matter how many gay people homophobes know—like the ones Russell and Aaron knew in Russell's girlfriend's family—gay people will continue to be seen as the enemy.

---

[1]*Meme:* In cultural anthropology, a unit that can be transmitted and reproduced from one generation to another (such as a fashion or a rule); the word was coined as a cultural analogy to *gene*, which can be biologically transmitted.

Picture the three of them at the Fireside, a bar downtown where   13
university and nonuniversity people mix. Even Aaron and Russell's
friends treat them like wimps—they often put Aaron in a headlock
and call him "the shrimp"—and tonight the Fireside's bartender is
shunning them because literally they have dirty hands.

And maybe also because they can't afford to tip. They don't even   14
have the $5.50 to pay for the pitcher of beer they just drank, and
they're turning their pockets inside out looking for it, annoying the
bartender. It's humiliating. All their cash is in nickels and dimes.
Then a beautiful boy at the end of the bar asks if he can help.

McKinney and Henderson are small men, but this boy is smaller.   15
He's the same age as they are but wearing incredibly stylish clothes, a
clean shave, shiny patent leather shoes. His hair is bleached; his
hands on the bar are white and flowerlike. He himself looks like an
emblem of everything they have never been allowed to be. He's a child-
man, or looks like one: still wearing braces, but with enough money
to pay for strangers.

The bartender loves him. Matthew thanks (and tips) him with a   16
marvelous politeness after every round. Russell and Aaron barely
know how to speak that way, like someone who's fluent in Arabic,
French, and German, who was able to be openly gay in high school
(at a fabulous private school in Switzerland), like someone who's already chosen a career in international human rights. They stare at
him across the bar (witnesses differ on whether they take his cash or
not). Matthew is, quite probably, being flirtatious. ("Matthew was
flirty *with everyone*," says Jason Marsden, who was a close friend.)

But these two boys have faces that might be read as gay, and   17
Henderson is actually cute. There are good grounds for believing that
something passed, both ways, between them and Shepard.

Media reports to the contrary, gay-bashing is an erotic crime, not   18
just a violent one. Most bashers, like Russell and Aaron on this
evening, proposition their victim before they kill. And it is easy to see
why Matthew would arouse these feelings. His very charm and gen-
erosity are seductive. Russell and Aaron could never give in to the allure of such flirtatious femininity in another man, but that doesn't
mean they haven't felt it: Most men do. For Russell and Aaron it is
an attraction tinged with envy. They have never been allowed to be
this feminine—or even, you might say, this nice. They have never
been allowed to take such pleasure in fabrics and textures as this boy
is taking in his expensive clothes, but they have wanted to.

Matthew's interest in them makes him infinitely more threatening; 19
this feminine boy has made a masculine pass by offering to pay for
their drinks. His wealth threatens to put them on the bottom where
they have always been, but this time, in relation to a tiny, femmy boy.

He tells them he is gay and they say that they're gay, too. "Let's 20
go back to Aaron's place," they say, "and get to know each other
better" (as Aaron's girlfriend will recount on *20/20*). Once he gets
into their truck, Aaron takes out his gun and smashes the butt of it
into Matthew's head. "We're not gay, and
you just got jacked," he yells.

I think it's significant I'm struck by how that sentence 21
that they killed Shepard resembles an equation: We're not gay
in such a beautiful *and* you just got jacked. Russell and
place. Aaron aren't "gay" — here, a synonym for
"powerless" — because Matthew just got
"jacked."

As they beat him with the .357 Magnum and their fists, Russell 22
laughs out loud. They take his wallet from him, further confirming
their superiority. Shepard begs for his life, which only makes him
more equivalent in their eyes to the piece of nothing that they want
him to be.

Henderson and McKinney drive him out to a prairie owned by 23
the Warren Livestock Company, where everyone in Laramie goes to
commune with nature. People bike and run and walk their dogs here;
and though the livestock company owns it, people act like it is everyone's. The prairie is windswept and rugged, and Russell and Aaron
would have seen incredibly beautiful stars at midnight when they
took him there.

I think it's significant that they killed Shepard in such a beautiful 24
place. Many people have noticed something strangely religious about
this crime, and the attack looks more and more so the more you walk
around the site. The fence to which they tied him is surrounded by
long, flat stones that look like altar stones. And the fence itself is
small, too tiny to keep out even a baby deer; it is purely symbolic,
like a gold cross on a chain. It is the idea of a fence, and that's
enough; they were demonstrating the idea of their election, their superiority. The press, in calling it a crucifixion, was not far off; it certainly looks like a site for holy sacrifice.

While they're whaling on Shepard, they repeatedly hit him in 25
the groin. They have to hit him in the groin: What else will finally

get across the idea that they are not the victims? One thing that is perpetually underemphasized in the discussion of gay-bashings is the sense of overcoming one's disgrace and terror. Almost all the antigay murderers in Arthur Dong's documentary *Licensed to Kill* mention their fear of being raped or beaten up, as they were by men in the past. In a major study of gay-bashers, almost all expressed fears of being raped by the men they sought to beat. In the minds of bashers, gay-bashing means *not being attacked anymore* (never mind that gay people haven't hurt them). Aaron and Russell, too, have been victims their whole lives, and now they want to be the opposite.

That's why they sacrifice him. Even after they force him to tell   26
his address so that they can rob his house, even after his nose is broken and his skull is cracked, there remains a taint of victimhood on them that they cannot expunge except by leaving Shepard tied there in their stead. They even remove his shoes, out of some insane fear that he might get up and walk away. He isn't spread-eagled, like Christ on the cross, but lying on the ground tied by his wrists, like an animal offering.

In that holy place, it feels like all their worthlessness has been re-   27
deemed. Shepard's face is covered in blood.

Vocabulary / Using a Dictionary

1. What does *inculcated* (para. 9) mean? It comes from the Latin word for *trample*. How are these meanings related?

2. Minkowitz uses the word *tinged* in paragraph 18 and the word *taint* in paragraph 26. How are these words similar? How do they contribute to the overall message of this article?

Responding to Words in Context

1. Why does Minkowitz establish herself as a *yuppie* in the first paragraph? What does the word mean?

2. Examine the context of the word *voluptuousness* in paragraph 9. How is this word normally used? Why does Minkowitz employ it in this paragraph?

3. Minkowitz calls the word *violates* a "fascinating verb choice" in paragraph 3. Why?

Discussing Main Point and Meaning

1. Why does the author think class distinctions are at least partly responsible for a crime more commonly perceived to be about sexual preference?

2. What is the significance of the deaf child crossing sign Minkowitz talks about in paragraph 6?

3. Why was Laramie the "likeliest place" in Wyoming for this crime to happen, according to the author? See paragraph 9 for help.

4. According to Minkowitz, why did Henderson and McKinney murder Shepard?

Examining Sentences, Paragraphs, and Organization

1. Describe the purpose of the juxtaposition (placing of unlikely things next to each other) in the following sentence: "If I weren't here to write about an antigay torture-murder, I would be buying pottery at Earth, Wind, and Fire, pricing silver at Green Gold, acquiring delicate, feathery pastries at Jeffrey's Too" (para. 4).

2. Why do you think that Minkowitz waits until the last sections of her essay to reveal the details of Matthew Shepard's murder?

3. "We're not gay, and you just got jacked," is a sentence that reminds Minkowitz of an equation (paras. 20 and 21). Explain what she means here.

Thinking Critically

1. Does Minkowitz's focus on class rather than sexuality minimize the nature of this crime? Does she make Shepard in some way responsible for his own death? Explain your answer.

2. Do you feel that you now understand what led Russell Henderson and Aaron McKinney to commit their crimes? How important should one's childhood be in evaluating adult behaviors?

In-Class Writing Activities

1. Write an essay that examines the relationship between class and gender discrimination or class and racial discrimination that, similar to this author's argument, attempts to get at some of the ways that class divisions can exacerbate other apparent divisions.

2. "In a major study of gay-bashers, almost all expressed fears of being raped by the men they sought to beat," Minkowitz writes in paragraph 25. Consider another famous homophobic murder: In 1995, Jonathan Schmitz murdered Scott Amedure after Amedure expressed romantic feelings for Schmitz while taping an episode of the *Jenny Jones* show on secret crushes. Schmitz was convicted after a criminal trial, and the *Jenny Jones* show was ordered to pay $25 million in damages to Amedure's family in a related civil suit. Write a short essay that examines the similarities and differences of these two murders as they relate to the above quote.

OPPOSING VIEWS

Do We Need Hate Crime Legislation?

Before You Read

Would Martin Luther King Jr. support hate crime legislation? Why or why not? Some think giving extra protection to some groups is discrimination, and should be stopped. Others believe that it's only fair for those more often targeted to receive more protection. What do you think?

Words to Learn [Editorial Board]

demographic (para. 3): statistical; population related (adj.)
polarized (para. 6): oppositional; extremely contrasting (adj.)

Word to Learn [Summers]

exacerbate (para. 1): aggravate; worsen (v.)

EDITORIAL BOARD

Hate Crime Laws Are Unnecessary

[THE DAILY UNIVERSE, BRIGHAM YOUNG UNIVERSITY/January 19, 2000]

How does one honor a great man whose life's purpose was to 1
demolish human barriers, a man who dreamed of equality for his
children and for all people?

President Clinton chose to honor that man by urging that we de- 2
fine more differences and erect more barriers. On January 15, 2000,
in honor of Martin Luther King Jr.'s birthday, Clinton announced his
intention to ask Congress to expand the number of categories that
would qualify under law as hate crimes. The current list includes
crimes committed against another on the basis of race, religion, color,
and national origin. Clinton wants to add homosexuals, women, and
the disabled to the list. To honor the spirit of equality, however, by
carving out more differences among people is not only ironic but
counterproductive.

Under the rule of law the United States is based on and is known 3
for worldwide, it appears that whenever a problem arises it can only
be addressed by means of additional legislation and subtler legal distinctions. Yet, rather than classifying us into various demographic
categories, shouldn't our laws protect human beings under the basic
premise that we are all just that—human beings? Isn't that what
King's dream was all about?

The classifications that hate crime legislation depends on are un- 4
necessary. In his speech, Clinton said that when people "take aim at
others for who they are . . . they take aim at America." But is targeting individuals because of their race worse than targeting individuals
because they are rich? Why is hate the defining factor? Surely any
crime against a fellow human being is not committed out of love for
that person.

A recent case before the Supreme Court involves a woman suing 5
her alleged rapist under the 1994 Violence Against Women Act. This
Act supports a dangerous distinction between the sexes, implying
that a violent act committed against a man is less serious than one

committed against a woman. The same implication can be found in hate crime legislation. It is wrong to say that one victim is somehow less important or less hurt than another.

> *When distinctions are drawn between races, religions, abilities, or sex, barriers are constructed, not demolished.*

When distinctions are drawn between races, religions, abilities, or sex, barriers are constructed, not demolished. Hate crimes were created in support of civil rights, but when differences are continually focused on, a backlash can occur. What we don't need are more polarized categories. What we really need is an increased awareness of prejudices that help us get to the roots of our problems. If Clinton wanted to honor King's dream of equality, creating more distinctions between people and defining more differences was not the way to go about it. Rather than run to the law books whenever a problem arises, we should try as a nation to raise our level of tolerance and prevent such problems from happening in the first place.

6

HEATHER SUMMERS

Hate Crime Legislation Is Necessary

[THE DAILY UNIVERSE, BRIGHAM YOUNG UNIVERSITY/January 24, 2000]

In response to your editorial concerning the Martin Luther King Jr. holiday, I wanted to take issue with your premise that hate crime legislation is unnecessary. If someone assaults or harasses me, it is generally for a reason—such as jealousy or anger—and there are often things I can do to prevent or exacerbate the offense. But when a person's color, religion, or sexual preference, rather than behavior, prompts someone to assault or harass that individual, then there is

1

HEATHER SUMMERS *wrote this article in response to the Brigham Young University* Daily Universe's *editorial reprinted here. The piece provides a hint of the continuing debate and controversy surrounding the need for hate crime prevention laws.*

nothing he or she can do to feel safe. A person's mere presence can be enough to make some bigots turn to violence. The fact that these perpetrators do not need a reason to commit violence makes them more of a danger to our community. For example, isn't a swastika painted on a Jewish family's door a more offensive act than some random graffiti? And aren't those who do the former more of a danger and risk to society?

> *For example, isn't a swastika painted on a Jewish family's door a more offensive act than some random graffiti?*

For those who feel that hate crime legislation punishes a "thought crime," please realize that much of our law is based on intention. The thoughts and motives of the defendant in a criminal trial, for example, can make the difference between murder and manslaughter.

Vocabulary/Using a Dictionary

1. What is a *demographic* (*Daily Universe,* para. 3) category? Can you list some of the *demographics* at your school?

2. The *Daily Universe* Editorial Board suggests that a *backlash* (para. 6) will result from the focus on differences. What do they mean by this?

3. What does it mean to *exacerbate* (Summers, para. 1) something? Give some examples of what Summers might be talking about in her use of this term.

Responding to Words in Context

1. What is the word *alleged* meant to signify in paragraph 5 (*Daily Universe*)?

2. What does Summers mean by the expression *thought crime* (para. 2)?

Discussing Main Point and Meaning

1. Why does the *Daily Universe* Editorial Board choose Martin Luther King Jr. Day as an opportunity to discuss hate crime legislation?

2. Do the authors of this editorial provide an alternative to the hate crime laws they criticize?

3. Why does Summers believe that hate crime legislation is necessary?

Examining Sentences, Paragraphs, and Organization

1. What is the main idea expressed in paragraphs 2 and 3 of the Editorial Board's essay? How is Martin Luther King's work used as evidence for that claim?

2. Paragraph 4 of the Editorial Board's essay examines the use of the word *hate* in hate crime legislation. What is the logic of the authors' analysis there?

3. What additional examples might be helpful to Summers's argument in paragraph 1?

Thinking Critically

1. The Editorial Board suggests that rather than using the law to stress the importance of social tolerance, "We should try as a nation to raise our level of tolerance and prevent such problems [hate crimes] from happening in the first place" (para. 6). What do you think they mean by this? Are you satisfied by this argument?

2. In paragraph 4, the Editorial Board asks whether targeting an individual because of race is worse than targeting an individual because of wealth. What do you think?

3. How do you think Summers would respond to the Editorial Board's complaint that hate crime legislation "polarizes" people and causes a "backlash"?

In-Class Writing Activity

1. "What we really need is an increased awareness of prejudices that help us get to the roots of our problems" says the Editorial Board in paragraph 6. Write a short essay suggesting some ways of achieving this awareness without the use of the law. Use Summers's argument as a jumping off point.

SALON.COM

[2000]

Before You Read

How do you define *politically correct?* Think of some examples of political correctness. Do they seem liberal or conservative to you? How do you define *hate crime?* Is it right to legislate laws designed to protect victims of hate crimes, or is this in itself prejudicial and hateful?

Word to Learn

instigation (sent. 7): provocation, a goading or urging forward (n.)

Vocabulary / Using a Dictionary

1. The last sentence in the advertisement reads: "Sorting Americans into specially protected racial and gender groups like a human 'endangered species' act, and designating whites and heterosexuals as 'oppressors,' is itself an *instigation* to commit. . . ." In this context, what does the word *instigation* mean? The ad ends midsentence. How do you think the sentence should end?

2. What does treating groups like "endangered species" instigate? What does the phrase *endangered species* connote?

Responding to Words in Context

1. Look up *alliteration* in your dictionary. Can you find any examples of it in this ad? Does this technique work? How?

2. What does *politically correct* mean, and how is it being used by Salon.com? Is the phrase being portrayed as negative or positive?

Discussing Main Point and Meaning

1. What type of company do you think Salon.com is? Why do they use this ad to promote themselves?

2. How does the picture of "love" and "hate" work for the ad? Does it enhance or detract from its effectiveness?

Examining Sentences, Paragraphs, and Organization

1. What is the purpose of ending the paragraph midsentence? Is this technique effective? Why?

Thinking Critically

1. What type of assumption is being made by this ad about supporters of hate crime legislation?

2. Do you think that hate crime legislation is only supported by "the self-righteous left"? Is the left being "self-righteous" by supporting these laws? Does the law, as the ad claims, really designate whites and heterosexuals as oppressors?

In-Class Writing Activity

1. Think about recent cases of race-motivated crimes or other hate crimes. Do you think they should be separated from other non-hate crimes? For example, the Amadou Diallo case in New York, in which police officers fired a hail of bullets at an unarmed black man, thinking he was reaching for a gun when he was actually reaching for his wallet. Should this case be tried according to any racist motivation the officers might have had, or purely according to the acts themselves? What if it was vice versa, and the officers were black and the victim white? Write about a recent hate-motivated crime and examine the problems with charging the defendant with a hate crime rather than just the crime itself.

Discussing the Unit

Suggested Topic for Discussion

Why do some people resort to violence to express their prejudices? The authors in this unit have some ideas. Gloria Steinem analyzes the socialization of white men, while Donna Minkowitz is interested in the catalyst of shameful poverty in a classist society. Whatever the causes, students at Brigham Young University grapple with the proper response to "hate crimes": special legislation or proper enforcement of existing laws. What do you think would prevent the Matthew Shepards and James Byrds of this world from being targeted by vicious predators?

Preparing for Class Discussion

1. The Editorial Board for *The Daily Universe* asks the question, "Is targeting individuals because of their race worse than targeting individuals because they are rich?" Discuss this question as it relates to the murder of Matthew Shepard as examined by Donna Minkowitz in "Love and Hate in Laramie."

2. How are Gloria Steinem's and Donna Minkowitz's analyses similar? How are they different?

3. How do you think the Editorial Board would comment on the murder of Matthew Shepard? How would they comment on the mass killings and serial killings referred to in Steinem's essay?

From Discussion to Writing

1. Try to define *hate*. Where does it come from? How do we acquire it? What can be done about it? Is society responsible for dealing with the effects of hate?

2. Hate crime legislation suggests that the federal government, rather than individual states, is responsible for protecting individuals from crimes motivated by discrimination. Do you think individual states should be able to address these crimes in their own ways? Or do you think that this kind of civil rights issue is best handled at the federal level? Explain your answer.

3. In addition to calling for more funding to women's shelters and counseling programs, and interstate exchange of criminal histories and charges, the 1994 Violence Against Women Act attempted to name crimes like rape, domestic violence, and sexual harassment as violations of the civil rights of the victims. Such a label would allow not only for criminal prosecution, but also for civil suits (where monetary damages can be awarded) in the case of violence against women where gender was a motivating factor. In May 2000, the provision for the civil remedies (lawsuits) portion of the act was struck down by the Supreme Court in a 5-4 decision. Where do you stand on this issue? Do you think women should be protected from violence by federal civil rights laws? Do you think, for example, that a rape victim should be able to sue her rapist for monetary damages, or is prison time punishment enough? Explain your position in a short essay.

Topics for Cross-Cultural Discussion

1. Is there anything similar to civil rights and hate crime legislation in other countries? If so, how does it compare to U.S. law? If not, why not?

2. All of these authors examine the consequences of belonging to various social groups. Is there similar concern with categories and groupings in other countries?

14

Can Violence Be Explained?

Does violent behavior in the media lead to violent behavior in real life? Does the availability of guns lead to more and more murders? Is the United States an exceptionally violent society, or is violence an innate characteristic of human behavior? Why do males appear more prone to violent acts than females? Why do children kill each other? We have grown accustomed to a barrage of questions like these, since they are repeatedly asked every time the nation is confronted with another deadly school shooting or when an enraged employee suddenly decides to kill his coworkers in cold blood.

This chapter examines some of the ways recent violent behavior has been explained. In "A Look at Terror with My Daughter," a media professor, Susan Douglas, describes how she talked about the Columbine High School massacre with her ten-year-old child: Like most of us, she says, "she at first wanted a simple, single-cause explanation." Such explanations may be compelling, she suggests, but the danger of oversimplification is that it encourages us to overlook the importance of two complex cultural factors—class and consumerism.

Also responding to recent incidences of school violence, Stephen M. Wolf agrees that there are no simple explanations, though in "Countering Violence" he offers a number of realistic measures that could be taken at many levels to "make our schools, our children, and our society a safer and more nurturing place."

A Tulane College student, Chris Wooten, in "As the Murder Rate Falls, Violence Soars," thinks most of the news media's explanations have missed the mark. The violent crimes, he argues, "are symptoms of a deeper, more fundamental problem in American society."

In the final selection, the Ad Council's National Campaign Against Youth Violence graphically suggests that adults may be continually exposing children to violence without even being aware of it.

SUSAN DOUGLAS

A Look at Terror with My Daughter

[THE PROGRESSIVE/June 1999]

Before You Read

How did the Columbine incident affect you? How would you explain the occurrence to a child in high school? Grade school? Would you explain the event at all? Have you discussed the incident with any children you know in the wake of the killings?

Words to Learn

patently (para. 3): clearly; obviously; openly (adv.)

pundits (para. 4): actual or self-professed authorities (n.)

ostracism (para. 5): a rejection or exclusion by general consent (n.)

stratification (para. 9): process of classifying people into groups (n.)

holistic (para. 11): relating to the principle that a part of a system is understandable only in

---

SUSAN DOUGLAS (b. 1950) is the Catherine Neafie Kellogg Professor of Communication Studies at the University of Michigan. She is author of, most recently, Listening In: Radio and the American Imagination *(1999), which won the Hacker Prize in 2000. She has also written for* The Nation, The Village Voice, Ms., In These Times, *the* Washington Post, *and* TV Guide. *Douglas lives in Ann Arbor, Michigan, with her husband and daughter.*

its relationship to the whole (adj.)

insatiable (para. 11): incapable of being satisfied (adj.)

pathological (para. 11): governed by compulsion; compulsive (adj.)

homogeneous (para. 13): of the same composition; alike; similar (adj.)

repudiated (para. 13): rejected as having no authority or binding force (v.)

preposterous (para. 16): absurd, fantastic (adj.)

My ten-year-old usually flees the living room as soon as Peter Jennings appears: "I hate the news! It's so boring."

But not on April 22 [1999]. She stood away from the set as if it were emitting something lethal. Though her back was against the wall, her intense, probing eyes were locked on the screen. She was riveted, just like millions of other kids that night who were trying to make sense of the enormity of the tragedy at Columbine High School.

Once the news was over, she didn't want to talk; she wanted to go off to her room to play and read. But I knew a talk was coming. And I knew the last thing she needed was some patently obvious "tell-them-violence-is-wrong" chat, as suggested by our president. She already knows this.

So I expected her to take us elsewhere, which she did. She and I lay in her bed with the lights out and talked for an hour about how these boys got the idea to do what they did. How could they want to do this, and then actually decide to do it? And like most of us—especially pundits and newscasters, it seems—she at first wanted a simple, single-cause explanation. But she was eager to consider various factors that might, together, have produced such a horror.

My daughter, like so many kids interviewed in the wake of the killings, thought it quite important that these boys had been made fun of in school—she understands the pain of ostracism, the enormous pressure to conform. She also thought their obsession with Hitler and war was telling.

What did I think made them do it, she wanted to know.

I didn't have a complete answer. But I did talk about what it means to have a society where it's very easy to get guns. I did mention the media, awash with violent movies, video games, and television shows. Computer and video games, in particular, that require you to enact murders with your own hands—yes, just a quick click, not unlike a trigger pull—may restructure some people's individual psychology in quite powerful ways so it becomes easier to do unspeakable things in the real world when you've rehearsed them so many times in a simulated one.

I think I had a good talk with my daughter, the little gem I send 8 off to school every day assuming she'll be OK, hoping she won't be afraid, and praying she won't get hurt. When my daughter finally went to bed that night, she insisted on having the hall light left on. She never has the hall light left on.

But I failed to link her concerns about the importance of friends 9 and the pain of being excluded to a discussion of sex roles and bigotry. Nor did I raise the complex issue of social stratification.

Some are now advocating school uniforms all around, others are 10 bashing the NRA (which it richly deserves), and still others are bashing the entertainment industry (which it deserves, too).

But I think the most important thing adults can do is to help our 11 kids, and others, to see this disaster in holistic terms: to see how the "culture of violence" is powerfully linked to our national religion, consumerism; how this fans an insatiable, almost pathological hunger for fame and celebrity; and how all of these are deeply sustained by a media culture that insists that winning the envy and even fear of others is the most important achievement there is.

It's not just "loners" or troublemakers who struggle with these 12 pressures—most kids do. Some, like the jocks and the cheerleaders, come out on top. But not without scars.

Cliques based on class—and the resentments that accompany 13 them—have existed in schools for decades. But distinctions based on conspicuous consumption and brand names have become more finely honed and obsessively policed since the 1980s. The press referred to Dylan Klebold and Eric Harris as middle class, but they were hardly part of some allegedly homogeneous "middle" in high school. Kids learn very early now—with the help of intensified advertising geared just to them—that as they grow up, they are supposed to learn how to make others envy, even resent them, and Ralph Lauren, Calvin Klein, Nike, and Tommy Hilfiger are there to do just that. Their parents, meanwhile, obsessed with what Barbara Ehrenreich brilliantly diagnosed as the "Fear of Falling," help them understand the pecking order based on the fine gradations between a Toyota Camry, a Ford Expedition, and a Lexus. The ones lower down on the ladder get razzed for not having the brand-name signifiers of those higher up. Wasn't this what we repudiated in the 1960s?

Wanting to be on top, while spitting on those beneath you, is a   14
desire that gained new legitimacy in the 1980s.

Amid this class intolerance, there is social intolerance. Too many   15
of our children—and boys in particular—are learning that words
like *bitch, nigger,* and *faggot* are accept-
able weapons to keep others in their place.

> *Admit to our children that it's not just violent kids who are affected by the media; we all are.*

Yes, we need to monitor violent   16
media fare, support gun control even
more fervently, and so forth. But let's also
sit down with our kids and a copy of the
Abercrombie & Fitch catalogue, or the
Sunday *New York Times Magazine,* and
talk with them about conspicuous consumption, conformity, snobbery, and ostracism. Admit to our children that it's not just violent
kids who are affected by the media; we all are. We must help them
understand that revenge fantasies and fantasies about preposterous
levels of fortune and fame are all of a piece.

Our kids are thinking about that most censored of topics in   17
America, class distinctions and how rigidly they are enforced. And if
we overlook this effect in them, we will have missed a lot.

Vocabulary / Using a Dictionary

1. While reflecting on the Columbine tragedy, Douglas states: "My
    daughter, like so many kids interviewed in the wake of the
    killings, thought it quite important that these boys had been
    made fun of in school—she understands the pain of *ostracism,*
    the enormous pressure to conform" (para. 5). What is *ostracism?*
    What does it mean to be *ostracized?* What is the origin of both
    words?

2. In paragraph 9 of her article, the author mentions the "complex
    issue of *social stratification.*" What does the term *social stratifi-
    cation* mean? Looking at the definition of the word *stratification,*
    how do you think we have arrived at this meaning?

3. In her conclusion, Douglas suggests that we need to "Admit to
    our children that it's not just violent kids who are affected by the
    media; we all are. We must help them understand that revenge
    fantasies and fantasies about *preposterous* levels of fortune and
    fame are all of a piece" (para. 16). With her use of the word *pre-
    posterous,* what is the author suggesting about the levels of for-

tune that these children think they will achieve? What is the origin of the word *preposterous?*

Responding to Words in Context

1. On April 22, 1999, Susan Douglas's ten-year-old daughter "stood away from the [television] set as if it were *emitting* something lethal. Though her back was against the wall, her intense, probing eyes were locked on the screen" (para. 2). Looking at her daughter's reaction, what do you think Douglas means in her use of the word *emitting?*

2. When concluding her argument, Douglas comments, "We must help them [our children] understand that revenge fantasies and fantasies about preposterous levels of fortune and fame are *all of a piece*" (para. 16). What statement is the author trying to make when she says that fantasies about revenge and great wealth are *"all of a piece"?*

Discussing Main Point and Meaning

1. Describe how Douglas's daughter reacted to the news of April 22, 1999. What did her daughter wish to do after the news broadcast? What did her daughter *actually* do?

2. According to Douglas, what is the most important thing adults can do to help their kids to see the disaster and terror of youth violence? Explain your answer in depth.

3. Besides monitoring the media and supporting gun control, what else does the author suggest we as adults need to do in order to keep our children happy and healthy? As a follow-up question, what (according to Douglas) is the most censored topic in the United States?

Examining Sentences, Paragraphs, and Organization

1. What is the topic sentence in paragraph 7? Why is this the topic sentence of that paragraph?

2. What do you make of Douglas's last paragraph? What is the tone of the paragraph? Does it leave the reader with a certain emotion or feeling? Do you consider it to be effective?

3. What is the thesis (main idea) of Douglas's essay? Where is it located?

Thinking Critically

1. In paragraph 10, Douglas claims that because of the recent increase in youth violence, "Some are now advocating school uniforms all around, others are bashing the NRA (which it richly deserves), and still others are bashing the entertainment industry (which it deserves, too)." Do you think it fair for Douglas to strongly state her opinion about the NRA and the entertainment industry? Do you think it detracts from her argument?

2. Do you agree with the author that "our kids are thinking about that most censored of topics in America, class distinctions" (para. 17)? Do you think most students are aware of class distinctions? To what extent?

In-Class Writing Activities

1. Write a letter to Susan Douglas's daughter, explaining to her your ideas of why the tragedy occurred at Columbine High School. Highlight certain points Douglas brought up that you think are relevant, but feel free to explore new areas that might help the young girl understand the incident.

2. "Amid this class intolerance, there is *social intolerance*. Too many of our children—and boys in particular—are learning that words like *bitch, nigger,* and *faggot* are acceptable weapons to keep others in their place," comments Douglas in paragraph 15. In a freewrite, describe what you think Douglas means when she uses the term *social intolerance,* and what problems are created by this narrow-mindedness? What are your experiences with *social intolerance?*

STEPHEN M. WOLF

Countering Violence

[ATTACHÉ/July 1999]

Before You Read

How did you react to the recent incidents in Littleton, Colorado, and Conyers, Georgia? Are there steps we can take to help young children through these tragedies? How do you think we can get this generation of American youth through these very violent times? What solutions can you offer?

Words to Learn

anecdote (para. 5): illustrative story, tale, episode (n.)

pervasive (paras. 6, 7): tending to spread throughout (adj.)

vicarious (para. 6): shared in by imagined participation in another's experience (adj.)

inculcate (paras. 7, 13): to impress upon the mind by frequent repetition (v.)

corollary (para. 7): a proposition that follows from another that has been proved (n.)

articulate (para. 10): to utter distinctly; pronounce carefully (v.)

diligence (para. 10): the quality of being constant; careful effort; perseverance (n.)

implementation (para. 10): fulfilling; execution; performance (n.)

accountable (para. 11): responsible (n.)

prevalent (para. 13): generally practiced, occurring, or accepted (adj.)

STEPHEN M. WOLF *is the chief executive officer of U.S. Airways. This piece was reprinted from* Attaché, *a U.S. Airways magazine in which he contributes a column titled "Chairman's Corner," which focuses on social and political issues.*

It was only a few months ago that we were sharing thoughts on a   1
seemingly unimaginable series of violent incidents in Arkansas, Pennsylvania, and Oregon that shook our nation's schools, and our nation. Now, sadly, we again have seen the wrenching images of frightened and tearful young people on our television screens asking the
question that haunts each of us: Why do these things happen? And
what are we, a society that can seek to build a space station, to do
about them?

As this is written in late May, there still is much we do not yet   2
know about that terrible April day in Littleton, Colorado, or about
the most recent incident in Conyers, Georgia. But we do know that
we stared in disbelief at our television screens and that we
unashamedly shed tears at what we saw. We do know that we said to
ourselves and our loved ones and our colleagues at work that the violence is unthinkable, indeed, unacceptable. We do know that the experts once again have made clear that there are steps that can be
taken—must be taken—if we are to stand a chance at recapturing a
vision and a future for our young.

As I listened to their solutions, common sense alone seemed to   3
dictate that we act simultaneously on several parallel tracks if we are
to stand any chance of success:

In her insightful book, *Mayhem,* a study of the impact of violence   4
in the media on society, Dr. Sissela Bok quotes a frightening statistic
from research done in the early 1990s that estimated by the time a
child left elementary school he or she would have watched 8,000
murders and more than 100,000 acts of violence on television, in the
movies, and on video games.

In a chilling anecdote, she quotes one mother who, with her hus-   5
band, had kept all violent programming out of their family TV viewing and refused to purchase the popular video games. Soon, she
began to notice that her seven-year-old son's friends would not come
to the house. The reason, according to one youngster: "There's no
killing there."

This is not to suggest that video games or violent movies or tele-   6
vision necessarily played a role in the tragic events at Littleton and
Conyers. And it is clear that many viewers realize the events they are
seeing are only on a screen and not part of life. Yet, it is equally clear
that the events in Littleton and Conyers were very real, and it seems
inescapable that there is today a pervasive and unacceptable level of
vicarious violence in the lives of our young. For the vulnerable individual, how many times can you see someone die in a video game or

on a screen before the mind tells you that somehow this is an accepted aspect of life?

Nor is the issue simply one of a willingness, even a desire, to resort to violence. As Dr. Bok points out, these screen images inculcate a pervasive fear that "enemies" will do violence to you if you do not do violence to them first. The corollary: Destroy your "enemy" before he or she destroys you.   7

> *For the vulnerable individual, how many times can you see someone die in a video game or on a screen before the mind tells you that somehow this is an accepted aspect of life?*

There clearly are basic and precious First Amendment issues linked to this subject, issues at the very heart of a democratic society. Perhaps the answer is a massive campaign to educate parents about the potential harm; perhaps the answer is elsewhere. Wherever it is, we must seek it out. But this is not the only issue.   8

To "destroy an enemy," a weapon is necessary. As Fred Hiatt points out in the *Washington Post*, 4,643 children and teenagers were killed with guns in 1996—2,866 murdered, 1,309 by suicide, and 468 in accidental shootings. That means 13 every day—a Littleton massacre every day, as Hiatt so aptly put it.   9

I do not intend to use this forum to articulate yet again the well-thought-out arguments on both sides of the issue of gun control. Yet, who can argue with the proposition that accessibility to guns should be limited to minimize the chance that they might come into the hands of people unable to understand their appropriate use, and especially young people? Acts of Congress are a start, but the real test will be in the diligence that each of us brings to their implementation.   10

Since the violent scenes and the guns will not disappear overnight, we also must equip our schools with the trained personnel necessary to help those who reach out for assistance and to try to spot those who might be close to the edge. As Kevin Dwyer, head of the National Association of School Psychologists, said in my last column on this issue, the recommended level of staffing is one school psychologist for every 1,000 students but the national average is one to 2,200. Of all the issues related to this painful subject, this is the easiest to address. We must insist that those with the ability to act be accountable.   11

For if we had the psychologists to identify and reach out, they perhaps could counsel both the vulnerable student—the one who is a   12 bit different—as well as the "average" student who sometimes is prone to isolate further those who seek to express themselves in different ways.

If the psychologists and teachers and, indeed, parents, can inculcate a culture of tolerance, and if the violent scenes are less prevalent on our screens to provide a seemingly acceptable avenue of expression, and if the weapons are not so readily available, then, perhaps, we will have begun to make our schools, our children, and our society a safer and more nurturing place.   13

We must have the wisdom. We must have the will. We reap that which we sow.   14

Vocabulary / Using a Dictionary

1. "For the vulnerable individual, how many times can you see someone die in a video game . . . before the mind tells you that somehow this is an accepted part of life? . . . these screen images *inculcate* a *pervasive* fear that enemies will do violence to you," comments Wolf in paragraphs 6 and 7. What does it mean to *inculcate* a *pervasive* fear?

2. Why does Wolf call the following line a *corollary:* "Destroy your 'enemy' before he or she destroys you" (para. 7)? What is a *corollary?*

3. When addressing the issue of gun control, Wolf mentions, "Acts of Congress are a start, but the real test will be in the *diligence* that each of us brings to their *implementation*" (para. 10). What does it mean to be *diligent?* What does it mean to be *diligent* in the *implementation* of the Acts of Congress?

Responding to Words in Context

1. In regard to the incidents in Littleton and Conyers, the author comments: "But we do know we stared in disbelief at our television screens and that we *unashamedly* shed tears at what we saw" (para. 2). What does it mean to do something *unashamedly?*

2. In his concluding statement, Wolf states: "We *reap* that which we *sow*" (para. 14). Translate the statement.

Discussing Main Point and Meaning

1. When discussing Dr. Sissela Bok's book *Mayhem* (para. 4), what frightening statistic does Wolf find? As a follow-up question, why does Wolf describe an anecdote from the book as "chilling"?

2. "To 'destroy an enemy,' a weapon is necessary," suggests Wolf in paragraph 9. What are the statistics Wolf (via Fred Hiatt of the *Washington Post*) gives for children being killed by guns?

3. Since violence and guns will "not disappear overnight," what action does Wolf suggest we take? Why? Explain your answer.

4. According to Wolf, what combined factors will begin to make our schools, children, and society a better place?

Examining Sentences, Paragraphs, and Organization

1. When discussing the unspeakably violent incidents that occurred in Arkansas, Pennsylvania, and Oregon, the author states: "And what are we, a society that can seek to build a space station, to do about them?" (para. 1). What does the author suggest to the reader in this sentence?

2. What is the effect of Wolf referring to Dr. Sissela Bok's book *Mayhem* for statistics and for an anecdote in paragraphs 4 and 5? How does this information affect the reader?

Thinking Critically

1. Do you agree with Wolf's suggestion that we must "equip our schools with the trained personnel necessary [that is, school psychologists] to help those who reach out for assistance and try to spot those who might be close to the edge" (para. 11)? Do you think we need more psychologists in the schools to "counsel both the vulnerable student—the one who is a bit different—as well as the 'average' student" (para. 12)?

2. The following statement could raise a lot of eyebrows: "For the vulnerable individual, how many times can you see someone die in a video game or on a screen before the mind tells you that somehow this is an accepted aspect of life?" (para. 6). Think back to your experience with violent television shows and video

games. Do you agree with Wolf that violent television programs and violent video games are influential?

In-Class Writing Activities

1. Think back to the "chilling" anecdote Wolf related about the family that allowed no violence in its household. Now pretend you are the head of a household. What rules and restrictions would you place on TV violence and ultraviolent video games, if any? Do you believe in making restrictions for the young people in your family? Does it restrict their freedom? Freewrite your ideas about how you would monitor violence in your household.

2. Wolf suggests that America's schools are in dire need of more psychologists to help reach troubled students. But this is just one suggestion that schools might take into consideration when addressing the epidemic of youth violence. Write a brief essay suggesting how you would better prepare America's schools to handle the recent violence in America.

CHRIS WOOTEN

As the Murder Rate Falls, Violence Soars

[THE TULANE HULLABALOO, TULANE UNIVERSITY/October 22, 1999]

Before You Read

Have violent crimes in America decreased in recent years? Do you think the murder rate has fallen? What factors do you think contribute to an increase or decrease in violent crimes in America? What part does violence play in our culture? What part does violence play in the media?

Words to Learn

comparatively (para. 4): relatively (adv.)
garner (para. 5): to collect or gather (v.)
fragged (para. 6): intentionally killed or wounded (v.)
stringent (para. 6): rigidly controlled, enforced; strict; severe (adj.)

Statistics issued by a recent FBI report showed that the U.S. murder rate in 1998 was the lowest since 1967. The 16,914 murders represent a general decline in crime that has been occurring since 1992. Political leaders were quick to point out that America is the safest it has been in a generation and, naturally, credited this achievement to their various pet crime-prevention programs.   1

The drastic fall in the murder rate is definitely worth celebrating, but it makes another trend in American society all the more disturbing. While the overall crime rate has plummeted in recent years, the number of mass murders, especially the news-friendly massacres in   2

CHRIS WOOTEN *(b. 1978) was a senior at Tulane University when he wrote this piece in "reaction to the succession of mass murders which occurred in 1999." The article first appeared in Wooten's editorial column "The Fool on the Hill" in the* Tulane Hullabaloo. *Wooten recently received a B.A. in international relations.*

schools, churches, and offices that have become so familiar, has sky-rocketed.

The decline of the murder rate is a direct result of the general fall   3
in crime, which is an immediate benefit of the booming U.S. econ-omy. (Although the FBI report also credits more and better trained police, mandatory sentencing laws that keep criminals off the streets for longer periods, and the strictest gun control laws the United States has ever seen.)

The rise in massacres has been blamed on violent movies and   4
video games, the breakdown of the American family, modern moral-ity's lack of respect for life, the high pace and high stress of today's lifestyles, and even a lack of religion in schools. None of these theo-ries, however, has been able to fully explain what turns compara-tively "normal," law-abiding Americans into hate and insanity-driven killers time and again.

After every workplace and schoolyard shooting spree, politicians   5
and theorists are ready to demonize movies and video games and to claim that even tougher gun control laws are the answer. But these seem to be convenient, inadequate explanations more designed to garner votes than actually solve the problem. Violence has existed in movies for as long as there have been moving pictures, and Western literature and theater have been filled with war and murder since time immemorial. Children's play, also, has mimicked the violence of adults probably ever since the first Cro-Magnon[1] child lifted a stick in imitation of his father's war club.

The perpetrators of these terrible crimes were surely influenced,   6
at least to some degree, by the movies they watched and the games they played, but it's foolish to believe that all of the blame can be laid on Hollywood and Silicon Valley. After all, many of the criminals were adults who couldn't find a hotkey[2] with both hands and who wouldn't know what a railgun[3] was if you fragged them with it. More stringent firearm laws don't seem to be the answer, either, as the number of mass killings has increased along with the "strength" of the gun control laws. Apparently, most of the weapons were either

[1]*Cro-Magnon:* Belonging to a prehistoric, caucasoid type of human who lived on the European continent, distinguished by tallness and erect stature and the use of bone im-plements.

[2]*hotkey:* A software program that customizes your keyboard to go to your favorite Web sites instantly.

[3]*railgun:* A device that uses electromagnetic energy to propel objects to tremendous ve-locities.

obtained through completely legal channels by people who passed all of the background checks and then went on to vent their rage through the trigger; or illegally, through theft, which bypassed the federal government's background check system, or on the black market where even a total ban on firearms couldn't have stopped them.

> *Segments of the American population are so cut off, so overlooked, and so marginalized that they are forced to simmer in their own anger, hatred, and insanity until they explode into fits of homicidal rage.*

Each time one of these horrible events graces the nightly news, whether from a high school in Colorado, an investment firm in Georgia, or a synagogue in California, the debate starts fresh, and it becomes more clear that there is no easy explanation for these crimes, which are symptoms of a deeper, more fundamental problem in American society. Segments of the American population are so cut off, so overlooked, and so marginalized that they are forced to simmer in their own anger, hatred, and insanity until they explode into fits of homicidal rage. 7

Every recent massacre could have been prevented had a parent, teacher, coworker, law enforcement official, or psychiatric worker noticed the warning signs. Excuses and legislation couldn't have stopped any of these crimes, but simple concern for another person's welfare could have stopped all of them. We live in an environment of our own creation. If we want to live in a country where our classmates and colleagues are more dangerous than junkies and carjackers, we will. 8

Vocabulary/Using a Dictionary

1. "None of these theories, however, has been able to fully explain what turns *comparatively* 'normal,' law-abiding Americans into hate and insanity-driven killers time and again," comments Wooten in paragraph 4. What is a *comparatively* normal, law-abiding American?

2. In paragraph 5, Wooten comments: "After every workplace and schoolyard shooting spree, politicians and theorists are ready to *demonize* movies and video games." What does the word *demonize* mean? How is it related to the word *demon*?

3. The author uses the expression *time immemorial* in paragraph 5: "Western literature and theater have been filled with war and murder since *time immemorial*." What does the expression mean?

Responding to Words in Context

1. "Political leaders were quick to point out that America is the safest it has been in a generation and . . . credited this achievement to their various *pet crime-prevention programs*," states Wooten in paragraph 1. Explain, from context, what a pet crime-prevention program is.

2. In paragraph 7, Wooten suggests that "it becomes more clear that there is no easy explanation for these crimes, which are symptoms of a deeper, more *fundamental* problem in American society." What does the author hint at by saying that there is a "more fundamental problem in American society"?

Discussing Main Point and Meaning

1. What are the recent statistics of murder rates in the United States definitely worth celebrating? According to Wooten, what trend do these statistics make all the more disturbing?

2. Generally speaking, what caused the decline in the murder rate in the United States? Again (generally speaking), what caused the rise in massacres in the United States? Is this explanation an adequate one for the author to accept?

3. What does the author mean when he says: "Children's play, also, has mimicked the violence of adults, probably ever since the first Cro-Magnon child lifted a stick in imitation of his father's war club" (para. 5)? Rephrase what the author is saying in your own words, using a different image.

4. After commenting that "there is no easy explanation for these crimes" (para. 7), Wooten suggests that these crimes are symptoms of a "deeper, more fundamental problem in American society" (para. 7). What does the author think this fundamental problem is?

Examining Sentences, Paragraphs, and Organization

1. What effect does the author's use of statistics have on his audience? Would you recommend this strategy to someone writing an essay? Why or why not?

2. At what point does the author reveal his opinion about the perpetrators of violent crimes? Why is this opinion placed where it is? Is the placement of his opinion effective?

3. If the organization of the entire essay revolves around the organizational strategy of *problem to solution,* what is the *problem* as stated by Wooten? The *solution?*

Thinking Critically

1. Do you agree with Wooten that we shouldn't be quick to blame movies or video games for influencing the increase in violent crimes among youth because "violence has existed in movies for as long as there have been moving pictures, and Western literature and theater have been filled with war and murder since time immemorial" (para. 5)? Explain your answer.

2. In his conclusion, Wooten states: "Excuses and legislation couldn't have stopped any of these crimes, but simple concern for another person's welfare could have stopped all of them" (para. 8). Do you feel that there is legislation that could have stopped some of these incidents? Further, do you think that "simple concern for another person's welfare" could have prevented all of these crimes?

In-Class Writing Activities

1. Wooten makes a powerful statement in the conclusion to his essay: "Segments of the American population are so cut off, so overlooked, and so marginalized that they are forced to simmer in their own anger, hatred, and insanity until they explode into fits of homicidal rage" (para. 7). Yet the author never goes into particulars about these groups. Freewrite some ideas about who some of these groups are and how society can better help them vent their rage and adjust their homicidal tendencies.

2. Rollo May, an existential therapist and humanist, once said: "Deeds of violence in our society are performed largely by those trying to establish their self-esteem, to defend their self-image, and to demonstrate that they, too, are significant. . . . Violence arises not out of superfluity [excessiveness] of power but out of powerlessness." Write a short essay agreeing or disagreeing with May, citing examples from your own life to support or disprove his point.

THE AD COUNCIL

[2000]

Before You Read

Do you think American children are subjected to too much violence?
Where do children gain access to violence in their everyday lives? Is
television too violent? Is music too violent? Do you ever "check"
your behavior when you are around children to make sure to censor
what you say or do?

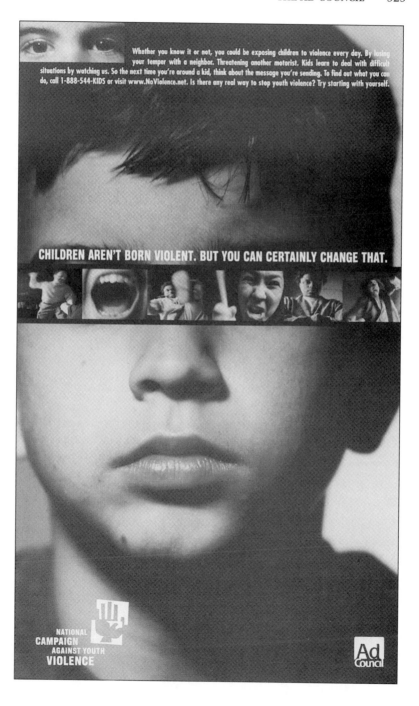

Discussing Main Point and Meaning

1. According to the advertisement, how do we expose children to violence every day?

2. What does the advertisement urge adults to "think about" (sent. 5)?

3. What is the answer to the question the advertisement raises: "Is there any real way to stop youth violence?" (sent. 7).

4. What double meaning is suggested by the title of the advertisement, "Children Aren't Born Violent. But You Can Certainly Change That"?

Examining Sentences, Paragraphs, and Organization

1. Who is the target of the advertisement? Why?

2. What effect does the constant repetition in the advertisement of the words *you* and *your* have on the reader?

Thinking Critically

1. Do you agree with the advertisement's conception of how children view violence? Are children like sponges, receiving data indiscriminately?

2. What contrast does the advertisement suggest between the images across the boy's eyes, and the face of the boy? Is there a specific reason why the boy is innocent-looking, healthy, and white?

In-Class Writing Activities

1. Ashley Montagu, an anthropologist and biologist once said: "Aggressiveness is taught, as are all forms of violence which human beings exhibit. . . . Aggression is the expression of frustrated expectation of love." In a freewrite, try and explain this quote to the best of your ability, bringing in elements of what has been previously discussed with the NCAYV's advertisement.

2. The National Campaign Against Youth Violence was started on May 10, 1999, at a White House summit. Their purpose is (according to the Web site) to provide "a new effort to address the epidemic rates of youth violence . . . to help private citizens, cor-

porations, and foundations to work against violence in their daily lives." Write a letter to the NCAYV giving them suggestions and comments about what you feel they can do to help lower the recent epidemic rates of youth violence in America.

Discussing the Unit

Suggested Topic for Discussion

The selections in this unit all discuss the relationship of children and violence. Do you feel that children are prone to being violent, or must they be led to violent actions? In the "blame game" of the twenty-first century, do you find yourself blaming certain influences for the sharp increase in youth violence? Who or what do you think is most responsible for youth violence? Why?

Preparing for Class Discussion

1. Do you think modern American society would be different if the Columbine tragedy had never happened? How have the recent incidents of violence in America changed our culture?

2. Susan Douglas suggests that we need to "sit down with our kids and a copy of the Abercrombie & Fitch catalogue ... and talk with them about conspicuous consumption, conformity, snobbery, and ostracism" (para. 16). After reading all the selections from this unit, how do you think consumerism and conformity play a role in the recent outbreaks of violence in America?

From Discussion to Writing

1. Write a letter to an imaginary "troubled youth" — a child who you feel may resort to violence to displace his or her inner turmoil. Seriously think about your word choice, what message you would want to relate to the child, and how you would go about organizing your thoughts. Take careful consideration when writing this letter.

2. Stephen M. Wolf gives us many steps with which we should be countering violence, and Susan Douglas wants a good answer as to why the Columbine shooting happened. The NCAYV wishes

us to model appropriate behavior for children, while Chris Wooten urges us to find a way to explain what turns law-abiding Americans into "insanity-driven killers." After reviewing all the selections you've read in this chapter, write an article that states your opinion about youth violence in America, examining whether or not you think violence can be "explained."

3. Describe an occasion when you resorted to violence or anger to cope with a problem. In retrospect, after reading the articles in this unit, how do you feel about the action you took? Looking back now, was your action justified?

Topics for Cross-Cultural Discussion

1. Have other cultures experienced a rise in violent crimes among their youth in the last few years? What do you think causes children in other cultures to be violent? How do other cultures deal with violence?

2. Do you find the United States has a reputation of being a violent country? Why or why not? In relationship to other cultures, how do the States compare in terms of violence? What do you think is the cause of youth violence in the United States?

15

Is the Death Penalty Necessary?

The death penalty has for decades been one of the nation's most controversial issues. Lately, however, with a rapid increase in the number of executions and recent DNA evidence casting doubt on the accuracy of guilty verdicts, the debate has grown even more urgent. Although opponents of the death penalty have been encouraged by a renewed skepticism over its fairness and justice, opinion polls still indicate that most Americans favor some form of capital punishment, especially for heinous murders.

The chapter opens with a statement from writer and journalist Ken Shulman about his participation in Bennetton's controversial photo campaign of inmates on death row at various prisons. Morally opposed to capital punishment—Shulman believes that it "contaminates all who come in contact with it"—in "We, On Death Row" he nevertheless does not romanticize the inmates and sympathizes deeply with their victims. In "What Do Murderers Deserve?" David Gelernter, a victim of the notorious "Unabomber" Theodore Kaczynski, examines responses to the death penalty from the perspective of modern America's "moral upside-downness."

The chapter also features two students with opposing views of the issue. In "An Eye for An Eye Doesn't Always Apply," Carl Villarreal, writing for the *Daily Texan* at the University of Texas, objects to the death penalty on the grounds that recent investigations have discovered too many innocent people on death row. Ann Knudson, in a column for the Bismarck State College *Mystician*, "Should the State

Kill?," reviews the many objections to the death penalty raised by advocate Sister Helen Prejean, and she isn't persuaded by any of them. (A brief excerpt from Prejean's best-selling book *Dead Man Walking* is reprinted in the Editor's Supplement.) In conclusion, an advertisement from the American Civil Liberties Union demonstrates in miniature the latest arguments being waged against the death penalty.

KEN SHULMAN

We, On Death Row

[BENETTON SUPPLEMENT / January 2000]

Before You Read

Should the state preserve and respect all life, even the lives of murderers? If the state chooses to execute some of its citizens, does it dehumanize all citizens?

Words to Learn

vestige (para. 2): trace; remnant (n.)

antithesis (para. 2): direct opposite; converse idea or statement (n.)

tenure (para. 2): term (n.)

catatonic (para. 3): in a stupor (adj.)

thrall (para. 7): servitude; bondage (n.)

consensus (para. 11): agreement; harmony (n.)

cynical (para. 11): pessimistic; skeptical (adj.)

cloying (para. 11): sickly sweet; nauseating (adj.)

mete (para. 11): to measure and deal out (v.)

placate (para. 11): soothe; pacify (v.)

myriad (para. 13): multitude (n.), or countless (adj.)

squalid (para. 15): foul; sleazy (adj.)

KEN SHULMAN *(b. 1965) has written for* Newsweek, *the* New York Times, *and* Artnews, *among other publications. He is also a regular contributor to* National Public Radio. *This article was distributed by Benetton as a supplement to the January 2000 edition of* Talk *magazine.*

How can you talk to them? How can you take their pictures, make them appear pious, contrite, thoughtful, benign, make them look and sound fully human, as if they were assigned to nothing worse than a third-rate holiday resort, as if the horrible deed that has defined and disfigured them far beyond remedy had never happened, or worse, had simply been forgiven? How can you ignore what they have done?

This project has tried my convictions, and repeatedly. I had always been against the death penalty. From my comfortable perch, from my distance, I saw capital punishment as a vestige of man's basest instincts. As the brutal suppression of a human life, helpless before a well-armed, faceless, vindictive state. I thought it the antithesis of justice, of the Christian ethic, of every noble sentiment that humankind has succeeded in kindling and nurturing during his brief tenure on earth.

And then I met the murderers. Murderers who were penitent. Murderers who were catatonic. Murderers who were arrogant, who proclaimed their innocence, or had genuinely forgotten just what they had done to land them on death row. They were as different as their cases, their upbringing, their race, their intelligence. Yet there was something all of them shared. I saw it on my first death row, stepping onto an enclosed, three-tiered cell block, the inmates dressed in hot pink scrub pants and T-shirts, out of their cells for their two-hour recreation.

It was in the way they noticed us without noticing, making us the intruders. It was in the way they sneered, or hid, or laughed, as if at a joke we could not possibly understand. It was something in their eyes, a light that shone neither outward nor inward, but hung suspended, like a bubble in ice. Something that rendered them diabolic and divine, as if having killed had lurched them into a new plane of being, a plane where nothing could embarrass or confuse them again, where they did not need to know anything they did not already know, where time did not flow but froze, cracking only when one of them was taken from the block to be executed.

These men, I saw, were different than you and I. Not in what they dreamed of doing, but in what they'd done. Some were pleasant, gangly, floppy-haired boys wishing they could be out on their mountain bikes, some fond, regretful men and women wishing they could be with their children. A few dreamed of taking to the pulpit, where they could preach the dangers of drugs and alcohol and godlessness to all who would listen. Some were charming. Some were soulful. Some were philosophical. All of them, in some ways, inspired pity.

And then I remember their crimes. The sexual assault and cold **6** blooded assassination of a teenage convenience store clerk for a few hundred dollars and three hundred cartons of cigarettes. The torturing and killing of a three-year-old girl. Four women kidnapped, raped, and murdered by the same man over a five year period. A teenage girl and boy clubbed to death during a robbery. If this had been your daughter, your wife, your brother, your child. . . .

Yes. Yes, I would. More than once, during my interviews, I fan- **7** tasized about doing them violence. There were times when I thought these inmates deserved to die. And worse, when I wanted to be their executioner. Yes, I knew, almost all of them were in the thrall of drugs and alcohol, almost all of them could tell stories of childhood abuse and neglect and depravity as unspeakable as the crimes they would later commit. But not every drug addict or childhood victim goes on to take a human life. Many of us have been tempted to cross that ultimate threshold.

And almost all of us have resisted. They broke the rules. They de- **8** fied the order. What a relief—what a thrill I realized—it was, for me not to have to resist anymore. To act out a script as old as life, to give in to a temptation as great as hunger, love, and power, the ultimate temptation that mankind has gradually and patiently broken in order to be able to live together in a civil manner. It is in our nature to be killers. And we are never far from that most primal region of our nature.

No. I was not interested in justice. I wasn't even interested in re- **9** venge—how could I be? I didn't know their victims, or the families of their victims. I was just inebriated by the opportunity to kill, freely, without the threat of punishment.

I am now more against the death penalty than ever. And not be- **10** cause I have sympathy for the killers. Many of them are likeable. Many of them are changed, especially after having found in prison, ironically and at last, the time and wherewithal to step out of their knotted lives and reflect on every step that has brought them here, to the valley of the shadow of death. Several of them are most likely innocent, although I cannot know which ones. A few might even be capable of leading constructive lives on the outside. Many of them are mentally ill, or deficient. But my sympathy goes to the victims, to their families and friends. These inmates, in most cases born badly, may have had very little control over their destiny.

I am against the death penalty because I believe it gives vent to **11** something very uncivilized within us. Because it makes us, by consensus, a little more like the men I met on death row, more abstract, more cynical, less human. I do not expect those who have lost a loved one to murder to agree with me, that they would want anything other than their pound of flesh—their closure, to use the most cloying, contemporary term. But our justice system does not exist to mete out closure, to placate the bereaved.

> *I am against the death penalty because I believe it gives vent to something very uncivilized within us. Because it makes us, by consensus, a little more like the men I met on death row, more abstract, more cynical, less human.*

It bears remembering that the plaintiff in a criminal suit is not the family of the victim, but the people of the commonwealth. Our justice system does not exist to barter revenge or blood lust. It exists to uphold the law, without which our society cannot function.

The death penalty subverts that law. And not only in the sanctioning of homicide. Due process is compromised in myriad ways, by elected officials pandering to the voting public with stepped up executions, by prosecutors avid enough to conceal evidence in order to wrest yet one more death conviction from a jury. By altering the severity of punishment to suit the race of the victim, and not the gravity of the crime. By making a community, a state, a nation, an accomplice to homicide. Even if the death penalty could be administered justly—and it cannot—each citizen is cheapened by it. As is our society, and the human race.

It is a strange, out of sorts congregation, this "death community." All who live there forfeit a great part of their lives. It is a place where assistant prosecutors give each other high-fives on the courthouse steps because a jury has just elected to send another poorly represented defendant to the death chamber. Where public defenders and pro bono defense attorneys sacrifice time, sleep, health, career, and in many cases their families in order to win their client's right to spend the rest of his natural life in prison. Where prison guards are forced to participate in the gassing or poisoning or electrocution of men and women with whom they have lived—and in some cases grown fond of—over the ten or twenty year period of incarceration.

The death penalty is punishment that contaminates all who come in contact with it. At times, during this long and often fascinating inquiry, it seemed that the inmates were the only balanced elements of this obscene region of the world, and only because their part in this squalid drama has already been spoken. Their role is to wait now, their lives effectively over, even if they should resist for fifty years in prison to die in their sleep as aged, forgotten, useless men. Even if they should, one day, get out. They know that having killed has changed them forever, and for the worst.

Vocabulary/Using a Dictionary

1. Shulman writes in paragraph 2 that he found capital punishment to be the "antithesis of justice, of the Christian ethic, of every noble sentiment. . . ." What is an *antithesis*? What would be its opposite?

2. In paragraph 4, Shulman calls the inmates "*diabolic* and *divine*." What do these two words mean? What is surprising about this description?

3. What does *myriad* mean? Use it in a sentence of your own.

Responding to Words in Context

1. Why does Shulman choose the word *inebriated* (para. 9) to describe himself? How do we normally use that word?

2. In paragraph 11, Shulman talks about the "cloying, contemporary" word *closure*. What do you understand *closure* to be? Do you agree with Shulman's description?

3. Why do you think Shulman chooses the word *congregation* in paragraph 14 to describe the death row community?

Discussing Main Point and Meaning

1. How does Shulman's experience observing death row inmates affect his position on the death penalty?

2. What is the "relief" or the "thrill" that Shulman describes in paragraph 8?

3. What does Shulman mean when he says that supporting the death penalty makes us, like death row inmates, "more abstract, more cynical" (para. 11)?

4. Explain what Shulman means when he says that the death penalty "subverts [the] law" (para. 13). Summarize the ways in which he believes that to be true.

5. Shulman describes the death row inmates as being "the only balanced elements" of the death row process and environment. What does he mean by this? Where else in the essay does he allude to this?

Examining Sentences, Paragraphs, and Organization

1. "How can you talk to them? How can you take their pictures. . . . How can you ignore what they have done?" These sentences appear in the first paragraph of Shulman's piece. Who is the "you" the sentences refer to?

2. When Shulman writes, "Yes. Yes, I would," in paragraph 7, what is he saying he would do?

3. When the author refers to the inmates he met during the time he spent observing them on death row, he often uses repetition — especially of sentence structure. Find some examples of this technique and explain how they affect the meaning of Shulman's piece.

4. "I wanted to be their executioner," writes Shulman in paragraph 7. Later in the essay, he announces that he is "more against the death penalty than ever" (para. 10). Where and how does Shulman reconcile these contradictory statements?

Thinking Critically

1. Do you believe, as Shulman does, that revenge has no place in the justice system? Or do you think that we must exact the heaviest price from murderers?

2. "Even if the death penalty could be administered justly — and it cannot — each citizen is cheapened by it" (para. 13). Examine the two points made in this sentence. Do you agree with either or both of them?

In-Class Writing Activities

1. Shulman says that the death penalty makes us "less human." Are there other issues you think have this effect? Does animal testing, euthanasia, pornography, or war make us as a society "less human"? Describe an issue you think does this, and why.

2. "They know that having killed has changed them forever, and for the worst," Shulman writes of death row inmates. Respond in writing to this statement. Do you agree with it or disagree? What

do you imagine it's like to have killed someone and to be in a
place that reminds one of that fact at every moment?

DAVID GELERNTER

What Do Murderers Deserve?

[THE UTNE READER/March–April 1999]

Before You Read

What is the moral way to treat murderers? Are we duty-bound to execute them? In a society where so many seem to have lost respect for
the lives of others, is execution the only answer? How do we protect
society as a whole from the evil of some individuals?

Words to Learn

penitent (para. 1): apologetic; re-
  morseful (adj.)
deterring (para. 3): discouraging;
  preventing (v.)
defiles (para. 4): pollutes; dishonors
  (v.)
catharsis (para. 4): purification;
  purging or cleansing of the emotions to relieve anxiety (n.)
equivocation (para. 5): avoidance of
  conclusion or certainty (n.)

anomaly (para. 7): irregularity; ab-
  normality (n.)
depraved (para. 8): wicked (adj.)
bent (para. 8): tendency or disposi-
  tion (n.)
cavalier (para. 11): casual; careless
  (adj.)
abhor (para. 13): detest; hate (v.)
apropos (para. 14): about; regarding (prep.)

DAVID GELERNTER *(b. 1955) is professor of computer science at Yale
University, chief scientist at Mirror Worlds Technologies (New Haven, Con-
necticut), and art critic at the* Weekly Standard. *He is the author of five
books and has been published in* Commentary, *the* New York Times, *the*
Washington Post, *the* National Review, *and* Time. *His new novel is appearing in serial form in* Commentary.

A Texas woman, Karla Faye Tucker, murdered two people with a pickax, was said to have repented in prison, and was put to death. A Montana man, Theodore Kaczynski, murdered three people with mail bombs, did not repent, and struck a bargain with the Justice Department: He pleaded guilty and will not be executed. (He also attempted to murder others and succeeded in wounding some, myself included.) Why did we execute the penitent and spare the impenitent? However we answer this question, we surely have a duty to ask it.

And we ask it—I do, anyway—with a sinking feeling, because in modern America, moral upside-downness is a specialty of the house. To eliminate race prejudice we discriminate by race. We promote the cultural assimilation of immigrant children by denying them schooling in English. We throw honest citizens in jail for child abuse, relying on testimony so phony any child could see through it. We make a point of admiring manly women and womanly men. None of which has anything to do with capital punishment directly, but it all obliges us to approach any question about morality in modern America in the larger context of this country's desperate confusion about elementary distinctions.

Why execute murderers? To deter? To avenge? Supporters of the death penalty often give the first answer, opponents the second. But neither can be the whole truth. If our main goal were deterring crime, we would insist on public executions—which are not on the political agenda, and not an item that many Americans are interested in promoting. If our main goal were vengeance, we would allow the grieving parties to decide the murderer's fate; if the victim had no family or friends to feel vengeful on his behalf, we would call the whole thing off.

In fact, we execute murderers in order to make a communal proclamation: that murder is intolerable. A deliberate murderer embodies evil so terrible that it defiles the community. Thus the late social philosopher Robert Nisbet wrote: "Until a catharsis has been effected through trial, through the finding of guilt and then punishment, the community is anxious, fearful, apprehensive, and, above all, contaminated."

When a murder takes place, the community is obliged to clear its throat and step up to the microphone. Every murder demands a communal response. Among possible responses, the death penalty is uniquely powerful because it is permanent. An execution forces the community to assume forever the burden of moral certainty; it is a form of absolute speech that allows no waffling or equivocation.

Of course, we could make the same point less emphatically, by   6
locking up murderers for life. The question then becomes: Is the
death penalty overdoing it?

The answer might be yes if we were a community in which murder   7
was a shocking anomaly. But we are not. "One can guesstimate,"
writes the criminologist and political scientist John J. DiIulio Jr., "that
we are nearing or may already have passed the day when 500,000
murderers, convicted and undetected, are living in American society."

DiIulio's statistics show an approach to murder so casual as to be   8
depraved. Our natural bent in the face of murder is not to avenge the
crime but to shrug it off, except in those rare cases when our own
near and dear are involved.

This is an old story. Cain murders Abel, and is brought in for   9
questioning: "Where is Abel, your brother?" The suspect's response:
"What am I, my brother's keeper?" It is one of the first human statements in the Bible; voiced here by a deeply interested party, it
nonetheless expresses a powerful and universal inclination. Why mess
in other people's problems?

Murder in primitive societies called for a private settling of   10
scores. The community as a whole stayed out of it. For murder to
count, as it does in the Bible, as a crime not merely against one man
but against the whole community and against God is a moral tri-
umph still basic to our integrity, and it should never be taken for
granted. By executing murderers, the community reaffirms this moral
understanding and restates the truth that absolute evil exists and
must be punished.

On the whole, we are doing a disgracefully bad job of adminis-   11
tering the death penalty. We are divided and confused: The community at large strongly favors capital punishment; the cultural elite is
strongly against it. Consequently, our attempts to speak with assur-
ance as a community sound like a man fighting off a chokehold as he
talks. But a community as cavalier about murder as we are has no
right to back down. The fact that we are botching things does not en-
title us to give up.

Opponents of capital punishment describe it as a surrender to   12
emotions—to grief, rage, fear, blood lust. For most supporters of the
death penalty, this is false. Even when we resolve in principle to go
ahead, we have to steel ourselves. Many of us would find it hard to
kill a dog, much less a man. Endorsing capital punishment means not
that we yield to our emotions but that we overcome them. If we favor
executing murderers, it is not because we want to but because, however much we do not want to, we consider ourselves obliged to.

Many Americans no longer feel that obligations; we have urged 13 one another to switch off our moral faculties: "Don't be judgmental!" Many of us are no longer sure evil even exists. The cultural elite oppose executions not (I think) because they abhor killing more than others do, but because the death penalty represents moral certainty, and doubt is the black-lung disease of the intelligentsia—an occupational hazard now inflicted on the whole culture.

Returning then to the penitent woman and the impenitent man: 14 The Karla Faye Tucker case is the harder of the two. We are told that she repented. If that is true, we would still have had no business forgiving her, or forgiving any murderer. As theologian Dennis Prager has written apropos this case, only the victim is entitled to forgive, and the victim is silent. But showing mercy to penitents is part of our religious tradition, and I cannot imagine renouncing it categorically.

> *Endorsing capital punishment means not that we yield to our emotions but that we overcome them.*

I would consider myself morally oblig- 15 ated to think long and hard before executing a penitent. But a true penitent would have to have renounced (as Karla Faye Tucker did) all legal attempts to overturn the original conviction. If every legal avenue has been tried and has failed, the penitence window is closed.

As for Kaczynski, the prosecutors say they got the best outcome 16 they could, under the circumstances, and I believe them. But I also regard this failure to execute a cold-blooded, impenitent terrorist and murderer as a tragic abdication of moral responsibility. The community was called on to speak unambiguously. It flubbed its lines, shrugged its shoulders, and walked away.

In executing murderers, we declare that deliberate murder is ab- 17 solutely evil and absolutely intolerable. This is a painfully difficult proclamation for a self-doubting community to make. But we dare not stop trying. Communities in which capital punishment is no longer the necessary response to deliberate murder may exist. America today is not one of them.

Vocabulary/Using a Dictionary

1. Explain the meaning of *catharsis* (para. 4), and provide one or two other examples of events that, like a trial, provide *catharsis*.

2. What are some antonyms for the word *depraved* (para. 8)? Some synonyms?

3. Use *apropos* (para. 14) in a sentence of your own.

Responding to Words in Context

1. What do you think is meant by the word *guesstimate* used in paragraph 7? What two words does it combine?

2. Examine the word *intelligentsia* (para. 13). What does it mean to you? To whom do you think it refers?

Discussing Main Point and Meaning

1. In the United States, Gelernter writes, "moral upside-downness is a specialty of the house" (para. 2). What does he mean by this? What are some of the examples he uses to illustrate his claim?

2. What is the relationship between murder and community integrity as expressed in paragraph 10?

3. One of the themes of this essay is "obligation." Find examples where Gelernter discusses obligation, or what we should be obliged to do. How does the theme contribute to the main point of the essay?

Examining Sentences, Paragraphs, and Organization

1. What is the topic of paragraph 9? Is there a topic sentence in that paragraph?

2. What does Gelernter mean when he says that "doubt is the black-lung disease of the intelligentsia" (para. 13)? How does he set up that point in the previous sentence?

3. Gelernter compares the cases of Karla Faye Tucker and Ted Kaczynski at the beginning of the essay, and then again at the end. Describe how the two parts of the comparison work together to form a whole. Why does Gelernter organize the comparison(s) this way?

4. What is Gelernter's main argument? Where do you find the most direct statement of that argument?

Thinking Critically

1. Gelernter alludes to being a victim of Ted Kaczynski in paragraph 1. How do you think that affects his ability to write objectively about this issue?

2. An "if/then" construction uses a kind of logic that suggests that for one set of circumstances there is one specific outcome. Examine the if/then logic that Gelernter uses in paragraph 3. What is the outcome for each set of circumstances Gelernter provides? Do you agree with his logic?

3. It was widely reported in the news that Ted Kaczynski suffered from schizophrenia, a mental illness characterized by visions and imagined voices as well as paranoia. Why do you think that Gelernter does not mention this fact? Is it relevant to death penalty sentencing, in your opinion?

In-Class Writing Activities

1. As Gelernter recounts, when Cain is asked about the whereabouts of his brother Abel, he says he is not his brother's keeper. Do you think that we ought to be each other's keepers? Or do you think each person should be responsible for him- or herself? Write an essay about this issue, explaining your position.

2. Gelernter writes, of American morality: "In modern America, moral upside-downness is a specialty of the house. To eliminate race prejudice we discriminate by race. We promote the cultural assimilation of immigrant children by denying them schooling in English. We throw honest citizens in jail for child abuse, relying on testimony so phony any child could see through it. We make a point of admiring manly women and womanly men. . . . [This] obliges us to approach any question about morality in America in the larger context of this country's desperate confusion about elementary distinctions" (para. 2). Analyze these ideas in a short essay, quoting or referring to the text where necessary.

OPPOSING VIEWPOINTS

Should Execution Be Abolished?

Before You Read
There has been much discussion recently about how many death row inmates have been found innocent—either before or after their executions. Given the possibility of human error in the justice system, can the death penalty ever be an appropriate sentence?

Words to Learn [Villarreal]
barbaric (para. 1): wild; crude; brutal (adj.)
antiquated (para. 1): outdated (adj.)
exonerated (para. 5): cleared; acquitted (v.)

Words to Learn [Knudson]
capital (para. 6): extremely serious; fatal; involving the death penalty (adj.)
cannibal (para. 9): person who eats human flesh; animal that eats its own kind (n.)

CARL VILLARREAL

An Eye for an Eye Doesn't Always Apply

[THE DAILY TEXAN, THE UNIVERSITY OF TEXAS AT AUSTIN/February 8, 1999]

There are numerous problems with the death penalty. It is not a   1
solution to the problem of violent crime. There is little proof that it is
a deterrent. It punishes the poor and minorities in grossly dispropor-

---

Carl Villarreal (b. 1975) is a member and cofounder of a campaign to end the death penalty in Austin, Texas. He is also currently a law student at the University of Texas at Austin, where he received his B.A. in microbiology and sociology. Villarreal wrote this piece for the Daily Texan *as a senior.*

tionate numbers. But perhaps the most compelling reason to abolish this unfair, barbaric, and antiquated punishment is because it kills innocent people.

According to Amnesty International, there have been over 400 cases of wrongful conviction for capital offenses in this country between 1900 and 1991. Although in most cases these individuals were able to prove their innocence in court, for 23 the evidence came too late.

> *Perhaps the most compelling reason to abolish this unfair, barbaric, and antiquated punishment is because it kills innocent people.*

Just last week [February 1999] Anthony Porter, a man who at one point had his execution stayed within two days of his death, was taken off Illinois death row because of new evidence and the confession of another man. Of course, there were plenty of reasons to pull him off death row, aside from an unfair justice system. Porter had an IQ of 51, but his innocence finally convinced the tough-on-crime state.

Some would say this shows that the system does work: An innocent man was finally freed. But it wasn't the system that freed him; it was a Northwestern University journalism class. The class, which was studying investigative reporting, questioned a witness who claimed her ex-husband was the shooter. Her ex-husband later confessed. The class could have decided to look at any number of controversial cases. But they chose this case and they did what no police, state, or federal agency thought was important or in their interests to do.

In fact, many people have been freed from death row, and usually it is pure chance at work and not a fair and just system. Last year *ABC News* reported on a group of 29 former death row inmates who met at Northwestern for the first-ever National Conference on Wrongful Convictions and the Death Penalty. It was revealed at the conference that since 1976, 486 prisoners had been executed in the United States and 75 had been exonerated before execution. This means that the policy that sends people to die is wrong at least one out of six times. Those are frightening odds when a bad bet means wrongful death.

Who pays for the mistakes and outright manipulation that put these innocent people on death row? Porter spent sixteen years on Illinois death row before he was freed. What will happen to the prosecutors and police that condemned him to die? They may be charged with obstruction of justice and perhaps sued in civil court, but they will never fear for their lives or go through what Porter had to go through. Yet, unlike Porter, they are truly guilty of a crime. It seems that an eye for an eye doesn't always apply.

A witness who testified against Porter later recanted, saying that   7
police had pressured him. This is a primary reason our justice system should not put people to death. The primary goal of prosecutors and police is often not justice but conviction. With this objective in mind, it's perfectly natural for them to ignore any evidence that doesn't point to the accused, especially if it comes out by the trial stage.

It seems that with just about every death row inmate in Texas,   8
the state's case is less than airtight. Imagine if the state paid for an independent team of investigators and reporters to review the cases of every death row inmate. It would be naive to think that no one would be found innocent. Some, like Porter, have been lucky. At the Northwestern death penalty conference, Randall Dale Adams, who was sentenced to death for killing a police officer in 1976, said, "I came seventy-two hours from execution. I was released in 1989. If the state of Texas had its way, I would be dead."

ANN KNUDSON

Should the State Kill?

[MYSTICIAN, BISMARCK STATE COLLEGE/February 24, 2000]

Texas is scheduled to execute Betty Lou Beets today. Sister   1
Helen Prejean would like to keep her alive.

Prejean is a nun who has acted as spiritual advisor to men on   2
death row. She wrote the best-selling book, *Dead Man Walking*,

---

ANN KNUDSON (b. 1952) likes to call herself an "OTA"—an older than average student. She holds two bachelor of arts degrees, one in communications from the University of Mary in Bismarck, North Dakota, and the other in ecological studies from the State University of New York, Syracuse. She also serves in the National Guard and says that her service in Croatia in 1997 "made me think about when it's right to kill and when it's not."

which was made into an award-winning movie.[1] She has been nominated twice for the Nobel Peace Prize.

Sister Helen presented her case against the death penalty at the University of Mary [in Bismarck, North Dakota] Prayer Day on February 16. I favor capital punishment, but in fairness I went to listen. I also read her book. Sister Helen says Beets was a battered woman who killed her abuser and was badly defended by her lawyer. Sister Helen would like to have the death penalty abolished for all, not just Beets. She says the death penalty does not deter crime, does not save money, kills innocent people, is cruel, and is applied unequally. Furthermore, she thinks the state should not kill its citizens.

So, does the death penalty deter crime? Quite simply, no. Neighboring states with and without the death penalty, such as Wisconsin and Illinois, don't show the difference in murder rates you would expect if it worked as a deterrent. Why not? Criminals don't think they'll get caught, and if caught, don't think they'll be executed. They have reason. The odds are less than one in a thousand that a murderer will get the death penalty. New York City lowered its crime rate, not by executing more criminals, but by putting more police officers on the streets.

> *Sister Helen believes that it is morally wrong for the state to kill anyone, ever, under any circumstances. I do not.*

Does the death penalty save money? It would certainly seem cheaper to execute convicted criminals than to house, feed, and guard them for the rest of their lives. Actually, the process of trials and appeals that ends in death row costs $2.3 million dollars (and up), whereas keeping an inmate in prison costs about $25,000 a year.

Are innocent persons executed? In Chapter Ten of *Dead Man Walking,* Sister Helen names six people sent to death row in error and later released: "Randall Dale Adams (released in March 1989, Texas) . . . William Jent and Earnest Lee Miller (released in 1988, Florida) . . . James Richardson (released in 1989, Florida)." She cites a study by Hugo Bedau of Tufts University and Michael Radelet of the University of Florida, which concludes that there are hundreds wrongly convicted of capital offenses.

Is capital punishment cruel? Her argument is that even if a lethal injection doesn't hurt, knowing that you are going to die on a certain

---

[1]An excerpt from the book follows this essay.

date produces agony in anticipation. She admits that murder is cruel, that victims suffer, and that the victims' families suffer.

Is the death penalty applied unequally? She cites another study, the "Chattahoochee Report," which shows that the death penalty was sought 85 percent of the time in murders of whites and only 15 percent of the time if the victims were black. Everyone on death row is poor. The rich hire better lawyers. 8

Should the state ever kill its citizens? That is a matter of belief. Sister Helen believes that it is morally wrong for the state to kill anyone, ever, under any circumstances. I do not. Some crimes deserve death. Perhaps a woman who kills her abuser might deserve jail instead. She may have had good reason to fear for her life. Most women who are murdered are killed by their husbands or boyfriends, often after trying to leave. However, Beets did it twice. What about the lifer who kills a prison guard while trying to escape? Without a death penalty, what's he got to lose? And what about someone like Jeffrey Dahmer, multiple murderer and cannibal? He doesn't deserve to live. What about the person who rapes and kills a nine-year-old girl? Prisons aren't perfect. He could escape, molest more children, perhaps kill again. If you execute him, you know for sure that he won't hurt any other children. 9

Vocabulary / Using a Dictionary

1. What are *capital* offenses (Knudson, para. 6)?

2. When Villarreal says that the poor and minorities are punished in "grossly disproportionate numbers" (para. 1), what does he mean?

3. What is the opposite of *exonerate* (Villarreal, para. 5)?

Responding to Words in Context

1. Knudson uses the word *lifer* in paragraph 9. What does this word mean?

2. What does the expression "an eye for an eye" mean? Why is Villarreal interested in it?

3. "The primary goal of prosecutors and police is often not *justice* but *conviction*" (Villarreal, para. 7). What's the difference between justice and conviction in your opinion?

Discussing Main Point and Meaning

1. "There are numerous problems with the death penalty," is the first sentence in Villarreal's article. Could it also be a sentence in Knudson's article? Why or why not?

2. Compare the content of paragraph 6 in Knudson's piece to paragraph 2 in Villarreal's. Both talk about wrongful convictions, but how does the content in each differ?

3. How do you think that Villarreal would respond to Knudson's arguments that "some crimes deserve death" and that because prisons are not perfect, the death penalty protects future victims from escaped murderers?

4. Are these authors interested more in justice or morality? Explain your answer.

Examining Sentences, Paragraphs, and Organization

1. Examine the basic structure of Knudson's essay. On what is it based? How does the structure evolve over the course of the essay?

2. Look at the first few paragraphs of Villarreal's essay. Can you find a thesis statement? Where is it? Is there a thesis statement in the beginning of Knudson's essay? If so, where is that?

3. Look at the sentence, "However, Beets did it twice" (Knudson, paragraph 9). What effect is this sentence meant to have? How is that effect related to the placement of this sentence?

4. Compare and contrast the final sentences of each of these essays. What feelings or thoughts is each sentence meant to inspire? Are the intentions behind these sentences fundamentally the same or fundamentally different?

Thinking Critically

1. Villarreal writes about one aspect of capital punishment only: the possibility that innocent people can be put to death. Do you think he should examine other issues as well—deterrence, for example? Or the need for justice for the victim?

2. Knudson waits until the final paragraph to reveal her rationale for supporting the death penalty. Do you think she does enough to make her case in that one paragraph?

In-Class Writing Activities

1. Write a letter to your school newspaper that examines these issues in light of any recent cases you know about. (For example, Gary Graham was executed in Texas in June 2000 based on the testimony of one eyewitness who believed she saw him kill another man.)

2. Write a response from one of these authors to the other. Think about how the responding author would rebut the arguments of their opponent, and try to keep the tone and style of their original piece.

Editor's Supplement

The most frequently cited book on capital punishment, Helen Prejean's *Dead Man Walking: An Eyewitness Account of the Death Penalty in the United States,* appeared in 1993 and two years later was made into a major film starring Sean Penn and Susan Sarandon (who received the Academy Award for best actress). Although the book is an impassioned indictment against the death penalty, Prejean never loses sight of the horrible criminal behavior of the accused and the awful loss experienced by the family and friends of the victims. A Catholic nun, Helen Prejean is a member of the Sisters of St. Joseph of Medaille and a community organizer in her home state of Louisiana. She has written and lectured extensively on the subject of capital punishment. She became closely involved with the issue when in 1982 she was asked to become a pen pal to a death row inmate, Patrick Sonnier, who was convicted of the brutal murder of two teenagers. In the following passage from the book's opening chapter Sister Prejean sorts out her feelings and beliefs about the morality of execution and the desire for retribution.

Helen Prejean, From Dead Man Walking

I cannot accept that the state now plans to kill Patrick Sonnier in cold blood. But the thought of the young victims haunts me. Why do I feel guilty when I think of them? Why do I feel as if I have murdered someone myself?

In prayer I sort it out.

I know that if I had been at the scene when the young people were abducted, I would have done all in my power to save them.

I know I feel compassion for their suffering parents and family   4
and would do anything to ease their pain if I knew how. I also know
that nothing can ease some pain.

I know I am trying to help people who are desperately poor, and   5
I hope I can prevent some of them from exploding into violence. Here
my conscience is clean and light. No heaviness, no guilt.

Then it comes to me. The victims are dead and the killer is alive   6
and I am befriending the killer.

Have I betrayed his victims? Do I have to take sides? I am acutely   7
aware that my beliefs about the death penalty have never been tested
by personal loss. Let Mama or my sister, Mary Ann, or my brother,
Louie, be brutally murdered and then see how much compassion I
have. My magnanimity is gratuitous. No one has shot my loved ones
in the back of the head.

If someone I love should be killed, I know I would feel rage, loss,   8
grief, helplessness, perhaps for the rest of my life. It would be arrogant to think I can predict how I would respond to such a disaster.
But Jesus Christ, whose way of life I try to follow, refused to meet
hate with hate and violence with violence. I pray for the strength to
be like him. I cannot believe in a God who metes out hurt for hurt,
pain for pain, torture for torture. Nor do I believe that God invests
human representatives with such power to torture and kill. The paths
of history are stained with the blood of those who have fallen victim
to "God's Avengers." Kings and Popes and military generals and
heads of state have killed, claiming God's authority and God's blessing. I do not believe in such a God.

In sorting out my feelings and beliefs, there is, however, one piece   9
of moral ground of which I am absolutely certain: If I were to be
murdered I would not want my murderer executed. I would not want
my death avenged. *Especially by government*—which can't be
trusted to control its own bureaucrats or collect taxes equitably or fill
a pothole, much less decide which of its citizens to kill.

AMERICAN CIVIL LIBERTIES UNION

[2000]

Before You Read

What is your position on the death penalty? Do you agree or disagree with this law? Is it right to sentence a person to death for a crime that he or she has committed? Further, is it the responsibility of the criminal justice system to protect and serve the public, or to render judgment and provide punishment for criminals?

Words to Learn

raspy (para. 1): gruff; hoarse; rough; harsh (adj.)

isolated (para. 2): inaccessible; lonely; remote (adj.)

competent (para. 3): capable; experienced; knowledgeable (adj.)

derailed (para. 4): disrupted; upset; wrecked (v.)

riddled (para. 4): punctured throughout (v.)

unscrupulous (para. 4): dishonest; unprincipled; corrupt (adj.)

moratorium (para. 4): suspension; halt; pause (n.)

dubious (para. 4): doubtful; uncertain; unsure (adj.)

inevitably (para. 5): unavoidably; inescapably (adv.)

miscarriages (para. 5): failures to carry out what was intended (n.)

imposed: (para 5): forced on another without right or invitation (v.)

fundamentally (para. 6): basically; essentially; primarily (adv.)

THANKS TO MODERN SCIENCE
17 INNOCENT PEOPLE HAVE BEEN REMOVED FROM DEATH ROW.
THANKS TO MODERN POLITICS
23 INNOCENT PEOPLE HAVE BEEN REMOVED FROM THE LIVING.

On April 15, 1999, Ronald Keith Williamson walked away from Oklahoma State Prison a free man. An innocent man. He had spent the last eleven years behind bars. "I did not rape or kill Debra Sue Carter," he would shout day and night from his death row cell. His voice was so torn and raspy from his pleas for justice that he could barely speak. DNA evidence would eventually end his nightmare and prove his innocence. He came within five days of being put to death for a crime he did not commit.

Williamson's plight is not an isolated one. Nor is it even unusual.

Anthony Porter also came within days of being executed. The state of Illinois halted his execution as it questioned whether or not Porter was mentally competent. Porter has an I.Q. of fifty-one. As the state questioned his competence, a journalism class at Northwestern University questioned his guilt. With a small amount of investigating, they managed to produce the real killer. After sixteen years on death row, Anthony Porter would find his freedom. He was lucky. He escaped with his life. A fate not shared by twenty-three other innocent men.

The Chicago Tribune, in its five-part series "Death Row justice derailed," pronounced, "Capital punishment in Illinois is a system so riddled with faulty evidence, unscrupulous trial tactics, and legal incompetence that justice has been forsaken." The governor of Illinois recently declared a moratorium on the death penalty after the state had acquired the dubious honor of releasing more men from death row than it had executed.

The unfairness that plagues the Illinois system also plagues every other state as well: incompetent lawyers, racial bias, and lack of access to DNA testing all inevitably lead to gross miscarriages of justice. As Supreme Court Justice William J. Brennan, Jr., stated, "Perhaps the bleakest fact of all is that the death penalty is imposed not only in a freakish and discriminatory manner, but also in some cases upon defendants who are actually innocent."

Even those who support capital punishment are finding it increasingly more difficult to endorse it in its current form. Capital punishment is a system that is deeply flawed – a system that preys on the poor and executes the innocent. It is a system that is fundamentally unjust and unfair. Please support our efforts to have a moratorium on further executions declared now. Support the ACLU.

american civil liberties union
125 Broad Street, 18th Floor, NY, NY 10004 www.aclu.org

Vocabulary/Using a Dictionary

1. What does the word *competent* mean? What is the origin of the word? What do you think the word *incompetent* means?

2. "Capital punishment in Illinois is a system so *riddled* with faulty evidence . . . that justice has been forsaken," states the ACLU's advertisement in paragraph 4. What does the word *riddled* mean? Restate the previous statement in your own words.

3. In paragraph 6 of their advertisement, the ACLU states that the capital punishment system is "*fundamentally* unjust and unfair." What does it mean when something is *fundamentally* unjust?

Responding to Words in Context

1. "The unfairness that *plagues* the Illinois system also *plagues* every other state as well," cites the ACLU in paragraph 5. What does the word *plague* suggest about the Illinois capital punishment system?

2. In the conclusion of the ACLU's advertisement, the first sentence of the final paragraph reads: "Even those who support capital punishment are finding it increasingly more difficult to *endorse* it in its current form" (para. 6). What does this statement suggest about the proponents (advocates) of capital punishment?

Discussing Main Point and Meaning

1. How was Anthony Porter proven innocent of his death row sentence? Why should this fact surprise the reader?

2. Why did the governor of Illinois recently declare a moratorium on the death penalty?

3. When discussing the death penalty, what did Supreme Court Justice William J. Brennan Jr. comment is the "bleakest fact of all" (para. 5)?

Examining Details, Imagery, and Design

1. What is the topic sentence of paragraph 1? Why is this the topic sentence of the paragraph?

2. Compare and contrast the opening and closing paragraphs of the advertisement. What is the tone of each paragraph? The purpose of each paragraph?

3. Do you think the advertisement suffers from a lack of examples wherein murderers—those convicted who *truly did* commit their crimes—are justly being put to death? Is the advertisement too one-sided?

Thinking Critically

1. Give some examples of the "plagues" on the state capital punishment systems. Why do you think these examples inhibit the effectiveness of the system?

2. In the concluding paragraph of the ACLU's advertisement, it states: "Capital punishment is a system that is deeply flawed—a system that preys on the poor and executes the innocent. It is a system that is fundamentally unjust and unfair" (para. 6). Do you agree with the ACLU's conclusions about capital punishment? If so, explain why. If not, what part (or parts) do you disagree with?

In-Class Writing Activities

1. If you were to construct a prison facility for death row inmates, what would it be like? Describe what you think is an appropriate environment for convicted murderers. If you think that there should be different environments according to the type, number, or reasons behind murder, point out these distinctions.

2. Write a definition of the word *punishment* without referring to a dictionary or other sources. What do you think is the purpose of punishment? How does a person know what a *just* punishment is? Are there benefits to a punishment? Are there benefits to such a punishment as the death penalty?

Discussing the Unit

Suggested Topic for Discussion

Presidential candidacies sometimes hinge on it, several movies have dramatized it, international coalitions have been formed because of it: Whether we favor or abhor it, the death penalty touches our rawest nerves. Where do you stand on this issue? Do you agree with

Ken Shulman that capital punishment robs all humans of some dignity, or are you persuaded by David Gelernter's opposing argument?

Preparing for Class Discussion

1. Right now, murderers can be executed in some states but not in others. Also, some states send a much higher percentage of convicted murderers to death row than others. Do you think this is fair? Should the death penalty be more uniformly applied, or abolished until it can be?

2. Where do you stand on this issue? Have any of these pieces helped you to fortify your own argument? Do you feel troubled by any of these authors' claims? Are there things you feel you still need to know about capital punishment before you take a position?

3. Are there crimes besides murder that deserve the death penalty, in your opinion? Treason once carried that punishment. Child molesters are sometimes murdered by their fellow inmates.

From Discussion to Writing

1. In groups of four, compose a dialogue between these four authors. Begin with the question, "Is the death penalty a morally appropriate punishment for murder?" Have each person assume the persona of one of the authors, and try to imagine how they would respond to each other.

2. Some opponents of the death penalty believe that life in prison is a better sentence because the convicted murderer has to live for years without freedom and with the painful knowledge that he or she has killed someone and cannot make amends. Using any of these essays as evidence, write an essay that compares life in prison without parole to the death penalty. Which is a better punishment, in your opinion?

3. Many who oppose the death penalty do so because they believe it constitutes an example of the "cruel and unusual punishments" prohibited by the Eighth Amendment to the Constitution. If the United States abolished the death penalty and substituted life imprisonment without parole as a more humane alternative, do you think that would satisfy the opponents of capital punishment or

would they then argue that life imprisonment without parole constitutes a "cruel and unusual" punishment?

4. What would you want to say to a person on death row? Write a letter to a death row inmate that explains how you feel about capital punishment and what you think his or her crime deserves. What do you think the inmate should be thinking about or doing in the years, months, or days leading up to execution?

Topics for Cross-Cultural Discussion

1. Do other countries you're familiar with have a death penalty? Why or why not?

2. How does public opinion about the death penalty in the United States compare with such similar opinion in other countries you know of?

Alternate Tables of Contents: Rhetorical Patterns, Working with Research and Information, and Motivations for Writing

I. Rhetorical Patterns

NARRATION

DESCRIPTION

EXEMPLIFICATION

DEFINITION

CLASSIFICATION

COMPARISON AND CONTRAST

CAUSE AND EFFECT

ANALOGY

PROCESS ANALYSIS

ARGUMENT AND PERSUASION

DEBATE: OPPOSING VIEWS

II. Working with Research and Information

FROM PERSONAL EXPERIENCE

III. Motivations for Writing

CLAIMING AN IDENTITY

CONSIDERING ISSUES AND IDEAS

PROPOSING SOLUTIONS TO PROBLEMS

OFFERING EXPLANATIONS

REPORTING INFORMATION

The Periodicals:
Information for Subscription

A. Magazine: Inside Asian America: bimonthly. $2.95/issue, $15/yr. A "national consumer magazine, by, for, and about Asian Americans, covering personalities, events, and experiences that shape the Asian American community." Subscription address: *A. Magazine,* 131 W. 1st St., Duluth, MN 55802; or call (800) 346–0085, ext. 558; Web site, *@LIVE/A Magazine Online:* <http://www.amagazine.com>.

American Prospect: bimonthly. $2.95/issue, $29.95/yr. "A national magazine of politics, business, and culture," with a liberal focus. Subscription address: *American Prospect,* P.O. Box 772, Boston, MA 02102-0772; or call (800) 872–0162; Web site, *American Prospect:* <http://www.epn.org/prospect.html>.

Attaché: monthly. $7.50/issue. In-flight magazine of US Airways examines travel-related topics. For information write: *Attaché,* Pace Communications, Inc., 1301 Carolina Street, Greensboro, NC 27401; Web site, *Attaché:* <http://www.attachemag.com>.

The Boston Globe: daily. Rates vary according to area; 50¢/issue, $35/mo. in New England; $45/mo. outside New England; student rates available. General newspaper covering local, national, and international news; sections include metro/region, business, living/arts, sports, and editorial. Subscription address: *The Boston Globe,* Subscription Dept., P.O. Box 2378, Boston, MA 02107; or call (617) 929–2215 or (800) 622–6631; Web site, *The Boston Globe Online:* <http://www.boston.com/globe>.

Brain, Child: quarterly. $18/yr. "Treats motherhood as a subject worthy of literature." Subscription address: *Brain, Child,* P.O. Box 714, Lexington, VA 24450; or call (888) 30–4MOMS; Web site: <http://www.brainchildmag.com>.

The Campus Times: A student newspaper of the University of Rochester. Subscription information: *Campus Times,* Wilson

Commons 102, University of Rochester, Rochester, NY 14627; or call (716) 275–5942; Web site, *Campus Times Online:* <http://www.ct.rochester.edu>.

Civilization: bimonthly. $6/issue, $20/yr. A magazine that examines contemporary social and cultural issues. Subscription address: *Civilization,* P.O. Box 420235, Palm Coast, FL 32142-0235; or call (800) 829–0427; Web site, *Civilization Online:* <http://www.civmag.com/index.html>.

Collegiate Times: daily weekdays. $35/semester, $50/yr.; free to Virginia Tech students. An independent student newspaper of Virginia Polytechnic Institute. Subscription address: *Collegiate Times,* 363 Squires Student Center, Blacksburg, VA 24061-0546; or call (540) 231–9860; Web site, *Collegiate Times:* <http://www.collegiatetimes.com>.

ColorLines: quarterly. $16/yr. "First national multiracial magazine devoted to covering the politics and creations of communities of color." Subscription address: *ColorLines* Subscription Dept., P.O. Box 3000, Denville, NJ 07834; or call (888) 458–8588; Web site, *ColorLines:* <http://www.arc.org/C_Lines/ArcColorLines.html>.

The CyberSignal: weekly. Student newspaper of the College of New Jersey. Web site, *CyberSignal:* <http://www.tcnj.edu~signal>.

The Daily Bruin: daily. A student newspaper of the University of California–Los Angeles. Subscription information: *The Daily Bruin,* 118 Kerckhoff Hall, 308 Westwood Plaza, Los Angeles, CA 90024; or call (310) 825–9898; Web site, *Daily Bruin Online:* <http://www.dailybruin.ucla.edu>.

The Daily Kansan: daily weekdays. $60/semester. A student newspaper of the University of Kansas. Subscription address: *The University Daily Kansan,* University of Kansas, 111 Stauffer-Flint Hall, Lawrence, KS 66045; or call (785) 864–4358; Web site, *Kansan.com:* <http://www.kansan.com>.

Daily Nebraskan: daily weekdays. $60/yr. A student newspaper of the University of Nebraska–Lincoln. Subscription address: *Daily Nebraskan,* 20 Nebraska Union, 1400 R. St., P.O. Box 880448, Lincoln, NE 68588-0448; or call (402) 472–2588; Web site, *Daily Nebraskan Online Edition:* <http://www.dailyneb.com/texis/scripts/vnews/newspaper>.

The Daily Northwestern: daily weekdays. $49/yr. A student newspaper of Northwestern University. Subscription address: *The Daily*

Northwestern, Students Publishing Company, 1999 Sheridan Road, Evanston, IL 60208; or call (847) 491–7206; Web site, *Daily Northwestern.com:* <http://www.dailynorthwestern.com>.

The Daily Texan: daily. The student newspaper of the University of Texas–Austin; Web site, *The Daily Texan:* <http://www.dailytexan.utexas.edu/webtexan/today/index.html>.

The Daily Universe: daily. $65/semester, $19/yr. "The official student newspaper of Brigham Young University with a readership of 30,000." Subscription address: 5538 WSC, *Daily Universe,* Provo, UT 84602; or call (801) 378–2957; Web site, *News-Net@byu:* <http://www.newsnet.byu.edu>.

DoubleTake: quarterly. $10/issue, $32/yr. Magazine of photography and visual arts. Subscription address: *DoubleTake,* P.O. Box 56070, Boulder, CO 80322-6070; or call (800) 964–8301; Web site, *DoubleTake:* <http://www.doubletakemagazine.org>.

Esquire: monthly. $3/issue, $15.94/yr., $30.94/2 yrs. A men's magazine that examines health, money, and fashion. Subscription address: *Esquire* Subscription Dept., P.O. Box 7146, Red Oak, IA 51591; or call (800) 888–5400; Web site, *Esquire:* <http://www.esquire.com>.

Essence: monthly. $2.75/issue, $18.96/yr. "The preeminent magazine for today's African American woman." Subscription address: *Essence Magazine* Subscription Dept., 1500 Broadway, 6th fl., New York, NY 10036; or call (800) 274–9398; Web site, *Essence:* <http://www.essence.com>.

Fourth Genre: semiannually. $8/issue, $15/yr. "A new journal devoted to publishing notable, innovative work in nonfiction." Subscription address: *Fourth Genre,* Michigan State University Press, 1405 South Hamson Rd., Suite 25, Manly Miles Building, East Lansing, MI 48823-5202; or call (517) 355–9543; Web site, *Fourth Genre:* <http://www.msu.edu/unit/msupress/journals/fourthgenre.html>.

Iowa State Daily: daily weekdays. $62/yr., students $40/yr. A student newspaper of Iowa State University. Subscription address: *Iowa State Daily,* 108C Hamilton Hall, Ames, IA 50011; or call (515) 294–2609; Web site, *Iowa State Daily Online Edition:* <http://www.iowastatedaily.com>.

Kansas State Collegian: daily weekdays. $115/academic yr. The official student newspaper of Kansas State University. Subscription address: *Kansas State Collegian,* Student Publications Inc.,

Kansas State University, 116 Kedzie Hall, Manhattan, KS 66506; or call (785) 532–6556; Web site, *eCollegian / Kansas State Collegian:* <http://www.collegian.ksu.edu>.

Life: No longer in print. Publishes special editions only.

Mother Jones: bimonthly. $3.95/issue, $18/yr. A journal of "investigative reporting and progressive points of view." Subscription address: *Mother Jones* Subscription Dept., P.O. Box 469024, Escondido, CA 92046; or call (800) 438–6656; Web site, *MOJO Wire:* <http://www.motherjones.com>.

Ms.: bimonthly. $5.95/issue, $28/yr. A feminist magazine that examines contemporary women's issues. Subscription address: *Ms.,* 20 Exchange Place, 22nd Fl., New York, NY 10005; or call (212) 509–2092; Web site, *Ms.* <http://www.msmagazine.com>.

The Muleskinner: weekly. $10/semester, $20/academic year. A student newspaper of Central Missouri State University. Subscription address: *The Muleskinner* Subscriptions, Martin 30, Warrensburg, MO 64093; or call (660) 543–4050; Web site, *The Muleskinner.org:* <http://www.muleskinner.org>.

Mystician: biweekly. Student newspaper of Bismarck State College; Web site, *Mystician:* <http://www.mystician.com>.

The Nation: weekly. $2.75/issue, $52/yr. "A liberal journal of critical opinion, committed to racial justice, anti-imperialism, civil liberties, and social equality," with commentary on politics, culture, books, and the arts. Subscription address: *The Nation,* P.O. Box 37072, Boone, IA 50037; or call (800) 333–8536; Web site, *The Nation Digital Edition:* <http://www.thenation.com>.

New Media Index: weekly. Web zine of Truman State University. Subscription information address: <subscriptions@index.truman.edu>; Web site, *New Media Index:* <http://index.truman.edu/issues>.

The New Republic: weekly. $2.95/issue, $39.99/yr. Student rates available. Opinion journal with a mix of liberal and conservative articles and commentary on American politics, foreign policy, literature, and the arts. Subscription address: *The New Republic,* Subscription Service Dept., P.O. Box 602, Mount Morris, IL 61054; or call (800) 827–1289; Web site, *The New Republic:* <http://www.thenewrepublic.com>.

Newsweek: weekly. $3.50/issue, $29.15/yr. News and commentary on the week's events in national and international affairs. Subscription address: *Newsweek* Subscriptions, P.O. Box 59967, Boulder, CO 80322; or call (800) 631–1040; Web site, *Newsweek.com:* <http://www.newsweek.com>.

The New Yorker: weekly. $2.95/issue, $39.95/yr., students $20/yr. Magazine of commentaries and reviews, current events, cartoons, biographical profiles, short fiction, and poetry. Subscription address: *The New Yorker,* P.O. Box 5231, Boulder, CO 80323-2312; or call (800) 825–2510; Web site, *The New Yorker:* <http://magazines.enews.com/magazines/new_yorker>.

The New York Times: daily, with large Sunday edition that contains *The New York Times Magazine* and *The New York Times Book Review,* as well as other supplements. Rates vary according to location and frequency of delivery. Considered the definitive source for current events; daily, national, and international news; and business and arts reporting. Subscription address: *The New York Times,* 229 West 43rd St., New York, NY 10036; or call (800) 631–2500; Web site, *The New York Times on the Web:* <http://www.nytimes.com>.

Notre Dame Magazine: quarterly. $20/yr. A publication of the University of Notre Dame addressing "institutional and Catholic concerns," and examining cultural issues and covering the university's discussion of science and the arts, society, and spiritual matters. Subscription address: *Notre Dame Magazine,* 538 Grace Hall, Notre Dame, IN 46556-5602; or call (219) 631–5335; Web site, *Notre Dame Magazine:* <http://www.nd.edu/~ndmag>.

The Progressive: monthly. $3.50/issue, $32/yr., $52/2 yrs.; $22/yr. for students. "A journal of cultural and political opinion from a left/progressive perspective." Subscription address: *The Progressive,* P.O. Box 421, Mount Morris, IL 61054-0421; or call (800) 827–0555; Web site, *The Progressive:* <http//www.progressive.org>.

Slate: daily. Online Web zine focuses on political and social issues and current events. For information write: *Slate,* 1 Microsoft Way, Redmond, WA 98052; or call (202) 862–4887; Web site, *Slate:* <http://slate.msn.com>.

The Spectrum: weekly. Student news source for Penn Valley Community College. For inquiries write: *Kansas City Spectrum,* Penn Valley Community College, 3201 Southwest Trafficway, Kansas City, MO 64111; or call (816) 759–4280; Web site, *Spectrum:* <http://www.spectrum.kcmetro.cc.mo.us/current/index.html>.

The Texas Observer: weekly. $32/yr., $59/2 yrs. An alternative nonprofit newspaper addressing local and national events, politics, and social concerns. Subscription address: The *Texas Observer,* 307 W. 7th St., Austin, TX 78701; or call (512) 477–0746; Web site, *The Texas Observer:* <http://www.texasobserver.org>.

Time: weekly. $3.50/issue, $69.92/yr. News and commentary on national and international affairs. Subscription address: *Time Magazine:* P.O. Box 60001, Tampa, FL 33660-0001; or call (800) 843–8463; Web site, *Time.com:* <http://www.time.com/time>.

The Tulane Hullabaloo: weekly. $35/yr. Student publication of Tulane University. Subscription address: *The Tulane Hullabaloo,* Room 25 Tulane University Center, New Orleans, LA 70118; or call (504) 865–5656; Web site, *The Tulane Hullabaloo Online:* <http://hullabaloo.tulane.org/20000428>.

The Utne Reader: bimonthly. $19.97/yr., $31.97/2 yrs. An alternative magazine with a focus on social change, the environment, gender, society, and politics. Subscription address: *Utne Reader* Subscriber Services, P.O. Box 7460, Red Oak, IA 51591-0460; or call (800) 736–8863; Web site, *The Utne Reader Online:* <http://utne.com>.

Washington Square News: daily weekdays. Subscriptions are unavailable. A student newspaper of New York University. For information write: 7 East 12th St., Suite 800, New York, NY 10003; or call (212) 998–4300; Web site, *Washington Square News:* <http://www.nyu.edu/pubs.wsn>.

The Western Illinois University Courier: weekly. $18/semester, $36/yr. A student newspaper of Western Illinois University. Subscription address: *University Courier,* Room 300, Heating Plant Annex, Sherman Drive, P.O. Box 6009, Western Illinois University, Macomb, IL 61455; or call (309) 298–1876; Web site, *Western Courier Online:* <http://www.westerncourier.com>.

Acknowledgments (continued from page iv)

American Civil Liberties Union (advertisement). "Driving While Black." Reprinted by permission of the ACLU. This advertisement is courtesy of The PlowShare Group.

American Civil Liberties Union (advertisement). "Thanks to modern science. . . ." Reprinted by permission of the ACLU. This advertisement is courtesy of Devito Verdi.

Anonymous. "A Gun to My Head." *Esquire*, February 1999. Reprinted by permission. ©1999 by Sara Corbett.

Anti-Defamation League (advertisement). "Religious freedom is only as strong as the wall separating church and state. . . ." © 1999 Anti-Defamation League, all rights reserved. Reprinted by permission.

Quang Bao. "My Unhoming." *A. Magazine*, February / March 2000. Reprinted by permission of the author.

Bill Batson. "In Africa, Men Hold Hands." *Essence,* December 1999. Reprinted by permission of the author.

Daniel Berkowitz. "Affirmative Action Scours Sincerity, Placing a Band-aid to Heal Injustice Is No Solution" ["End It"]. *Campus Times*, University of Rochester, March 25, 1999. Reprinted by permission of the author and the *Campus Times*.

Deborah Blum. "What's the Difference between Boys and Girls?" *Life*, July 1999. Copyright © Time Inc. Reprinted by permission.

Carmen Cerra (cartoon). "Poison Ink." *Iowa State Daily*, Iowa State University, April 24, 2000. Reprinted by permission of the artist and the *Iowa State Daily*.

Chinese for Affirmative Action (advertisement). "Charged with Being Ethnic Chinese." © Public Media Center. Reprinted by permission of Public Media Center.

Lindsay Cohen. "Reno's Show of Force in Miami Was Justified" ["A Tale of Two Images"]. *Daily Northwestern*, Northwestern University, April 28, 2000. Copyright © Daily Northwestern. Reprinted by permission of the author and the *Daily Northwestern*.

Edward Cohn. "Are Men's Fingers Faster?" *The American Prospect*, April 24, 2000. Reprinted with permission from *The American Prospect*, vol. 11, issue 11, April 24, 2000. Copyright 2000. The American Prospect, P.O. Box 772, Boston, MA 02102-0772. All rights reserved.

Common Sense for Drug Policy (advertisement). "Just Say Not Guilty?" Reprinted with permission.

Ellis Cose. "Our New Look: The Colors of Race." From *Newsweek*, January 1, 2000. © 2000 Newsweek, Inc. All rights reserved. Reprinted by permission.

Rachael Cowley. "King or Queen of the Road: A Girl's View" ["Women Stop for Directions"]. *Spectrum,* Penn Valley College, December 8, 1999. Reprinted by permission of the author and the *Spectrum*.

Steve Dalton. "King or Queen of the Road: A Guy's View" ["The Mirror Is Not for Makeup"]. *Spectrum,* Penn Valley College, December 8, 1999. Reprinted by permission of the author and the *Spectrum*.

Camille DeAngelis. "Pondering the Profundity of 'Love'" ["Pondering 'Love'"]. *Washington Square News*, New York University, October 26, 1999. Reprinted by permission of the author and the *Washington Square News*.

Susan Douglas. "A Look at Terror with My Daughter." *The Progressive*, June 1999. Reprinted by permission of *The Progressive*.

Brandon Eckenrode. "It's Time for Humans to Settle from Within" ["The Next Frontier"]. *Courier*, Western Illinois University, January 29, 1999.

Barbara Ehrenreich. "Will Women Still Need Men?" *Time*, February 21, 2000. Reprinted by permission of International Creative Management, Inc. Copyright © 2000 by Time Magazine.

Wendy Ewald. "The Best Part of Me." *DoubleTake*, Winter 1999. Reprinted by permission of the author.

James E. Garcia. "War and Hypocrisy." *Texas Observer*, January 21, 2000. Reprinted by permission of the author.

David Gelernter. "What Do Murderers Deserve?" *Utne Reader*, April 1999. Reprinted by permission of the author.

Nathan Glazer. "Should the SAT Account for Race? Yes." *The New Republic*, September 27, 1999. Reprinted by permission of *The New Republic*, © 1999, The New Republic, Inc.

"Hate Crime Laws Are Unnecessary." *The Daily Universe* Editorial Board, Brigham Young University, January 19, 2000. Reprinted by permission.

Adrian Haymond. "Legalization Logic Fails to Solve Problem" ["Can Legalization Solve America's Drug Problem?"]. *Daily Bruin*, University of California, Los Angeles, October 28, 1999. Reprinted by permission of the author and the *Daily Bruin*.

Andrea Hein. "Religious Paranoia Harms Nation" ["Do the Ten Commandments Violate the First Amendment? No"]. *New Media Index*, Truman State University, September 2, 1999. Reprinted by permission of the author.

Jack Hitt. "The Hidden Life of SUVs." *Mother Jones Magazine*, July / August 1999. © 1999, Foundation for National Progress.

Jeff Jacoby. "The ACLU and the G-Word" ["Can We Use the G-Word?"]. *Boston Globe*, June 1, 2000. Reprinted by permission of The Copyright Clearance Center, Inc.

Robin Kelley. "The People in Me." *ColorLines*, April / May 1999. Reprinted by permission of *ColorLines* magazine.

Ann Knudson. "Should the State Kill?" *Mystician*, Bismarck State College, February 24, 2000. Reprinted by permission of the author and *Mystician*.

Anya Lakner. "In Op-Ed Debate, Racial Misjustice Is Misunderstood" ["What Should We Do about Affirmative Action? End It"]. *Campus Times*, University of Rochester, April 28, 1999. Reprinted by permission of the author and the *Campus Times*.

Los Angeles Times front page, April 23, 2000. Reprinted courtesy of the Los Angeles Times.

Breeze Luetke-Stahlman. "Local Activists Can Serve as Role Models for Kids" ["Real People Make Real Role Models"]. *University Daily Kansan*, University of Kansas, February 7, 2000. Reprinted by permission of the author and the *University Daily Kansan*, University of Kansas.

Miami Herald front page, April 23, 2000. Reprinted by permission of the *Miami Herald*.

Donna Minkowitz. "Love and Hate in Laramie." *The Nation*, July 12, 1999. Copyright © 1999 by Donna Minkowitz. Reprinted by permission of Georges Borchardt, Inc., for the author.

John Monczunski. "Cornered." *Notre Dame Magazine*, Spring 1999. Reprinted by permission of the author.

Mothers Against Drunk Drivers (advertisement). "Do You Really Want Jim, Johnnie, José or Jack Riding Shotgun with Him?" Photo courtesy of Mothers Against Drunk Driving. Reprinted by permission.

Eric Nagourney. "A Verbal Way to Stand Tall." *New York Times*, June 4, 2000. Copyright © 2000. Reprinted by permission of the New York Times Co.

National Abortion Federation (advertisement). "Making Abortion Safe." Reprinted by permission of the National Abortion Federation.

Brenda Neff. "Living Together." *Muleskinner*, Central Missouri State University, September 9, 1999. Reprinted by permission of the author and *Muleskinner*.

Negative Population Growth (advertisement). "Remember when this was heavy traffic?" Reprinted by permission of Negative Population Growth.

New York Times front page, April 23, 2000. Reprinted by permission of the New York Times Co.

Lesley Owusu. "Weighty Issues." *Daily Nebraskan*, University of Nebraska, February 1, 2000. Reprinted by permission of the author and the *Daily Nebraskan*.

Thea Palad. "I'm Filipino, Not New York" ["Fighting Stereotypes"]. *Unbound*, the College of New Jersey, Fall 1999. Reprinted by permission of the author.

Helen Prejean. "The Morality of Retribution." From *Dead Man Walking* by Helen Prejean. Copyright © 1993 by Helen Prejean. Reprinted by permission of Random House, Inc.

Anna Quindlen. "The Drug That Pretends It Isn't." *Newsweek*, April 10, 2000. Reprinted by permission of International Creative Management, Inc. ©2000 by Anna Quindlen.

William Safire. "In the Dead of Night." *New York Times*, April 24, 2000. Copyright © 2000. Reprinted by permission of the New York Times Co.

William Saletan. "The Elián Pictures." *Slate*, April 24, 2000. Copyright © Slate. Reprinted by permission of the New York Times Special Features / Syndication Sales.

Salon.com (advertisement). "Why is it a hate crime . . . ?" Reprinted by permission of Salon.com. All rights reserved.

Penelope Scambly Schott. "Report on the Difference between Men and Women." *Fourth Genre*, Fall 1999. Reprinted with permission of the author.

Ken Shulman. "We, On Death Row." United Colors of Benetton, January 2000. Reprinted with permission of the author.

Peter Singer. "The Singer Solution to World Poverty." *New York Times Magazine*, September 4, 1999. Copyright © 1999. Reprinted by permission of the New York Times Co.

Gloria Steinem. "Supremacy Crimes." *Ms.* magazine, August / September 1999. Reprinted by permission of the author.

Heather Summers. "Hate Crime Legislation Is Necessary." *The Daily Universe*, Brigham Young University, January 24, 2000. Reprinted by permission.

Deborah Tannen. "Contrite Makes Right." *Civilization,* April / May 1999. Copyright Deborah Tannen. Reprinted with permission.

Jim Tella. "Sipping Coffee." *Newsweek.com*, November 5, 1999. © 1999 Newsweek, Inc. All rights reserved. Reprinted by permission.

"Ten Commandments Not a Public Symbol." ["Do the Ten Commandments Violate the First Amendment? Yes"]. *Collegiate Times* Editorial Board, February 11, 2000. Reprinted by permission of *Collegiate Times*, Virginia Polytechnic Institute and State University.

Abigail Thernstrom. "Should the SAT Account for Race? No." *The New Republic*, September 27, 1999. Reprinted by permission of *The New Republic,* © 1999, The New Republic, Inc.

Carl Villarreal. "An Eye for an Eye Doesn't Always Apply." *Daily Texan*, University of Texas at Austin, February 8, 1999. Reprinted by permission of the author and the *Daily Texan*.

Travis Weigel. "Being Politically Correct Corrupts Unity of Once-Strong American Society" ["America's Identity Crisis"]. *Kansas State Collegian*, Kansas State University, February 4, 2000. Reprinted by permission of the author and *Kansas State Collegian*.

Stephen M. Wolf. "Countering Violence." *Attaché*, July 1999. Reprinted by permission of the author.

Chris Wooten. "Murder Rate Falls — Number of Homicidal Maniacs Increases" ["As the Murder Rate Falls, Violence Soars"]. *Hullabaloo*, Tulane University, October 28, 1999. Reprinted by permission.

Howard Zinn. "Unsung Heroes." *The Progressive*, June 2000. Reprinted by permission of *The Progressive*.

Index of Authors and Titles